John Patrick

Reflexions upon the devotions of the Roman church

With the prayers, hymns & lessons

John Patrick

Reflexions upon the devotions of the Roman church
With the prayers, hymns & lessons

ISBN/EAN: 9783337223656

Printed in Europe, USA, Canada, Australia, Japan

Cover: Foto ©Lupo / pixelio.de

More available books at **www.hansebooks.com**

REFLEXIONS
UPON THE
DEVOTIONS
OF THE
𝕽𝕺𝕸𝕬𝕹 𝕮𝕳𝖀𝕽𝕮𝕳.

REFLEXIONS
UPON THE
DEVOTIONS
OF THE
𝕽𝕺𝕸𝕬𝕹 𝕮𝕳𝖀𝕽𝕮𝕳,
WITH THE
PRAYERS, HYMNS & LESSONS
themselves, taken out of their
Authentick Books.

𝕵𝖓 𝕿𝖍𝖗𝖊𝖊 𝕻𝖆𝖗𝖙𝖘.

This *First Part*, containing their *Devotions* to 𝕾𝖆𝖎𝖓𝖙𝖘 and 𝕬𝖓𝖌𝖊𝖑𝖘.

ALSO

Two Digressions concerning the *Reliques* and *Miracles* in Mr. *Cressy*'s late 𝕮𝖍𝖚𝖗𝖈𝖍-𝕳𝖎𝖘𝖙𝖔𝖗𝖞. *by Bishop Patrick*

Utinam tam facilè vera invenire possem, quàm falsa convincere. Cicero *apud* Lactantium *de Orig. erroris, Lib. 2.*

LONDON,

Printed for *Richard Royston*, Book-seller to His most Sacred Majesty. 1674.

THE AUTHOR'S Advertisement TO THE READER.

A Great Part of the Devotions mentioned in this Book, is taken out of the *Breviary*, and other *Offices* now in use in the *Roman Church*; the rest chiefly out of those *Publick Offices* that were used in the *English Church* before the *Reformation*; such as the *Breviary* and *Hours* of *Sarum*, and other Books heretofore in great reputation.

If any one shall object against the frequent citation of those old Books; My Answer is this: No reasonable man can think it strange, that they should be charged with the Absurdity of those Devotions which they have laid aside: for since they were formerly allowed, and recommended and enjoyned, their Church must be always accountable for them, or else confess that she was once mistaken. If she hath at any time taught her Children to invocate for Saints *Romantick names*, such as S. *Christopher* and the 7 *Sleepers*; or to insert in their Prayers *Ridiculous Tales*, such as S. *George's* killing the Dragon, &c. These either errours or wilful forgeries,

geries, can never confist with her *pretended Infallibility* in Canonizing of Saints, and directing as well the *Worship* as the *Faith* of Christians. But they understand too well the consequence of acknowledging mistakes, ever to be guilty of so much ingenuity: and therefore though they have removed many of those *scandalous Legends* out of the *common Offices*, it is without disclaiming them, and with the pretence of other reasons, such as may save the reputation both of the *Legends* and of the *Church* that received them for *true Histories*. Thus *Carthagena* informs us, "That the Office

Citat. à Martyrol. Francisc. p. 351.

"of S. *Roch* and S. *Anne* (and he might have "said the same of the rest) was not left out "of the *Roman Office*, because it contained "any untruth in it, but that all things might be reduced to "the ancient order.

Most of those Saints whose *Histories* are omitted in the *Breviary* reformed by Pope *Pius* V. have proper offices for them, appointed to be used in some particular Churches. The Allowance is particularly remarkable which this Pope gave to the *Franciscans*; of whose *chief Saints* little is said in the *common Breviary*, but very many of their old Lessons are still retained in the *Proper Offices* of that *Order*. There is no mention made of S. *Crispin* and *Crispinian* in the *Roman Breviaries*; in that of *Sarum* they have three short Lessons, *Octob*. 25. But in the *proper Offices* of the Church of *Lisbon* (Printed there 1625) we have three long Lessons concerning them; wherein they relate, that they were of *Noble Parentage*, that in the Persecution of *Diocletian*, they set up the Trade of Shoo making, in which they were so extraordinarily assisted by God, that they exceeded all the Practitioners of the *Gentle Craft*, and mended poor peoples Shooes for nothing, *&c.* S. *Gabriel* the Archangel, is also left out; but he hath a very solemn Office performed by the Order of the *H. Trinity* for the *Redemption of Captives*, on *March* 18. with several *Hymns* and Nine *Lessons*: Examples

The Author's Advertisement to the Reader.

ples of the same kind are to be found in the *proper Feasts* of all the several Orders. It's plain too by the practice of the Vulgar, what judgment they are taught to make of the omission of some Names and Histories that were used before in their *publick Devotions*: The Saints are numerous, and their number increases every day; the old ones have had a fair time to receive the honour and veneration of the People, and may perhaps think it reasonable to resign their places to others; any thing will more easily be imagined, than that the Histories were omitted because they are Fabulous. S. *Roch* is left out of the *Kalendar* in the *present Breviaries* and *Missals*, who had a place there before: but he is still prayed to; Altars and Churches are dedicated in honour of him; his Images and Pictures set up; and when a Plague was at *Arles* in *France*, a *Fraternity* was erected to his honour, 40 Days of Indulgence given, that Sodality confirmed with many Indulgences by *Urban* VIII. *an.* 1629; a *Martyrol. Francisc. ad Aug.*16. *p.* 350. fair Church was built, and a silver and gilt Statue of S. *Roch* given by the *Fraternity*; and a form of Prayer in time of the *Plague*, relating to his help, remains in the *French Office* of the *Bl. Virgin*, Printed at *Paris*, 1615, which I shall after mention. So it is too in the case of S. *Margaret*: Her *old Legend*, how she was put in Prison by the Heathen Tyrant *Olybrius*, how the *Devil* in the shape of a *Dragon* swallowed her up, *&c.* is all expunged; and though she has a place still in the *Kalendar*, yet there is neither *Proper Lesson* nor *Proper Prayer* remains for her: and yet still it is made use of, it is read to *Women in Labour* (that bursting of the belly of the *Dragon*, out of which she came forth, being interpreted, I suppose, for a kind of Child-birth) and Women with Child are girded with her *Girdle*, kept in S. *Germans Abbey* at *Paris*, where the *Friers* perform that charitable office for them. Since therefore these old and Fabulous Devotions have the *countenance of common practice*, and the *favourable connivance*

The Author's Advertisement to the Reader.

connivance at least of *their Church*, there can be no reason to blame me for giving an account of them.

Especially when the many *false Reliques*, which give life to the superstition of the Vulgar, are every where publickly exposed and venerated, those of the most *Romantick Saints* not excepted: If they intended that their Histories should be no longer believed, when they left out their old Lessons; why did they not at the same time prohibit any farther showing of their pretended remains? Can *these* be justified by any Tradition, that will not justifie *all the rest* that is said of *them*? Will it be enough, when I set down the Romance of *Ursula*, and the 11000 *Virgins* out of the *old Breviaries*, to tell me, that there is not a word of their story remains in the *New*; when at *Colen* all passes as current as ever, and a thousand of their Reliques are there and at other places still produced? Can this Church be thought to intend, that men, if they please, may disbelieve the *Acts* of S. *George*, and yet at the same time countenance the showing of his *Arme*? If they really design the reformation of abuses, why do they not begin it where the cheat is most notorious, and where the People still hear and read more Fables, than in all the Lessons of the *old Breviary* put together? I do not hear that this Trading with Reliques is as yet set up publickly by them in *England*; but it will, no doubt, be used in due time, if they succeed in their hopes: it cannot be amiss therefore to let *our People* understand the way of this Traffick, and what *taking commodities* they expose in *other places*: and because the following Book will afford the Reader many rarities of the Saints Reliques; I will therefore here only give him one *small Collection*, with their Speeches to the People at the showing of them, as I find them in a *Print* of theirs of a Procession at *Aquisgranum* or *Aken*, 1650. Part of the *Wood of the Cross*, and a *Nayle* of the same. Some of the *Manna* in the Wilderness, and of the blossoms of *Aaron*'s Rod. Part of the *Sudarium*, of the *Reed* and *Spunge* of our Lord. A

Girdle

The Author's Advertisement to the Reader.

Girdle of our Saviour's, and another of the Bl. Virgins. The *Cord* with which *Christ* was bound at his Passion. Some of the *Hair* of S. *John* Baptist. A *Ring* of the *Chain* of S. *Peter*. Some of the *Blood* of S. *Stephen*, and of the *oyle* of S. *Catharine*. The *Arme* of S. *Simeon*. The *Image* of the Bl. *Virgin* drawn by S. *Luke*. The Reliques of S. *Spes* (or S. *Hope*.) Some of the *Hair* of the *Bl. Virgin*. (methinks the having her Hair, should have made it very fitting to have purchased one of her Combs; since the last Age was furnished with 2 of them, one at Rome, and another at Besancon in Burgundy; and at a place near Lyons they showed the Combs of all the 12 *Apostles*.) These and some others which I forbear to mention, are Yearly produced. But there are 4 Reliques besides, which they seem to account more sacred than the rest, being showed but once in *seven* Years, viz. The shift (*indusium*) of the Bl. Virgin. The *Swathes* of our Saviour. The *Linnen Cloth* upon which S. *John* Baptist was beheaded: and the *Cloth* with which our *Saviour* was covered on the Cross. When these are exhibited, there are these *solemn Proclamations* made to the People. (*thus translated out of the French.*)

1. *Proclamation.* " You shall have a sight of the *Shift*, that
" holy Garment, which the Virgin *Mary* the Mother of God
" had on, upon the Night of our Lord's Nativity: where-
" fore let us humbly pray to God, to be able to behold such
" Reliques to his glory, to the end that we may partake of
" his Grace for the attaining salvation. 2. *Proclam.* You
" shall have a sight of the *Swathes*, those holy Clothes, in
" which our Saviour *Jesus Christ* was wrapped on the night
" of his Nativity: wherefore let us pray Almighty God,
" to behold these Reliques to the increase of his Honour,
" to the end that we may never be separated from him. 3.
Proclam. " You shall have a sight of the Holy *Linnen-cloth*,
" upon which S. *John* Baptist was beheaded, with the marks
" of his blood spilt upon it, to whom God gave testimony,
" that he was the most holy Person that ever was born of a
" Woman: Let us therefore pray our Lord *Jesus Christ*,
" that

The Author's Advertisement to the Reader.

"that we may behold it to his honour, and that by his grace
"we may be saved. 4. *Proclam.* You shall have a sight of
"that *holy cloth*, which was put before our Lord's Body, and
"veiled it upon the Tree of the H. Cross, when he suffered
"death for our sins on Good *Friday.* Pray we therefore
"our Lord *Jesus Christ,* that we may behold it with such
"Devotion, that we may be partakers of his Death and Pas-
"sion, and may be delivered from all evils and sins.

These things I perceive are never likely to be reformed, though the shameful abuses have been often discovered; and if there were Liberty throughly to examine them, we should find most of them, no doubt, to be such cheats as Mr. *Calvin* mentions (and may sure be trusted in a matter of Fact, belonging to the Church where he lived) about Part of the *Brains of S. Peter,* which was shown for a precious Relique at *Geneva,* but upon examination was found to be onely a *Pumice-stone.*

Calvin admon. de reliquiis inter Tractat. Theologic.

I need add no more, to justifie what I have here set down out of their *old Devotions,* after I have told the *Reader,* that I hope I may have leave to do that, which their *own Authors* do with so much Approbation. Mr. *Cressy* has published, not long since, a great *Church-History,* where he has again revived many of the old Legends (such as that of *S. Winefrid* and others) and supplied the World anew with a prodigious heap of *Fictitious Gests*: nay, there seems to have been a Late Conspiracy to bring the Ridiculous stories of their *Saints* into vogue again, by other Writers of *their Lives;* witness the work of *Johannes Colganus* in his *Acta Sanctorum Hiberniæ* (whose first Volume in Fol. came forth at *Lovain, An.* 1645.) and especially the vast undertaking of the Jesuite *Johannes Bollandus* in his *Acta Sanctorum,* containing the Lives of all the *Saints*: whose first Volume was Printed at *Antwerp,* 1643, and was continued after his death by

Hens-

The Author's Advertisement to the Reader.

Henschenius and *Papebrochius* of the same *Society*: which Work if it be carried on sutably to the first draught, will amount to above 30 great Volumes in Folio. He has taken liberty to collect in Latin what he pleased out of a vast number of old *Breviaries* he mentions (and can it be any fault in me to do the same in *English?*) and he has had the hardiness, after all that Churches reformation, to defend the *Golden Legend* of *Jacobus de Voragine*; nay, he has told us, how that an Angel taught the *Roman* office (which must be the *old one*) to *S. Veronica*, and bore a part with her in reciting the *Responsals* and *Antiphona's*, which is more I think than they can alledge for the countenancing of the *New one*.

And now that I may prevent, if possible, their usual clamours about false citation of *Authors*, I will here once for all set down the Editions of some *Books* cited most frequently.

Books of Devotion.

Horæ B. Virginis secundum *usum Sarum. Paris.* 1519. *Horæ* sec. usum *Romanum. Paris.* 1570. *Breviarium* (seu Portiforium) sec. us. *Sarum* (pars Æstivalis & Hyem.) *Paris.* 1555. *Missale* secundum usum *Sarum. Rothomagi,* 1554. *Missale Romanum* Antiquum. fol. *Paris.* 1520. *Breviarium Roman.* Antiq. always refers to an Edition, 1543. *Sacrarum Cæremoniarum* Rom. Eccles. Libri tres. *Venetiis,* 1516. Where you at any time find in the Margin, *Missale Rom.* or *Breviar. Rom.* or *Rituale Rom.* without the Addition of *Antiq.* it always signifies the *Missal, Breviary,* and *Ritual* now in use.

Some other Books often made use of.

Baronii Annales Ecclesiast. Antverp. apud Plantinum. 1st. Vol. 1610. *Baronii Notationes* in Martyrologium Romanum. Antverp. 1613. *Matth. Paris. Londini,* 1640. *Martyrologium Franciscanum. Paris.* 1638. *Ribadeneiræ*

The Author's Advertisement to the Reader.

Flos Sanctorum. Coloniæ, 1630. *Surius*. Coloniæ, 1617. *Bibliotheca Patrum Cisterciensium*, unà cum Dialogis *Cæsarii de Heisterbach*. Bonofonte, 1660. *Gononi Chronicon SS*. Deiparæ Virg. Lugduni, 1637. *Dauroutii* Catechism. Historial. Tom. 2dus. Duaci, 1616.

The Editions of other Authors shall be mentioned, if there be any need, as they occur in the Book.

Dolenter hoc dico potiùs, quam contumeliosè, multò à Laertio severiùs vitas Philosophorum *scriptas, quam à* Christianis, vitas Sanctorum ; *longéque incorruptiùs atque integriùs* Suetonium res Cæsarum *exposuisse, quam exposuerunt* Catholici, *non res dico* Imperatorum, *sed* Martyrum, Virginum *&* Confessorum : *illi enim in probis aut Philosophis aut Principibus, nec vitia nec suspiciones vitiorum tacent ; in improbis verò, nec suspiciones virtutum produnt. Nostri autem plerique vel affectibus inserviunt, vel de industria quoque ita multa confingunt, ut eorum me nimirum non solùm pudeat, sed etiam tædeat.* Melchior Canus. Loc. Theolog. Lib. 11. Fol. 333.

Im-

IMPRIMATUR,

Sam. Parker R. in Christo Patri ac Domino, Domino Gilberto, Archi-Episc. Cantuar. à sac. Dom.

Jun. 1: 1673.

Faults to be Corrected.

Pag. 29. Line 8. for *and* read *or.* p. 32. Marg. r. *Art.* 4. p. 40. l. 29. dele *the.* p. 66. l. 15. dele *farther.* p. 70. l. 33. r. 3 *Thumbs.* p. 77. l. 15. r. *Futhwara.* p. 199. l. 11. r. *Cenomans.* p. 207. l. 14. r. *Celestine III.* p. 208. l. 12. r. *points.* p. 251. l. 22. r. 20 *of July.* p. 276. l. 3. r. *with in.* p. 309. l. 2 ult. r. *tell us.* p. 310. l. 29. r. *surlily.* p. 318. l. 5. r. *complaining.* p. 342. l. 16. r. *Aldelme.* p. 354. l. 29. dele *one of.* p. 359. l. ult. r. *tivity.* p. 385. l. 4. r. *rape.* p. 432. l. 19. r. *what was.*

The Reader may also, if he thinks it more proper, change the Latin Names of some places, into those of more ordinary use; as p. 32. l. ult. r. *Barcellona.* p. 40. l. 30. r. *Veii.* p. 97. l. 31. r. *Strasburg.* p. 201. l. 26. r. *Sens.* p. 263. l. 9. r. *Clervaux.* p. 279. l. 17. r. *Valentienes.* Ib. l. 19. r. *Hainault.*

CHOICE DEVOTIONS OF THE ROMAN CHURCH,

With some Reflexions upon them.

PART I.

N the Hours of the Bl. Virgin, according to the use of *Sarum*, fol. 124. I find this Prayer.

Peto Domine Jesu Christe, largire mihi in amore tuo, modum sine mensura, effectum sine modo, languorem sine ordine, ardorem sine discretione: Amen.

If I had Mr. *Cressy*'s faculty of understanding mystical Divinity, and commenting upon Non-sense (which I observe by a late Book of his, he is very good at) I should then have translated this Prayer; but till then, I can onely look upon it as a piece of pure Fanaticism; and having long since learnt, never to admire that which I cannot understand, I have nothing farther to wonder at, save onely the excellency of the contrivance, that the very Prayer it self against prudence, should be so foolish a one in the make of it. And there

there being many more of the same sort, I now begin to think the Church of *Rome* has some reason on her side for keeping her service in Latin; for surely nothing is more fit, than that absurd Devotions should be in an unknown Tongue, and that such Prayers as are made without Discretion, should be said without understanding. That this is not a slander against that Church, I desire the unprejudiced Reader to suspend his censure so long, till he has perused the numerous instances of it, that now shall follow.

Devotions to Fabulous Saints, or where the ground of them, is Fabulous.

Horæ. sec. usum Sarum.

De *S.* Wilgefortis, *Virg. & Martyre.*

On S. *Wilgefortis,* **Virgin and Martyr.**

Antiphona.

Ave Sancta famula *Wilgefortis* Christi,
Quæ ex tota anima Christum dilexisti,
Dum Regis Siciliæ nuptias sprevisti,
Crucifixo Domino fidem præbuisti.
Jussu patris carceris tormenta subiisti;
Crevit barba facie, quod obtinuisti,
A Christo, pro munere quod sibi voluisti,
Te volentes nubere sibi confudisti.
Videns pater impius te sic deformatam,

Hail Holy Wilgefort,
Maiden of Christ,
Who with all thy heart thy Saviour didst love,
While to match with Sicily's King thou deny'st,
To thy crucify'd Lord thou faithful dost prove.
While thy Father in Prison procures thy woe,
A miraculous beard on thy Face did grow.
Christ gave it in lieu of the heart he had had,
The design of the Match-makers quite was marr'd,
Thy Father observing this change grew so mad,

Elevavit

Devotions of the Roman Church.

Elevavit acrius in cru... ratam;
Ubi cum virtutibus reddidisti gratam
Animam, toties Christo commendatam.
Quia devotis laudibus tuam memoriam virgo colimus,
O beata *Wilgefortis* ora pro nobis quæsumus.

Vers. Diffusa est gratia in Labiis tuis.

Resp. Propterea benedixit te Deus in æternum.

Oremus.

Familiam tuam, quæsumus Domine, beatæ *Wilgefortis*, Virginis & Martyris tuæ Regis filiæ, meritis & precibus propitius respice, & sicut ad preces ipsius, barbam quam concupivit sibi cælitus accrescere fecisti, ita desideria cordis nostri supernæ gratiæ digneris beneficiis augmentare.

Per Christum.

Pater noster. Ave Maria.

...rmons any whit behind their Prayers... : Of which take Thy Soul so o... Homilies.
To Christ, went to Heaven;
There need be no fear
Of thy welcome there,
When so many graces enrich thee;
And for us that here raise
Devout Hymns to thy praise,
Pray for us St. Wilgefort, we beseech thee.

Vers. *Grace is poured into thy Lips.*

Ans. *Therefore God hath blessed thee for ever.*

Let us Pray.

We pray Thee, O Lord, look graciously upon thy Family, for the merits & pray'rs sake of S. Wilgefortis thy Virgin & Martyr, the Kings Daughter; and as in answer to her Prayers, thou madest the beard which she desired to have, miraculously to grow; so vouchsafe to augment the desires of our hearts with the benefits of supernal Grace.

Through Christ, &c.
Our Father. Hayl Mary, &c.

Judicis examen fac mite sit omnibus, Amen.

Verſ. Ora pro nobis B. Martyr *Chriſtophore.*
Reſp. Ut digni efficiamur promiſſionibus Chriſti.

The great *Judg*'s ſtrict examen,
Make eaſy to all of us, Amen.
Verſ. Pray for us, O Bl. Martyr Christopher.
Anſ. That we may be made worthy of the promiſes of Chriſt.

Oratio.

Miſſale Sar. de S. Chriſtoph. COncede quæſumus, omnipotens & miſericors Deus, ut qui Beati *Chriſtophori* Martyris tui memoriam agimus; ejus piis meritis & interceſſione, a morte perpetua & ſubitanea; a peſte, fame, timore & tempeſtate, clade & paupertate, & ab omnibus inimicorum inſidiis liberemur. Per te, Jeſu Chriſte, Salvator mundi, Rex gloriæ, quem ipſe meruit in brachiis portare.

Pater noſter. Ave Maria.

A Prayer.

GRant, we beſeech thee, Almighty and merciful God, that we who keep the memorial of S. Chriſtopher thy Martyr, may by his holy merits & interceſſion, be delivered from ſudden Death, from Peſtilence, famine, Fear and Tempeſt, deſtruction and poverty, and from all the ſnares of our enemies: Through thee, O Jeſu Chriſt, the Saviour of the world, the King of Glory, whom he merited to carry in his Armes.

Our Father, &c.
Hail Mary, &c.

Alia de S. Chriſtophoro.

Horæ ſec. uſ. Roman. SAncte *Chriſtophore* Martyr Dei pretioſe, rogo te per nomen Chriſti Creatoris tui, & per illud prærogativum quod

Another of St. *Christopher.*

O St. Christopher, the precious Martyr of God, I intreat thee by the Name of Chriſt thy Creator, and by that Prerogative tibi

tibi contulit, quando nomen suum tibi soli imposuit; te deprecor in Nomine Patris, Filii, & Spiritus Sancti, & per gratiam quam accepisti; ut erga Deum & Sanctam ejus Genetricem mihi famulo tuo *N.* sis propitius peccatori; quatenus tuo pio interventu, facias me vincere omnes, qui cogitant mihi mala; & per illud leve onus, quod est Christus, quod trans marinum flumen in humeris tuis feliciter portare meruisti, alleviare dignare præsentes meas angustias, paupertates, tribulationes, malas & perversas machinationes, fraudulentas conspirationes, mendacia, falsa testimonia, occulta sive aperta consilia, & alia quæ contra honorem meum cogitando vel conspirando veritatis æmuli, mihi servo tuo inferre conantur; ut vita comite & salvo honore, tecum gaudere valeam in secula seculorum.

he bestowed on thee, when he put his own Name on thee alone; I beseech thee in the Name of the Father, Son, and H. Ghost, and by the grace thou didst receive; to make God and his holy Mother propitious towards me thy servant N. a sinner; so that by thy pious intercession thou may'st make me to overcome all those who think ill against me; and by that light burden (which is Christ) which thou didst merit happily to carry on thy shoulders over the Sea-river, vouchsafe to alleviate my present distresses, poverties, tribulations, evil and perverse machinations, fraudulent Conspiracies, lies, false testimonies, hidden or open Councels, and those other things which the haters of truth think or conspire to inflict on me thy servant, against mine honour; that so my life and honour being in safety, I may be able to rejoyce with Thee for evermore.

Oremus.

Deus, qui B. *Christophorum*, Martyrem tuum, virtute constantiæ in passione roborasti; quique unigenitum tuum Dominum nostrum Jesum Christum, in suis humeris mirabiliter portari voluisti; concede propitius, ut qui ejus commemorationem agimus, ipsius meritis ad regna cœlestia pervenire mereamur.

Per Dominum, &c.

Let us Pray.

O GOD, who did'st strengthen S. Christopher thy Martyr, with the vertue of constancy in suffering, who also wouldst have thy only begotten Son Jesus Christ our Lord, to be wonderfully carried on his shoulders; favourably grant, that we who make a commemoration of him, by his merits we may merit to come to the Celestial Kingdom.

Through Christ, &c.

NOTES.

Those are pretty big requests, one would think, considering the Saint to whom they are presented; concerning whose story, of his carrying Christ over the River upon his back, we are forced, for want of ancient Authorities, to resolve our faith into the *Aurea Legenda*, and his Pictures upon the Sign-posts. There indeed he is made a mighty Gyant, with a great Beam in his hand, as he must in all reason be, when he carries Christ over the *marinum flumen* (as it is in the Prayer) an arme of the Sea. *Mantuan Lib. 7. Fastor.* says, he was 12 Ells high; and *Ludovicus Vives* * tells us, that in a Church, a tooth was shown him for one of St. *Christophers*, bigger then his fist: which might have given some credit to this Saint, if unluckily the Jesuit *Kircher* had not lately told us of a place in *Sicily*, where he and another Noble-man in his

* *In lib. 15. cap. 9. August. de civit. Dei. Mund. subter. lib. 8. p. 58.*

his Company, saw whole Cart-loads of such Teeth. And as his stature was great, so were his deeds mighty, for *Jacobus de Voragine*, quotes it out of a Preface of S. *Ambrose*,* that S. *Christopher* by his bright Miracles converted Forty-eight Thousand *Gentiles* to Christianity. But *Serarius* (*Litaneutic.* 2. *qu.* 20.) says, he never could see that Preface yet, and he believes *Baronius* never saw it neither, by his silence concerning it; and I do firmly believe as much. But *Baronius* has luckily delivered us from all fear; *Quod pertinet ad Giganteam Staturam qua pingi consuevit, quid dicam non habeo*: He knows not what to say to his Giantly stature; and he inclines to the Opinion of *Hieronymus Vida*, who has turned all to an Allegory: but alas! these Allegorical Saints will do nothing to salve the credit of the Prayers. If this Saint had had the good Fate to have been born in *England*, or that report had ever made him stalk over our narrow Seas, in all probability he had come off better than thus: and we should have had a pleasant account of his Adventures from Father *Cressy*, and this his carrying Christ upon his back, would have suited rarely well with the word *Gests*, so often used by him. Of his inclinations to pleasure us in this particular, I am pretty well assured; because he has set down as great a Romance as this is in his Church-History, in the Tale he has there told of S. *Winefrids* head, which after it was cut off by her Brutish Lover, came tumbling down the Hill into the Church among all the Assembly, and being carried up the Hill again, where her dead Body lay, and joyned to it; by the Prayers of the Church, she arose and lived again; and no sign remained of her ever having lost her head, save onely that where the head was rejoyned to the body, there appeared a white Circle compassing her Neck, small as a white thread, which continued so all her Life; and as for him that did the fact, upon the

* Surius *also mentions the same Preface, in the life of S.*Christoph. *on* July 25.

Baron. *notis in* Martyrolog. Rom. *ad* Jul. 25.

Ch. History. lib. 16. c. 8.

Prayer

Prayer of the Holy-man, that God would punish his detestable crime, he immediately fell down dead; and which was more strange, his body presently disappeared, and many say that it was swallowed up by the Earth, and with the wicked Soul sunk into Hell: and in the very place where her Head fell, immediately sprung out of the Earth that famous Well, which took both its Name and Vertues from the Miracles that then were showed upon her. This Mr. *Cr.* takes, as he says, from *Robert Abbot* of *Shrewsbury*, who lived 500 Years ago; from whom also I must suppose the Author of the *Salisbury* Breviary took it, for all this I find there almost Verbatim, in several Lessons on S. *Winifrids* Day, *Novemb.* 3. The truth is, when I consider the large swallow of Mr. *Cressy*'s faith, and find in his History the story of *Guy* of *Warwick* and *Colbrand* the *Danish* Gyant set down out of *Harpsfield*; I pitty the hard luck of Sir *Guy*, that he was onely a poor Pilgrim, and not a Bishop of his Church; for if he had been so, I doubt not but he would have made a shift, to have salved the Objections he mentions against the Truth of that Legend, and have given us as good an account of it, as of S. *Winefrid*; and then his landing at *Portsmouth*, just in the nick of time, when K. *Athelston* was in such distress for a Champion, should have been not the effect of a lucky chance, but of a Vision, or a Revelation, which he is very free upon all occasions to produce. If I could be assured that Mr. *Cr.* way of writing Histories, was like to be in any great vogue, a little matter would tempt me to Translate the Lives of the Saints, as I find them in the ancient Breviaries of the *Romish* Church, (whereas now I shall onely touch upon them as they fall in my way) for that they are in good credit with him, I cannot question, since I find him adding the Authority of the Breviary of *Sarum*, to that of *Baronius*, in the case of *Ursula*, and the Eleven Thousand Virgins, to justifie an Opinion he mentions, about the time of their Martyrdome.

Lib 31. *cap.* 5.

Lib. 9. *cap.* 20.

Longini

Devotions of the Roman Church.

Longini Martyris Memoria.

Oratio.

Brev. Rom. Antiq. Martii 15.

OMnipotens sempiterne Deus, qui pretiosissimo tui sanguinis liquore, oculos Sancti Martyris tui Longini illuminasti; quæsumus, ut dono tuæ gratiæ mentes nostras illustrare digneris, quatenus post hanc vitam in æterna beatitudine te perfrui mereamur.

Qui vivis, &c.

St. Longinus Martyr.

The Prayer.

ALmighty everlasting God, who by the most precious liquor of thy blood, didst inlighten the eyes of thy holy Martyr Longinus; we pray Thee, vouchsafe to illustrate our minds with the gift of thy grace, so that after this life we may merit to enjoy thee in eternal blessedness.

Who livest, &c.

NOTES.

THis Prayer is founded upon so excellent a Fable that follows there in the forecited Breviary, that I cannot omit to translate it, especially because the Lessons are but short.

Lesson 1.

"We have it by Tradition, that *Longinus* a Free-man, "and belonging to the *Roman* Souldiery, his Eyes being al-"most blind, with his Lance pierced our Lord Jesus on the "Cross, and by the touch of that blood (which fell, it is "supposed on his eyes) immediately recovered his sight, "and believed; who forsaking his Military profession, be-"ing instructed by the Apostles, lived 38 Years a mona-"stick life in *Cesarea* of *Capadocia*; and continuing in all "sanctity, by Doctrine and Example converted many to the "Faith. At length he finished the glorious strife of Mar-
"tyrdome,

"tyrdome, for the Confession of *Christ*, under the Presi-
"dent *Octavius*. [This story of blind *Longinus* piercing
Christ's side, & recovering his sight, & being converted, they
would countenance by the *revelations* of
S. *Veronica*; but *Baronius* looks upon the
story of *Longinus* the Souldier that was
blind and pierced *Christ*'s side, as taken
out of Apocryphal writings. *Bollandus*,
though he has given us his life, yet confesses that his name
was not heard among the *Greeks*, till the Year 715. and a-
mong the *Latines* not till the writing of the
Martyrologies, and those too not the most
ancient, for that of the Genuine *Bede* has it
not. It is also farther remarkable, that though this Lesson
and many Martyrologies, agree in making *Longinus* to be
a Martyr of *Cappadocia*, yet the *Mantuans* maintain a strong
contest, that his Martyrdom was at *Man-
tua*, and that there his Body was long a-
go found (viz. *an.* 804.) together with a Vessel having
some of the Blood of *Christ* in it, which he brought thither; and they say, that *Mantua*, or a place hard by it, was
of old called *Cappadocia*. They of *Sardinia* do the like, and
maintain that *Longinus* was born among them, suffered under *Nero*'s persecution there, and that the Body of this
Romantick Saint, was found and digged up by them, *an.* 1626.
but to go on with the Lessons.]

*Bolland. Act. Sanctor.
ad Januar.* 13. *p.* 912.

Ad. an. 34. *num.* 127.

*Bolland. Ibid. ad
Mart.* 15. *p.* 376.

See Bolland. loc. citat.

Lesson 2.
"When he was brought before the President, while he by
"various Arguments sought to draw him to the Worship
"of Idols, among other things he said to him; Sacrifice to
"the Gods, for I perceive that through thy too great ab-
"stinence, thou art not able to endure torments. But
"while he continued still to preach *Christ*, the President in
choler commanded all his Teeth to be struck out, and his
tongue to be cut off. *Longinus* notwithstanding this, did not*

* *Qui res humanas a Divis, quorum historias scribendas sumunt, alienas
fore censent, hi Divos ipsos ne homines quidem fuisse videntur credere.
Melch. Canus. Loc. Theol. l.* II. *c.* 6.

lose

"lose his speech, but said to the President; If thou believest
"the Gods which thou worshippest to be truly such, suffer
"me to be punished by them, whilst I break them in pieces,
"and then I will believe them to be true Gods; but if after
"this they do me no harm, I will believe still in my God.
"The President gave him leave, who taking an Axe, hew-
"ed in pieces all the Images, and whatsoever was in the
"Temple. Whereupon the Devils presently going out of
"the Images, entered into the President and into his Ser-
"vants; who raving, and barking, and falling prostrate at
"*Longinus* his feet, upon the request of the People that
"made great acclamations, that the Saint would drive a-
"way the Devils, he healed them; and a great number of
"the by-standers, seeing this wonder, believed.

Lesson 3.

"But a little while after, the President being instigated
"by the Devil, and accounting all these things to be but il-
"lusions of the senses, he spake thus to S. *Longinus*; When
"the Emperour shall hear, that through the Magical Arts
"of Christians, this City has departed from the Sacrifices
"of the Gods, he will destroy us all. The President being
"sharply reproved by *Aphrodisius Commentariensis*, for
"tormenting a Man of God, who had delivered them all,
"and the City; the President thereupon commanded the
"said *Aphrodisius* his Tongue to be cut out. But by the
"judgment of God he presently hereupon was struck blind,
"and being tortured in his whole Body, he began to cry
"out and desire, that the Man of God *Longinus*, against
"whom he confessed he had acted foolishly, would pray
"for him. To whom *Longinus* answered, if thou wilt be
"saved, kill me, and then I will pray for thee, and thou shalt
"be healed. Immediately by his command he was behead-
"ed, and the President prostrating himself, upon his repen-
"tance received his sight, and burying the Saint honourably
"continued in the Faith. [*Thus far the Legend.*] *Baronius* in his Annals (*ad an.* 38. *f.* 2.) seems plainly to doubt
of the truth of this story, when he questions whether he
may

may give credit to *Metaphrastes* the relator of it. "If, "says he, we may give credit to the Acts of *Longinus* the "*Centurion*, recited by *Metaphrastes*, it is plain, that by "*Pilate*'s cruelty the said *Centurion*, together with other 2. "Souldiers, were beheaded, becaufe they freely confeffed "Chrift. And yet upon the *Roman* Martyrology (*Martii*, 15.) he is not afhamed to tell us of the venerable Body of S. *Longinus*, that is kept at *Rome* in the Church of St. *Augustine*. As another Author informs us, that his Head and Arm are preferved at *Prague*, among the numerous Reliques that were brought thither by *Charles* IV. but I think, a Man may believe as he pleafes, when he obferves in the Catalogue fuch particulars as thefe, *viz.* fome Reliques of *Abraham*, *Ifaac*, and *Jacob*. The Arm and fome part of the Body of *Lazarus*; Two pieces of two Girdles of the Bl. Virgin: A part of the Body of S. *Mark*, and a part of his Gofpel of his own hand-writing: A piece of S. *John* the Evangelift's Coat: A piece of the Staff of S. *Peter*, and another piece of the Staff of S. *Paul*: A part of S. *Peter*'s chain: A finger of S. *Anne*: A part of the B. Virgins Vail. The Head of S. *Luke* the Evangelift (though that alfo is fhow'd in a Church at *Rome*) fome of the Reliques of S. *Katherine* of *Alexandria*. The Head and Finger of S. *Stephen*; and an Arm of one of the Holy Innocents, &c. We are told alfo by the fame Author, of the *Vatican* Church having his venerable Arm, with a Ring upon his Ring-finger, and of feveral other places where his Reliques are preferved. One may the lefs wonder that fuch ridiculous Fables as thefe fhould be pinn'd upon the Gofpel Hiftory, by thofe that have taken the boldnefs in their publick Books of Devotion to alter and corrupt even the very Gofpel-Text it felf; for then there can be no fecurity againft fuch abfurd comments as this of *Longinus*, and Twenty other like it. To give a few inftances of both.

Bollandus Vol. 1. Append. ad Jan. 2.

Vit. fanct. ad Mar. 15.

In the old *Roman* Miffals and Breviaries, upon the *Feria 5. poft.*

5. *post Dominicam* 2 *in Quadrages.* the Gospel (*Luc.* 16. v. 19.) begins thus, *In illo tempore dixit Jesus Discipulis suis parabolam hanc.* Homo, &c. The Missal of *Pius* 5. 1580. reads, *In illo tempore dixit Jesus discipulis suis*, and leaves out *parabolam hanc.* The present Missals and Breviaries have it, *In illo tempore dixit Jesus pharisæis.* But there is not one word of any of these, chuse which you will, in the Text.

Thus upon the *Sabbatum post Domin.* 2 *in Quadrag.* (*Luc.* 15. 11.) The old ones have it, *In illo tempore dixit Jesus discipulis suis parabolam hanc. Homo quidam, &c.* The new ones say, *In illo tempore dixit Jesus Pharisæis & Scribis parabolam hanc. Homo, &c.* But there is nothing more in the Text, then, *Et dixit, Homo, &c.*

So *Domin.* 3. *post Pentacost.* (for the Gospel, *Luc.* 14. 16.) the old Missals have added, *Dixit Jesus Discipulis suis parabolam hanc.* The new, *Dixit Jesus Pharisæis parabolam hanc,* which are also both false, for our Saviour spake to one particular Man.

So, *Dominic.* 4. *post Quadrages.* (Gospel is *Joh.* 6. v. 1.) Instead of *Posthæc abiit Jesus, &c.* Both old and new read, *In illo tempore abiit Jesus.* Which is not to be turned off, by saying that *In illo tempore*, is a common beginning of the Gospel-Lessons, (as *In diebus illis,* commonly begins the Lessons of the old Testament) to signify I suppose to the people, who do not understand *Latin,* when the Gospel begins. For surely the Church ought not for any such pretended convenience of the people, be so uncivil to the Scripture as to contradict it, and put *At that time,* for *After that time.*

But the most remarkable instance of corrupting the Text I meet withall, is in the *Feria* 3. *post. dominic.* 3. *in Quadrages.* where all the old Breviaries and Missals I have seen begin the Gospel for the day (*Matth.* 18. 15.) in this manner: *In illo tempore, respiciens Jesus Discipulos suos, dixit Simoni Petro, si peccaverit, &c.* And so it is in the Reformed Breviary of *Pius* V. *Antverpiæ,* 1580. The reason of this

this addition is plain, becaufe the Gofpel fayes prefently, *Whatfoever ye fhall bind on Earth, fhall be bound in Heaven, &c.* and they thought it not fit, that Chrift fhould fay thefe words to any but to *Simon Peter*, to whom the Keys of the Kingdom of Heaven were committed. Now in the prefent Books it is altered thus. *In illo tempore dixit Jefus difcipulis fuis*, which is an addition to the Text ftill, for there are no fuch words there, though more tolerable, becaufe it is true, that Chrift did fpeak them to his Difciples.

And as they have endeavoured to abufe the Text, fo they have alfo made lewd comments in feveral places upon it. Of which I'le give the Reader a few remarkable Inftances, as I find them in a Book called the *Feftivale* (or Homilies upon the Feftivals before the Reformation:). We read in the Gofpel that the Bl. Virgin was aftonifhed when the Angel *Gabriel* brought his happy Meffage to her; now that Book gives this reafon for it. "There was in that Coun-
"try a Man that coude moch Witchcraft, and fo with help
"of *Fiendes*, he made himfelf like an Angel, and came to
"divers Maydens, and faid he was fent from God to them
"on his Meffage, and fo often times lay with them, and did
"them great villany: Then when our Lady heard tell of
"that Man, fhe was addread left it had been he, for fhe had
"fpoke with none Angel before. *fol. 93.*

So *fol. 72.* in the Sermon upon the Circumcifion of our Lord, it fays, "The flefh which was cut from Chrift's mem-
"ber at his Circumcifion, an Angel brought it after to King
"*Charles* for the moft precious Relique of the World, and
"for the greateft worfhip he could do thereto, he brought
"it to *Rome*, to a Church that is called *Sancta Sanctorum*. (concerning this fore-skin we fhall have a fit occafion to fpeak more afterwards.)

Ibid, *fol. 67.* "When our Lord lay in the *Cratch*, the
"Oxe and the Affe fell down on their Knees and worfhipped
"Him, and eat no more of the Hay.

Ibid

Ibid. fol. 66. "*Thomas* the Apostles (*a*) hand that was in *Christ*'s side, would never go into his Tomb, but always lay without, which hand had such vertue in it, that if the *Priest* when he goes to Mass, put a branch of a Vine into his hand, the branch putteth forth grapes, and by that time that the Gospel be said, the Grapes been ripe, and he takes the Grapes and wringeth them into the Chalice, and with that Wine houselleth the people.

(*a*) It is no doubt *this hand* that is meant, in that story *Stapleton* tells of this Apostle, how *John* the Patriarch of the *Indies, An.* 1120. declared publickly to the Pope, *Sanctum Thomam Apostolum omni anno communicare populum suum, manu propriâ porrectâ dignis & retractâ ab indignis. Stapleton de tribus Thomis.* p. 19.

Idem, fol. 108. Concerning the death of the two great Apostles *Peter* and *Paul,* it says thus. "St. *Poule* for that he was a Gentleman born, for the more worship they smote off his head, but crucified *Peter* with his head downward.

So, *fol.* 91. (speaking concerning *Judas* his bursting asunder) "The *Fiende* could not draw out the Soul of *Judas* when he hanged himself, out of his mouth, because he had lately kissed the mouth of *Christ,* therefore the *Fiende* brake his Womb and shed out his Guts, and then he took his Soul and bare it to Hell. But surely the foul Fiend, imployed about this work, was not such a fool as this Writer, not to remember a certain Back-door very proper for such a foul soul as *Judas* his was, to issue out at, and so to no purpose at all for this end to take such needless pains.

A Prayer to the 3. *Kings of Colen.*

Horæ Sec.
usum Sa-
rum.

TRium Regum trinum munus Christus homo Deus unus unus *in* essentia trina

SInce I can make no sence of some part of this, I shall therefore make no Rithme upon any of it, let him do it, that has a mind.

dona tres signent Rex in auro, Deus thure Myrrha mortalitas. Colunt reges propter Regem summi Reges servent Regem coloni Coloniæ. Nos in fide sumus rivi, hi sunt fontes primitivi, gentium primitiæ.

Tu nos ab hac Christe valle
Duc ad vitam recto calle
   per horum suffragia,
Ubi Patris, ubi Nati,
Tui & amoris Sacri
   Frui mereamur gloria.

Instead thereof, I'le give you an excellent account concerning the 3. offerings of these wise Men, out of the *Festivale* on *Epiphany* day, which is this. " *Joseph* kept of the Gold as " much as him needed, to pay " his tribute to the Emperor, " and also to keep our Lady " with while she lay in child- " bed, and the rest he deeled " to the poor. The incense " he brent, to put away the " stench of the stable there as " she lay in: and with the " Myrrhe, our Lady anointed " her Child, to keep him " from Worms and Disease.

Oremus.

Deus qui tres Magos Orientales, Jaspar, Melchior & Balthasar, ad tua cunabula, ut te mysticis venerarentur muneribus sine impedimento stella duce duxisti; concede propitius, ut per horum trium Regum pias intercessiones & merita commemorationum, nobis famulis tuis tribuas, ut itinere quo ituri sumus, celeritate lætitia gratia & pace teipso sole vera stella vera luminis luce, ad loca destinata in pace & salute, & negotio peracto

Let us Pray.

O God, who by the guidance of a star didst lead without impediment the 3 Eastern Magi, Jaspar, Melchior and Balthasar to thy Cradle, to worship thee with mystical gifts; mercifully grant, that by the pious intercessions of these three Kings, and by the merits of their commemorations, thou wouldst afford unto us thy servants, that in the journey which we are undertaking, with speed, joy, grace and peace, thou thy

cum

cum omni prosperitate, salvi & sani redire valeamus.

Qui vivis, &c.

Amen.

*Horæ sec. usum Romanum,*1570.

O Rex *Jaspar*, Rex *Melchior*, Rex *Balthasar*, rogo vos per singula nomina, rogo vos per Sanctam Trinitatem, rogo vos per regem regum, quem vagientem in cunis videre meruistis; ut compatiamini tribulationibus meis hodie, & intercedite pro me ad Dominum, cujus desiderio exules facti estis: & sicut vos per Angelicam nunciationem de reditu ad Herodem eripuit, ita me hodie liberare dignetur ab omnibus inimicis meis visibilibus & invisibilibus, & à subitanea & improvisa morte, & ab omni confusione mala, & ab omni periculo corporis & animæ.

self being the Sun, the true star, the true light of the day, we may come to the places we design to go to, in peace and safety; and after the dispatch of our business, may be able to return safe and sound with all prosperity. Who liveth, &c. *Amen.*

O King Jaspar, King Melchior, King Balthasar, I intreat you by every of your names, I intreat you by the holy Trinity, I intreat you by the King of Kings, whom you merited to see crying in his Cradle; that you would compassionate this day my tribulations, and intercede with the Lord for me, for the desire of seeing whom, you were made exiles; and as he delivered you by the Angels message from returning to Herod; so he may vouchsafe to deliver me this day from all mine enemies, visible and invisible, and from sudden & unforeseen death, and from all evil confusion, and from all danger of body and soul.

Oremus.

Oremus.

Deus illuminator omnium gentium, da populis tuis perpetua pace gaudere; & illud lumen infunde cordibus nostris, quod trium Magorum mentibus aspirasti.

Per Dominum, &c.

Let us pray.

O God, that dost enlighten all Nations, grant unto thy people that they may rejoyce in perpetual peace, and infuse that light into our hearts, which thou didst breath into the minds of the three Magi.

Through our Lord, &c.

NOTES.

This piece of Devotion is so great an instance of the folly and gross superstition of this Church, that I cannot but make some considerable Remarques upon it, before I go farther: and especially because this tale of the 3 Kings of *Colen*, is again revived by Mr. *Cressy* in his late Church-History, who I see is resolved (such is his discretion) to play all the lost Games of the Church of *Rome*, and would fain give veneration to a story, which for its ridiculousness (and without any other design) has been set to a Tune in the Catch-Book, after it had been blotted out of the Devotions of the Church.

It cannot but seem very strange to all but those who are for *Devotion* without *Discretion*, that any should in their addresses to Almighty God, presume to tell him their idle and uncertain stories; especially when they have his own direction (who sure best knows what is pleasing to himself) what name they are to use, and to whom they are to go in all their prayers, that they may speed in Heaven. We have oft heard of the *Son of God*, in the Scripture, as a prevailing *Advocate* with the *Father*, but never a word there of the *Mother of God*, as destined to such an Office; or an instance of any there, that ever *came to God* by *her*, or by any other

other *departed Saint*. A man might well suspect, that these men who thus apply themselves to them, imagined that either *Christ*'s hands were too full of Petitions, or that his heart was not so tender as theirs; (which I shall after show, is indeed their plain sence concerning the Bl. *Virgin*,) or that some Courtiers in Heaven had lately stept into greater honour and favour with God than he. But how I pray come these 3 Kings of *Colen* to be in so much vogue for intercession? The Scripture, I am sure, neither tells us, that the Men who came from the East to visit our Saviour, and to offer gifts to Him, were either Kings, or that their number was onely three (their three offerings do not prove it, for each one might offer all three) or that their names were *Jaspar*, *Melchior* and *Balthasar*; and yet all this must be put (as if it were unquestionable) into a Prayer. But, it may be they will say that Tradition will supply all these defects. If it were such a Tradition as has delivered the Bible to us, and the names of the several Writers of that Holy Book, we might and would accept it; that is, if it were ancient enough, and agreed with it self. But the learned *Isaac Casaubon* (not to mention others) has said enough in his second Exercitation, number the 10th. against *Baronius*, to show the folly of this pretence. For to pass over their being (a) Kings, (which if they were, they must be onely truckling and petty ones) the ancient Writers have not pronounced their number to be onely three, and neither Ancient nor Later have agreed that these were their Names.

(a) Concerning which see *Maldonate* upon the 2d. of S. *Matthew*, v. 1. who sayes thus, *Ecclesia Magos fuisse Reges non certa & Catholica fide, sed probabili opinione credit. Licuit enim Christiano poetæ (sc. Mantuano) salva Religione dicere: Nec reges ut opinor erant.* (the more shame their prayers should be so positive that they were so) *Licuit multis nostro tempore Catholicis & eruditis Theologis idem scribere:* and then he mentions such arguments as these; *Non fuisse Evangelistam silentio nomen Regum, si reges fuissent, præteriturum, cum id ad honorem adorandi Christi magnopere pertineret: majore apparatu excipiendos ab Herode, Reges à Rege.*

I think if I had their perswasions, that the Saints are mightily pleased with the addresses that are made to them, and reflected withall upon the slender assurance that is given, that they were but three in number, I should be afraid, lest there should happen to be a fourth, and he as deserving a King as any of the other; and that every time I invoked the three, I should be in danger of disobliging him, by seeing his fellows venerated and courted perpetually, and himself without regard, and having nothing to do. But what if they have guessed right at their number, and have been out in their names? Are they sure that the Saints will not take it ill to be miscall'd? And what if they should not know, whether you have any thing for them to do, till they hear their own true names? What will this prayer then do good to *Jaspar*, *Melchior* and *Balthasar*, when another tradition says their names were, *Apellius*, *Amerus* and *Damascus*; a third, that they were, *Magalath*, *Galgalath* and *Saracin*; and a fourth calls them, *Ator*, *Sator* and *Peratoras*? which last I should chuse (in this uncertainty) to call them by, as having the more Kingly sound, if it had not been for a scurvy story *Casaubon* mentions out of an old *Greek* book, that these three, together with *Misael*, *Achael*, *Cyriacus* and *Stephanus* (the names of the 4. Shepherds that came to visit our Lord in *Bethlehem*) had been used (and he tells how) for a charm to cure the biting of Serpents and other venemous Beasts.

But it may be I needed not have offered all this about their names, since neither Mr. *Cressy* nor *Baronius* (who has so large a discourse concerning them) have undertaken to justify this prayer in that respect, or so much as to mention how they were called. Let us come therefore to the main matter, wherein Mr. *Cressy* is to be considered, and that is concerning their Reliques to be seen at *Colen*, which is the reason they are called the 3 Kings of *Colen*; for I hope the Laity of the *Romish* Church, though they are very ignorant, yet do not imagine, that these three ever raigned in that place together, like the 2 Kings of *Brentford*.

A

A Digression concerning Reliques.

IT seems to be a story very hard, without great proof, to be believed, that these *three* dead Bodies should ever come to this City; But we need go no farther for the resolution of this doubt, than to Mr. *Cressy*, who thus informs us out of the supplement of the *Gallican* Martyrology.

"At *Colonia Agrippina* (or *Colen*) is cele-
"brated the memory of the *three* holy Kings,
"who on this day (*Jan.* 6.) adored our Lord
"in his Cradle at *Bethlehem*. The Bodies of these Saints
"were by the care and devotion of the holy Empress *He-*
"*lena*, brought out of the East to *Constantinople*; where in
"the Temple of *Sancta Sophia* (afterward more magnifi-
"cently repaired by *Justinian*) they remained to the times
"of the Emperour *Emanuel*; who bearing a great affecti-
"on to *Eustorgius* Bishop of *Milan*, by birth a *Grecian*, at
"his earnest prayers bestowed on him those sacred pledges.
"*Eustorgius* presently conveighed them to *Milan*, placing
"them in a Church of Religious Virgins. But in the year
"Eleven-Hundred sixty and four, the Emperour *Frederick*,
"having by force reduced *Milan* to his obedience, granted
"to his Chancellour *Raynaldus*, Arch-Bishop of *Colen*, at
"his most earnest suit, the same *three* sacred Bodies, which
"he transferr'd to *Colen*, where he reposed them in the
"principal Church, in which place they are to this day ce-
"lebrated with great veneration. *Thus far he.*

Ch. Hist. lib. 7. *cap.* 16.

When I first read this story, it seemed to me, just such a made idle speech, as the shewer of the Tombs would say over the Bodies of King *Arthur*, or *Guy* of *Warwick*; and I wish it be not the very Tale that is told over them, to those that visit those holy Reliques, at the Metropolitan Church of *Colen*. I think I do not despise this story without a great deal of reason; for *Guil. Neubrigensis,* * who lived at that

* *Lib.* 2. *de reb. Anglic. cap.* 8. *Nec notum est à quibus personis sacræ illorum reliquiæ illuc dilatæ, ibique repositæ fuerint.*

very time when *Milan* was taken by *Frederick*, and who mentions, that these Bodies of the *Magi* were found in an old destroyed Monastery, yet adds, *That this Treasure was not known to the Monks and Clergy that ministred there, but was found when the Church was overturned to the foundation, and revealed by manifest tokens, to whom they did belong* (but what those tokens were he says not a word of) and a little after,—— *Nor was it known by what Persons their holy Reliques were brought and laid there* ; (it seems there was not a word said about *Helena* at this time.) Besides, it is scarce imaginable, if this story were true, that not one word of it should be mentioned either by *Eusebius* or *Socrates*, and especially not by his beloved *Baronius*, who with so much care has collected out of all Authors the progress of *Helena* into the East, to the holy Land ; who certainly was led to it in her extream Age of above Fourscore, out of Devotion to the Sepulchre, and to visit the places, that were so famous for the actions and sufferings of our Lord ; and when she had found what she went in Quest of, he tells us of no journey forward, or circuit she made into the East, but there, for ought we can learn, her steps rested till her return. And indeed, by what those Authors relate of her, we may easily conceive, how she might spend a *Twelve-moneth* (if she had so long a time both for her progress and return) without going farther. For we hear, when she came to *Jerusalem*, of her curious search after the Cross, for the finding of which, she was fain to dig some while, and of her building two Churches, one at *Bethlehem*, and another at Mount *Oliver*. And as her great Age must needs make it improbable, that she should take much pleasure in farther journeying, when this great curiosity was satisfied : so the *little time she lived after*, makes it still more : for *Valesius* makes it out, that *Helena* must end her days, either *an.* 326. (which was the year she came to *Jerusalem*) or *an.* 327. with whom Mr. *Cr.* here agrees, saying, "She "seems to have ended her life, either the same year, or in

Valef not. in Eusb. de vit. Constantin. l. 3. cap. 47.

the

the beginning of the following year; and both he and *Baronius* will have her to dye at *Rome*, after her return to *Constantinople*, which, considering her Age, could not be dispatched in a little time. I might also add farther, that if really *Helena* had been informed of the place of the burial of these 3 *Magi*, and had brought their Bodies along with her to her Son to *Constantinople*, (as this story pretends) it could scarce have been possible, (considering that Age of Learned men, and the fame of the thing) but that a more certain Tradition of this would have remained in the Church: Besides, we now see so little evidence of the place where they were *buried*, that scarce any thing has more exercised the Pens of Learned Criticks, than to determine what Country that is, which the Scripture calls the East, from whence they *came*; some thinking it was *Chaldæa*, some *Persia*, and some *Arabia*; and all giving probable conjectures for their several Opinions; and when not onely Later Writers, but even the *Fathers* themselves are divided in this matter, as any who will but consult *Maldonate*, in the forenamed place (to omit many others) may see.

But I have not yet done with Mr. *Cr.* but must add a few words more to tell him, that he quite mistook his Cue, in stuffing and swelling his History to such a great bulk, by such a prodigious number of Legends, concerning the Reliques of the Saints and Miracles about them: that his Faith is a great deal too big (for so charitable I'le be, though some I doubt will imagine him to have none at all) and his Discretion apparently too little for the inquisitiveness and Learning o the Age he lives in. That in this wild way of promoting his Faction, he has done infinite disservice to our common Christianity, and that in an Age, wherein too many, God knows, are inclined to Infidelity, by prejudicing them against the belief of the undoubted Miracles; by which our Christianity is proved, when they see such an heap of wonders produced, to countenance apparent fooleries and superstitions, but little differing from that of the

Heathens,

Heathens, and things contrary to the sense of all sober Man-kind. If he had lived in the 9, or 10 Century (as his Talent seems to be fitted for such a credulous Age) I am inclined to believe that he would not onely have been famed for a *Writer* of others Miracles, but some *Monk* or other, would have made him a *worker* of them too. What pitty was it, that Mr. *Cr.* was not in Being 2 Ages ago, when that important Controversy was menaged with such zeal about the Bl. Virgins Ring wherewith she was espoused to *Joseph*, and 2 Towns went together by the ears, in contesting to whom it did belong (which story I'le give the Reader afterwards.) There could not have been pickt out such a man as Mr. *Cr.* to have made a *Prologue* to that *Play*: He could have represented, what vast expences *Princes* were at heretofore, to obtain such holy Treasures, as they were now concern'd about: How the Reliques of S. *Austin*'s body had been purchased with a 100 Talents of Silver, and a Talent of Gold: How great a Summe the Arm of S. *Bartholomew* cost Queen *Emma*, when she purchased it of the Bishop of *Beneventum*: He could have told them, that there could scarce be any hard bargain in buying the precious Arm of S. *Sampson* Arch-Bishop, which was taken from such a shoulder, upon which, when he received the Order of Priesthood, a Pillar of Light from Heaven was seen to rest, till the whole Office was finished. And what could he not have said in representing the mighty concern of *Henry* the Emperour, who when he could not with Promises and Rewards, obtain from *Rodulph* Duke of *Burgundy*, the Lance with which our Lord's side was pierced, and to which was fixed one of the Nails of his Cross; at last with threats of an Invasion extorted it from him, and how he after rewarded the *Duke*, not onely with store of Gold and Silver, but with bestowing on him a great part of the Province of *Suevia*. Here was a pious Emperour indeed, who to obtain (as he thought) the Lance

Ch.Hist.l.34.c.3.

Ibid.

Id.l.31.c.10.

Ibid.

Lance which pierced our Saviour, could have been contented to have really murthered Thousands of Christians, in which it is hard to say, whether he had expressed more kindness to our Lord, or his Members. These stories, no doubt, would have been very acceptable in that Age; but Mr. *Cr.* must exercise a little patience, if we now should chance to smile at the fooleries of his History in this particular of Reliques; and we promise him to be contented to be called *Jews*, and be ranged by him in the society of evil spirits (I give you his own language) or any thing else he pleases in his Frantick fits to call us; so he will but give us leave to look, before we turn purchasers, and not quite lay aside our *reason*, when he calls upon us to believe and venerate.

To begin therefore with the last instance I named, concerning the Spear and Nailes of the Cross, which the Emperour had. As for the Spear; since the story of *Longinus* (who was once said to pierce our *Saviour*'s side, and to be converted at the cross) may well be lookt upon by all as a Fable; this Spear too I doubt must now follow his fate; especially since the Historians, *Socrates, Sozomen* and *Theodoret*, who have told us of *Helena*'s finding other Instruments of *Christ*'s passion (and some of them have related, how she found and disposed of the Nailes, as by and by we shall hear) yet say not a word of her finding the Spear among the rest, that were digged out of Mount *Calvary*, where she found the Cross. And as for the Nailes, by which our *Saviour* was fastned to the Cross; *Baronius* has confessed, that there could be but 3, or at most 4 of them, and he also informs us how *Helena* disposed of them: With two she caused a Bridle * to be made for the Emperor *Constantine*; the *Third* she put in his Crown; and the *Fourth* (*which in my Opinion was best bestowed*) was thrown in a great Tempest into the *Adriatick* Sea, to becalm it: But

---

* *Theodoret* applies to this the Prophecy of *Zachary* (*cap.* 14. *v.* 20.) where, following the 70, he reads, *Holiness shall be upon the Bridles of the Horse*: but the *Hebrew* מצלות, (which signifies *Bells*, not *Bridles*) quite spoiles the conceit, if nothing else did.

then

then any one may see how the Cardinal is put to it, to answer for all the other Nayles that are shown in several places. Thus he attempts it. *Sed fortasse accidit, &c.* "Perhaps it so fell out, that to

<small>*Baron. ad an.*
326. *nu.* 54.</small>

"every one of those Nayles (*that are shown*) "there might a small portion of Iron be taken from a true "Nayle, (*that pierc'd his body*) and added to it, (the least I "can imagine, is, when two Nayles are rubb'd one upon another, and so one may be sanctified by the other) or rather, "when the ancient Monuments were lost, that testified the "matter, then those Nayles by which the pieces of the holy "Cross were joyned, were taken for those by which *Christ*'s "Body was fastned to the Cross: And perhaps in some pla- "ces it so happened, that a Nayle kept among the sacred "Reliques, whereby one of the mystical members of *Christ*, "*viz.* a Martyr, was pierced, was taken for one of the very "Nayles of the Passion of *Christ* (*a fine fetch to save a* "*lye, the Nayle that pierces Christ's mystical members, pier-* "*ces his body*) *and then he concludes, Quicquid sit, fides* "*purgat facinus*; whatsoever becomes of it, faith purges "the crime (*not of those that cheat with it, nor of the Church* "*that connives at it*) for none of the faithful worships the "Iron, but rather venerates and adores the Passion of "*Christ* in the Iron: (*which pretty excuse of the Cardinal,* *may as well serve for all the stupidity and cheats of the Heathen Idolatry; for they never worshipp'd any thing, but with relation to that which they verily believed to be a Deity.*) But to return to Mr. *Cressy*: He tells us out of *Matth.*

<small>*Ch. Hist. l.*2.
Cap. 13.</small>

Paris, "that the Master of the Hospital of St. "*John* at *Jerusalem*, sent a portion of the Blood "of *Christ* shed on the Cross, in a certain cry- "stal Glass, by a Brother of the Temple, well known to "*Henry* III. the which present was confirmed by the Te- "stimony of the Patriarch of *Jerusalem*, of Arch-Bishops, "Bishops, Abbots, and Noblemen dwelling in the H. Land, "and with what reverence the King and Nobility enter- "tained the said holy Treasure; as also (in the same Chap-
"ter)

"ter) that S. *Joseph* of *Arimathea* brought with him into
"*Brittany* two Silver Vessels, filled with the Blood of our
"*Saviour*, which precious Vessels, by his order, were buri-
"ed with him in his Tomb: and he gives two excellent rea-
"sons, why he would have them thus buried with him.
"1. Because, if they should have been consigned to any par-
"ticular persons in those times, before Christianity was set-
"led in this Island, either a losing and profanation of them
"could scarce have been avoided: (*by the same reason we
should never more have heard of the Spear; and why could
not a Miracle, such as is show'd perpetually in preserving and
increasing the Wood of the Cross, have preserved them?*)
"Whereas a certainty that they were reserved in that place,
"would be an occasion to stir up the Devotion of present
"and succeeding Christians to frequent it, and reap benefit
"by the vertue of them. 2. Again, Saint *Joseph* had no
"doubt the same design herein, that the Emperour *Con-
"stantine* exprest, who made (as *Eusebius* tells us) the Re-
"liques he had collected of the Apostles, be laid up in his
"Tomb, to the end that being dead, he might be partaker
"of the Prayers, which there in honour of the Apostles
"should be offered to God: [both which reasons are confuted by himself in the foregoing Chapter, where he tells
us, that the particular place where *S. Joseph* was buried is
unknown, and that though one *John Blome*, (thinking he
had a Revelation) obtained leave from the King to search
for it, yet his labour was in vain, and that his Reliques could
never be discovered; insomuch as some anciently doubted,
whether he was indeed buried at *Glastonbury*.] But however highly he may seem to estimate the Blood of *Jesus*,
while it is thus preserved in Glasses and Silver Vessels;
yet I doubt he forgot one thing, which argues it, in my
Opinion, to be more sacred, and too precious to be deposi-
ted any where on Earth; and that is, (what the Apostle to
the *Hebrews* insists on) that this Blood was to be presented
in the most holy place, being that of an expia- *Heb.*9.*v* 11,
tory Sacrifice; and that the Heavenly things 12, & 23.
were to be purified by it. It

It may be worth Mr. *Cressy*'s resolving, whether the blood that was shed on the Cross, after it was poured out, had any relation to our *Saviour*'s Body: if it had; whether, when his Body became glorious * and immortal, after his entrance into the holy place, that is, into Heaven, we must not say the same of his Blood too: unless we will make a strange and incongruous difference between the Body and Blood of *Christ*; which would be more still, if some part of his Blood (as we must suppose some remained in his Body, and was not wholly evacuated when he dyed) suffered such a glorious change, and other parts of it remained as they were before; some of it translated above, and some of it remaining still below: If he say that all of it was made like unto his glorious Body; I ask then, whether he may not as wisely think, to fill a Bottle with the Sun-beames, as with this Blood?

* Dr. *Jackson* on the Creed, Book 10. cap. 46. pag. 3258. *To inquire, says he, what should become of all our Saviours blood, whether shed in his Agony or upon the Cross, will seem I know a curious Question, specially to slothful Students in Divinity. On the other side, it would argue a drowsie fancy, either voluntarily to imagine, or to be by others perswaded, that this most precious blood being shed in such abundance, should be like water spilt upon the ground, or mingled with dust, or dispersed by the heat of the Sun, and resolved into vapours: Seeing every drop of it was truly the blood of God, it can be no sin to suppose, nay to believe, that all of it was by his death, made, as his body now is, immortal; that all of it was preserved intire and sincere, and brought either by his own immediate power, or by the Ministry of his holy Angels, into those Heavenly Sanctuaries, which were to be consecrated by it, to be the Seats and Mansions of Everlasting Bliss unto all true Believers, and thus brought in at the time of his entrance into Paradise, in Soul, though not in Body, which was immediately after he had commended his Spirit unto his Heavenly Father.*

I foresee Mr. *Cr.* will have a hard task, to resolve this with satisfaction; because I observe how the great *Jesuites* of his Church are at a loss in a like case, though of less difficulty, to wit, about the *Præputium* of our Saviour, which was cut off at his Circumcision. How this sacred Relique was preserved and found we shall have occasion to mention

after-

Devotions of the Roman Church. 31

afterwards; but they are not agreed, where it is kept.* *Costerus* says, it was kept at *Antwerp* many years, till the fury of *Hereticks* took it away, in the Year 1566. *Cardinal Tolet* says, to this Day it is kept at *Calcata* in the Church of Saint *Cornelius* and *Cyprian*, where it has been worshipped from the Year 1559, to 1584. *Salmeron* out of the Legend of *Jacobus de Voragine*, will have it to have been given by the Bl. Virgin, first to *Mary Magdalen*, and afterward to have been brought by an Angel to *Charles the Great* at *Aken*, and after came to be laid up in the *Lateran*; Hence those Verses.

* See *Bollandus Act. Sanct. ad Jan. 1. de præputio Christi.* And *Rivets Apologia pro S. Maria virgine lib. 1. c. 17.*

Tolet in cap. 2. Luc. annot. 31.

Salmeron in Evang. Tom. 3. Tract. 36.

*Circumcisa caro Christi, Sandalia Sacra,
Atque umbilici viget hîc præcisio chara.*

That is,

Christ's foreskin and blest Sandals are kept here,
And what was cut from off his Navel dear.

But for all this, the Church of *Antwerp* seems to say the most for themselves, that they were the owners of this Treasure; if we either consider the Miracles they also pretend to, or the numerous testimonies *Bollandus* has mentioned: *First*, that of the *Chapter of Antwerp*, an. 1416. of *Theobald Arch-Bishop of Bisonti*; an. 1427. of *John Bishop of Cambray*, an. 1428. (in whose presence, we are told the wonder appeared, of *three* drops of blood, which distilled from the *Præputium* upon the Corporal on which it was laid) of Pope *Eugenius*, an. 1446. and the Bull of *Clement* VIII. an. 1599. in which the *Confraternity of the Circumcision* is confirmed, which was long before there instituted. There is another place still that pretends to this Relique, for those of *Podium*

Loc. citat.

do

do carry it about with great Veneration on the Feast of the *Ascension*; but the Knife of the Circumcision is shown to the people at Compendium.

Bollandus in Appendic. Vol. 1. ad. 1. Januar.

But then comes a farther doubt; If this be true, says *Salmeron*, it is very wonderful; for since *that* Flesh is of the truth of his humane Nature, we believe that upon the Resurrection of *Christ*, it returned to its glorified place. *Suarez* the Jesuite is also put to it, to resolve the Question; who notwithstanding all the Revelations to S. *Briget* concerning the preservation of this Relique, concludes; "That the Body of *Christ* rising from the dead, had a fore-" skin; because this is a particle of Man's body, belonging " after a sort to its intireness; therefore it is not wanting " to the Body of *Christ* now in Heaven, in which there is " no imperfection: Besides, *Adam*, and other beatified " Saints have their Bodies intire, without the defect of this " part, &c. As to the Objection, that the foreskin of *Christ* is still preserved in the Church, he answers, " 1. That *Innocent* the III. called it in Question. 2. He adds that the " foreskin belongs to the intireness of the Body *formally* and " not *materially*; therefore some material part may remain " on Earth, which was supplied to the Body of *Christ* in " Heaven, from other matter that was sometimes of his " Body, and had been resolved by continual Nutrition. *Thus he.* Now if all this difficulty appears in salving this Relique, which is a less considerable part of our *Saviour's* Body; the difficulty must increase when we speak of this Relique of his Blood; especially because it was that very individual Blood, which was last in his Body when he dyed, and then a part of it: And it ought to abate Mr. *Cr.* confidence still more; when he calls to mind, that it is the most common Opinion of the *School-men*, that the Blood of *Christ* was *Hypostatically* united to the *Word*, not only when he was alive, but also *in Triduo mortis*; and that a Divine of *Barcinona*, who preached that the Blood of *Christ* shed in his Passion,

Suarez. in 3 part. qu. 54. Act. 4. disp. 47. Sec. 1.

Passion, was separated from his Divinity, was condemned for preaching Heresie, and a Book written against him, by the command of Pope *Clement* VI. and he was made to recant his Sermon, as you may see in *Vasquez*, who asserts it as his own Opinion,* that, *No portion of the blood of Christ did remain on Earth under the form of blood*, but onely *under its colour, amissâ formâ sanguinis*. *Aquinas* also is positive, "What-"soever, *says he*, belongs to the nature of a humane body, "was wholly in the body of *Christ* "when he rose, as his flesh and bones "and blood, *&c*. and therefore all "those were in the body of *Christ* when he rose, and that "intirely without all diminution, otherwise it had not been "a perfect resurrection. And more fully afterward, "all "the blood that flowed from the Body of "*Christ*, since it belongs to the verity of "humane Nature, rose in the body of "*Christ*: as for that blood which is preserved in some "Churches for Reliques, it did not flow from *Christ*'s side, "but is said miraculously to have flowed from a certain I- "mage of *Christ* that was pierced. Which last words refer to that story that is told in a Book attributed to *S. Athanasius* (though falsly, as *Bellarmine* confesses, *de Scriptor. Eccles. p.* 116.) wherein he relates how a *Jew* at *Berytus* pierced the Image of *Christ* upon the Cross, and blood issued from it. *But enough of this matter*. As Mr. *Cressy*'s discourse is weak and childish (to say no worse) about the Blood of our Saviour, so it is too, about the Bodies of the Saints. The *Roman* Church celebrates the Martyrdome of Eleven Thousand Virgins upon the 21 of *October*, all slain at one time: I shall now only deal with Mr. *Cr.* about their *Reliques*, deferring to speak to their *Story*, which I intend to give afterward. If we suppose what he says about their slaughter and the circumstances of it, to be true, one may then allow the place pretty easie to be found where they

Vasquez. in 3 part. Thomæ Qu. 5. Artic. 2. Disp. 36. cap. 4.

* *Ibid. cap. 8.*

Thomas part 3. qu. 54. Artic. 2. respondeo ascendum.

Ibid. ad Tertium.

Ch. Hist. l. 9. cap. 20. were buried, and we'l suppose it, as he says, to be near *Colen*; and that that might be done about 10 Years after, which he says the Arch-Bishop of *Colen* did, taking their Bones out of the ground, and reverently burying them again in Chests hewn out of stone (which is hard to be believed, the number is so great; but if *Colen* could show 1100 such Chests, allowing 10 Bodies, which is fair, to one Chest, that doubt might cease) we might then also grant, that several of those Bodies and parts of them, might have been preserved a long time, (though without a Miracle, they that have been dead 12, or 1300 Years, will scarce look so fresh, as I suppose their pretended remains do at *Colen*, and other places, where they show more than stone chests.) Grant too, that these Reliques have been dispersed, as he would have them, all over the World, and let the Town of *Maydenhead*, take its name from the Head of one of the Virgins, there (*I know not how long since*) kept and venerated. But now comes that wherein my faith is crampt (which yet Mr. *Cr.* runs off as roundly as any part of the story) *viz.* his confident pretending, that the body of such a one of these Virgins, naming her, lies at such a place, and he mentions above 40 of them, with the distinct places, where their Reliques are preserved. "The body of S. *Ursula* her self (the Leader of them) is still preserved at *Colen*, * " but her Head " was translated to *Paris*, where the Colledge of *Sorbon* ac- " knowledge her their Patroness: (*having got so choice a* " *part of her, as her head*) At S. *Denis* in *France* is a com- " memoration of *Panefredis, Secunda, Semibaria, Florina* " and *Valeria* companions of *Ursula*, whose Reliques re- " pose there: In *Flanders* the Monastery of *Marcian* pos- " sesses some part of the Body of *Cordula*, &c. Now I desire Mr. *Cr.* to satisfie me in this one demand; since these

Ibid. lib. 9. cap. 23.

---

* *As certainly, as that very Gold-Ring is still kept there, with which* Ursula *was betrothed to Prince* Connarus, *which* Laurus *sayes he saw shewn at* Colen *among their Reliques.* Laurus de annulo pron. B. Virg. pag. 2.

bodies undoubtedly were buried at first, as rudely as they were slain, and that in a strange Countrey far distant from their own, where they were known to none; and are not pretended to have been stirred out of their first grave, till about 10 Years after their burial; Let him tell me without flying to a Miracle (which is as foolish in this case, as idle talking of Occult Qualities in a Question of Philosophy) how could any one know the body of S. *Ursula* from that of S. *Cordula*; S. *Babcaria* from S. *Semibaria*; and so distinguish any of the rest? If he thinks the Question hard, I'le give him time to send to *Colen* to be resolved farther about it, and if he pleases too, about the 3 Kings there; and he would do well to inquire whether *Ursula* had not more bodies and heads than one; since in the Index of the Reliques of *Glastonbury* Abbey, it is thus recorded. *In a coffin, the Reliques of S. Ursula the Virgin are contained satis plenè, and in the same coffin is contained a third part of the Reliques of S. Daria the Virgin* (who yet in the Visions of S. *Elizabeth* is said to be the Mother of *Ursula*, which creates a farther doubt worth resolving) the gift of Henry Bishop of *Winchester* (who was Abbot there, and lived at that time when the Sepulchral Titles were discovered, that gave occasion to the dispersing the Reliques of the 11000 Virgins, in the Year 1156.) The *Bergomenses* also firmly believe, that they have the head of S. *Ursula*, as well as they of *Colen*. But to go on.

Bish. Usher de Britan. Eccles. primord. p. 626, 627.

He tells us of S. *Audoens* Reliques, that being applied to one almost consumed with the Leprosie, and to another half dead with the Palsey, by the hand of S. *Odo* Arch-Bishop of *Canterbury*, they were immediately restored to health. Now though I could have wished, that any other hand had applied them, than S. *Odo's*, because some may doubt, considering how great a Miracle-worker (as we shall see afterwards) S. *Odo* was, whether it was his hand, or the others *Reliques* that wrought the cure; yet I shall be so civil, as to make

Lib. 32. cap. 3.

no farther scruple about either *Adon* or his other two Brothers, they may all work miracles, I'le not question it, when *Adon*, *Dado*, and *Rado*,* are their names.

* *Capgrave* calls them *Ado*, *Bado*, and *Dado*. *in vit. S. Audoen.*

He says, concerning S. *Brigid*, (*lib.* 10. *c.* 12.) that in Testimony of her Virginity, having touched the wood of an Altar, it became presently green: But I shall take leave to suspend my faith in it, till I am told, who ever called her Virginity in Question (for that he says not a word of) and I cannot upon my Principles imagine that any such miracle would have been shown, unless that which it gave testimony to, had been opposed; any more than that there would have been any miracles in the Primitive Church, if there had been neither *Jews* nor *Heathens*, who blasphemed and contradicted the sacred Doctrines of *Christ*; for these are not for them that believe, but for them that believe not. I'le also give him another miracle of S. *Brigid*, to make my peace with him, (if he can believe it he may; for I cannot) which I find in the Breviary of *Sarum*, *Les.* 2. of S. *Brigid* (where also that about the Wood being made green is mentioned) "S. *Brigid* being sent by her Mother a milking, in "order to the making of Butter, she gave all the Milk to the "poor; and when the rest of the Maids brought in what "the Cows afforded, she prayed to the Lord, and he be-"stowed Butter upon his Virgin in great abundance. (As if God would miraculously incourage that which he has so expresly forbidden, the doing of evil, that good may come of it? this sure is only fit for them to believe who very often practise it.) We are farther informed also, that she used to divide the Butter she gave away into 12 parts, as if it were for the 12 Apostles, and one part she made bigger than any of the rest, which stood for *Christ*'s portion: though its strange she forgot to make another inequality, by ordering one portion more of the Butter to be made bigger than the remaining ones, in honour of S. *Peter* the Prince of the Apostles.

Bolland. Act. Sanct. ad Febr. 1.

Apostles. These Butter-miracles, I was apt to fancy, could afford no *Sure Footing* to a wise Man's faith; and yet I observe, that the only wonder that we are told, of another *She-Saint*, (to wit, *S. Haseka*) is but this, that at a meal, by her prayers she made stinking butter sweet. *Boland. ad Januar. 26.* But Mr. *Cressy* calls us to harder tasks of believing still in some other instances he gives about the Saints bodies. The one is concerning St. *Baldred*, out of the *English* Martyrology. Where it is said, *Lib. 14. c. 3.* " That he was wonderfully buried in *three* places, " seeing *three* Towns, *Aldham, Tinningham*, and *Preston*, " contended for his body. The meaning of which is, that his whole body unremoved was buried in *three* places, else it was no wonder at all. This Mr. *Cr.* believes, and so do I, only we differ in this small circumstance, that I believe it to be a stupid and notorious lye. But I seem plainly to apprehend, that he did not intend that we Protestants should much trouble our selves about it; for he knew well enough, that this was too hard a morsel for us to swallow down, upon the meer credit of a Martyrology: but oh this is a sweet story for his Catholicks, who are resolved to believe in spight of all their reason, that the whole Body of *Christ* may be at the same time in a thousand places; and let them take the comfort of it, I shall not envy them. Another is somewhat to the same purpose, concerning *S. Theliau*: " After he was dead, the Inhabitants of *three* se- *Lib. 11. c. 13.* " veral places contended earnestly which of them " should enjoy his body: those of *Pennalum*, where his an- " cestors had been buried; those of *Lanteliovaur*, where he " dyed; and those of *Landaff*, among whom he had been " Bishop. When therefore no agreement could be made " amongst them, there appeared presently *three* Bodies so " like to one another, that *three* eggs could not more per- " fectly resemble. So each of these People took one of them, " and by that means the controversy ended. *But then it fol-* " *lows*, That by frequent miracles at his Tomb it appeared, " that the Inhabitants of *Landaff* possessed the true Body.

This

This story neither need create us but little trouble, since, as good luck will have it, it confutes it self. For can any one imagine, that when three Towns are with equal zeal and devotion contending for the possession of so great a Treasure as his Body was, that only one of them should glory in the prize? or that the same miracle which gave it them, should give them occasion to laugh at the other two, who were fobb'd and cheated with an aery Image, and made to embrace a *cloud* instead of *Juno*? I can allow easily that God might *deny* 20 Towns, who should have put in for it, but I cannot believe that he would thus *deceive* one: This was a trick fit for none but the Devil to play, who delights in cousenage and abusing of Man-kind: but rather than thus to think of God, I'le sooner be perswaded that a tender hearted Father, when *three* of his hungry Children cry to him for Bread, will fill the Belly of one of them, and still the complaints of the other two, only with a painted Baby or a Rattle. And now me thinks I begin to be weary of considering these follies, and it's well if I have not made the Reader do some penance too; since therefore I hope I have sufficiently secured him, from giving too hasty a credit to Mr. *Cressy*'s Legends, I dare now trust him with such idle tattle, as this that follows. (Only premising, that if there were 20 more such miracles told us, though we should hear of the finding Children unhurt on the tops of Trees in Eagles nests, as in the case of *Nesting*, (lib. 32. c. 19.) if they have the seal of St. *Dunstan*'s age, or the next upon them, that is, refer to 900, or a 1000 Years after *Christ*, the Reader may give them a pass in course, and need not examine them farther, or stop them.)

Lib. 33. c. 17. "The Lungs of King *Edward* the Martyr "continued fresh for many Ages, and seemed "to pant.

Lib. 33. c. 15. "The Chariot in which the body of S. *Edmund* was carried, passed over a Bridge, "narrower than it self, without any harm, so that one wheel "rolled in the Ayr. (*pure Capgrave.*)

"A

"A Monk of *Glastonbury* named *Ailsi*, "refusing to bow, as others did, to a Cruci- *Lib.* 32. *c.* 19. "fix; at last either out of compunction, or "by command of his Superiour, he bowed himself: but a "voice proceeding from the Image, said these words di- "stinctly; *Now too late Ailsi, now too late Ailsi*, which "voice so frighted him, that falling down, he presently expi- "red: And so that which follows of a cross shaking over King *Edgar*'s head, and a Crown falling. So (*lib.* 32. *c.* 25.) After a great debate between the Seculars and Monks, when a great many things had been alledged against the Monks, and every one expected S. *Dustan*'s resolution, who was present; an Image of *Christ* on the Cross, which was fastned above in the Room, spake these words distinctly in the hearing of all. *It must not be, it must not be, you have ordered things well, you shall do ill to change them.* Every one was amazed, and S. *Dunstan* said, my Brethren, what would you have more? you have heard the affair decided by a Divine sentence: They answered, we have indeed heard it: and upon this the Monks of *Winchester* remained secure, and were never after disturbed in their possession. But Mr. *Cressy* adds, though the Debate ended, the minds of the contrary party were not yet satisfied, but they still pursued their pretensions; that is, I suppose, they were crafty knaves, and knew more than others did of the secret of speaking Images; and so * *Polydore Virgil* mentioning this very matter, says, that some thought this voice was rather formed by the fraud of men, than by the ordering of God: and indeed any man without much breach of charity may have liberty to suspect these things of contrivance, since this device of moving Images was practised no longer since, than the Age before us; when the famous Image of the *Rood of Grace*, was brought forth and publickly show'd at

---

* *Pol. Virg. Anglic. Histor. l. 6. in fine, atque sic monachi ope divina vel humana potius (nam etiam tum non defuerunt, qui id oraculum Phœbi magis quam Dei fuisse, hoc est, hominum fraude, non dei nutu, editum putarint) utcunque parta retinuerunt.*

St. *Paul*'s cross with all its tricks and Mechanisme (*a*): and we could (if need were) tell Men of Books, that will direct them how all such things may be done; and how even the Image and representation of *Christ* in the form of a child, (a thing talked of not long ago, as a wonder in *France*, and which Mr. *Cressy* relates an instance of, *lib. 9. c. 11.*) may at Noon-day be made to descend, to remain unmoveable and fixed upon an Altar, to ascend up again without wires, or any visible hand to move it, or possibility of stirring it one inch out of its place, (if any by-stander should attempt it) and all without either conjuring or miracles. But if any stiff Catholick be resolved to believe these voices to be miraculous, and thinks they mightily serve for a proof of their way of Religion and Worship; he may do well to bethink himself, that whether he will or no, the old *Gentile Religion* will come in for a share in the demonstration, and an equal kindness in all reason should be expressed to their superstitions, which have been long since recommended to the world by just such wonderful attestations; for, what's the difference, I pray, between the voice that said in the case of the Monks, *Ye have ordered all things well, &c.* And that which *Valerius Maximus* mentions, of the Image of Fortune, which spoke to the Matrons that had by their prayers hindred *Coriolanus* from destroying the City, and spake it twice, *You Matrons have rightly seen me, and rightly dedicated me.* And the same Author tells us, that when *Camillus* took the *Veia*, "the Souldiers by the command of the "General, being about to remove from its "seat, and bring into the City the Image of *Juno Moneta*, "which was there chiefly worshipped; when one of the "Souldiers jestingly asked the Goddess, whether she would "remove to *Rome*, she answered, *She would remove*: which "voice being heard, the jest was turned into admiration; "and now believing that they carried not the statue of *Juno*, "but

(*a*) *L. Herbert. H. 8.* pag. 432.

Val. Maxim. lib. 1. c. 12. n. 4. Ritè me Matronæ vidistis, ritè dedicastis.

Val. Max. ibid. Num. 3.

"but the very Goddess come down from Heaven, with
"great joy, they placed it in that part of *Mount Aventine,*
"in which now her Temple is to be seen: that is, they had
as good reason (if not better after the hearing such a voice)
to be perswaded that *Juno* was pleased, and that this translation of her image would turn to the advantage of their City; as the devout People of the *Roman* Church have confidently to presume the Patronage of that great Saint, whose
Image or Reliques they carry about with so much joy and
triumph in a solemn procession.

And now methinks I fancy, without pretending to one
of Mr. *Cressy*'s visions, that I see him not a little angry and
chafing at me, as one very profane, pert and presumptuous,
who have dared thus irreverently to handle the Holy Treasure (as he oft calls it) of the Saints, attempted to enervate
the force and spoil the credit of so many miraculous stories, which it cost him so much time and pains to bring to a
general Muster in his History; and have told the world in
effect, that a *deleatur* might have been put to one half of his
Book.

I am willing to fancy also, that when the angry fit is o-
ver, and he will calmly hear me speak for my self, I shall be
able, if not to make him my Friend, yet at least make him
have a better opinion of me: In order to which, I first of
all assure him, that I have a mighty veneration for true Miracles, true Saints, and true Histories, and, which may make
his pique the less against me, that I am none of the *Married
Clergy.* But then I add farther, that if I am spoyl'd as to
my faith in his history, he himself has helpt to do it: he is
the Person who has taught me to be cautious, and to suspend
my belief, to consider the nature of the things, as well as the
number or fame of the Writers that assert them, before I
give credit to them. I'le give him an instance of his own,
which, as I take it, gives any man liberty to believe as much,
or as little as he pleases, about the Reliques and Miracles
that are recorded in his Book: it is that which I find, *Lib.*
9. *cap.* 6. concerning the *Staff of Jesus:* which I will set
down,

down, word for word, as it is there, and hope to make good use of it afterwards. It is thus:

"St. *Patrick* by Divine Revelation, passed over to a certain solitary *Hermit*, living in an Island of the *Tyrrhen Sea*, whose name was *Justus*; which he made good by his actions, being a Man of a Holy Life, great Fame and much Merit. After devout salutations and good discourse, the same man of God gave to S. *Patrick* a Staff, which he seriously affirmed, had been bestowed on him immediatly by the hand of our *Lord Jesus* himself, who had appear'd to him. Now there was in the same Island at some distance, other men also who lived solitary lives, of which some seem'd very fresh and youthful, and others were decrepit old men. S. *Patrick*, after some conversation with them, was informed, that those very old men, were children to those who appeared so youthful. At which being astonisht, and inquiring the occasion of so great a miracle, they thus acquainted him, saying; We from our Child-hood by Divine grace, have been much addicted to works of mercy, so that our Doors were always open to all Travellers which demanded Meat or Lodging. On a certain Night it happened, that a stranger having a *Staff* in his hand, was entertained by us, whom we used with all the courtesie we could. On the Morning after he gave us his Benediction, and said, I am *Jesus Christ*: my members you have oft hitherto ministred to, and this Night entertained me in my own Person. After this he gave the Staff which he had in his hand, to a Man of God, our Father both spiritually and carnally; commanding him to keep it, till in succeeding times, a certain stranger named *Patrick* should come to visit him, and to him he should give it: Having said this, he presently ascended into Heaven; and from that day we have remained in the same state of youthful comeliness and vigour to this hour; whereas our Children, who then were little Infants, are now as you see become decrepit old men. *Thus far the story.*

Now

Now I desire any man that has read Mr. *Cressy*'s Church-History, to tell me, whether he look upon this as the most strange and improbable story in his Book; and whether there be not 40 others, as unlikely to be true? But now that which amazes me, is, that in all the prodigious things Mr. *Cr.* has related, and those few of them I have set down before; I never to my remembrance found his faith at a stand, but only here. This he leaves uncharitably to shift for it self, and take its chance; *Whatsoever fortune so stupendious a Story may find in the mind of the Reader*, (they are his words) and before he tells it out of *Joceline*, he says thus, *Without interposing my credit for the truth of it.*

Now I thank Mr. *Cr.* with all my heart; this was the passage I waited for a great while, but could not meet with it before; I thought I should have heard something like it, when he told us of the Blood of *Jesus* kept in Silver Vessels and Crystal Glasses; but that was too near the beginning of his Book, and every Catholick Reader would have cry'd shame on the Jadishness of Mr. *Cr.* faith, if at the first going out from easie trot into full speed, it should have lagg'd or drawn a lame Leg after it: But here it does you see; he dare not attest the truth of this. Why, what's the matter? Is not *Joceline* a man fit to be relyed upon? he has never told, that I know, any stories in favour of Hereticks; however I am sure this is none of them: and suppose it depended upon his single testimony, yet that's no news at all for Mr. *Cr.* to assert a miracle upon the credit of one witness. *Capgrave*, I am sure, has many a time been trusted, in matters as hard to be believed as this. But the case is not so here; We have Saint *Bernard* and *Giraldus Cambrensis*, both of them speaking home to the point, as to this *Staff of Jesus*, and if there were need of farther witnesses, the whole *Irish Nation* is ready to depose for it; so that (as *Cambrensis* tells us) in their Opinion, it was with this very Staff, that S. *Patrick* cast out of the Island all venemous beasts. I might add also, that Mr. *Cressy* knows not what he does, when he goes about to question the miracles of

Staffs,

Staffs, since a great part of the Religion of the *Irish*, seems to be supported by wonders of this nature. For how many of the dryed Staffs of Saints being fixed in the ground, have taken Root afresh, and grown into great Trees? So we are told of S. *Florentine's*, (a) of S. *Treſſan's*, (b) S. *Indract's*, (c) S. *Fingar's*, (d) S. *Mochoemoc's*. (e) St. *Furſe's* (f) staff, being stuck in the ground, produced presently a Fountain of fresh water, which was of such vertue, that it cured all the diseases of such as washed therein. When S. *Fechinus* wanted water to drive a Mill he had built, he fetcht it from a Pool a mile distant, only by throwing *two* staves (g) into it, which like Quick-silver bored their way through a Mountain which was between the Pool and his Mill, and so supplyed it ever after with Water. But what talk I of staves; any *bit of the Wood* of S. *Colmanus*'s famous Tree that he planted, being carried about a Person, who has confidence in the Saint, is a miraculous security against the most imminent dangers of death; insomuch that we are told that not long ago, a certain Malefactor adjudged to dye, before he was hanged up, having a piece of the wood of that Tree about him, he put it into his mouth, and was found alive after he had hanged the usual time; and so he was a 2d. and a 3d. time hanged up, yet could not be strangled; but the Officers examining the matter farther, found the bit of that wood in his mouth, which when they had taken out, he then quickly dyed: So ill advised was Mr. *Cr.* to begin his doubts with S. *Patrick's* staff. However I am resolved to tell his Catholicks the news: Mr. *Creſſy* himself dares not be a fourth man, to vouch for a story, where S. *Bernard* is one of the witnesses, and where he has Tradition too, and the veneration of so wise a Nation to back it. This is his hour of Temptation; he has been listening to the whispers of carnal reason, that great enemy to faith, and *credo quia impoſſibile*, is now no part of his Divinity: He has let go his hold of that Staff, which

Colganus Act. Sanct.
(a) *p.* 157.
(b) *p.* 272.
(c) *p.* 254.
(d) *p.* 390.
(e) *p.* 592.
(f) *p.* 295.
(g) *p.* 132.

Colganus. Ibid. p. 246, 247.

which if it had been well menaged, might have given the Hereticks such a blow, as they could not in hast have recover'd it; but now they turn the weapon with great advantage against himself, and there is no Circle, that he can ever hope to conjure us into; but by the help of this *Staff* of *Jesus*, we shall make our way out, and dissolve the charm: and so I take my leave at this time, and I hope fairly, of Mr. *Cressy*; and give him over to *Father Patrick* to be chastis'd by him, not only for his gross infidelity, but for his insolent affront of the whole *Irish Nation*.

And now I think it is high time to remember my promise, and give the Reader as short an account as I can of that famous Controversie two Ages ago, concerning the *Ring* with which the *Bl. Virgin* was espoused to *Joseph*; which story I hope will somewhat refresh him; and shew him into what folly and madness People will run, when their Religion degenerates into superstition.

The famous Controversie about the Sponsal Ring of the Bl. Virgin.

The story was first written by *Joh. Baptista Laurus* the *Pope*'s Protonotary of *Perusia*, and one of the Bed-chamber to *Urban* the VIII. His Book was Printed at *Rome*, *An.* 1622. (and afterwards put by *Bzovius* into his *Annal. Ecclesiastic. ad an.* 1480.) I shall give you the substance of it, leaving you to consult him in his large excursions.

Laurus begins his story with this supposition; that in contracting of marriages, Rings were in use, not only among the *Romans* and *Grecians*, but also among the ancient *Hebrews*, as a testimony of Faith and Conjugal affection: (which because it is the foundation of all that follows, we'l consider the truth of it in the Conclusion) He then adds, that those Ancient Rings of the *Hebrews*, were not of *Gold* (that he knew would not so well agree to the meanness of *Joseph*'s condition) but of baser mettals, as *Iron*; or were made of an *Onyx-stone*, to shew the frugality and parsimony of the ancient manner of living. And he says, that this of the B. Virgin, must not be thought like those Rings, we

read

read that Christ often used in myſtical marriages with holy Virgins, as S. *Agnes*, S. *Catharine* of *Sena*,&c. which were Rings in *appearance*: nor of the ſame kind with that, wherewith S. *Joachim* was married to S. *Anne* the Mother of the Bl. Virgin, and is kept at *Rome* by the Nuns of S. *Anne*, (*another precious treaſure*) for that is a rude Silver one, *&c.* but it is the *true* Ring with which the Bl. Virgin was eſpouſed to *Joseph*, made of an ord'nary *Onyx*, or *Amethyſt* (for it is ſomewhat doubtful, ſays he, which it is) which being very old, ſeems to have ſomething obſcurely ingraven on it, where ſome fancy they diſcern flowers, repreſenting the budding of old *Joseph's* Rod: (which is an old Fable, mentioned in the old *Roman* Breviary on S. *Joseph's* Day, *March* 19. that to know to whom the Bl. Virgin was to be eſpouſed, the High-Prieſt commanded, that all that were unmarried of the Houſe of *David* ſhould appear at the Temple, and bring dry Rods in their hands, which *Joseph* alſo did; but in the preſence of all, his Rod had green Leaves preſently upon it, and ſome add (which this Author mentions) that a Dove deſcending from Heaven, ſat upon the top of his Rod.

Theſe, you'l ſay, are good preparations, and now follows the Hiſtory of this wonderful Ring. Of which there is not one word ſaid, till the days of Pope *Gregory* the V. and of the Emperor *Otho* the III. who both began their Raign together, *an.* 996. So that we are fallen again into the Fabulous Age, and I'le warrant you the ſtory will work right which commences there, eſpecially after that the Ring had lien dormant a 1000 Years before.

At this time then, *Judith* the Wife of one *Hugo* a Marqueſs of *Etruria*, being a great Lover of Jewels, imployed one *Ranerius* a Jeweller of *Cluſium*, and a ſkilful Lapidary, and to whom ſhe gave good ſtore of Money, to go to *Rome* to make a purchaſe for her. Here it was, by the favour of Heaven, that *Ranerius* meets with a Jeweller come from *Jeruſalem* to *Rome*, from whom (you ſhall hear preſently how) he obtained this Ring: and (as the Author adds) it was

not

not fitting, that any where elſe, ſave at *Rome*, (which is the great Market of ſacred Reliques, and already poſſeſſed the Manger where *Chriſt* was laid) this Sponſal-Ring of his Mother ſhould be brought to light. After then that *Reinerus* has furniſht himſelf, and was now ready to depart and take his leave of his Merchant, the Jeweller profeſſing a ſtrange love to him, takes out this Ring and preſents it to *Reinerus*, as a pledge of their future kindneſs: which he looking upon as a thing of little or no value, would have put off the receiving it with a ſlight complement. But the Jeweller bid him not to contemn it, though its aſpect beſpoke it to be of no great value, for it was the Ring by which the Virgin was eſpouſed to *Joſeph*: and ſo made him take it with this charge, that he ſhould carefully ſee, that it did not come into the hands of any wicked perſon. But *Reinerus* not regarding what he ſaid, when he came home, careleſly threw it aſide in a little Cheſt, among other things of ſmall value. [And, to add that before I go on, he had indeed no great reaſon to mind his words much, for if the cunning Merchant, had known it really to have been what he pretended, he would unqueſtionably rather have made a preſent of it to the *Pope* himſelf, (who would ſure have rewarded him well for ſuch a treaſure, if he could have made it out, that it belonged to the B. Virgin) than have given it to one who was wholly a ſtranger to him, and whoſe whole purchaſe of Jewels bought of him, could not come near the value of this one Ring; but to proceed.] *Ranerius* at his return to *Cluſium*, gives an account to *Judith*, how he had laid out her Money, but forgot to ſay a word to her of the Ring, and if he had at that time, it might have ſignified little, for ſhe was more addicted to Pride than Religion, being of her Husbands humour, who minded little elſe but his pleaſure and ſports: but he in a Viſion of the B. Virgin to him, at a time when he had been wearied with Hunting, was ſeverely chidden; and the effect of it was, that he became a devout Perſon, and built many Religious Houſes, and a very venerable one at *Florence*, in honour of the B. Virgin;

his Wife *Judith* also became remarkable afterwards for her Piety.

But the forgetfulness of *Ranerius* cost him very dear; for having only one Son of 10 Years old (and so long it was that he had disregarded the Ring of the Virgin) he fell sick and dyed, and was carried out to be buried at the Church of S. *Musthiola* hard by *Clusium*. As the Herse went forward, on a sudden the dead Body of his Son rises in the Coffin, bids the Bearers stand still, and calls to his Father to come to him, to whom he spake to this effect. That by the favour of the B. Virgin, he was come to him from Heaven (whither after he had delivered his message, he must return again) to convince him of his contempt of Religion, for letting that most holy Jewel be in a common heap, he having never show'd it to any body, no not so much as to him: that now he must send for it, and produce it publickly, that it might be venerated; and that he might not doubt of the truth of what he said, he gave him a sign, by telling him of his secret vows of taking a Pilgrimage to Mount *Garganus*, and to *Siponto*, and of repairing a Church, which he had not performed.

Immediately the Chest is sent for, and delivered into the Son's hand, who amidst a number of other stones, presently findes the Ring (though he had never seen it before) and fervently kissed it, and openly show'd it to the company, who were all in readiness to venerate it; and the Bells, as some say, of their own accord rung a joyful Peal, as a sign of publick happiness. * After having dispatched this weighty business, which he came from Heaven on purpose about, and having directed them to the place where he would be buried, and delivered the Ring to the Curate of the Parish, the Child laid himself down in the Coffin, and went to Heaven, and his Body was buried. The fame of this drew a great

---

* *The like Story is told us of St.* Pega, *that going from England on Pilgrimage to Rome, as soon as she entred the City, the Bells of every Church rung out, of their own accord, for an Hours space, and told all the City the merits of her sanctity.* Bollandus ad Januar. 8. vol. 1. p. 533.

conflux

Devotions of the Roman **Church.**

conflux of People to visit this holy Relique wherefore binding a Gold-Chain to the Ring, they prepared a Coffer to keep it in; but before it was laid up, it wrought several wonders. For a Woman of Royal Extraction called *Vualdrada*, in a sudden pang of zeal, snatching the Ring, and putting it on her Ring-finger, immediately that Finger (*a*) withered, and so continued to her death. It is said also, that one *Contulus*, who was troubled with a *Sciatica*, made an impression of the Ring in wax, and applying it to his Hip, when the pain afflicted him, always found ease by it. And the Author says, that he, at the intreaty of some great Women, caused some Ivory Rings to be touched with that sacred one, and they received such vertue from it, that being put upon the finger of Women that had hard Labour, they

(*a*) *These are just such lying wonders, as* Card. Tolet *mentions* (*in the forenamed Comment. on* Luke 2. *annot.* 31.) *concerning the foreskin of our Saviour, found an.* 1557. *which at the sacking of* Rome, *an.* 1527. *was taken away, with several other Reliques, out of the Lateran Church, and hid by a Souldier in a Cellar at* Calcata, *who afterwards confessed where he had laid them, and after search made by the command of Pope* Clemens VI. *they were found, and brought by a Priest to* Magdalena Strotia: *which* Magdalene, *going about to unty a silken bag, in which the præputium was, found her hands grow stiff; and trying a second time, she found still a greater benummedness seize upon them; and upon a third tryal, two of her fingers were stiff and hard: then with tears by the advice of the Priest, she committed the undoing of it, to her Daughter* Clarica *a young Virgin, who presently without any difficulty unlosed the string, and laid the præputium in a Silver Vessel, which says he,* Densum ac crispum erat instar rubri cicêris. *Then follow other Miracles; how an.* 1559. *certain Women coming to* Calcata, (*the Town where it was preserved*) *went to see it with lighted Candles in their hands, and as soon as the Priest laid it on the Altar, a Cloud filled the Church, and hid the Reliques for* 4 *Hours time, so that nothing could be seen, save only the Cloud, Stars and Flames of Fire. And when one* Pimpinellus, *a Canon of the Lateran Church, tryed with two of his fingers, whether the præputium was soft or hard, by the pressure of his fingers, he brake it into two parts; upon the doing of which, says he,* Oh wonderful, *what Thunders there were, what Lightnings, how dark the Ayre was over the place, so that even all the by-standers were even dead for fear. All which being related to the Pope, they confirmed them for true Reliques; and for the greater fame of the place,* Sixtus V. *anno* 1584. *granted a plenary indulgence in that Church of* Calcata, *on the day of Christ's Circumcision, for Ten Years.*

E

were

were presently relieved: The Ring also was found beneficial for defects in the eyes, and for reconciling the affections of married People that lived at odds, and the freeing several from the vexation of evil spirits.

Thus this Sponsal Ring of the B. Virgin, remained in the possession of the *Clusians* 484 Years.

After this it came into the hands of the *Perusians*, an. 1473. in this manner following.

The Church of *Musthiola* becoming ruinous, where it had remained, it was brought into an House of the *Franciscans* in *Clusium*, and freely enough shown to the People; which a certain *Franciscan* Frier, a *German*, observing, whose name was *Wintherus*, a very crafty Knave, under the shew of great devotion, he begs of the Magistrates of *Clusium* to have the office of showing the Ring, who granted his petition. One time, after he had made a Sermon and showed it to the People, stooping, as if he intended to put it up in the place provided for it, he secretly conveighs it into his sleeve, and locking the Door, gives the Key boldly to the Magistrate, and privily conveighs himself away from *Clusium*, taking the Ring along with him. He had no sooner crossed the River, but the Field was fill'd with so thick a Mist and Darkness, that he knew not which way to turn himself or go: At last, his conscience smiting him for what he had done, taking the Ring out of his bosome, he hang'd it by the Chain upon a little bough of a Tree, and falling on the ground, with tears he accuses himself, and expostulating his sad condition to the Ring, if he should return to *Clusium*, he prays to the Ring, that it would send forth such light, as to dispell the Mist, and direct him by it, in the way wherein he should go: Presently he took the Ring again, and there came so great a light from it, as show'd him the way to *Perusia*, where he put in among the *Augustan* Friers.

A while after he attempted to go into *Germany*, his own Country, (whither he at first designed to carry it) but he was hindred in the same manner by the darkness that again came suddenly on him, so that he was forced to stay: and

this

this not only infested him, but the whole City for 20 Days, till at last he unbosom'd himself to his Landlord, one *Lucas Jordanus*, and declared to him all the adventure of the Ring; who with great craft and cunning, by representing the danger he was in from the *Clusians*, and the benefits he would receive from those of *Perusia*, he prevailed with him at last to bestow it upon this City; and as soon as ever it was showed to the People, all the Mists and Darkness was presently scattered and dispersed. The *Friar* was well rewarded; but for his better security against the *Clusians*, he was brought into the House of the Chief Magistrate, where, though in shew a Prisoner, he was well provided for.

In the mean while they of *Clusium* understood his theft and their loss, and dispatch over their Bishop to *Perusia*, who indeavoured partly by Intreaties, and partly by Threatning to regain the Ring. They ingage also the Citizens of *Sena* (a confederate City) to assist them in recovering of it, who sent Letters about it to *Perusia*, and after that an Embassador of theirs, one *Barth. Bonaspirius* to plead the cause before them; whom the Citizens of *Perusia* received with great respect; but told him, that since it pleased Heaven to bestow upon them that Ring, which they by no sacrilegious Arts had endeavour'd to procure, that they might not be thought injurious to the Mother of *Christ*, they would defend it with their Arms, and admit it not only within their Walls, but their Breasts, and receive it as they would do the Ark of the Covenant, or if there were any thing more sacred.

When this course would prevail nothing; at last the *Clusians* bring their cause before Pope *Sixtus* IV. and they of *Sena* gravely prepare for a Holy War. Neither were the *Perusians* idle, but send their Embassador to *Rome*; whose first work was to secure the favour of *Cardinal Petrus Riarius*, and Count *Hieronymus* his Brother, who were of the *Pope*'s Kindred, for they did not at all doubt of the *Pope*'s good inclinations to favour their City, having begun his studies among them, and been enrolled in their Colledg of Divines,

vines, and declared the chief Prelate of the *Franciscans*, in the General Assembly. 1464.

In the mean time, *Wintherus*, by the importunity of the *Clusians* to the *Pope*, is put into closer hold, but there maintained at the publick charge, and the heat of prosecuting him in a while being over, he lived merrily 30 Years in *Perusia*; and when he dyed, there happen'd another Religious quarrel, between the *Franciscans* and the *Canons* of S. *Laurence*, who should dispose of this Ring-stealers body, and it was carried for the latter; in whose Chappel, before the Altar dedicated to *Joseph* and the Bl. Virgin, he was buried, *an*. 1506. upon whose Tomb they wrote an Inscription, wherein they acknowledg that *Perusia* owed no less for the sponsal Ring of the Virgin, though a casual gift, than if he had offer'd it of his own accord; nay perhaps it was the sweeter for being stoln. They allowed also an Annual Pension to the Brothers of *Luke Jordan*, who had done them such good service in procuring the Ring: and now their next care was to provide by all possible securities, that the Ring should never more be taken out of their possession: It was kept therefore under 4 Locks, whose Keys were delivered to 4 Fraternities, of the *Dominicans, Franciscans, Servitæ, & Augustinians*, and was never to be show'd, but when they were by: it was also decreed, that it should not be in the Liberty of any Mortal to carry it any whither out of Town, nay it was Banishment for any one to propose so much. They also, the better to grace the solemnity of showing it, ordered the Fathers to appear in costly Habits; Drums, Trumpets, Organs, Bells, and a Musical Consort to sound at that time; and they took a publick Oath of those, to whose care it was committed (confirmed by taking the Sacrament in the presence of the Bishop, and Magistrates, and all the Clergy) to look carefully to it. Three appointed times of the Year, they decreed it should be shown, the Fraternities accompanying it from the Palatine Chappel to S. *Laurence* Church; and there in a Pulpit, one of the chief Prelates, should hold it to be seen, the space of one Hour, Morning and

and Afternoon: After this it was ordered to be shown only once a Year; but that Law was abrogated a while after, upon the clamorous Petitions of devout People. But now the Controversie grew hot, between the *Senenses* (whose Clients the *Clusians* were) and the *Perusians*: and one while the Pope hears of the Miracles that were done by the Ring, since it came to *Perusia*, and how fit it was, that famous City should still retain it: Then the Embassadors of *Sena* were brought to him, by means of Cardinal *Riarius* and *Ursinus*, to whom they had promised 25000 Pieces of Gold, in case by their means the *Clusians* should get the day, (*which I much wonder that it did not determine the business*) and they represent to him, how much the *Perusians* had been heretofore beholden to them, how ungrateful they had been to them in this affair, and sacrilegious in detaining that which they had got by theft, &c. The Pope appoints Eight Cardinals to hear the matter, and to weigh the Reasons on both sides, and in the mean while enjoyns the contending Parties to live in peace, telling them how absurd a thing it was, that the Ring which was a pledge of Love and Conjugal affection, should now be an occasion of contention and strife: (*and it was absurd enough in all conscience, without this witty Reason which the Pope gives.*) The Embassadors on both sides returned, and were gladly received, the *Perusians* especially rejoyced, thinking their cause was the better supported. But the two forenamed Cardinals, being allured with the great promises which the *Senenses* made to them, in case they could overthrow the *Perusians*, went thither to sollicit their cause; where being honourably received, they, in the name of the Pope, began to urge the *Perusians* to restore the Ring, that had, for so many Ages, belonged to them of *Clusium*, and in generosity, not to suffer such a reproachful mark of injustice to lye upon them; this they discoursed at first more privately, afterwards openly, and at last came so far as to threaten them with the sad effects of War, in case they refused. But while these things were thus transacted, Cardinal *Riarius* dies in the flower of his Age, being began some skirmishes against the *Clusians*, who preyed upon their flocks, and laid hands on the Countrey-men they met, and put them in hold; neither did the *Perusians* spare the Fields of the Bishop of *Clusium*. (Though dull and carnal men, who do not understand the worth of Reliques, would be apt to think it had been much better, that this Ring had at first been thrown after one of the Nayles of the Cross, into the Sea, than that such a stir should have been made about it.) But the *Perusians* had reason to take more heart, because they were favoured by many great ones, and at that time Cardinal *Fortebrachius* made attempts of war upon the *Senenses*. The *Perusians* after this, endeavour to oblige the *Pope*'s Kindred, especially *Hieron. Bassus* the Nephew of *Sixtus*, who was newly made Cardinal, and favoured their affairs. But they of *Sena*, being perplex'd with many troubles that befell them, grew more cold in their prosecutions; and some at *Rome* gave the *Pope* counsel (which he had also before threatned) to demand, that the Ring should be brought to *Rome*, and placed in one of the two Houses dedicated to the Bl. Virgin, which he had repaired : accordingly by a Letter dated, *Dec.* 18. 1480. the *Pope* desired the *Perusians* to deliver the Ring to *J. Baptista de Sabellis*, his Cardinal Legat, promising to put it in some venerable Temple of the City, and to give them holy Reliques in recompence to their content. But when the Legat came to urge the *Perusians* to comply with the *Pope*'s desires, instead of answering to what he said, they burst out into teares and howlings, cast themselves to the ground before him, and with sighs, and beating their breasts, in the most pitteous manner, beseeched and begg'd of him, to implore the favour of the *Pope* on their behalf. He was so moved with their teares and sad complaints, that he became a suppliant by his Letters

to

to the *Pope* on their behalf, which joyned with a moving Oration, of *Hieron. Riarius*, made the *Pope* alter his determination, and let the Ring still abide there. Also by the *Pope*'s interposing, the differences betwixt the *Senenses* and the *Perusians* were composed, and by agreement, they were to have no more words about the Ring ; and *Marcus Barbus* is perswaded to mitigate by his Authority the unpeaceable minds of the *Clusians*. But while these things are menaging, Pope *Sixtus* IV. dies ; and the Controversie was not fully decided, till the 3d. Year of Pope *Innocent* the VIII. *an.* 1486. When, the contending Parties agreed, being weary of squabling, to leave the matter to be determined by the *Pope*, and Cardinal *Piccolominæus*, who did that which *Eight* Cardinals before could not effect, and the Ring was adjudged to *Perusia:* who testified how welcome the News was which their Embassadors brought them, by making Bone-fires, and turning the very Night into Day, by Flames and Torches, and showing all other imaginable expressions of joy, *&c.* And now for the greater honor of the sacred Ring, the *Perusians* removed it from the *Palatine* House, to a more worthy place ; for to this end they built a Chappel in S. *Laurence* his Church ; and caused this Inscription to be placed on high.

> *Hîc sociata suo colitur Regina marito,*
> *Et facili justas accipit aure preces.*
> *Hâc sacer intactæ Matris jacet annulus æde,*
> *Qui dedit, est custos muneris ille sui.*

That is,

> Here Heav'ns great Queen is worshipt with her Spouse,
>   A gracious Ear to all just Pray'rs she lends.
> The untoucht Mother's Ring lies in this House,
>   And he that gave't, his Gift with care defends.

Also against the Festival dedicated to *Joseph* and *Mary*, they caused a curious Piece to be drawn, by one *Peter*, a *Perusian* Painter; in which was elegantly represented the Temple of *Jerusalem*; and in the open Court of the Temple was drawn on one side a Chorus of Virgins, and on the other side a Chorus of young Men, with withered Rods in their hands, and one of them breaking his Rod upon his Knee in anger, seeing *Joseph*'s Rod to flourish: Also the High-Priest was represented taking hold of the hands of *Joseph* and *Mary*, and preparing with the Ring to espouse them. There was also instituted a Society of *Seculars*, called the Sodality of S. *Joseph*, who together with the Clergy of S. *Laurence* Church, were perpetually to serve in the Chappel where the Ring was, and a Statue was placed at the right hand of the Altar, dedicated to S. *Joseph*, which was publickly produced upon his Festival, on the 19 of *March*. Thus the *Perusians* being inriched with their prey triumphed over the carelesness of the *Clusians*. [*Thus far the account of Laurus.*]

This story, I think upon the very relating of it, without any further commentary upon it, must needs appear to any judicious and unprejudiced Reader, to be the most egregious piece of Foolery, that ever entertained the World for so long a time: and I will be very thankful to Mr. *Cressy*, if for the credit of his Religion, he will be pleased to match this story with any thing equally ridiculous among *Turks*, or *Heathens*: for it grieves me, that any that bear the name of Christians, should run into such extravagant Follies, as the most absurd Religions in the World were never guilty of. It might be sufficient to stagger the Faith of any wise Man in this *Perusian* Ring; to tell him what *Bollandus* (or his Continuer) has observed; that in *Burgundy*, a Priory pretends to have had the Sponsal Ring of the Bl. Virgin, the space of Eight hundred Seventy-seven Years: And another Monastery in *Holland*, puts in strongly for the honor of having it, and have the countenance of miraculous examples,

Commentar. Historic de S. Joseph. ad 19. Mart. Sec. 8.

examples, of Women, who in the sharpest pangs of Travel, have by this Ring found present ease. But I have one thing farther to offer, which must needs utterly spoil the credit of this *Onyx* Ring of the Virgin, and also of that Silver one, mentioned at the beginning of the story, as the Sponsal Ring of *Joachim*, and S. *Anne*, the Parents of the Bl. Virgin, (though this too is countenanced with a pretended Miracle, that being stole from *Rome*, when the City was sacked in the Days of Pope *Clement* the VII. it was brought again, and laid upon a Stone in the view of many, by a Crow.) and both of them must fall into *Bolland. Act. Sanct. 21. Mart. in vit. S. Santuccia. p 363.* the Number of those cheating Bawbles, with which this Church abuses the World and Religion. And that which I shall offer, is a quite contrary story, to that which *Laurus* has laid as the foundation of all his discourse, *viz.* That this Custome of espousing by a Ring, though it was used by other Nations, yet was not practised by the ancient *Hebrews*. Which we are sufficiently assured of, by two as learned Men, as can be named in matters of this Nature, and as well acquainted with the *Jewish* Customes.

The one is *Buxtorfius* (in his Book, *De Sponsalibus & divortiis*, Sect. 45. *De forma & modo desponsandi*) where he shows, that their Espousals were performed these 3 ways; by Money, by an Instrument in Writing, or *Concubitu:* which last way as less honest, though they suppose it lawful according to the Law of *Moses*, yet has no longer place, but is prohibited under the penalty of beating [*]. He tells us indeed (*Sect.* 57.) of their confirming espousals by a Ring, out of some of their later Authors, but he expressly adds, that *Maimonides* never mentions any thing of it. And though he mentions, out of a Book of *Victor de Carben*, a baptized *Jew*; (Printed at *Colen, an.* 1509.) that the *Jews* take great care, to put the Ring upon the Fore-finger of her that is espoused, because they write, that *Mary*, when she was espoused to *Joseph*, wore her Ring on the Middle-finger,

[*] *See of this more largely, Seldens Uxor Hebraic. lib.2. cap.2.*

whence

whence no *Jewish* Woman will put hers to this day upon that Finger; yet, says *Buxtorf*, I could never meet with any such thing in their Books: and indeed he was not worthy to be Baptized into *that Church*, that could not invent such a story of his own head, with all his old *Jewdaisme* to help him.

The other Author is the Learned *Selden*, who tells us, that though there are to be found some slender *Sellens Uxor* Testimonies in the *Jewish Rituals*, of the use *Hebraic.lib.2.* of a Ring among the *Jews*, yet he says, it is ex-*cap. 14.* presly asserted by *Leo Mutinensis*, the Ruler of the Synagogue at *Venice*, that the use of a Ring is very rare among that Nation: and *Selden* says, he never remembers the least mention of a Sponsal Ring in the whole body of the *Thalmud*: But the ancient way among them was, to give to the Woman a Piece of Money (or its value) as a pledge of their contract of Marriage: but the Later *Jewes* observing, that other Nations used a Ring for such a Token *Uxor Hebr.* and pledge, brought in its use by imitation, and *lib.2.cap.2.* graved on it מזל טוב, wishing them good luck; but still this Ring was not used *quà annulus*, under that notion, but only to supply the place of the Money mentioned before; which he proves out of their Rituals, showing that *two* witnesses were called in, to inquire, whether the Sponsal Ring then produced, were of equal value with the פרוטה or Money, whereby Marriage-contracts were wont to be made. And whereas we heard *Laurus* before telling the story, that the *Jews*, to shew their frugality, caused their Sponsal Rings to be made of Iron or *Onyx*-stone: *Buxtorf* says clean contrary, that this Ring was to be made of pure Gold, † without any stone in it, lest any cheat should happen, by offering an adulterate Jewel for a true one, a common for a precious one, and so the Espousals become erroneous and void.

* *Annulus autem debet esse ex auro puro, sine gemma inserta, idque ideo, ne fraus aliqua intervenire possit, adulterinam sc. gemmam pro vera, vilem pro pretiosa sponsæ offerendo, & hac ratione desponsatio fiat erronea & vana. Buxtorf. loc. citat. sec. 57.*

As

As for such as have, with *Laurus*, the faculty of running up the use of such Sponsal Rings, as high as *Moses* his days, because that among the offerings of the Children of *Israel* to the Tabernacle, we read of Rings and *Onyx*-stones; they may next, for ought I know, be pleased with that Blasphemous fancy (mentioned by the *Elder Buxtorf* out of the *Talmud*, and altogether as wisely collected out of the Text) that God himself, at the Marriage of *Eve*, made up finely the Hair of her Head, and adorned it, sang before her, and danced with her in Paradise; which they deduce from *Gen. 2. 22.* where it is said that God brought *Eve* to *Adam*; that is, say they, he brought her as a Bride is wont to be brought, elegantly dressed, and her Hair curled (*calamistratam*) with leaping and dancing. There is nothing indeed more common in this Church, than to seek to countenance their Fables and Follies, by Texts of Scripture, where only the sound of one Word, without the least regard to the sense of it, is enough to serve their purpose; of which take an instance or two. We are told concerning St. *Endeus*, that leaving his Government, and taking the habit of a *Monk*, his Companions came to endeavour to draw him from his purpose, but upon the prayers of St. *Fanchea*, and her making the sign of the Cross, their Feet immediately stuck to the Earth like immoveable stones; but hereupon becoming sensible of their fault, and promising repentance, their Feet were again loosed, and they went their way; in which (says the Author of the Life) was fulfilled that of our Lord, *Whatsoever ye shall bind on Earth shall be bound in Heaven, and whatsoever ye shall loose on Earth shall be loosed in Heaven.* We have another pleasant instance of this kind, in the Letters of the Church of *Antwerp*, concerning the *Præputium* of our Saviour, cited by *Bollandus*; where relating how a Chaplain of *Godfrey* of *Bullen*, had brought this Relique from *Jerusalem* to *Antwerp*, they add,

Exod. 35. 22, 27.

Synagog. Judaic. cap. 28.

Colganus Act. Sanctor. in vit. S. Fancheæ. ad 1 *Januar. p.* 1, 2.

Bollandus Act. Sanct. ad Januar. 1. *p.* 14. 6.

Esa. 37. 32. add, For God said by the Prophet, *De Jerusalem exibunt reliquiæ*; out of *Jerusalem* shall go forth Reliques, (instead of, *a remnant*) And in another place, *Disperdam de loco hoc reliquias*, I will *Zephan.* 1.4. disperse Reliques from this place, (that is, from *Jerusalem*) but they left out the word *Baal* which follows, and we rightly translate, *I will cut off the remnant of Baal from this place*: And in another Prophet, *Possidere faciam reliquias populi hujus*; I will *Zachar.* 8. 12. make them to possess the Reliques of this people; instead of, *I will make the remnant of this people to possess all these things*. If this way of playing with Scripture were allowable, they might have added another out of the Prophet *Micah* (chap. 2. 12.) *In unum conducam reliquias Israel — tumultuabuntur à multitudine hominum*: *I will gather together the Reliques of Israel — they shall make a noise by reason of the multitude of men*; which last words might serve as well as the rest, to countenance their singing, when the Reliques are carried in procession, with a multitude attending them: *But this by the way*. And now, after all these things I have said, are well considered, I hope, without any dishonour to the Bl. Virgin, we may take leave to set a far less price upon her pretended Ring, than those of *Perusia* have done; and to laugh at their folly, for contending in such good earnest about it. I will refer the Reader (lest I should tire him) to consult another

Bzovius Annal. Eccles. ad an. 1463. *parag.* 60.

Controversie in *Bzovius*, (almost like this of the Ring) about the Body of S. *Luke*, which the *Duke of Venice* had obtained from the *Grecians*, with a very strong certificate of the Truth of it, and of Miracles wrought by it; but it was upon examination found to be a cheat, and that his true body was at *Padua* long before, only without a head (which the *Venetian* body was supplyed with) and his head had been long preserved at a Church in *Rome*. *Rivet* also gives us ano-

Rivet, Apologia pro S. Virg. Maria. lib. 2. *cap.* 9.

ther fine entertainment in what he presents us with, concerning the Figure

gure of the Sole of the *Bl. Virgin's* Shoe, graven in *Spain*, and set forth with Licence; which, he says, he preserves by him, and has caused the Figure of it to be graved, after the *Spanish* Original, in the foresaid Book. * In the midst of the Sole is written this. *The measure of the most holy Foot of our Lady*; And then is added. *Pope John XXII. hath granted to those that shall thrice kiss it, and rehearse 3 Ave Maries with devotion to her blessed honour and reverence, that they shall gain 700 Years of Pardon, and be freed from many Sins.*

* *I have measur'd the length of the Sole in our inches, and it is just 7 inches ¼; perhaps some Ladies of the Romish perswasion may find much comfort, in finding their Feet just fitting this measure.*

I cannot well omit a memorable passage in *Baronius*, which if duly considered, may serve to abate and lessen our Adversaries high Opinion both of their Reliques and of the Miracles that are said to be done by them. *Annal. Ecclef. ad an.*1027. p.89. Thus he writes. *Cum autem Reliquias Sanctorum tam caro pretio, &c.* "A "certain crafty Knave, understanding that the Reliques of "the Saints were sold at so dear a rate (*he mentions before, how the Arm of S. Austin, was purchased at Papia, at the rate of a Hundred Talents of Silver, and a Talent of Gold*) "he "set up a wicked Trade of merchandizing with the coun- "terfeit Reliques of the Saints, of whom *Glaber* relates this "story. There was at that time a certain ordinary Fellow, "a crafty Huckster, of an unknown Name and Countrey, "who that he might not be discovered, gave himself divers "Names, at several places where he skulked. This man "secretly taking up the Bones of dead Men out of their "Graves, sold them for the Reliques of *Martyrs* or *Confessors*. After he had played many such cheating tricks in "*France*, at last he came among the *Alpes*, where a sort of "sottish people inhabit. There he called himself *Steven*, "who otherwhile used to go by the name of *Peter* or *John*. "There, after his wonted manner, he gathered by Night in

"a sorry place, the Bones of an unknown person, which put-
"ting into a Chest, he had it by Revelation from an Angel,
"that those were the Reliques of the Martyr *Justus*. All
"the idle Countrey people flock together at the report,
"and the cheater was troubled, if there wanted at any time
"diseases to be cured. Then he leads the weak, bestows his
"little gifts, watches whole Nights, expecting sudden mi-
"racles, which (*mark well*) are sometimes permitted to be
"wrought by evil spirits, to try men that before have been
"sinful, which doubtless did evidently then appear, *&c.*
And a little after, *Baronius* mentions the complaint of S. *Austin*, that in *Africk*, many Impostors, pretending to be *Monks*, went up and down selling Reliques for gain, which they called the Bones of *Martyrs*. And methinks he himself, if he had been ingenuous, might have put into the number of cheating remains, that which he mentions upon the Roman *Martyrologie*. "That the most holy

August 29. "Fore-finger of *John* the Baptist, wherewith
"he pointed to *Christ* the Lord, saying, *Behold*
"*the Lamb of God*, &c. was brought from *Jerusalem* into
"the Island of *Melita*, by the Brothers of S. *John*'s Hospi-
"tal, and there is had in great veneration. To draw towards an end of this Digression about Reliques; I cannot but approve the saying of *Isaac Casaubon*. *Hodiernas reliquias*, &c. "The most of the Modern

Exercit. 16. *Sect.* 104. "Reliques, are either of uncertain credit,
adv. Annales Baronii. "or plainly counterfeit and false, which
"ought not to have been dissembled by the defenders of
"them, if they had taken care to approve their piety to-
"wards God; which is well matched with the wise discourse of *Cassander* in his *Consultation*, con-
Cassandri opera cerning the Veneration of Reliques; (who
pag. 973. being a person of their own communion, his words may perhaps meet with greater regard from the *Romanists*) Thus then he discourses. *Hodie vero cum passim*, &c.
"At this day, when all places every where seem to be filled
"with the Reliques of Saints, it is to be feared, lest, if Bi-
"shops

"ſhops and Princes would uſe that diligence they ought, in
"inquiring and judging of true Reliques, great and abomi-
"nable Impoſtures would be diſcovered, as it has fallen out
"in ſome places, and as it happened of old to S. *Martin*;
"who coming to a place of his Dioceſs, famous for the Mo-
"nument of a certain *Martyr* ſo accounted, he found the
"Tomb of a wicked *Thief (not of a Martyr)* frequented and
"venerated by the People, which preſently he commanded
"to be overturned and demoliſhed: Though they alſo
"ought not to be approved, who through hatred of ſuper-
"ſtition, have violated the certain Monuments of pious men,
"and with the greateſt Ignominy have thrown away and
"diſperſed thoſe Bones and Aſhes, which even the moſt bar-
"barous people have ſpared. Since therefore the true and
"unqueſtionable Reliques are very few, eſpecially in theſe
"Provinces; and many of thoſe that are ſhown, may with
"great reaſon be ſuſpected; ſince the frequenting and ve-
"neration of them, ſerves piety but a little, but ſerves ſu-
"perſtition or gain very much; it ſeems a great deal more
"adviſeable, that there ſhould be no ſhowing of Reliques;
"but that the people ſhould be provoked to venerate the
"true Reliques of the Saints, that is, to imitate the examples
"of their piety and vertues, which are extant in Books writ-
"ten by themſelves, or of other Men concerning them.
It were a moſt eaſie thing, if this diſcourſe did not ſwell too
big, to ſhow that theſe two great Men laſt named, had juſt
occaſion thus to cenſure the Modern Reliques. I'le give the
Reader a taſt only out of a late Book; that he may ſee and
deteſt the horrible affront, this Church is
reſolved ſtill to put, not only upon Religi- *Laſſels his voyage into Italy.*
on, but the common diſcretion of Mankind,
while they preſume to ſhow ſuch things as theſe which follow, deſigning to have them believed for true Reliques, *viz.*
The holy Syndon (or Linnen) in which Chriſt's body was buried; ſhown at *Turin*. *The Diſh* in which Chriſt ate the
Paſchal Lamb, made of one *Emerald*; at *Genua*. *A Nail*
of our Saviour's Croſs, fixt on the Roof of the Church at
Milan. At

At *Rome* these are shown.

The *Stone* upon which *Abraham* offered to Sacrifice his Son, and another Stone upon which our Saviour was placed, when he was presented in the Temple. The top of the *Lance* with which Christ's side was pierced, and the Statue of *Longinus* under it. The *smock* of S. *Prisca*, in which she was Martyred, above 1400 Years old. A *Thorn* of that Crown of Thorns, which was put upon our Saviour's Head. The *Head* of the Woman of *Samaria*, who was converted by our Saviour. The *Arm* of S. *Anne*, Mother of the Bl. Virgin; and the *Chain* of S. *Paul*. The *Table* upon which our Saviour did eat the *Paschal Lamb*. *Scala Sancta*, or the 28. steps of white Marble, up which Christ was led in his Passion to *Pilate*'s House, and upon some of which are shown the marks of his blood, sent by *Helena* from *Jerusalem* to *Constantine*. A *Picture of our Saviour*, said to be begun by S. *Luke*, and finisht miraculously by an Angel, or (as others say) that S. *Luke* preparing to draw it, and falling to his prayers to God, that he might draw his Son aright, when he rose he found the Picture finished. The *holy Crib* of our Saviour. *The Pillar* at which our Saviour was whipped.

At *Venice* these are shown.

Some of our Saviour's *blood*, gather'd up at his Passion, with the Earth it was spilt upon. A *Thorn* of the Crown of Thorns. A *Finger* of S. *Mary Magdalen*. A piece of S. *John Baptist*'s skull. A *Tooth* of S. *Mark*: also one of his *Fingers*, and his *Ring* with a Stone in it. A piece of S. *John Baptist*'s habit. Some of the Bl. Virgin's Hair. The *Sword* of S. *Peter*. A piece of Christ's *white Robe*, when he was set at naught by *Herod*. One of *the Stones*, wherewith S. *Steven* was stoned. To which you may add, the *Hough* (or breath) of S. *Joseph*, which an Angel inclosed in a Vessel, as he was cleaving Wood, shown as a Relique in *France*. And now methinks I wonder, it never came into their heads to pretend to one Relique more, that would have been as considerable and miraculous as any of these; *viz.* The *Dust* upon which our Saviour wrote, with the

Devotions of the Roman Church.

the Characters still upon it, very fair and legible: but I hope, now they are put in mind of it, they will take care to procure it. *So I put an end to this long Digression.*

But now it is fit we should return to our 3 Kings, whom we may seem to have forgotten; If you look back again upon the prayer to them, you will find a piece of old *Rome*'s Heathenism * revived; I mean, in invocating them for success in Journeys. For every one knows, that as they had their *Tutelar Gods* for Countreys and Cities (wherein too they have been seconded by this Churches practice of assigning particular Saints to the Patronage of Places and Nations; as S. *George* for *England*, S. *James* for *Spain*, S. *Denis* for *Paris*, S. *Patrick* for *Ireland*, S. *David* for *Wales*, &c.) So also they appropriated particular Imployments and Offices to their Deities; and one was to be called upon in War; another in Sickness; one was more powerful by Land, and another by Sea; one taught Eloquence, and another Physick: onely the superstition and folly of *New Rome*, is worse than that of the *Old* in this regard, that *they* could content themselves with one *Æsculapius* in all matters that related to Physick and Diseases; but *these* must have almost as many Saints to invoke, as there are Maladies to be cured. One Saint is good for sore Breasts (a), and another to help in the Tooth-ach (b); one for Feavers (c), and another for Inflammations (d); and if they do give a more general Licence about Diseases, they will not trust

(a) *S. Agatha.*
(b) *S. Apollonia.*
(c) *S. Sigismund.*
(d) *S. Anthony.*

* *Lud. Vives notis in Augustin. de civit. Dei. lib. 8. c. 27. Edit. an. 1596.*
" *Multi Christiani in re bona plerumque peccant, quòd Divos Divásq; non*
" *aliter venerantur quàm Deum. Nec video in multis quid sit discrimen*
" *inter eorum opinionem de Sanctis, & id quod Gentiles putabant de Diis*
" *suis.* This saying the *Louain* Divines thought the Church of *Rome* so much concerned in, that they censured it there, and it was left out of a *Paris* Edition. an. 1613. It had as little kindness for them, as that part of the 10 Commandements, Thou shalt not make to thy self a Graven Image, &c. Which therefore they use to leave out of their Catechismes, and so it is left out of the *Manual of Godly Prayers*, and the Institutio Christiana, before the *Office of the Bl. Virgin*, omits it.

F

it in the hands of one alone, but he shall have a Fellow-saint joyned with him, and then *Cosmus* in Consultation with *Damian*, will not fail to help: and so in the desperate case of the Plague, for the greater encouragement of the Patients, S. *Rocch* is joyned with S.*Sebastian:* In the pains of Child-birth, S. *Margaret* no doubt can do as much as *Lucina*, and in the danger of shipwrack, S. *Nicholas* as *Neptune*; but however it will do well to have *two* strings to ones Bow, and the Bl. Virgin in both is to be called in at a dead lift: in the latter case indeed, now that it comes into my mind, *they* had their *Venus orta mari*, sprung from the Sea, to invoke; and now, not to be a whit behind them, this Church sings, *Ave maria maris stella,* Hayl *Mary* the Star of the Sea.

But let us hear a little farther their addresses to the *three Kings*; (for of that great *Queen* we shall have occasion to speak more hereafter) Thus then I find it, in the Hours of the Bl. Virgin on *Epiphany* day, *January* 6.

O Rex *Jaspar*, Rex *Melchior*, Rex *Balthasar*, rogo vos per singula nomina, rogo vos per Sanctam Trinitatem, rogo vos per regem regum, quem vagientem in cunis videre meruistis; ut compatiamini tribulationibus meis hodiè, & intercedite pro me ad Dominum, cujus desiderio exules facti estis: & sicut vos per Angelicam nunciationem de reditu ad Herodem eripuit, ita me hodie liberare dignetur ab omnibus inimicis meis visibilibus &

O King Jaspar, King Melchior, King Balthasar, I intreat you by all your names, I intreat you by the holy Trinity, I intreat you by the King of Kings, whom you had the honour to see when he was a crying infant in his Cradle, that you would compassionate my tribulations this day, and intercede for me to the Lord, for the desire of seeing whom, you became exiles; and as he by the message of an Angel, preserved you from returning to Herod, so may he vouch-
invi-

Devotions of the Roman Church. 67

invisibilibus, & à subitanea & improvisa morte, & ab omni confusione mala, & ab omni periculo corporis & animæ.

safe to deliver me this day from all mine enemies, visible and invisible, and from suddain & unforeseen death, and from all evil confusion, and from all danger of body and soul.

Thus it hath pleased this Church, to grace these 3 with the special Patronage of Travellers, and to use their names, together with the Guardian Angel. Therefore in the fore-named Hours of *Sarum*, we have this Direction given. *Whan thou first goest out of thy House, bless thee, saying thus.*

CRux Triumphalis Domini nostri *Jesu Christi*; ecce vivificæ crucis Dominicum signum; fugite partes adversæ. In nomine Patris & Filii & Spiritus Sancti.

Amen.

THe Triumphal Cross of our Lord Jesus Christ; behold the Lords sign of the Life-giving cross; fly away all ye adverse powers; in the name of the Father, and the Son, and the Holy Ghost.

Amen.

DEus qui tres Magos Orientales, Jaspar, Melchior & Balthasar, ad præsepe Domini stellâ duce conduxisti, conduc me ad loca proposita, sine totius adversitatis impedimento; & qui eos conduxisti Angelo nunciante, reduc me teipso auxiliante,

Per eundem Christum, &c.

OGod, who didst lead the 3 Eastern Magi, Jaspar, Melchior and Balthazar, to the cratch of our Lord, by the guidance of a star; conduct me without any afflictive impediment, to the places I design to go to; and thou that didst conduct them by an Angels message, bring me back by thy help.

Through Jesus Christ, &c.

Angele qui meus es custos, pietate supernâ, Me tibi commissum serva, defende, guberna.	O Angel Guardian, unto thee my self I have commended; May I by thy great kindness be kept, govern'd & defended.

Now I profess, such is the weakness of my small wit, that I cannot possibly see how it follows, that because these 3, by a Divine direction, took a long Journey, to visit the New-born Saviour of the World, that therefore we, without any such direction should invoke their conduct in our Travels; [For I hope no wise man will think this Invocation sufficiently warranted by the Tale of *Picardus* (out of *Erhardus Winheims Sacrarium Coloniæ Agrippinæ*) concerning one *John Aprilius*, who when he was hanged, implored the patronage of the holy *Magi* (I suppose because of the long journey he was going to take, when he should be turned off the Ladder) and after 3 days was found alive, & being taken down, came to *Colen* half naked, with his Halter about his Neck, to return thanks to his Deliverers.] If there were any consequence in this, I would fain know, why the 12 Patriarchs, or the 12 Apostles, who were all very great Travellers, and went too upon God's errands, might not expect this Honor, and have this Office as soon as they, and especially the latter before them. But enough of the *three Kings*, proceed we to other Instances.

Piccardi notæ in Lib. 2. cap. 8. N. ubrigensis.

De S. Dionysio & Sociis.	*Of S. Denys and his Companions.*
Brev. Rom. ad Octob. 9. *Oratio.*	The Prayer.
DEus, qui hodiernâ die Beatum *Dionysium* Martyrem tuum atque pontificem virtute constantiæ in passione roborasti; quique illi ad præ-	O God, who this day didst strengthen thy Martyr & Bishop S. Denys, with the vertue of constancy in suffering; and who didst dicandum

Devotions of the Roman Church.

dicandum Gentibus gloriam tuam, Rusticum & Eleutherium sociare dignatus es ; tribue nobis quæsumus, eorum imitatione, pro amore tuo prospera mundi despicere, & nulla ejus adversa formidare.

Per Dominum.

vouchsafe to joyn with him Rusticus and Eleutherius for to preach thy glory to the Gentiles; Grant us we beseech thee, in imitation of them to despise, for the Love of thee, the worlds prosperities, and to fear none of its adversities.

Through our Lord.

NOTES.

This *Saint*, who is the great *Patron* of *France*, is supposed to be the same that is mentioned in the *Acts*, under the name of *Dionysius* the *Areopagite*, though there is great reason to believe the contrary, if we give any credit to *Sulpitius Severus*, who tells us, that under the Reign of *Aurelius* the Son of *Antoninus*, *tum primùm inter Gallias martyria visa*; the first Martyrdomes in *France* were under his persecution; long before which the *Areopagite* must have been dead; which testimony of *Severus* is so strong, that even their own men have defended it, and pleaded for a distinction betwixt the *Parisian Dionysius*, and the *Areopagite*; (see *Joh. Launoy* his 3 Dissertations.) But if they were right as to the person, yet the Breviaries have made a fabulous story of him, which it would be too tedious to recite in all its circumstances, but I'le give a tast, out of the Breviary of *Sarum*. He is said to be sent into *France*, by Pope *Clemens*, to preach the Gospel, accompanied with *Rusticus* and *Eleutherius*; and preaching with great zeal at *Paris*, in the time of *Domitian*'s persecution, they were laid hold of by the *Roman* Governour *Sisinnius*, (the later Breviaries call him *Fescenninus*) who inflicted various torments on them, and cast them into prison; where S. *Denys* consecrated the Eucharist, and at the time when the Holy Bread was broken, so great a Light

Severus l. 2 Hist. Sacr. cap. 46.

Light shone upon him, that all greatly wondered. In this light Jesus Christ himself came, and took the Bread, and gave it to him, saying, Take this, my dear *Denys,* (*chare meus*) and incouraged him with the promise of great rewards to him and his hearers in God's Kingdom. After this, he and his two Companions refusing to sacrifice to the *Heathen* Gods, they were all beheaded in one and the same moment, whose Tongues, after their Heads were cut off, did still confess the Lord. And to declare the merits of the Martyr *Denys,* after he was beheaded, he stood upon his Feet, and taking up his own Head in his Arms, he carried it to the place where it now lies buried. Thus *France* glories in the Reliques of this Saint; yet *Baronius* tells us, that *Ratisbonne* in *Germany* has long contested with them about it, and show his Body there; and Pope *Leo* IX. set out a Declaration, determining that the true Body of S. *Denys* was entire at *Ratisbonne,* wanting only the little Finger of his right hand, yet they of *Paris* cease not their pretences to it; so that here are two Bodies venerated of the same individual Saint * : and both of them are mistaken, if they of *Prague* have not been cheated; among whose numerous Reliques I find the Arm of S. *Denis,* the Apostle of *Paris,* reckoned. A following *Antiphona* tells us, that a Multitude of the Heavenly Host accompany'd the dead Body of S. *Denis,* who carried his own Head, praising God, and saying, *Glory be to thee, O Lord.* The *Roman* Missal also in Folio (*Paris.* 1520) tells the very same story in a long *Prosa* (where there is mention of *Sisinnius*) of which take a few Verses towards the end.

Baron. ad an. 1052.

Bollard. Act. Sanct. in Append. ad Januar. 2.

---

* *But why not 2 Bodies as well as 2 Thumbs of one Saint: for the Virgins of a Nunnery in Ireland, that were very desirous of Reliques, found the Thumb of S. Senanus lying on the ground by his dead Body, and yet (which was the miracle) neither of his hands wanted a Thumb or a Finger. Oh the Thumb!* Colganus in supplement. vit. S. Senani. nu. 42.

Seniore

Devotions of the Roman Church.

Seniore celebrante
Missam, turbâ circumstante
Christus adest, comitante
    Cœlesti frequentiâ.

Specu clausum carcerali
Consolatur, & vitali
Pane cibat, immortali
    Coronandum gloriâ.

Prodit Martyr conflicturus,
Sub securi stat securus,
Ferit Lictor, sicque victor
    Consummatur gladio.

Sed cadaver mox erexit,
Truncus truncum caput vexit
Quo ferente hoc direxit
    Angelorum concio.

Tam præclara passio
Repleat nos gaudio.

      Amen.

While round the saint in crouds
   the people stand,
As he the Mass devoutly
   celebrates,
Christ he himself appears, a
   glorious band
Of the Celestial Host upon
   him waits.
He cheers th' imprison'd Saint
   with joys divine
His own hand feeds him with
   immortal bread;
He tries him now, but after
   does design
To set a glorious Crown upon
   his Head.
And now the Martyr bravely
   comes to fight,
Under the sharpned Axe he
   stands secure,
The Lictors blow, though 'twas
   directed right,
Did only make this Champi-
   ons conquests sure.
He fell indeed, but presently
   arose,
The breathless Body findes
   both feet and way,
He takes his Head in hand, and
   forward goes,
Till the directing Angels
   bid him stay.
Well may the Church trium-
   phantly proclaim
This Martyr's Death, and
   never dying fame.

Lesson 6. The present Breviary also retains this ridiculous passage concerning his carrying of his Head, and determines his walk more expresly to have been two miles. *Ribadeneira* in his Life, adds, that he delivered his Head into the hands of a Woman called *Catula*.

And now it may not be amiss to make a few farther Reflexions upon some pieces of his Legend; and I shall begin with that of *Christ*'s miraculous appearing in the Administration of the Eucharist. Now though I think no body need be much concerned in relations of this kind, that are made by those who tell us that People can speak when their Tongues are out of their Heads *, or can carry their Heads in their hands; yet I find Mr. *Cressy* is very fond of such passages; and I doubt he might take it ill, if I should pass over a story he tells to the same purpose, and lays a great deal of stress upon it, for the establishing his Catholick Faith. It is concerning S. *Odo*, who celebrating the Mass, in the presence of certain of the Clergy of *Canterbury* (who maintained that the Bread and Wine, after Consecration do remain in their former substance, and are not *Christ*'s true Body and Blood, but a Figure of it) " When he was come to confraction, presently the fragments " of the Body of *Christ*, which he held in his hands, began " to pour forth Blood into the Chalice; whereupon he shed " (Good Man!) tears of joy, and beck'ning to them that " wavered in their faith, to come near and see the wonder- " ful work of God, as soon as they beheld it, they cryed " out, O holy Prelate, to whom the Son of God has been " pleased to reveal himself visibly in the Flesh, pray for us, " that the Blood we see here present to our eyes, may again " be changed, lest for our unbelief the Divine vengeance fall " upon us. He prayed accordingly; after which looking " into the Chalice, he saw the Species of Bread and Wine, " where he had left Blood. [To which may be added a story in the *Festivale*, which may make a good Comment

* See the 2d. Lesson of Longinus.

Ch. H. p. l. 31. cap. 20.

ment upon this of Mr. *Cressy* concerning these Mi-   *Fol.* 52.
raculous Changes of the Elements in the Sacra-
ment. "A *Jew* once went with a *Cristen* man into a Church
"and heard *Mass*; when the Mass was done, the *Jew* said
"to him, If I had eaten as much as thou hast, I would not
"be a hungred, as I trow, in *three* days. Forsooth said the
"Christian, I eat no manner of Meat this day. Then said
"the *Jew*, I saw thee eat a Child, the which the *Priest* held
"up at the Altar: Then came there a fair man, that had ma-
"ny children in his Lap, and he gave each *Christen* man a
"child, such as the *Priest* eat. The same also we are told
of S. *Wittekindus*, that in the Administration of the Eucharist, he saw a child enter into every ones
mouth, playing and smiling when some   *Bolland. in vitæ ejus,*
received him, and with an abhorring   *ad Jan.* 7. *p.*384.
countenance, when he went into the mouths of others, that
is, *Christ* showed this Saint in his countenance, who were
worthy, and who unworthy receivers.] To let pass that
which *Baronius* tells us (which Mr. *Cr.* durst not mention,
lest it should spoil the Saints credit) concerning S. *Odo*, that
when a Thief was brought before him, who
had stollen a Horse in the Night * (though   *Baron. ad an.*
his Monk *Godofred*, who saw him do it, while   936. *num.*13.
he was reciting his Canonical Hours, durst not cry out to
take him, lest he should break his Rule of Silence) S. *Odo*
commanded, in stead of punishing him, *Five* shillings to be
given the Thief, in consideration that he had watched all
Night, taken a great deal of pains, and endured much hard-

* *Thus they have abused* Macarius (*who deserved better*) *by telling us, that finding a Thief plundering his Cell, he, as if he had been a stranger, helped him to load his Horse with his own goods, saying these words of Job,* We brought nothing into this World, and it is certain we can carry nothing out, the Lord gave, and as the Lord pleases every thing comes to pass, blessed be the Lord in all things. *Of whom the Legenda has left also this wise Memorial, that* Macarius *having on a time killed a Flea that bit him, he was so penitent thereupon, that he went six Months naked in the Wilderness, that the Fleas by biting him might have their revenge upon him at full.*

ship;

ship; which argues S. *Odo* not over-fit to decide a greater controversie without a miracle. Waving this, I say, I cannot be moved by this miracle, or *twenty* other fine stories that are told me about this time, though it was a time mighty fruitful of Monkish wonders. For I consider (as I intimated before in the case of Reliques) that this Century was remarkable above all others for Ignorance *, Sottishness and Superstition; wherein by reason of the Barbarism and illiterateness of the Age, Lies and Fables must needs meet with a good Market to put them off.

* *Baronius ad an.* 900, *has given us its character at the beginning of it, thus*; *Novum inchoatur seculum, quod sui asperitate & boni sterilitate ferreum, malique exundantis deformitate* plumbeum, *atque inopia Scriptorum appellari consuevit* obscurum.

And the truth is, if my Faith were staggering upon the hearing Mr. *Cr.*'s story, yet the very next Page to it, would settle it again; where he informs us, that S. *Dunstan* saw the H. Ghost descending from Heaven in the likeness of a *Dove*: and the *Sarisbury Breviary* edifies me still farther, telling me,

Less. 6. of S. Dunstan.

that he saw the Holy Spirit in this shape twice, and heard the Angels chanting *Kyrie Eleison* in the praise of the Trinity; and that his Harp that hung at the Wall, was by Angels hands made to sound that *Antiphona*, *Gaudent in Cœlis animæ sanctorum*, which he only understood. And *Lesson* 5, I hear more such wonders, which me-thinks sound as well as Mr. *Cressy*'s. How, when a mighty Beam from the Top of the Church, threatned the destruction of many by its fall, S. *Dunstan* with his right hand, making the sign of the Cross, lifts it up again *; and that as this Saint was praying one Night, the Devil assailes him in the shape of a Bear, and endeavoured with his Teeth,

* *Which may well be credited, when we read of S.* Aidanus, *that his Cart and two Oxen laden with Wood, as he drove them, falling down a high Rock into the Sea, he only made the sign of the Cross as they fell, and received all safe and sound out of the Waters. And* S. Maidoc *did the same to a fallen Cart-load of Ale*: Colganus vit. S. David. 1 Martii. p. 427. and S. Maid. p. 210.

to snatch the Staff out of his hands, upon which the Man of God leaned; he unaffrighted lifts up his Staff, and followed the horrid Monster beating him, and singing these words; *Let God arise, and let his Enemies be scattered*, and the ugly Phantasme vanished. And no doubt from this Age of S. *Odo*'s Miracle (for it could not so well be from any other) came that Tradition to us from Father to Son, in Mr. *Sergeant*'s sure way, how S. *Dunstan* held the Devil by the nose with a pair of Tongs. Mr. *Cressy*'s miracle then shown in S. *Dunstan*'s days, is like to do feats to establish the Churches Faith concerning the Eucharist, to convince and confound all Opposers, especially when S. *Odo* has to do in it, that known Miracle-worker, who as Mr. *Cr.* records it, when the Roof of his Church was to be repaired, suspended all Rain for the space of *three* Years, that it should not hinder the Work. And now I have begun with Mr. *Cr.* about this Argument, I will *Ch. Hist. lib. 32. cap. 5.* call him a little farther to account, for some of the many wonders he relates.

A Brief Digression concerning some of the Miracles related in Mr. Cr.'s History.

IT is an Ingenuous Confession, which is made by *Melchior Canus*, concerning the *Miracles* of the Saints. "We "cannot deny, says he, that sometimes even the most grave "Men, especially in describing the "Miracles of the Saints, have both "pickt up scattered rumors, and "also related them in their wri- "tings to Posterity. In which thing, "it seems to me, they have either "indulged themselves too much, or "at least the vulgar sort of Believ-

Quanquam negare non possumus, viros aliquando gravissimos in Divorum præsertim prodigiis describendis, sparsos rumores & excepisse, & scriptis etiam ad posteros retulisse. Loc. Theol. lib. 11. c. 6. &c.

"ers;

"ers; becaufe they thought that thefe would not only ea-
"fily believe, but alfo earneftly defired fuch Miracles:
"Therefore holy Men have recorded feveral figns and pro-
"digies, not as if they willingly themfelves believed them,
"but left they fhould feem to be wanting to the wifhes of
"the faithful.

Mr. *Creffy*, I fuppofe, has a mind to be taken for a grave Author; and every one that turns over his Hiftory, cannot but fee that it was the great defign of it, to gather together whatever he could meet with, that was prodigious and wonderful, relating to the *English* Saints. I have fo good an Opinion of his wit, that I cannot bring my felf to believe, that he could poffibly think half that which he has related, to be meafured truth; and I'le give him but one Inftance among many of this, in his Life of S. *Suibert*, which he has given us out of *Marcellinus* : He might have eafily known (if he had not rather chofen to follow *Surius*, and his good Father *Alford* blindfold) how the learned Men of his own Church have defpifed this Hiftory, fome calling him *Auctorem Stramineum* (as *Labbe* does) others look upon it as a *late Fable* (as *Holftenius*) and if any one has a mind to fee the Arguments which cannot be anfwered, to prove this *Marcellinus* to be a foolifh Writer, and his Relation impoffible to be true, as contradicting both Hiftory and Chronology, he may only look into *Bollandus* (who has alfo been fo ingenuous as to leave out, all that Mr. *Creffy* has foolifhly inferted) and *Colganus* *.

Ch. Hft. lib. 20, &c.

Recentius commentum.

Bolland. Commentar. Hiftoricus de S. Suibert. ad 1 Martii.

It's moft likely then, that *Canus* has hit right, and that Mr. *Cr.* (as well as others before him) hath herein complied too much with the humor and defires of vulgar Catholicks, and refolved to ferve his Church by the old way of pious frauds, without any regret for the difhonefty of it. Yet however, methinks he fhould have better fecured the reputation of his difcretion.

* *Colganus in notis ad vit.* Suitberti, *pag. 436.*

For

For I could not but imagine, that the foregoing story of S. *Denis*, was such a stretcher, that no body would ever have had the confidence (not to say conscience) to put a Man's faith to it, to believe that there was above one Saint, that could endure his Head off as well as his Hat, or clap it under his Arm and walk, as if nothing ailed him: and I was ready to comfort my self, that this story was only calculated for the *French*-men, and that an *English* Faith was not much concerned in it. But alas! I found quickly that I was mistaken; for there are two *English*-men, *Capgrave* and Mr. *Cressy*, that are resolved, I think, that no *French* Saint should have the better of those of our own Nation, in showing these Feats. Mr. *Cressy* has produced S. *Clarus* (a) an *English* Hermit, S. *Ositha* (b), S. *Decumanus* (c), and S. *Juthwera* (d), who all carried their Heads in their Armes after they were smitten off: but if he had left out all these, that one story he relates concerning S. *Justinian* (e), may suffice to silence the fame of S. *Denys* his adventure; who after he had been slain, and his Head cut off, by the wicked rage of his own Servants, his Body presently arose, and with his Head between his two Arms, walking thence to the Sea, passed over to a Port called by his name, and fell down at a place, where a Church is built to his memory.

Ch. History.
(a) *lib.* 17. *c.* 3.
(b) *l.* 17. *c.* 5.
(c) *l.* 21. *c.* 4.
(d) *l.* 23. *c.* 9.
(e) *l.* 11. *c.* 8.

I shall now make bold, in the name of Mr. *Cressy*, to challenge any *French*-man of them all, to produce any Saint of theirs, that ever did the like: For alas! their S. *Denys*'s journey, as you have heard, was not above *two* Miles, and that too upon plain firm ground, and what's that, I pray, to going over Sea without ones head?

But I have a farther request to Mr. *Cr.* which upon this occasion, I think fit to make, and methinks it is a very reasonable one: it is this. That he would give us leave, without swaggering, to put upon the Head of several of his Chapters, (instead of Gests) *The Fables of S. Justinian and the Fables of S. David, &c.* as he himself has done to
the

the famous *Arthur:* lib. 11. c. 16. *Fables concerning King Arthur censured.* I dare say the Writers of these things he calls Fables in *Arthur*'s case, such as *Geoffery Monmouth**,

* A grave Author with Baronius in the case of the 11000 Virgins.

and *Matthew Westmonast.* are of as good credit as his great Authors *Capgrave* and *Harpsfield*; and these Acts too of his Chivalry, which he calls prodigious, in the Conquest of so many Countreys, are not near so incredible and ridiculous, as his story of S. *Alban* (though mentioned by *Bede*) drying up a River for this foolish reason, that People might more commodiously behold his Martyrdom, or the Mountain rising under the Feet

Ch. Hist. lib. 6. cap. 12.

of S. *David*, (of which we shall say more afterward in his life) or this of S. *Justinian*'s going over Sea without a Head. He has given us some excuse for excessive praises, in *Arthur*'s case, from the custome of People to magnifie Romantickly some one of their Princes; as the *Grecians* their *Alexander*; the *Romans* their *Octavian*; the *English* their *Richard*; and the *French* their *Charles*. But there is no excuse for pretending to advance Religion, by telling incredible stories, and for producing wonders as absurdly, as if this power were given, to inable a Saint to show tricks of *Legerdemain*, or to alter the Laws of Nature in sport, and without any apparent and considerable necessity. *Magnum sit necesse est, propter quod natura leges exceduntur.*

To come a little closer to Mr. *Cr.*'s History, by presenting him with a few Instances of his own, to this purpose.

Can he answer it to his own reason, why a Saints bad memory in forgetting a cloath, upon which he had consecrated the Eucharist, should, after he was gone to Sea, be so far incouraged, as that the Divine power should inable him to walk upon the Sea to fetch it, as he tells us of

Lib. 15. c. 4.

S. *Birinus*? When any one else, I dare say, with his conceipts about the Corporal, would rather have expected, that this his carelesness should by a Divine hand have been punisht? I know not indeed how

far

Devotions of the Roman Church. 79

far another story of this Saint, after his death, may invite us to believe the former in his life-time. For *Capgrave* relates, that a young Man that was born deaf and dumb, was cured by being brought to his Tomb, and spake *English* presently, and within *three* days more spake *French* perfectly as well. I read of *Christ* and his Apostles working Miracles, to supply the pressing necessities of other Men; but I do not remember any one instance, wherein they endeavoured to ingage the extraordinary power of God, to help themselves meerly, or that God did it for them, without their requesting, when the thing might be done by ordinary ways. Was it never heard that *two* Men in a hot Countrey took a long Journey, without a Screen to defend them from the scorching of the Sun? Or, if it were necessary, was there no way for them to procure a shade, but that God must send a mighty Eagle * with her Wings to over-shaddow them, til they came to their Journeys end? Yet thus, he tels us, it was done upon their Prayers, for *Roger* of *Cannæ*, & *Richard* of *Andria*, when they went to *Siponto*. Can any one be so foolish as to think, that if Water could have been constantly supplied to the Children of *Israel*, in their Travels through the Wilderness, by fetching it at the distance of a Mile or two, that God would miraculously have made it follow them, to save that pains? Yet Mr. *Cr.* writes, as if he would have us believe this following story. That the Monastery of S. *Eanswitha*, had only one incommodity, that being seated on the top of high Rocks, there was a penury of sweet Water. "The holy Virgin "was sensible of this inconvenience, and after she had by "Prayer sollicited our Lord, she went to the Fountain more "than a Mile remote from the Monastery; and striking the "Water with a Staff, commanded it to follow her: The "deaf Element heard and obeyed the Sacred Virgin's voice, "and against the Inclination of Nature followed her steps, till

Li.10. c.18.

Lib.15. c.8.

---

* *So we are told of S. Lutwin, that lying along upon the ground asleep, an Eagle with her shady Wings defended his Face from the hot scorching Sun. Bollandus in vita S. Basini ad 4 Martii.*

over-

"overcoming all the difficulties of the paſſage, it mounted "up to the Monaſtery, where it abundantly ſerved all their "uſes: One particular more increaſed the admiration of "the Event, for this little Rivolet in the way being to paſs "through a Pool (ſhe muſt be ſuppoſed to do ſo too, be- "cauſe it was ſaid to follow her ſteps, but that's a ſmall mat- "ter, for a Virgin in *Capgrave*'s ſtory to tread Water) it "flowed notwithſtanding pure and free from all mixture. Mr. *Creſſy* might have told us alſo, that which immediately precedes this ſtory in *Capgrave*, how ſhe triumphed over a King of the *Northumbers*, who courted her for his Wife; by making this the condition of having her, (which he accepted) that he ſhould *pray* a great Beam *three* Foot longer than it was, (for ſo much it was too ſhort for the reſt of the Timber that was prepared to build her Oratory) which he failing to accompliſh, after long invoking his Gods, he departed from her aſhamed, and ſhe eſcaped him; but by her *own Prayers*, immediately the Beam became a Yard longer *; and I ſuppoſe it may be every whit as fit to believe, that by another Prayer, without the help of any Carpenters, all might be joyn'd and fram'd into a Houſe.

* *Which is no great matter to believe, when we read that* S. Hildutus *with his Diſciples living in a ſtrait Iſland, they obtained by their Prayers, that the Iſland was inlarged and made bigger.* Colganus vit. Gildæ Bidonic. *p.* 182.

Neither can I ſee much need of a Miracle, in another ſtory he tells us, about the conveighing S. *Cuth-* *Lib.* 28. *c.* 19. *bert*'s Body from the Sea ſide: where firſt he ſays it was told a Monk in a Viſion, that upon a certain Tree they ſhould find a Bridle hanging, which if they held up in the Ayr, an Horſe would come to them of his own accord, to aſſiſt them! They did ſo, and a Bayhorſe preſently offered his ſervice, which they joyning to a Waggon, conveighed it away. The ſtory tells us not a word how the Waggon came there; and yet one would think it had been as eaſie to get a Horſe without a Miracle as a Waggon;

Waggon; but what need was there of either, when there were 7 *Monks* that did attend it? and if they could not carry S. *Cuthbert*'s Body, let him call them what he pleases, I shall make bold to say they were lazy Lubbers; and a Vision of a Whip for them, was rather needful, than of a Bridle for the Horse: especially considering, that there is reason to believe, that S. *Cuthbert* was no fat Man; which is easily collected, from what I find in Mr. *Cressy*, that he was very much given to fasting, even before he entered into the Monastery, (much more you may be sure afterwards) and that he took so little care about Victuals, that in a Journey he was miraculously supplied with a Meal, after having fasted all day, by means of his Horse; which pulled down from the Roof of a House, half a Loaf of warm Bread, and a piece of Flesh, wrapped up in a Linnen-cloth. *Lib.* 15. *c.* 16.

I hope the Reader is not tired with these Relations, and therefore, with his good leave, I'le add *two* or *three* more. My next shall be in S. *Wereburga* and her *Wild-geese*: which story Mr. *Cr.* is much concerned for, and takes it ill from Mr. *Camden*, that he should insinuate his unwillingness to believe it. The substance of it is this. *Ch. Hist. l.* 17. *cap.* 17.

"The Steward of S. *Wereburga*'s Monastery, complaining
"that in a Farm that belonged to it, the Corn was much in-
"jured by Flocks of Wild-geese: S. *Wereburga* commands
"the Steward to go and shut them all up together in a
"House. He, though at first he wondered at the command,
"thinking (as any one else would have done) that she had
"spoke those words in jest; yet perceiving her to renew
"her command, he went to the Wild-geese, which were in
"great numbers devouring the Corn, and with a loud voice
"commanded them, in his Mistress's name, to follow him.
"They obeyed, and all in one Drove were shut up together;
"only one of the Number was privily stoln by a Servant,
"with an intention to eat it. The next Morning the Holy
"Virgin went to the House, and after she had chidden them

"for usurping that which belonged not to them, she com-
"manded them to fly away, and not to return. Immedi-
"ately the whole Army took Wing; but being sensible that
"one of their Number was wanting, they hovering over
"the Virgins head, complained of their loss: she hearing
"their clamours, understood by inspiration the cause of it;
"and after search, made the Offendor confess his theft, and
"after the Bird was restored to her Companions, they all
"flew away, and not any Bird of that kind was afterward
"seen in that Territory.

What fine circumstances are here to invite a Man to believe? The Saints interest in this devoured Corn, which belonged to her own Monastery: The sawciness of these Geese, that durst make so bold with *her* Corn: The great charity of the Virgin, in giving the Geese so fair an admonition, to make them sensible of their crime before she punisht them: Their wonderful sagacity, quite exceeding the pitch of that Fowles understanding in our days: The seasonableness of an inspiration to advance her duller understanding, and make her apprehend *their* Language, as well as they did *hers* before: Her honesty, in restoring the stoln Bird to her Companions, and that rather than they should be defrauded (if *Malmesbury* be in the right that the Bird was killed) restoring it to life again by a Miracle: and yet her terrible severity towards them (which may be a fair warning to all succeeding Geese that hear it, to take heed of such trespassing) debarring not only that individual Flock, but the whole Race of Geese, and not only for her life time, but for ever after, from being seen, and so consequently never to make a Meal more, in that Territory. These circumstances, I assure you, do so far obstruct my faith in this Miracle, that, to be plain with Mr. *Cressy*, this one Flam of S. *Wereburga*, seems to me more incredible, than all the Tales of K. *Arthur*, and his Knights; and for the sake of her Wild-geese, I am inclined to disbelieve another story I

Act. Sanctor. Mart. 3. *p.* 251.

meet with, of a Tame-Goose in the Life of S. *Winwaloe*, whose Sisters eye being
pluckt

Devotions of the Roman Church. 83

pluckt out, as she was playing, by a Goose; he was taught by an Angel a sign, whereby to know that Goose from the rest about the House, and having cut it open, found the Eye in its Entrails, preserved by the power of God unhurt, and shining like a Gemm; which he took and put it again in its proper place, and recovered his Sister; and was so kind also to the Goose, as to send it away alive, after it had been cut up, to the rest of the Flock. I know Mr. *Cressy* may pick up out of the Saints Lives *Twenty* parallel stories, how they have commanded Birds and Beasts, and punisht the injuries they have done to the Saints upon them: He may tell us perhaps that of S. *Brigid*, who seeing Wild-Ducks sometimes swimming in the Water, and again flying in the Ayr, she called them *Act. Sanct. in vit. Brig. ad Feb. 1.* to her, who without any fear obeyed, and came to her hand, who after she had stroked and imbraced them a while, she let them fly away again. Of S. *Genulph*, whom they bring in chiding a Fox, that had stoln one of his Hens, and commanding him to lay it down just in the place whence he took it, all which the Fox performed; but could not so escape, but was *Boll. Act. Sanct. in vit. Genulph. ad Jan. 17.* miraculously punisht for his Theft, for as he was running away by the Door of his Church, he fell down dead. He may tell us of S. *Kierans* admirable arguing the case with the Fox too, that had stoln his Shooes, with a purpose to eat them; To whom the holy Man said, Brother, why hast thou done this ill thing, which it becomes not a *Monk* to *Colganus. vit. S. Kieran. 5 Mart. p. 459.* do? (*he had several Beasts that served him tamely, besides this Fox, whom he called by the Name of Monks*) Behold, our Water is sweet and common, and our Meat is divided in common among us all, and if thou hadst a mind according to thy Nature to eat Flesh, God Almighty for our sake would have made it of the Barks of Trees; which melting speech so wrought upon the Fox, that he begged his pardon, did Penance by Fasting, eating nothing till the holy Man bad him. He may instance in the *Weasel*, that for its sawciness in gnawing the Frock of S. *Peter* the *Abbot*, was found dead upon it. But if he can be contented that the Saints should be brought in foolishly treating Birds and Beasts, and discoursing to them like rational Creatures, and that they should use a miraculous Power to punish them as Transgressors, which for want of choice, are uncapable of any other Laws than their Natural Inclinations; yet we cannot so easily believe that God will lend his Power to countenance such ridiculous and trifling designs.

Ibid. in ejus vit. ad Mart. 4.

Indeed such idle Tales we meet with, of wonderful Birds among the Heathen, such as those which S. *Augustine* (a), and *Pliny* (b) relate, concerning *Diomedes* his Birds, which abiding at his Tomb in *Apulia*, courted and flattered the *Græcians*; but infested, and with their hard Beaks killed strangers that were not of their race; that sprinkled and purified his Temple with Water, which they brought in their Bills and Feathers, &c. If any will be so kind to these stories, as not to look upon them as Fictions, yet he need go no farther for satisfaction about them, than to S. *Augustine*, who in the next Chapter, resolves them into the cheating Arts and Tricks of the Devil; and thither I should refer Mr. *Cressy*'s Wild-geese, if the matter of fact were proved, since, as I said before, I cannot be perswaded, that God will lend his Power to effect such ridiculous things.

(a) *S. Augustin de civ. dei. lib. 18. c 16. speaking concerning the Story of Diomedes his Companions turned in Birds, and frequenting his Tomb in Apulia, near to Mount Garganus; Hoc Templum aiunt, circumvolare atque incolere has alites tam mirabili obsequio, ut rostrum aqua impleant & aspergant; & eo si Græci venerint, vel Græcorum stirpe progeniti, non solum quietas esse sed & superadvolare; si autem alienigenas viderint, subvolare, & capita eorum tam gravibus ictibus, ut etiam perimant, vulnerare; nam duris & grandibus rostris, satis ad hæc prælia perhibentur armatæ.*

(b) *Plinius Nat. Hist. l. 10. c. 44. He tells much what the same Story, Advenas Barbaros clangore insistant, Græcis tantum adulantur, miro discrimine, velut generi Diomedis hoc tribuentes: ædemque eam quotidie pleno gutture madentibus pennis perluunt atque purificant, unde origo fabulæ Diomedis socios in earum effigies mutatos.* He lays before, *Eis esse dentes, oculosque igneo colore, cætera candidis.*

Saint *Ivo* his appearing to the *Abbot* of *Ramsey* after his death, is told us in another place; how he seemed to draw on his Leggs a pair of Boots, with care to make them fit smooth and handsome, telling him that he must wear them for his sake, and that they would last a good while; upon which the *Abbot* awaking, felt such horrible pain in his Leggs, that he was not able to walk or stand, and Fifteen Years he remained in this Infirmity. A sad punishment, considering the offence, for which it is said to be inflicted, which was, that this *Abbot* did not presently give credit to the pretence of a Vision of S. *Ivo*, that required that his Body should be translated to *Ramsey*, and cast out this hasty speech, *Must we translate and venerate the Ashes of I know not what Cobler?* He must have a forward faith, that can believe, that the Saints departed are either so *Sportive*, or so *Spightful*, as this story represents them.

Ch. Hist. lib. 13. cap. 9.

In the next Chapter, Mr. *Cressy* gives us this account of S. *Paul de Leon*, "That on a time visiting a Sister of his, who devoutly served God in a Cell, seated near the Sea of the *British* shore, at her request he obtained of God by his Prayers, that the Sea should never swell beyond the bounds marked by her, by placing a Row of Stones. by which means the Sea was restrained the space of a Mile from his usual course, and continues so to this day. In this story, (besides the prejudice I have against it, as related by *Capgrave*, whom I cannot think of without a Pique against him, for making so many Saints carry their Heads in their hands) there appears no reason at all, why the Sea should be forced out of its ordinary road, only that a devout Sister had toyingly placed a Row of Stones, and thought it pretty, if this could be made a Sea-bank, and accordingly God's Power must be called in to make good this fancy, which seems to be directly such a playing with Miracles, as Boys play at *Ducks* and *Drakes* with Stones upon the surface of the Water; but Mr. *Cressy* has omitted another wonderful circumstance.

Lib. 13. c. 10.

stance, which *Capgrave* mentions concerning those Stones; that as he and his Sister returned home, they saw on a sudden that those little Stones, by the Divine Power, were turned into Pillars of Stone of a vast Magnitude; indeed all things done by this S. *Paul de Leon* are so great, that they quite put down those of the Scripture Saint *Paul*; for a Dragon of an Hundred and Twenty Foot long, is another kind of Beast, than that he fought with at *Ephesus*; yet such a one

Folland. Act Sanct.
ad Mart.12, f.118.

this Saint (we are told in his life) overcame, and when he had done, made it to follow him to the Sea-side like *a Dog*.

Bollandus indeed makes it a matter of his wonder, that it should be told of almost all the *Irish* Saints,

Id. Ibid p.110.

and those of *Little-Brittany*, that they killed *Dragons* of vast Size; for my part, I believe there is no difference at all in the Size of the *Dragons* of those Countreys, from what they are elsewhere; but the Invention of the Writers of the Lives is vast, and their Conscience large, and the toyishness of their fancy in feigning wonders is admirable indeed, and beyond all compare. Mr. *Cressy* is an argument of the one, *viz.* the bulkiness of their Miracles, for though his swallow be as large as most Men's I know, yet you may remember an *Irish* miracle (that about the Staff of *Jesus*) stuck so vilely by the way, before it could get down, that I was afraid it would have choakt him: And for an instance of their toying and childish playing with Miracles, you may take that of S. *Mochua*; who, they tell us, seeing a Company of Lambs running

Colganus, Vit. S.
Mochua Mart.
28. p.780.

hastily to suck their Damms, as he was walking by them and praying, he suddenly stept before them, and with his Staff drew a Line upon the ground, which none of the Lambs, as hungry as they were, durst pass, but there stopt.

Idem. vit.
Fintani p.11.

The like was done by S. *Fintanus* to the Calves, parting them and the Cows asunder, onely by the Interposition of his Staff. But the most excellent story I have met with of this kind, is in the Life of

S. *Fin-*

S. *Finnianus*, where we find him, and S. *Ruadanus* bandying Miracles as sportfully, as Tennis-Balls are tossed from one to another with a Racket. Thus it is related: S. *Ruadanus* obtained this special favour of God, that from a certain Tree in his Cell (*Tilia* it's call'd) from the Hour of Sun-setting to *Nine* a Clock the next Day dropt a Liquor, of a peculiar tast, pleasing to every Palate; which then fill'd a Vessel, which sufficed for a Dinner for him, and all his Brotherhood: and from *Nine* a Clock to Sun-setting, it dropt half the Vessel full, with which Strangers were entertained. Upon the fame of this Miracle, many of the Saints came to S. *Finnian*, desiring him to go along with them to that place, and perswade *Ruadanus* to live a life common with others. S. *Finnian* went with them, and when they came to the Tree that gave the admirable Liquor, he signed it with the sign of the Cross, and after *Nine* a Clock the Liquor ceased to flow. S. *Ruadanus* hearing that his Master S. *Finian*, and several others were come to him, he called his Servant, and bad him prepare a Dinner for his Guests; who going to the Tree, he found the Vessel that stood under it wholly empty, and told his Master how it was; who bad him carry his Vessel to the Fountain, and fill it to the top with Water, which when he had done, presently the Water was changed into the tast of that Liquor, that dropt from the Tree: Moreover he found a Fish of a great bigness in the Fountain, and carried all to the Man of God; who commanded him to set these Gifts before S. *Finnian*. He seeing what was done, crossed the Liquor, and it was changed again into common Water, and said, Why is this Liquor of a false name given to me? The Disciples of S. *Finnian* seeing all this, desired their Master to go to the Fountain and cross it, as he had done the Tree: (*they had a mind to see more of this sport*) But S. *Finnian* answered them; My Brethren, do not grieve this holy Man, for if he go before us to the next Bog, * he

Colganus vit. Finniani 23 Febr. p. 395.

---

* *Ad vicinam grunnam*: which *Colganus* explains, net. 17. ad Vit. Maidoc. p. 216. *Gruuna alias grunda, capitur hîc pro terra humida & inaquosa, in qua cæspites & glebæ effodiuntur, &c.*

will be able to do the same that he did in the Tree and the Water, (*i.e.* make such Liquor flow thence.) Wherefore S. *Finnian*, and the rest, all intreated S. *Ruadanus*, that he would live as others did; which he yielded to, and (*not depending upon miracles*) he held the common course of living.

Give me leave to mention one wonder more out of Mr. *Cressy*, concerning *Austin* the Monk, who dis-
Ch. Hist. l. 13. cap. 18. puting with the *British Bishops*, about the Observation of *Easter*, and arguing that they did not keep it in its due time; when the *Britains*, after a long disputation, would not be moved to give their assent, but would follow their own Traditions; *Austin* brought the Dispute to this Conclusion, saying; "Let us beseech our "Lord, who makes Brethren of one mind in the House of "his Father, that he would vouchsafe by Celestial signs to "make known unto us, which of these Traditions is to be "followed, and which is the right Path leading to his King-"dom: Let some sick Person be here produced among us, "and he by whose Prayers he shall be cured, let that Man's "faith and practice be believed acceptable to God, and to "be followed by Men. This Proposition being accepted "with much ado, a blind Man was brought before them, "and was first offered to the *British* Bishops, but by their "endeavours and Ministery found no cure and help: At "length *Austin*, compelled thereto by just necessity, kneel-"ed down, and prayed to God to restore the blind Man "his sight; whereupon immediately the blind Man (upon "his Prayer) received sight, and *Austin* was proclaimed "by all a true Preacher of Celestial Light; (and *People were afterwards put in the right Path to Heaven, so far as concerned that saving Point, of the time of observing Easter.*) This story, though related by *Bede* *, cannot obtain my be-

---

* *His own Melch. Canus has betrayed his doubting of the certainty of many of his, and Gregories relations. Beda in historia Anglorum, & Gregorius in Dialogis, quædam miracula scribunt, quæ hujus præsertim seculi Arista chi incerta esse censentur: Equidem historias illas probarem magis, si earum authores, severitati judicii curam in eligendo majorem adjunxissent. Loc. Theol. lib. 11. pag. 337.*

lief,

lief, that God thus decided this Controversie; because I am sure *that* is false, which I read in the very story it self, that *Austin* went to pray for this Miracle, *being compelled thereto by just necessity*: this was well put in indeed, if it had been true (for I all along go upon this Principle, that there must be a manifest and great necessity, for such great alterations of the course of Nature) but there was no necessity at all, that this Controversie (upon what Day *Easter* should be kept) should be decided, where two contrary customes had long obtained, and both sides were agreed to keep it: but the *Eastern* Church following S. *John*'s practice, may determine the time one way, and the *Western* following the Traditions of S. *Peter*, may in this particular go another way, and yet both be pleasing to God. Mr. *Cr.* himself has told us out of *Bede*, "That this dissonance in the "observation of *Easter*, was patiently tolerated "by all, whilst Bishop *Aidan* lived; because it "was well known, that though those who sent him, would "not permit him to celebrate that Feast otherwise than they "were accustomed, yet he was zealous to perform all Chri-"stian Duties of Faith, Piety and Charity, according to the "Custome prescribed by all God's Saints; and therefore "he was deservedly loved by all, even by those who differ-"ently celebrated *Easter*. *Ch. Hist. l.16. c.16.*

Besides it seems to me a ridiculous thing, and a tempting of God to go to imitate *Elijah* (as it is plain in this thing *Austin* did, by proposing to have it miraculously decided) when the case and necessity is no ways alike, of bringing a People off from Idolatry, to worship the true God; and both worshipping the same true God and Saviour, to agree in an uniform observance of a Day, or of a Ceremony. Yet a frequent practice this is upon any sleight occasion to tell miraculous stories of their Saints, bringing in any example of the Scripture, that has any resemblance to them, and taking care commonly that the Scripture-instance be out-done. To give a few Examples. A pleasant story they give us of S. *Gonsalvus*, building a Bridg over the River *Tamaca*. And
first,

first, they make the place where he should build it, to be shown him by the revelation of an Angel; then how he got Money for his work, particularly of a Gentleman, who passed by, of whom *Gonsalvus* asked his Charity towards it; who upon his importunity wrote a Letter to his Wife, to whom he bid him carry it, and she would give him his Almes: the Contents were, that she should give him so much Money, as the weight of his Letter came to; which she looking upon as a Jear, wished him to go his way; But *Gonsalvus* insisted that she should do as her Husband required; and when she weighed the Letter, by a Miracle the weight of it was so increased, that he got a considerable Summe of Money for his Work. After this, wanting Provisions for his Workmen, upon his Prayers, and making the sign of the Cross upon the Waters of the River, a Multitude of Fishes covered the surface of it, and he taking up as many of them as he needed, sent the rest of the Fishes away with his blessing, and thus he did more than once. And as they were thus wonderfully supplied with Food, so also with Drink; for as another *Moses* (says the story) he with his Staff brought Water out of a Rock (I wonder why River-water might not have served the turn) which became a perpetual Fountain; but now that *Moses* may be sure to be out-done, he brought Wine also out of the Rock to serve their needs, but (as it is wisely put in) that was dryed up when the Bridg was finished. Another instance we have in S. *Endeus* his going by Sea to the Island *Arann*; He coming to the Sea-side, and finding no Vessel to conveigh him over, he commanded 8 *Friers*, to take up a great Stone that lay near hand, and put it in the Sea; and in the vertue of him who walked dry-shod upon the Sea, he got upon that stone, and Christ causing a fit Wind to blow, he was brought safe upon it to the Island. S. *Mochua* is another example of the same nature; who having a visit given him by S. *Kyenanus*, and 15 of his Clergy;

Marginal notes:
Bolland. vita S. Gonsalvi. 10 Jan. p. 646.
Colganus vit. S. Endei. 21 Mart. p. 707.
Bolland. Act. Sanct. 1 Januar. p. 46, 47.

Clergy; in their return, they came to an unpassable and impetuous River, and wanted a Boat; whereupon S. *Mochua* spread his Mantle upon the Water, being mindful of *Elijah*'s Mantle that divided the River *Jordan*, and *Kyenanus* and his 15 Men were carried over the River upon this Mantle, as safely as in a Vessel, and it returned back to its owner, without wrinkle or wetting. After this *Mochua* going to the Consecration of a Church *Kyenanus* had built, he saw 12 Harts in a Mountain, and brought them tamely along with him loaden with Wood, and after that with Water to boil their Flesh, upon which they feasted; only he commanded all their Bones to be reserved: which the next Day he commanded (in the virtue of him that raised *Lazarus* from the dead) to rise in their proper form, and they did so; and were sent away by him alive into the Mountains. This, it's plain, which way soever you take it, was a greater Miracle than the raising of *Lazarus*, for his Flesh was neither new created Flesh, nor devoured: Nay, and upon the same account, it is a greater Miracle, than the Resurrection of *Christ* from the Dead, which is the main confirmation of the Christian Religion; and yet there is no imaginable reason for this great Miracle of the Resurrection of the 12 Staggs. There was some little occasion for their coming along with the Saint, to furnish the Consecration Feast; but that good work being done, there appears no reason at all for that extraordinary Miracle afterwards; unless it were to prove the Immortality of Beasts, as the Resurrection of our Saviour, and others, was particularly designed to prove the Immortality of Men.

To instance only in one more; *viz.* S. *Severus* a Bishop in *France*, of whom they tell in his Life this Wonder: As he was passing by the House of a poor Widdow in a Journey, he heard her making sad moan; he stopt, and went in to inquire the cause; which was this; That as she was setting Bread into her Oven, the Peel was left in it, and was burnt; and she knew not how either to draw out the Loaves that were

Bolland. vit. Sanc. 1 *Feb. p.* 189, 192.

were already in, or put in those that were still out: upon which S. *Severus*, without any dread, went into the hot Oven, and took in and placed in order the remaining Loaves; and when they were all baked (for he stayed in the Oven till then) he reached them all out to the Woman; and came forth, as the *Three Children* out of the Fiery Furnace, untouched by the heat, either in his Body or Cloaths. This is such a Rapper, that I cannot but admire at the wanton fancy of the *Monks*, those Fathers of Lies, in the invention of this and other Miracles. Can any Man believe, that to save an old Womans Batch of Bread, God Almighty should work so extraordinary a Miracle, as in some circumstances of it, is beyond that of the *Three Children*, wrought by him in Vindication of his own honour against Idolatry? But, in the name of wonder, what need the Bishop stay in the Oven till the Bread was baked? Besides, I doubt the Criticks will have a hard task to determine, whether of the two we are to believe, either that the Oven was a very large one, or that the Bishop was very little. Herein then the *Three Children*, and this Saint scarce stand upon equal terms; but in another respect he far out-did them: for S. *Severus* was as miraculously preserved from starving, as from burning. (*which we never read of them*) For being shut out of doors in a sad snowy Night, having nothing on but Drawers (for he had given away the rest of his cloaths) a Herd of *Mares* which he used to keep in the Field, came round about him, and turning all their heads to him, by their breath kept him warm all Night, and the Snow that came down, all fell without that Circle.

But to conclude this Digression. I am sure there are Controversies of more importance, depending betwixt us and the Church of *Rome*, than that fore-named was, about the time of observing *Easter*: If Mr. *Cr.*'s Collection of Wonders, upon far less occasions, were true; methinks we might, without any imputation of sawciness, desire and hope, that when such showers of Miracles have fallen in the Ages before us, which have made Mountains to spring up; we

might

might but have some few drops fall upon us, such as would produce at least a Mole-hill. I dare say the *English* Protestants, though they have, I believe, more skill to avoid being cheated, yet they are as willing to be determined by a real Miracle, as the old *Brittish* Christians were: I know not therefore what should hinder it, unless the Prayers of the present *Romish* Saints, who are the great Pretenders to Miracles, are not so acceptable and prevalent with Heaven as heretofore; and I'le give Mr. *Cressy* leave to guess at the true reason of that.

De S. *Georgio*.

Horæ sec.
uf. Sarum.

Antiphona.

Georgi Martyr inclyte,
Te decet Laus & gloria
Prædotatum militia:
Per quem puella regia
Existens in tristitia,
Coram Dracone pessimo
Salvata est. Ex animo
Te rogamus corde intimo,
Ut cum cunctis fidelibus
Cœli jungamur civibus,
Nostris ablutis sordibus;
Ut simul cum lætitia
Tecum simus in gloria;
Nostraque reddant labia,
Laudes Christo cum gratia.

Of St. George.

(*Translated by Dr.* Heylin.)

George Holy Martyr,
praise and fame,
Attend upon thy glorious name;
Advanc'd to Knightly dignity,
The Daughter of a King by Thee
(*As she was making grievous moan*
By a fierce Dragon all alone)
Was freed from Death. We thee intreat
That we in Heaven may have a Seat.
And being washt from every stain
May there with all the faithful reign;
That we with Thee together may
Sing gladly man) a sacred lay.

The

Verſ. Ora pro nobis B. *Georgi* Chriſti miles.

Reſp. Ut hoſtes viſibiles & inviſibiles, ſint contra nos valde debiles.

Oremus.

OMnipotens ſempiterne Deus; qui deprecantium voces benignus exaudis; Majeſtatem tuam ſupplices exoramus, ut ſicuti in honorem beati & glorioſiſſimi Martyris tui *Georgii*, Draconem à puella ſuperari voluiſti; ita ejuſdem interceſſione, hoſtes noſtros viſibiles & inviſibiles, ne nocere valeant, à nobis ſuperari concedas.

Per Dominum, &c.

The gracious Throne of Chriſt before,
To whom be praiſe for ever more.

Verſ. Pray for us S. George the Souldier of Chriſt.

Anſ. That our enemies viſible and inviſible may be very weak in oppoſing us.

Let us Pray.

ALmighty everlaſting God, who mercifully heareſt the requeſts of thoſe that pray to Thee; we humbly intreat thy Majeſty, that as in honor of thy bleſſed and moſt glorious Martyr George, thou wouldſt have the Dragon to be vanquiſht by a Maid *, ſo grant that by his interceſſion, our enemies viſible and inviſible may be overcome by us, that they may have no power to hurt us.

By our Lord, &c.

---

* *This I ſuppoſe refers to that in the Legend, mentioned in the Feſtivale, f. 96. that when S. George had bore down the Dragon with his Spear to the ground, he bad the Damoſel to bind it with her Girdle about the Neck and lead it into the City, which ſhe did, and the Dragon followed after her as it had been a Hound.*

NOTES.

NOTES.

I Need not meddle with the Controverſie, whether S. *George* were an Imaginary Saint, or an *Arrian* Heretick, concerning which you may ſee enough both of the Opinions of Proteſtants and Papiſts, in Dr. *Heylin*'s Hiſtory of S. *George*. But theſe things concerning the Dragon, and the King's Daughter mentioned in the Prayer, are plainly taken out of the Golden Legend of *Jacobus de Voragine* *, as *Baronius* himſelf acknowledges in his Annotations on the *Roman Martyrologie*, April 23. and (which is obſervable) the *Breviary of Sarum*, though it abound with ſo many fabulous Legends, yet does not mention any thing in the Leſſons for S. *George*, about the killing of the *Dragon*; but tells a dull ſtory in compariſon concerning him, as a Martyr of *Cappadocia*; And *Baronius* inclines rather to make him a Symbolical Saint. And yet you ſee in the Prayer, that this Fable of the Dragon is made the ground of that which follows, that by the Interceſſion of this Dragon-killer (*ejuſdem interceſſione*) they may prevail over their enemies viſible and inviſible; for they then thought, that no other Saint or Martyr could do their work ſo well as he *, eſpecially ſince their Great Enemy is ſo formidable, and is repreſented as an old Dragon. *Ribadeneira* tells us, in his life, that Generals and Kings when they go to the Wars, take him for their ſingular Patron; and that the *Roman* Church invokes S. *George*, S. *Sebaſtian*, and S. *Maurice*, as the moſt powerful Captains and Defenders, againſt the enemies of the Chriſtian Faith. But a more ſpecial honour was done to him here, when a Conſtitution was made by *Henry* Arch-Biſhop of *Canterbury*

* *Who is called by Melch. Canus, homo ferrei oris, plumbei cordis, animi certé parum ſeveri & prudentis.* Loc. Theol. l. 11. p. 337.

* *Maxime bellorum Rector, quem noſtra juventus Pro Mavorte colit.* Mantuan. Faſt. lib. 4.

Canterbury, an. 1415. that a great Festival should be kept to his Memory (*Sub officio duplici, Et ad modum majoris duplicis festi*, are the words) as to the special Patron and Protector of the *English* Nation (and it was just at the time when *Henry* V. begun his Warr in *France*) undoubtedly believing, that by his intercession the Arms of the Nation would fare the better in time of War, and the Clergy, its spiritual Militia, in times of Peace. To this confidence in S. *George*, the Legends at that time, and the Relations of Visions betrayed them. But long before this, even very anciently, we find that his story had been corrupted with Fables, insomuch that Pope *Gelasius*, in the first *Roman* Council reckons the *Passion of George*, among Apocryphal Writings. And the 4*th*. Canon of *Nicephorus* the Confessor, requires the 2 *Martyrdomes* of *George* not to be admitted, but rejected. But though all be in the dark, and uncertain as to the Acts of this Saint (and therefore the reformed Breviaries have no special Lessons for him, nor any mention is made of his Acts, because as *Ribadeneira* well observes, there is no truth appears in those that are extant) though his feats of Arms prove all fabulous; yet however, Armes his Body had; and if they wrought no Miracles while he lived, they cannot fail to effect wonders now he is dead: one of them they have got at *Paris* in the Church of S. *Vincent*, and the other they keep at *Colen*, where (says the Writer) many and great Miracles are wrought by it (as good a place for it to do feats in, as any it could have been lodg'd at) His *Head* is shown in *Rome* at a Church called after his Name; and it's great pitty that they have not told us of

some

Tom. 12. *Concil. Labbe.* p. 295.

Hujus namque, ut indubitanter credimus, interventu, nedum gentis Angligena armata militia, contra incursus hostiles bellorum tempore regitur, sed & Cleri pugna militaris in sacrae pacis otio, sub tanti patroni suffragio celebriter roboratur. Ibid.

Tom. 4. *Concil. Labbe.* p. 1265.

Tom. 7. *Concil. Lab.* p. 1297.

Ribadeneira in vit. Georgii. p. 170.

Ribaden. Ibid.

Devotions of the Roman Church.

some place, where we might have seen too, at least a part of the *Dragon*'s Tayl. For my part, till I see some better account of the History of this Saint's Life, I shall content my self with the mysteries and Moral Lecture, the Legend has given us upon his Name. (which is another *Passion of George* and *Martyrdom of Greek*.) "*Geor-*   Legend. aurea de S. Georg.
"*gius* comes from *Geos*, which signi-
"fies the Earth, and *Orge* to Till, *as if you should say, one*
"*that* tilleth the Earth, *that is*, his Flesh. S. *Augustine* says,
"that good ground is in the Altitude of Mountains, in the
"temperament of Hills, in the Level-ground of the Fields:
"The first is good for green Herbs, the second for Vines,
"the third for Fruits. Even so S. *George* was *high* by despi-
"sing inferiour things, and therefore he had the greenness
"of purity. He was *Temperate* by discretion, and there-
"fore he had the Wine of inward jucundity. He was *plain*
"by humility, and therefore brought forth the Fruits of
"good Works. Or thus, *Georgius* comes from *Gerar*, that
"is *Holy*, and *Gion*, that is *Sand*, as if you should say, *Holy*
"*Sand*: for he was *Sand*, because *ponderous*, by the gravi-
"ty of his manners, and *small* by humility, and *dry* (by ab-
"stinence) from carnal pleasure. Or else thus, *Georgius*
"comes from *Gerar*, i. e. Holy, and *Gion*, which signifies
"*Striving*; as much as to say, *Holy Combatant*, because he
"combated with the *Dragon*, and the *Executioner*. Or,
"(Lastly,) *Georgius* is derived from *Gero*, that is, a *Stran-*
"*ger*, and *Gir*, i. e. *precious*, and *Us* a *Counsellour*. For
"he was a stranger in his contempt of the World, precious
"in his Crown of Martyrdom, and a Counsellour in the
"Preaching of the Kingdom. Thus far the Golden Legend, Printed at *Argentine*, an. 1502. which has a Hundred more such pleasant accounts of Names *, which because they

---

* Such as, *Fabianus*, *quasi* Fabricanus, sc. *fabricans beatitudinem supernam*. S. *Vincentius*, quasi vitium incendens. S. *Gregorius*, qu. Egregorius, *ab* Egregius & Gore *pradicator*, i.e. *Egregius prædicator*. S. *Vitalis*, qu. *Vivens talis*. sc. qualis erat in corde. S. *Euphemia*, qu. *bona fæmina*, ab eu bonum & *femina*. S. Francis was *first* called John, but after

H   were

his name was changed to Franciscus, of which one reason is, Quia ipse per se & per filios suos, multos servos peccati & Diaboli debeat francos & liberos facere, &c.

were very edifying, they were brought after this into Sermons; and the People were told that *Vaspatian* (a) was named from hence, because he had a malady in his Nosthrils, and there dropped out of his Nose Wormes like Waspes. And the Sermon on the Day of *Pentecost* begins thus. (b) Good Men and Women, this Day is called *Whitsunday*, because the Holy Ghost brought *Wit* and *Wisdome* into *Christ*'s Disciples, and so by their Preaching after into all Christendome. *But enough of this.*

(a) *Festivale, fol. 99.*
(b) *Ibid. fol. 43.*

Memoria de 7 Dormientibus.	The Memorial of the 7 Sleepers.
Oratio.	The Prayer.
Breviar. sec. us. Sar. 27. Julii. & Missale Sarum an. 1554. Deus qui gloriosos resurrectionis æternæ præcones septem dormientes magnificè coronasti; præsta quæsumus, ut eorum precibus, resurrectionem sanctam quæ in eis mirabiliter præostensa est, consequamur. Per Dominum, &c.	O God, who didst magnificently crown the 7 Sleepers, who proclaimed the eternal resurrection; grant we beseech thee, that by their Prayers, we may obtain that holy resurrection, which was wonderfully foreshown in them. Through, &c.

NOTES.

NOTES.

To show the Reader, what great care the Heads of this Church had in those Days of Mens Souls, how well they instructed them, and by what fine stories their Devotions were then conducted; I cannot but translate the History of these 7 Sleepers, as I find it in the *Salisbury* Breviary in the forecited place: which if it had been designed to entertain Youth, as the History of the *Seven Champions*, it might have deserved a less severe censure; but this was read in the Church to the People, as Chapters are out of the Bible, and divided into so many Lessons, which take in *English* just as I find it.

1. *Lesson.*

"Under the Reign of *Decius* the Emperor, when a grievous Persecution fell upon the Christians, there were Seven Christians Citizens of *Ephesus*, whose Names were *, *Maximianus, Malchus, Martianus, Dionysius, Johannes, Serapion* and *Constantine*, who to avoid the fury of the Persecutors, hid themselves in a Cave in Mount *Celius*; appointing *Malchus* *, in the Habit of a Beggar, to buy them Victuals; in which Cave they slept for many Ages.

* Surius out of Metaphrastes, gives us but two of these names, viz. Denys & Johns; the other five are, Maximilianus, Jamblicus, Martinus, Exacustadius and Antoninus.

* *Metaphrastes calls him Jamblicus.*

2. *Lesson.*

"At the end of Three Hundred Sixty two Years, in the Reign of the most Christian Emperour *Theodosius*, there arose a detestable Heresie, that endeavoured to root out the Faith of the General Resurrection. These Saints then awaking, and thinking they had slept only the space

Ribadeneira in their life, corrects this as a mistake in Chronologie, and makes it 177 Years.

"space of one Night; they sent *Malchus* to the City, to
"buy necessary Provisions for them; who seeing a Cross
"erected over the Gate of the City, and all Men invoking
"the Name of God, began greatly to wonder; and when
"he pull'd out his Money, those that beheld it said, admiring,
"This young Man has found a Treasure: and they brought
"him to the *Proconsul* of the City.

3 Lesson.

"When the *Proconsul* inquired of him, where he found
"that Treasure, *Malchus* falling at his Feet, said; I intreat
"you to tell me, where is *Decius* the Emperour, for I and
"my Companions to avoid his Persecution, hid our selves
"in a Cave of Mount *Celius*. *Marinus* the Bishop of the
"City, hearing this, said: Let us go with him to the place;
"and coming to the Cave, they beheld the Servants of God
"sitting, and their Faces were as fresh as a Rose. They a-
"dored them, and sent for the Emperour, who when he was
"come, worshipped them and wept. Whereupon they spake
"thus to him: For thy sake our God has raised us up be-
"fore the Day of the Great Resurrection, that thou, with-
"out farther doubting, mightest believe the Resurrection
"of the Dead. And when they had said thus, they gave up
"the Ghost at God's bidding. Then the Emperor weep-
"ing, and kissing their holy Reliques, gathered together a
"great-many Bishops, and others of the Faithful, who made
"in the same place a worthy Memorial of them.

Thus far the Lessons.

Now though a great deal of this Stuff is to be met with
in *Greg. Turonensis, de gloria Martyrum*; yet if any have
a mind to see the ground of the Prayer, and this Legend of
the *Seven* Sleepers confuted, he need go no farther, than to
Baronius his Notes upon the *Roman Martyrologie, July* 27.
Where he shows, that there was no Heresie about the Resurrection in the Days of *Theodosius jun.* And that it was
no Confirmation of the Resurrection, to say that these *Seven*

ven were raised from a long sleep, and yet were not truly dead; besides that none of the Writers that lived in that Age, mention any such wonder, which it is no ways likely they could have been ignorant of, if it had been true.

Memoria S. Davidis *Episcopi & Confessoris.*

Brev. Sarum.
1 Martii.

Oratio.

DEus, qui B. Confessorem tuum atque pontificem (*sc. Davidem*) angelo nunciante, triginta annis antequam nasceretur prædixisti; tribue nobis quæsumus, ut cujus festivitatem colimus, ejus intercessione ad æterna gaudia perveniamus.

Per Dominum, &c.

The Memorial of St. David Bishop & Confessor.

The Prayer.

O God, who by an Angel didst foretell the Nativity of thy B!. Confessor and Bishop (S. David) thirty years before he was born; Grant to us, we beseech thee, that we who celebrate his Festival, may by his intercession attain to joys everlasting.

By our Lord, &c.

NOTES.

This Prayer is plainly grounded upon the story of *S. David*'s Life; a short account of which we have in the *Salisbury* Breviary: which we shall comment upon out of Mr. *Cressy*, and *Capgrave*, who has given it more largely, with a great many Wonders, which the Breviary pretermits. The Summe of the Lessons in the Breviary is as follows.

Lesson 1, *&* 2.

S. *Patrick* returning from *Rome* into his Native Countrey of *Brittany*, he came into a Valley called *Rosina* [which

H 3

place

Colgan. 1 Mart. p. 425. place, says his Life in *Colganus*, he beheld as fit for him to serve God, and to abide in] "To "whom an Angel appearing, said to him; O "*Patrick*, God has not provided this Seat for thee, but for "one that is not yet born, but shall be born 30 Years hence; "so the Vale of *Rosina* was left by him for S. *David* not yet "born, as it was told him by the Angel. [*Capgrave* tells us, that when S. *Patrick* heard this Message he was grieved and angry, that God should chuse and prefer one not yet born, before himself, who had served him from his Infancy; and in a peevish humour he was preparing to fly away and forsake Christ: but an Angel was sent a second time to him, to smooth and flatter him *, and (just as crying Children are

* Ut ill'um verbis familiaribus blandiretur. stilled with the sight of some fine gayes) the Angel said, Rejoyce O *Patrick*, for the Lord hath sent me to thee, to show thee all the Island of *Ireland*, and thou shalt be an Apostle of all that Countrey, &c. And when he had said this, lifting up his eyes from the place in which he was (which was a great Valley in which was a Stone upon which

* Call'd Sessio S. Patricii, sayes his Life in Colganus. he stood *,) he beheld all the Island. Which was a pretty Miracle, out of a Valley to show him a whole Countrey, unless the Stone swell'd into a great Mountain under him, as we shall hear the place did, where S. *David* once preached.]

Lesson 3, & 4.

"S. *David* before he was born, even while he was yet in "his Mothers Womb, was fore-shown by God how great "a Preacher he should be: for when a certain Master na-
"med *Gildas*, (sc. *Albanius*) was Preaching to the People, "and the Mother of S. *David*, great with Child, entred the "Church; *Gildas* of a sudden held his peace, and presumed "not to Preach any farther. Who when he was asked by "the People, why he left off Preaching and was silent; he "answered: that he could have discoursed to them in com-
"mon talk, but could not Preach; because that Woman,
"which

" which now by intreaty went out of the Church, came in
" by a Heavenly warning, while I declared to you the Word
" of God, to demonstrate (by my being put to silence) the
" excellency of her offspring. [This passage of *Gildas*
his being dumb, is farther explained by *Colganus* and *Capgrave*; how that when he could not go on in his Preaching, he desired all the People to go out of the Church, and he remain within, and try whether then he could

Colganus ut supra. Capgrave in vita Gilda Confessor.

go on: The People did so, but she alone lay hid within the Church, out of a desire to hear the Word of God, or being detained by God for the showing the Miracle. But when the Man of God endeavoured to Preach, he could still do nothing; so that being amazed at the Miracle, he cryed out, saying: If there be any one that lies hid in the Church, I adjure thee by God, that thou show thy self quickly to me. Then she answered, Behold here I lye hid. Then said he, Do thou stand without Doors, and let the People return into the Church; which being done, the impediment of his Tongue was loosed, and he Preached as he was wont: and when upon his questioning her, she confessed her self to be with Child; he by this sign understood and foretold that the Child should be so eminent in Sanctity, that none in those Parts should be comparable to him. Thus by childish and unlikely circumstances, they make Prophecies as ridiculous, as they do their Miracles; they intended some likeness in *Gildas* his dumbness, to that of the Father of *John the Baptist*, as I conjecture: but it would have been a strange sign of his Son's *future Devotion*, if *Zacharias* should have been able to talk of *any affair* with his Neighbours, but should not have been able to speak at all, when he came to say *his Prayers*; me-thinks they should have either made *Gildas* wholly dumb, or raised his Oratory in Preaching above his common pitch, at the Presence of him that was to be so great a Preacher; especially since not being able to go on in a Sermon, when a Man can otherwise speak, may be imputable to other causes than a Divine hinderance. But the

H 4 *Monks*

Monks will play at small Games, rather than their invention shall hold out: Of which me-thinks we have a remarkable instance in the story of S. *Cuthbert*, of whom *Capgrave* says, that when he was a Boy, he walked out with the Bishop that educated him, to see his Cattel in the Field; and as he came by a Cow ready to Calve, *Cuthbert* attentively beheld her and smiled; the Bishop asked the cause of it, and he told him, I see a wonderful thing, for since this Cow is altogether black, it's strange what hidden cause in Nature should prevail to conceive a Calf so unlike, which seems to be of a reddish colour with a white Star in its Forehead: presently after the Cow calved, and brought forth such a Calf as the Boy had foretold. This Prediction, as worthy a one as it was, I suppose was intended, to be a sign too of *Cuthbert*'s eminent future sanctity, contrary to what might have been expected, considering, as we are told just before, that he was begot on a deflowred Virgin.] But to go on with S. *David*.

Capgrave vit. S. Cuthbert. f. 69.

Lesson 5.

" When the Days wherein he should be born, according
" to the Angel's Prediction, were fulfilled, S. *David* sprung
" from a generous Stock, was the Son of a Prince of the
" Province of *Leretica* (*it should be Ceretica*) When he was
" born, Divine Miracles were not wanting. [This is a very fair account of S. *David*, which the Breviary gives; and any one that reads it alone, would conclude that he was the Son of a Prince lawfully begotten. But Mr. *Cressy* has commented scurvily upon this Passage. " A
" Prince of the Region called *Ceretica*, travel-
" ling to *Demetia*, met by the way a Religious
" Virgin called *Nonnita*, of great beauty, which he lusting
" after, by violence deflowred her: Hereby she conceived a
" Son (which was this *David*) and neither before nor after
" ever had knowledge of any Man; but persevering in cha-
" stity, both of Body and Mind, and sustaining her self only
" with Bread and Water from the time of her Conception,
" She

Ch. Hist. l. 10. cap. 8.

Devotions of the Roman Church. 105

"she led a most holy Life. I doubt all the commendations of the after abstinence and chastity of the Mother, which Mr. *Cr.* gives, will not make an amends to the Welch-men, whose great Patron S. *David* is, for telling them, what either they never knew before, or had willingly, I presume, forgotten, that *S. David was a Bastard.* Capgrave indeed has made some amends, by Miracles that concerned the Mother: for in the place where she was deflowred, and at the very time of her conception, 2 great Stones, says he, appeared, which were never seen before, the one at her Head, and the other at her Feet; (though he leaves us to guess what they signified) and when she was in Labour *, she leaned with her Hands upon a Stone which lay by her, which shows the Print of her hands, as if it had been made in Wax, and by being divided in the middle, the Stone did as it were condole with her in her Pangs: as certainly true, as that of S. *Ængussius*, who when he had chopt off his left hand as he was cleaving Wood, the Birds came flocking about him with a great and loud noise, to testifie their condoling the mishap that had befallen him, though they need not have been so much concerned, for it was but taking his hand, and clapping it on to the Wrest again, and he was perfectly cured without more to do.]

Capgr. vit. S. David, f. 83.

Colganus vit. S. Ængus. p. 580.

* *Thus they tell us that the Mother of S. Senanus, when she was in Travel held a piece of dry Wood in her hand, which presently waxed green, and flourished with leaves, and became a Tree which is seen at this day; (when the Wood of the Altar S.* Brigid *touched waxed green, it was a sign (we heard) of her Virginity; I wonder what this greenness of Wood upon a Mothers touching it will signifie.) Colgan. in supplement. vit. S. Senani. nu. 6.*

Lesson 6.

"When he was Baptized by *Elveus* (called *Relveus* by
"*Cambrensis*) Bishop of *Menevia*, as he returned out of
"*Ireland*, and then came just into the Port called *Gleys*; at
"his Baptism a Fountain of clear Water flowed out, which
"was

"was never seen before. [Here is a material doubt, how this *Relvius* or *Elvius*, who by *Cambrensis*, the Breviary and Anglican Martyrology is said to be the Bishop of *Menevia*, could be so, when none sate in that Seat before S. *David*, and this Bishop baptized him? *Alford* gives 2 Answers to this doubt (though Mr. *Cressy* his Transcriber mention but one of them) the first is very ingenuous; that there are many things that occur in the Lives of the Saints, which deservedly stumble the Reader; for the Writers of those Lives, were so wholly taken up in rehearsing their vertues and miracles, that they were little sollicitous about other things that pertained to History (*i.e.* they were more concerned to set down their own fabulous inventions, than to take care how they agreed with the truth of things) his second answer is, that instead of *Relveus* of *Menevia*, we ought to read *Ælbeus* of *Mumenia*, because he finds a Bishop there of that Name: but cites not one Author, who writes this story, that agrees with him, and so may as fairly be rejected as proposed.]

Alford Ann.l. Eccl. Britan. ad an. 462.

Lesson 7.

"A certain old Man blind from his Child-hood, having a
"defect in his Nose, which did not a little deform his Face,
"washed the Child at the Fountain; whom as he held in his
"Lap, understanding the sanctity of the Infant, he took the
"Water in which he was *three* times dipped, and therewith
"sprinkled his face *three* times, and presently he wonder-
"fully obtained the sight of his eyes, and the intireness of
"his Face. [Such another wonderful cure of eyes, *Capgrave* relates, he wrought upon his Master *Paulens* (or *Paulinus*) who through too much grief having lost his sight, he desired every one of his Scholars to look into his Eyes, and bless them: all the rest did so, but in vain; but when S. *David* touched and blessed them, he recovered his Eyes: by the same token that he desired to be excused from looking into them, for such was his excessive modesty, that for 10 Years space he never once had the confidence to look
him

Devotions of the Roman Church. 107

him in the Face. Yet so powerful was his blessing, that, coming to the Town of *Bath*, he bestowed by his Benediction a perpetual heat upon those Waters there, making them fit to bath in, which before were mortiferous.

Capgrave in ejus vit. fol. 83.

Lesson 8, & 9.

" Thus the Child grew, being full of the Holy Ghost;
" and being addicted to the study of Learning, by the quick-
" ness of his sharp wit he made proficiency, beyond all his
" equals in age: for he was so replenisht with grace, that
" his School-fellows testified, they often saw a white Dove *
" with a Golden Bill, as it were teaching him. His me-
" rits thus increasing, the Saint being brought into Holy
" Orders, at last he was raised to the dignity of a Bishop;
" and when he was almost an Hundred Forty seven Years
" old, after he had received the Body and Blood of *Christ*,
" after the Christian manner, he rendred his most holy soul
" to his Creator.

* *So the Disciples of S Ambrose of Sena, affirmed that they saw a Dove at his eares as he preached, Act. Sanct. 20. Mart. p. 192. as if they had a mind to justifie the Fable of Mahomet's Pidgeon.*

[This story of the *Dove* is told us with an admirable addition in *Colganus*, how that his School-fellows saw the *Dove* often teaching him, and (which is more) *singing Hymns with Him*. But there are a great many other remarkable passages of S. *David's* Life, which the Breviary has overpassed, some of which it may not be amiss here to insert. Such is that usage of S. *David*, which *Capgrave* mentions, that presently after Mattens he went into cold Water, and by staying therein a good while, he tamed the heat of his Flesh. A common practice I find this was with the *Irish* Saints. S. *Scutinus*, we are told, when at any time he found any lustful motions within him, he used to leap into a Tub of cold Water, and there

Colganus in vit. David. p. 426.

Capgrav. ut supra fol. 84.

Colganus vit. S. Scutin. pag. 9. sec. 4, 5.

continue

continue in Prayer, till he had almost lost all vital sense; but he was miraculously rewarded; for he could tread water so well, that he was often seen to walk upon the Sea, without any Vessel to carry him. S. *Ænguſſius* did the same, standing in cold Water, till he had repeated a third part of the *Psalmes*: S. *Cuanna* out-did him, who by Night used to go into a Fountain of cold Water, and there sing the *Psalter* from the beginning to the end: but S. *Fechinus* had the advantage of them all, who using this Cold-water Penance, his Butler *Paſtolius* had one time a mind to try it with him, but as soon as his Body touched the Water, he began to shiver and his Teeth to chatter; but upon his approaching nearer to *Fechinus*, and joyning in Devotion with him, by vertue of their fervent prayer, the Cold water was so intensly heated, that *Paſtolius* not being able to endure it, was fain in haste to leave the Bath; whom the Man of God charged, for the avoiding of vain-glory, that he should not discover it to any one whil'st the Saint lived: (*and he might tell what Lies he pleased of him, wherein he was only a Witneſs, after he was dead.*) But to return to S. *David*. The most famed Miracle, (related by *Colganus*, *Capgrave*, and Mr. *Creſſy*) is that which hapned at a *Synod* in *Wales*, met about the *Pelagian Hereſie*, where there was an Assembly of 118 Bishops (I wonder where their Sees were in *Brittany*) and an innumerable Multitude of Abbots and Clergy-men, Kings, Princes and People (says the Life in *Colganus*) so that they seemed to cover all the Land; where they were greatly concerned, lest by reason of the Multitude, which neither Voice nor Trumpet (in an ordinary way) seemed capable of reaching all their eares, the People not hearing the Sermon (which was the way according to this account of determining the Controverſie) might still remain in Hereſie. It was therefore agreed, that raiſing a heap of Garments on high, one standing upon them should begin to Preach, and

Idem. p. 579.

Idem. in vit. S. Cuanna. p. 250.

Colganus vit. S. Fechini 20 Januar. p. 132. n. 17.

Devotions of the Roman Church.   109

and whosoever obtained the grace to be heard by all the People, (*Capgrave* says, *to be heard by all equally*) he should be all their Metropolitan and Patriarch. Then one of the Bishops began to Preach, but was scarce heard by those that stood next him, by reason of the Tumult of the People; and so it fared with a great many more; at last they agree to send for S. *David* to preach at the *Synod*, who twice or thrice humbly refusing; at length he consented to go thither, but not designing to *Preach*, only he told them he would give them some assistance in *Prayer*. But when he came thither, they prevailed with him to Preach; and commanding a Child which attended him, and had been lately restored to life by him, to spread his Handkerchief under his Feet, standing upon it, he began (says Mr. *Cressy*) to expound the Gospel and the *Sudarium suum.* Law to the Auditory: All the while that his Oration continued, a Snow-white Dove, descending from Heaven, sate upon his shoulders; and moreover the Earth on which he stood, raised it self under him, till it became a Hill, so that he was seen by all, and his voice like a Trumpet was equally heard by all, both near and afar off; on the Top of which Hill a Church was afterwards built, which remains to this day. By this Sermon he confounded Heresie, and establisht the Orthodox Faith, and by the consent of all, was made the Arch-Bishop of all *Brittany*. *Thus far the Story.* Which I think, as to this last part, needs not any comment to proclaim it to be a Fable; that a Hill should here be miraculously raised, only to serve S. *David* for a Pulpit: for though I deny not this to be a good substantial Miracle, yet me-thinks a Man of Mr. *Cressy*'s wit (if the rest had none) should have found out a fitter place for it. Had S. *David* been to preach upon *Salisbury Plaines*, there might have been more reason for it; but it is not easie to imagine how the wit of Man could have hit upon a more pleasant absurdity, than to put God Almighty to the expence of a Miracle, for the making up the want of a Hill in *Wales*.

After

After S. *David's* death, we are told by *Capgrave*; that a great Plague happening in *England*, a Bishop of *Menevia* (or S. *David's*) brought with him the Arm of S. *David* (after a fruitless tryal of other Reliques) which being washed in Water, the Water appeared as if it were guilded with fat, and a Golden Cross upon it, which he causing the People to drink, the Mortality presently ceased.

Capgr. ubi supra, fol. 85.

He also relates, that a *Welch-man* (together with an *Almain*) being taken Prisoner by the *Saracens*, and bound with an Iron-Chain, he invoked the Saint Day and Night in the words of his Countrey-Language, *Dewi wareth:* i. e. *David help*; and he was suddenly restored to his Countrey: His Fellow-Prisoner, remembring how the *Welch-man* often repeated the words *Dewi wareth*, he resolved to say so too, though he understood nothing of their meaning: He did so, and immediately he also was snatched away from that place, and brought home, though how he was carried, he could give no account: For producing which example, I expect the *Romanists* thanks, since it is so very pat an Instance, to prove the Vertue of Prayers in an unknown Tongue.

Capgr. Ibid.

Ad undecim Millia Virginum.

Horâ sec. us. Sarum.

Antiphona.

O Vos undena millia,
    Puellæ gloriolæ,
Virginitatis Lilia
    Martyriique rosæ;
In vita me defendite
    Præbendo mihi juvamen;

To the Eleven Thousand Virgins.

Eleven Thousand Maids!
    O glorious Company!
Ye fairest Lillies of Virginity,
Roses of Martyrdome; *in life defend me,*

In

Devotions of the Roman Church. 111

In morte vos ostendite
Supernum ferendo solamen.

And at my Death Celestial Comforts send me.

Vers. Orate pro nobis Sponsæ Dei Electæ.
Resp. Ut ad vestrum consortium valeamus pervenire.

Vers. Pray for us ye Elect Spouses of God.
Ans. That we may be able to come to your Society.

Oremus.

O Dulcissime Domine Jesu Christe, qui es Sponsus Virginum, præmium Martyrum, & piissimus exauditor omnium Sanctorum tuorum; precibus & meritis gloriosissimarum sponsarum tuarum, sanctissimæ *Ursula*, sociarumque suarum Virginum & Martyrum, concedere digneris mihi & omnibus eas venerantibus, singulorum suorum peccatorum veniam, in adversis expedientem protectionem, in prosperis congruam directionem, & gratiam conformandi ad tuam voluntatem; inque fine vitæ illarum visibilem consolationem, & cum illis transitum securum ad gloriam sempiternam.

Qui tecum, &c.

Pater Noster. Ave Maria.

Let us Pray.

O Most sweet Lord Jesus Christ, who art the Spouse of Virgins, the reward of Martyrs, and the most merciful Hearer of all thy Saints; by the Prayers and Merits of thy most glorious Spouses, the most holy Ursula, and her Companions, Virgins & Martyrs, be pleased to grant unto me and to all those that venerate them, the pardon of all their sins; expedient protection in adversity, convenient direction in prosperity, and grace to conform to thy will; and when life is ended, their visible consolation, and a secure passage with them to Eternal Glory.

Who liveth, &c.

Our Father. Hail Mary.

Oratio.

Oratio.   A Prayer.

Breviar. Rom. reform. 21 Octob.

DA nobis, quæsumus Domine Deus noster, sanctarum Virginum & Martyrum tuarum *Ursulæ* & Sociarum ejus palmas incessabili devotione venerari, ut quas digna mente non possumus celebrare, humilibus saltem frequentemus obsequiis.

Per Dominum, &c.

GRant unto us, we beseech thee, O Lord our God, that we may with unceasant Devotion venerate the Palmes (victory) of thy holy Virgins and Martyrs, Ursula & her Companions; that so, whom we cannot celebrate with a worthy mind, we may at least visit them often with humble observance.

Through our Lord, &c.

Hortul. animæ sec. us. antiq. Eccles. Roman.

O Præclaræ vos Puellæ,
Nunc implete meum velle;
Et dum mortis venit hora
Subvenite sine mora.
In tam gravi tempestate
Me precantem defensate
A Dæmonum injuria.

O *Ye ever famous Maids,*
To my wishes say no Nay,
When I enter Death's black shades,
Succour me without delay.
In that Tempests sad Alarm
Let no Devils do me harm.

Vers. Pia Mater *Ursula,* Sponsa Christi decora,
Resp. Cum tuis sodalibus semper pro nobis ora.

Vers. *Christ's lovely Spouse, blest Martyr* Ursula,
Ans. *With thy Companions ever for us pray.*

Oremus.   Let us pray.

DEus, qui affluentissimæ bonitatis tuæ prudentia, Beatissimam *Ursulam* cum

O God, who in the wisdom of thine abundant goodness didst vouch-

undecim

undecim millibus Virginum, triumpho Martyrii coronare dignatus es; concede propitius, ut earum precibus ac meritis, cum ipsis in æterna beatitudine collocari mereamur.

Per Dominum.

safe to Crown Bl. Ursula, and the Eleven Thousand Virgins with the triumph of Martyrdom; mercifully grant that by their Prayers and Merits, we may merit a place with them in Eternal felicity.

Through our Lord, &c.

NOTES.

IT was no doubt a very comfortable time in the *Roman* Church, when the Inventions of the Monks could never run on so fast, in wonderous stories; but the Faith and Devotion of the People could keep pace with them, nay rather run before them: but the Later Ages have unluckily been given to examine matters more than before, and by *scrupling* implicite faith, and *bogling* at contradictions, have put the Writers of that Church to a great deal of troublesome work; in defending impossible stories, and in setting a good Gloss upon Fables, and countenancing long practised Devotions, which in civility to their Fore-fathers, they must not *acknowledg* to be either absurd or impious, though they are really so. We have found it so in many foregoing instances; and this of the Eleven Thousand Virgins is a very remarkable one. For if you call them to an account about this matter, you'l find little agreement among their Authors, which way to make it look like a probable story; though all of them would fain hold the Conclusion, and have it believed to be true. *Harpsfield* complains sadly;
" That the injury of Men and Times, has
" deprived us of the accurate and exact
" knowledg of this matter, as well as of
" many other things; instead of which, certain idle People,
" abusing their leasure shamefully, and the too forward cre-

Harpsfi-ld. Hist. Eccl. Anglic. p. 35.

" dulity

"dulity of the Age they lived in (*an excellent character of* "*the former Monks*) have obtruded meer Fables, and those "too perfectly disagreeing one from another; and have "forced us that live so many Ages after, to follow not un- "doubted truth, but slender conjectures. And yet (*see the power of a strong faith above reason!*) the same Author there breaks out into this expression. "Would to God that the "History of *Ursula* were so certain and free from difficul- "ties, as I easily and certainly perswade my self, that she "and her Companions are blessed Martyrs in Heaven. If the History of them be not certain, then there is nothing left, but Tradition to ground his certainty of Perswasion upon, that they were at all in being, or that they were Martyrs; and if he is forced to rely upon Tradition for this which is the main thing, why not for the rest too, without taking the needless pains of conjecturing uncertainly about them? he was bound to it in civility, unless the story that Tradition tells, prove impossible; and his not following it throughout, argues that he thought it so: but any one instance of that nature does our work; for a witness loses his credit in the whole, when he would obtrude an absurd or impossible thing upon our faith. Whether the Oral Tradition concerning these Virgins does not so, I shall examine afterwards: First beginning with the Historical account out of Authors, because this way of proof must needs be more satisfying to any inquisitive Person.

Baronius tells us, that he took a great deal of pains to find out the truth of their story, turning o-ver the Books of the *Vatican*; and yet that whole Library did not afford him a better Author to pitch upon, than our trusty *Geoffrey* of *Monmouth*: for which he makes this Apology in his *Annals*; "That though this Author has ma- "ny fabulous stories, so that he must be read "with great care, yet being forced to sit as an "Arbitrator, among the refuse of Apocryphal Writers, he "thought fit to chuse the most probable story, and there- "fore

Baron. not. in Rom. Martyrol. 21 Octob.

Baron. Annal. ad an. 383.

"fore readily imbraced the Relation of *Geoffrey*, because it was supported by the most likely conjectures: but, says he, the other Acts of these Virgins that are publisht, must appear to any prudent Man to be stuft with abundance of Fables. *Baronius* his account then out of *Geoffrey*, is this in short.

When *Maximus* the Tyrant in his Invasion of *Gaul*, had expelled the Inhabitants of *Armorica*, he invites a Colony over thither of *Brittish* Souldiers, and settles them there, and thence it was called *Little-Brittany*: And now the next care was, to get Wives for them in their own Country. *Ursula* the Daughter of *Dionotus* Prince of *Cornwall*, is designed for *Conanus* their Chief Leader, and she and her 11000 Virgin-Companions were shipt at *London*, though unwillingly, upon this design to go for *Armorica*: but a cruel Tempest drove them to the *German* shore; where falling into a Navy of Pyrates, under the command of *Melga* a Pirate of the *Picts*, and *Gaunus* of the *Hunns*, they consulted to offer violence to their Chastity; but by the perswasion of *Ursula*, they chose all with a Christian constancy to dye, rather than be deflowred, and so were all barbarously slain together; and he fixes the time of this cruelty, *An. Dom.* 383.

This account Mr. *Cressy* can by no means allow, and gives these Reasons: (or his Friend *Alford* for him.) Because *Maximus* his short Reign, after his passing into *Gaul*, and his continual imployments in Warre, could not permit him to settle Colonies in *Armorica*, whither himself never went. Besides the *French Historians* refer the erecting of a Principality of *Brittains* in *Armorica* to a much Later Date, when *Meroveus* was King of the *Francks*, which was *An.* 448. As also because *Dionotus* the Father of *Ursula*, is acknowledged by our best Historians, to have lived long after the Emperor *Gratianus* his time, who was slain by *Maximus*; so that *Ursula* could not be alive, much less marriageable in those days: neither lastly, is there any mention among Historians, of *Hunns* so

*Ch.Hist.l.*9. *cap.* 20.

early

early infesting *Germany*, or exercising Piracy on the River *Rhene*, or the *Western Ocean*. Indeed these Objections against *Baronius*, seem very hard to be answered; and so we are fairly quit of him without more ado. Let us now see what Mr. *Cr.* gives us in the room of it. He agrees with *Baronius* in the main substance of the History; only differs from him in the following particulars. He has placed their slaughter in the Year 453. when *Attila* King of the *Hunns* wasted *Italy*, and the Western Regions: he makes it to happen in the days of *Maximus* the Tyrant, but not of him who slew the Emperor *Gratianus*, but of that *Maximus* who invaded the Empire, and succeeded *Valentinian*, and appointed *Avitus* to oppose those Barbarous People. He has joyned together *two occasions*, why this numerous Company of Virgins departed out of their Countrey: the one was, the fore-named design of Marrying their own Country-men in *Armorica*, (or *Little Brittany*) the other occasion was, the Cruelty exercised upon the *Brittans* by the *Saxons*, who were first called in by *Vortigern* to assist the *Brittans* against the *Picts*, but after making Peace with them, turned their Arms against their Benefactors, and exercised all manner of cruelties upon them, and made many fly the Land, among whom he supposes these 11000 Virgins. A very pretty conjecture! but yet not strong enough to plead for the truth of their story, nor to justifie the Devotions of the Church to them. For as to the pretended cause of their Voyage, from their intended Marriage in *Armorica*; their own *Harpsfield* has plainly and honestly confessed, "That he should easily acquiesce in this "Narration, but that they who are of this Opinion, bring "no certain and approved Author that te-"stifies about this Marriage; and, says he, "though I my self have laboured never so, "I could never yet light upon any, that has any testimony "of Antiquity and fidelity; only I have seen an *Anonymous* "*Brittan*, translated by *Geoffrey* into Latine, that says some "such thing; but he is a man, who as in many other things, "so

Harpsf Hist Angl. Ecclef. p. 35.

"so in this Narration concerning the affairs of *Maximus*,
"is guilty of more than one lye.   [From whence, by the
way, one may conclude that the Testimony cited by some out
of *Sigebert*, concerning that intended Mar-
riage, was not looked upon by him as an   *Surius, and the old
Authentick Authority, but as an Interpo-   Rom. Breviary.*
lation *, especially since I find him, more than once upon
other occasions, citing *Sigebert's Chronicon*.]   But *Harpsfield* (in the same place) has hit upon another worse Objection, against the Marriage story, when he adds; *Neque
sanè adhuc video justam Martyrii in superiore narratione
causam.* He does not see in the foregoing narration any just
cause of *Martyrdome*: (and yet you know, the thing that
Church celebrates them for, is for their being Martyrs.) He
was so wise, as not to think that a *Massacre* meerly made a
Martyrdome, for then he knew that *Hereticks* (in his sence)
might boast of numbers beyond Eleven Thousand, and that
one in his time at *Paris*, would then have out-vied *Colen*:
and all the account that the story he opposes gave farther,
was only, that these slaughtered Persons were *Virgins*; but
that could not make them *Martyrs* neither, because it will
not alone make any one a *Christian*; and in *this case*, their
Virginity was the less considerable also, because they intended no longer to be fam'd for that sort of Chastity, than till
they could get good Husbands, which they were now in

---

* Bishop *Usher* calls the Author of that account of *Ursula*, *Sigebertini
Chronici interpolator.* (de Primord. Eccl. Br. p. 624, 631.) And he had great
reason to say so; for in *Miraus* his Edition of *Sigebert, Antwerp. an. 1608.*
that story *Surius* mentions out of him, is in a different character from the
rest; of which *Miraus* gives this account, in his Preface to the Reader:
That what is so Printed in a small character, was either not in the *Codex
Gemblacensis* (which he calls the most ancient) or if it were, was added
by a Later hand; *Qualia sunt*, says he, *quæ à racemaltoribus plerumque
indoctis adjecta, aut ex nugis ac quisquiliis Galfridi Monumetensis seu A-
saphensis, insperse leguntur.* And so it is expresly said in *H. Steven's* Edition of *Sigebert, an. 1513. Sigeberti Gemblacensis Chronicon, ab an. 381.
ad an. 1113. Cum insertionibus ex historia Galfridi & additionibus Ro-
berti Abbatis Montis, &c.*

Quest after. But Mr. *Cr.* seems to rely more upon the story of the *Saxons* barbarous usage, which first gave occasion for the flight of these Virgins, and after to the slaughter of them by the *Hunns*. But, whatsoever he may imagine in his performance, I think he has no ways assoyled the Objections that lye against this account too. For is it credible, that what is pretended to be acted in the *middle of an Age*, should not so much as be mentioned by one who lived *in that very Age*, and wrote about this very matter, concerning the destruction of the *Brittans* by the *Saxons*, at the end of it? I mean by *Gildas*? no nor afterwards taken notice of by *Beda* in his History? I see indeed Mr. *Cr.* endeavours to apologize for this omission, but so pittiful are the excuses he makes, that I wonder he had the confidence to insert them. As for *Gildas*, he says, " his design being to

Ch. Hist. l. 9. cap. 22.

" bewail the general destruction of the *Brittish* " state, and to declare the horrible crimes that " provoked Almighty God, to give them up to " the fury of a barbarous People; no wonder if he did not " in so short a narration, involve occurrents happening a- " broad. Not *every occurrent*, I grant, that happened abroad; but such as were *remarkably destructive*, one would think he might; especially such a one as this was, being a story, such as no Age, I think, can parallel, either for the number of Virgins slain (Eleven Thousand in one Day and Place) or for the barbarous fury of those that slew them (which he confesses was one part of *Gildas* his design Tragically to express) nor any particular *occurrent* that gave such a deadly blow to the *Brittish State*; and he must sure be in great hast, and affect strange Brevity, that could not afford the place of one Line in his Book for such a story, which though acted *abroad*, yet not at that distance, but that the report of it would quickly arrive, and ring aloud in the ears of those, that were so much concerned in it *at home*. But Mr. *Cr.* would perswade us, that *Gildas* has general ex-

Ch. Hist. l. 9. c. 20.

pressions that seem to point at their story, and he pretends to give you their express words that
speak

speak thus. "Very many passed over Sea into Foreign
"Countreys, with grievous howlings and lamentation, and
"in their Voyage by Sea, they joyntly with mournful voi-
"ces, repeated those sad words of the Psalmist, *Thou hast,*
"*O Lord, given us up as Sheep to be devoured, and hast dis-*
"*persed us among the Nations.* This, says Mr. *Cr.* seems
"to be a description most proper to the condition of the
"weaker Sex (he thought that it could not be so proper for
"*Men* to run away and cry) which no doubt by the provi-
"dent care of their Parents and Friends, was in the first place
"secured from the violence of their Barbarous Enemies;
"and those words, *Thou hast dispersed us among the Nati-*
"*ons,* do most fitly suit to these Virgin-Martyrs, whose sa-
"cred Reliques have been dispersed among all the Nations
"of Christendome.

Excellently guessed! and well translated, by him that pretends to give us his express words! as any one will see,
when I give you *Gildas* his words in his own Language, with
a little more, which goes before that which he has cited.
Thus then *Gildas.* "*Itaque nonnulli miserarum reliquia-*
"*rum* * *in montibus deprehensi (quò nimirum fugerant) acer-*
"*vatim jugulabantur: alii fame confecti accedentes manus*
"*hostibus dabant, in æternum servituri; si tamen continuò*
"*non trucidarentur, quod altissimæ gratiæ stabat loco: alii*
"*transmarinas petebant regiones, cum ululatu magno, ceu ce-*
"*leusmatis vice, hoc modo sub velorum sinibus cantantes;*
"Dedisti nos tanquam oves escarum, & in gentibus disper-
"sisti nos: *alii montanis collibus, minacibus præruptis, valla-*
"*tis densissimis saltibus, marinisque rupibus, vitam suspectâ*
"*semper mente credentes, in patria licet trepidi perstabant.*
These words of *Gildas,* follow after the sad story he had

---

* So *Bed.*1, Lib.1.Hist.Eccles.cap.15. *Itaque nonnulli de miserandis re-*
liquiis in montibus comprehensi, acervatim jugulabantur. Alii fame con-
fecti procedentes, manus hostibus dabant, pro accipiendis alimentorum sub-
sidiis, æternum subituri servitiam. Alii transmarinas regiones dolentes
petebant: alii perstantes in patria trepidi pauperem vitam in montibus,
silvis, vel rupibus arduis, suspectâ semper mente agebant.

told, concerning the destruction which the *Saxons* made, depopulating Cities and Fields, destroying Priest and People with Fire and Sword, whose Bodies lay mangled and unburied, a prey for Beasts and Birds. " Then, says he, of the " *miserable remnant (mark that)* some being caught in the " Mountains (whither they fled) were slain on heaps, others " went into Foreign Regions, &c. I never thought before, that when one is dividing a *remnant* of People, and describing the several miseries of them so divided, that *Nonnulli* or *alii*, could be translated *very many*; rather of the two it might be Englisht *some few:* but the other translation was necessary for his purpose, of Eleven Thousand Virgins going away at once in one company. It was well guessed too, to ascribe their voyage to *the provident care of their Parents and Friends to secure them in the first place, from the violence of their Barbarous Enemies*, by this sending them away: when *Gildas* rather, describes a company of People, scattered, and at their wits end, not knowing which way to shift for their own Lives. Besides, I observe another passage in *Gildas*, which, if you could suppose a Body of so many Thousand Virgins gathered together, and by reason of the feebleness of their Sex fit to be made a *Sacrifice*, yet implyes, that it was scarce possible to find so many, fit to make *Martyrs* of at that time: For when he there tells us, of *the Bodies* of abundance of People, lying mangled and unburied; he presently adds his doubt, that there were but a few *pious Souls* among them fit to go to Heaven: (there was at that time such a horrid corruption of manners among the *Brittans*, even worse than that of their Enemies that butcher'd them.) " *Si tamen multa inventæ sunt* (sc. sanctæ animæ) " *quæ ad ardua cœli, id temporis, à sanctis Angelis veheren-* " *tur, &c.* If there could be found any number of holy " Souls at that time, that were fit to be carried up to Hea- " ven by holy Angels: For, says he, *Ita degeneraverat tunc* " *vinea illa olim bona, in amaritudinem; ut raro, secundùm* " *prophetam, videretur quasi post tergum vindemiatorum aut* " *messorum, racemus aut spica.* i.e. The Vineyard that was
" once

"once good, was then so degenerate, that as the Prophet
"speaks, after the Grape-gatherer or Mower, could scarce
"be found a Cluster, or an Ear of Corn. But Eleven
Thousand would have been a pretty Cluster of Virgins.
Wherefore I conclude that *Gildas* in his story, never
dreamt of any thing like such a number of Virgin-Martyrs. I hope Mr. *Cr.* does not think there lyes any
strength in those words he added, that when they mournfully cryed out, "*Thou hast dispersed us among the Nati-*
"*ons,* this most fitly suits these Martyrs, whose Reliques
"have been dispersed all over Christendome. For why
should he perswade us, that *they* differ'd so much from *other*
Saints, and *sorrowfully* pronounced that, which S. *Francis*
so much *triumph'd in?* Who being cast into Prison by the
Perusians, he was so full of joy, that his
Fellow-prisoners were offended at it; to
whom he gave this account, *Ideo me exultare noveritis, quia adhuc Sanctus per totum seculum adorabor:* He leapt for *joy,* because after all this he should be worshipped for a Saint all over the World *. Why should we
not believe that they had the spirit of S. *Francis* in them
while they lived, and rejoyced in the thoughts of that which
they prophetically foretold? especially when their stories
tell us, that they are so hugely pleased to have their Reliques dispersed and venerated now they are dead? Two of
their Bodies that were digged up
at *Colen,* and translated to an Abby
in *Thuringia,* removed *themselves*
back again to *Colen,* because their

Jac. de Vorag. Legend.de S.Franc.

Cæsarii Dialog.diß.8. c.85. in Biblioth. patrum Cisterc. edit. an. 1662.

* Lest any should deny S. *Francis* to be the Author of this saying, as
not thinking *Jac. de Voragine* to be a competent witness; let the Reader
take notice, that the same is put among S. *Francis* his *Prophecies,* who is
said to speak thus to his Fellow-prisoners, who were offended at his pleasantness. *Etsi vestra condoleam miseriæ, magis tamen de propriâ exultandum est felicitate. Humile quid de me cogitatis. Quem modò in carcere vinclis videtis adstrictum, per totum mundum posthac agnoscite respiciendum. Prophetia* 4. *inter opusc. S.Francis. p.* 81. *edit. Paris. an.* 1641. *per Joh.de la Haye.*

Reliques

Reliques were in the other place neglected. And when a Sister had a mind to some of their Reliques, and pressed with her Knee upon a great Stone that lay upon one of their Graves, the Stone, that *six* Men could scarce stir, gave way and opened the Grave to let her put in her hand to take out the Bones, and then laid it self down again in the place it was in before. Nay, when one of the *Monks*, having got some of these Virgins Heads to his Monastery, washed them in Wine, and kissed them in Devotion; one of them appeared that Night to him in his sleep, and embracing him, said, *Yesterday when you washed my Head, you friendly kissed it, and now I come to repay your kindness*, and saluted him; though when she offered it, he considering his profession, to avoid the Maids kiss, drew back his Head. Who can be of another mind, but that they now have just the same passions and affections they had when they were alive, when he reads how that a Comb being found together with one of the Bodies mentioned before, which Comb was secretly conveighed away by one *Frederindis*, who came by, as the Body was digging up; the Night before the Body was to be removed by an Abbot, the Virgin appeared to him in a dream, and refused to have her Body removed; and when he humbly asked her the reason, she told him, *because she had lost her Comb which her Mother gave her, when she went out of her Countrey.* There is one doubt remains, which Mr. *Cressy* is concerned in, who talks so much of the *dispersing of their Reliques over all Christendome*, viz. What security we can have that false Bodies and Bones, have not been scattered up and down for *theirs*: I know that *Cæsarius* of *Heisterbach* has told us a fine story, how that when certain *Monks* were washing many of their Bodies and drying them, there arose suddenly an intolerable stink; whereupon the Abbot *Goswin* suspecting it to be a trick of the Devils, to extinguish the *Friers* devotion towards their Reliques, adjured the Devil to discover if he had any hand in the stink; and

Id. Ibid. c. 87.
Id. Ibid. c. 88.
Ibid. cap. 85.
Cæsarius, Ibid. cap. 89.

and immediately a great Horse-bone leaping from the midst of the Reliques, was thrown out of the place, as if it had been driven with a Whirl-wind. But I am a great deal more afraid of the *Monks* tricks to abuse Men into their Devotion, than of the Devils to extinguish it; and I doubt that when *they* design to cheat, the Bones will neither *stir* nor *stink*, to inable us that way to discover it. But I have too long considered Mr. *Cressy*'s foolish pretences out of *Gildas*. I shall be shorter in answering what he says for the silence of *Bede*, who makes no mention of them neither in his History. "It is no wonder, says he, if *Beda*'s "History, intended only to relate the affairs of "the *Saxons*, does not recount such particular oc- "currents of the *Brittans*. *Ch. Hist. ut supra.* Well reasoned again! What? when the *Saxon* affairs at this time were Acts of Barbarous Cruelty, and the *Brittans* were the subjects of it, is it no wonder if one pretend to give an account of the *one*, and should leave out the *other*? This would be, just as if a *Carthaginian Historian* had designed to give an account of the affairs of his own Countrey, and should have said little or nothing of *Hannibal* and his Army in *Italy*, or have passed over in silence that most famous Battle at *Cannæ*, never so much as naming the *Roman General* there, or the number of those that were slain. Well, but says Mr. *Cr.* "*Beda* in "other Treatises, twice expresly mentions the Celebration "of Eleven Thousand Virgin-Martyrs, suffering for their "Faith and Chastity at *Colen*, to wit, in his *Martyrologie*, "and in his *Ephemeris*. It's true indeed, if you look into *Beda*'s *Works*, you will find in his *Martyrologie* 12 *Cal. Novemb.* these words, *In Colonia sanctarum virginum undecim millium*: and in his *Ephemeris* these, *In Colonia sanctarum Virginum*; but all this will not do Mr. *Cressy*'s *work*: For the Authority of these Books is very slender, and the Interpolation and abuse of them certain and evident * : If I had

---

* *Martyrologium quod Bedæ nomen modò præfert, haud sincerum est, multorum subinde additionibus locupletatum, ut ex præfatione* Usuardi *colligunt viri eruditi.* Phil. Labbe de Scriptor. Ecclef. vol. 1. pag. 185.

no other way to know that there are Names of Saints in those Books, which *Bede* never put in, I might be sufficiently assured of it, only by examining the Persons there inserted for Saints and Martyrs. To give Mr. *Cr.* an Instance or two, very near the place where the 11000 Virgins stand. In his *Martyrologie,* 7 Idus Novemb. *Depositio Vuillibrordi Episcopi, de gente Anglorum, viri sanctissimi & miraculorum gratiâ admodum insignis; qui à Sergio Papa Romæ ordinatus est, & in Germaniam ad prædicandum destinatus, ibidemque requievit.* In his *Ephemeris,* 8 Idus. *Willibrordi Episcopi.* I suppose that Saints were not put into the *Calendar* before they dyed; and it would be pretty if any one could believe that *Bede* should put into his *Martyrologie* the death of a Saint who out-lived him. But according to Mr. *Cressy**, *Bede's* death is placed, *an.*731. (*Calvisius* Chronol. says 734.) and he has placed S.*Willibrords*, an.736.

* *Ch. Hist. l.22. c.25. and lib.23. c.6.*

To add another: *Bedæ Martyrol.* 16 Cal. Decemb. *Depositio beati Othmari Abbatis* (in his *Ephemeris* 16 Cal.Dec. *Otmari confessoris*) who dyed (as both *Surius* and *Calvisius* agree) *an.* 761. that is, according to Mr. *Cr.'s* account, 30 Years after *Beda.* But, what talk I of *Thirty* Years? if you look into his Martyrology, 17 Calend. *Januar.* there you find, *Viennæ, Beati Adonis Episcopi*: and yet this *Ado Viennensis* lived after *Bede,* above an Hundred and *Thirty* Years. If all this will not yet satisfie Mr. *Cr.* but that he still thinks no such tricks have been plaid with the 11000 Virgins, I then must farther tell him, that in the most correct *Martyrologie* of *Bede* (Printed in *Bollandus* his second Vol. of *March,* and which was set forth after comparing a great many Antient Manuscripts) I say in his *Genuine Text,* Printed in a larger character, there is nothing to be found of these 11000 Virgins; but it's put in a smaller character afterwards, to show that that passage was inserted by others since; and I must conclude too, that it was inserted a good while after his time; since *Usuardus* in his *Martyrologie* makes no mention of these

Bellarm. de Scriptor. Eccles.

these Virgins; nor *Ado Viennensis* in *his*, no nor in his *Chronicon* neither, though he there takes notice of the sufferings of many other Martyrs, and had a fair occasion to mention *them*; for he speaks of *Maximus* his drawing almost all the armed Youth of *Brittany* into *France*; and if *Baronius* his conjecture had been true, *there* sure he would have mentioned them, if he had known any thing concerning them: and afterwards he takes notice of the *Saxons* destroying *Brittany* from the East, to the West side of the Island with Fire and Sword (which is Mr. *Cressy*'s time of placing their flight and Martyrdome) and yet not a syllable of them *here* neither. And if the *Martyrologie* of *Bede* does not say any thing about it, his *Ephemeris* which is collected out of it in short, if it say more, may deservedly be suspected: But he might as well (in this case) cite the *Almanack* for the Year when he wrote his Book; for there he might find the name of S. *Ursula* against the 21 of *October*, but no such name in *Bede's Ephemeris*.

Adon. Chronic. in Biblioth. Patr. Tom. 7. pag. 353, 356.

Thus we have seen the lame account and groundless conjectures, which they that would make a *formal History* of these Virgins, go upon. Now, in the next place, let's consider whether they that build their faith upon *Oral Tradition*, and the current story that passes at *Colen*, where they are said to have been Interred, have mended the matter.

Here first, it is worth observing, that the Late *Romish* Writers are much more inclinable, I perceive, to follow the Traditional account, than the other: (only excepting the Jesuite *Alford*, who writing a *History* thought it not so proper to mention Revelations; and living, as he sayes, among Heterodox Persons (being then in *England*) he thought that telling stories of Miracles, unless they were vouched by Classick Authors, would not be a means to convince them; for the Age he lived in was no ways favourable to them.) Therefore though *Ribadeneira*, when he first put forth the Lives of the Saints in *Spanish*,

Alford. Annal. Eccl. Brit. ad an. 453. p. 585. and p. 598.

followed

followed *Baronius* and our *Geoffrey*; yet when his Book was Printed at *Colen* in *Latine*, an. 1630. they put out that Life of his, and inserted another, after the Traditional way: For so the Reader, before that life, is admonished; that instead of that, "They thought good rather to adjoyn another Narration, far more certain, which was composed with great labour and diligence, out of several Monuments of the Ancients, out of the *ancient Tradition* of the Church of *Colen*, and out of the very footsteps of places that are to be seen both at *Colen*, and elsewhere on the *Rhene*, by a Father of the Jesuites Colledge in *Colen*. This *Father* was *Philippus Bebius*, as *Alford* informs us; between whom there had some Letters passed touching this matter: in *Bebius* his Letter to *Alford* he says, that he began to write the Life of S. *Ursula*, and her companions in the *Latine* and *German* Tongue by the command of his Superiours; and not living perfectly to finish it, *Hermannus Crombachius* succeeded him in his work, and opinion, (being for Tradition and Revelations) in a large Volume, entitled *Ursula vindicata*. This way therefore, having the greater countenance of the Church, is now to be set down; and there is scarce any thing more needful; (it looking all along so like a Romance) to confute it. We are told then, that in the Year *One Thousand One Hundred Fifty Six*, there were found at *Colen* certain Inscriptions or Titles on Grave-stones (*Tituli Sepulchrales* they are called) bearing the Names of divers of the *Ursulan Virgins*, and of the Men that did accompany them: *Gerlacus* the Abbot of *Tuitium*, who was present when the Tombs were opened, made an Index of their Names, which is still kept there. This gave occasion the same Year to the Revelations of *Elizabeth* of *Schonaw* concerning *Ursula*, and her Army of Virgins, as she her self says. Who speaking, how in several

Ribad.Flor.Sanct. 21. *Octob.* p. 501.

Alford.Ibid. p. 590.

* *Alf.ad an.*237. p. 228. 230.

See Bish. *Usher de Britan. Eccl: primord.* p. 619.

*Elizab.Vision. lib.*4 *c.*2.

ral

ral Graves there were found Stones having Titles upon them, signifying to whom those Bodies did belong; "The "Chief and most remarkable of them, says she, the Abbot "*Gerlacus* sent to me, hoping that something might be re- "vealed to me, by the grace of God, concerning them: for "he had a suspicion of the finders of those holy Bodies, lest "for gain sake they might have craftily caused them to be "written. S. *Elizabeth* then understood, God revealing it to her by S. *Ursula*, and S. *Verena*, by whom and when these Titles were written and put into their Graves. She says, that at that time when the H. Virgins came from *Rome* to *Colen*, there was in their company, one *James* Bishop of *An-tioch*, who being divinely inspired, did *Vid. Bebii vit. Ursul. inter Flor. Sanctor. Ribaden. p. 504.* inquire into the names and state of the chief Persons of that Company, and diligently noted them. This *James*, when the H. Virgins were slain, he hid himself in a certain Cave that was in a Hill of that Field; but by the Providence of God, the Enemies after the slaughter withdrew themselves, and the People of *Colen* going out of the City to bury the Sacred Bodies, this Bishop came forth to them, and showed them the Names of the chief Persons, to the end that being cut in certain Stones, they might be placed together with their Bodies in their Graves; who himself was slain by the same returning Enemies, on the third Day after the common slaughter of the Virgins; just as he was giving order for his own Name to be ingraved; from whence it came to pass, that in *Gerlacus* his Catalogue of Names, there appears nothing for *Him*, but the bare Name of *James*. A pretty story, and well hanging together I assure you! well may the Jesuite that relates this, boast of the truth and certainty of these *Colen* Reliques, when such stones as these lye at the foundation to support their faith; only I could have wished that these stones had been somewhat bigger than I perceive they were: by the great noise of these *Tituli Sepulchrales*, I was ready before to fancy, that they were stones laid over their Graves; but the *revelation* has spoiled that

conceipt,

conceipt, by telling us that they were put *into* their Graves; for now they might be such, for ought I know, as might be put in ones Pocket, and I am not wholly freed from *Gerlacus* his jealousie of the Diggers cheat. But I must not forget that besides these *Revelations* of S. *Elizabeth* after her death, one *Richardus Præmonstratensis* had new Visions concerning these Virgins, wherein by the admonition of the Bl. *Virgin*, and of *Ursula* her self, many defects of the former revelations were supplied; these happened *An. Dom.* 1183. and these are they that make up the life of *Ursula*, and the 11000 Virgins in *Capgrave*; so that when I shall hereafter cite him for any part of their story, you must remember that in time past, that went in the *Roman* Church for Vision and Revelation; and indeed the whole story of *Ursula* in the *Colen* way of Tradition, and that which we have in the old Breviaries, is wholly beholden to them, being borrowed from them. Nay, we are told out of *Winheim*, that the very Church of S. *Ursula* in *Colen*, was vulgarly called the *Church of the Revelations*, S. *Elizabeth*'s Visions having given such great credit to her story. Let us now see, what it is they say; and I think the best way will be, to make the Lessons of the *Breviary* our Text, and the other will serve to explain them.

A. Bish. Usher, Ibid. pag. 631.

Winheim. Sacrar. Agrippin.

Lesson 1.

Brev. Roman. Antiq. 21. *Octob.*

"St. *Ursula* the only Daughter of a most
"Noble and Rich Prince of the *Brittans*,
"extreme beautiful, and of great wit, when she was Mar-
"riageable was demanded in Marriage by a Son of the
"King of *England*; at which, seeing her most Christian
"Father extreamly troubled, as well because it was no ways
"consonant to Reason to force his Daughter to marry who
"was devoted to God, as also because if he did not consent
"to the Proposal, he feared the cruelty of the *Pagan*;
"She, being divinely inspired, perswaded her Father to con-
"sent to the Tyrant, if he would yield to these following
"Conditions,

"Conditions. *viz.* That he the Son of the King of *Eng-*
"*land* would deliver to her *Ten* Virgins, choice ones in
"Age, Form and Parentage; and that as well to her self,
"as to each of the other *Ten*, might be joyned a 1000 Vir-
"gins more; and that 11 Ships being prepared according
"to their number, he would grant her the truce of *Three*
"Years for the *Dedication* * of her Virginity, and that
"this Young Spouse of hers in this
"3 Years space, should be instructed
"in the Faith. *Ursula* used this new
"counsel of the H. Ghost, that so ei-
"ther by the difficulty of the proposed condition she might
"take off his mind from his design, or that by this oppor-
"tunity she might dedicate all her Virgins, together with
"her self, to God.

* The pretended *Sigebert* in *Surius* has it, *ad exercitium virginitatis suæ.*

NOTES.

This Lesson of the *Breviary* gives us no name of any of these Persons, save only that of *Ursula*, but the rest are sufficiently supplied out of the Revelations, and elsewhere. As for the name of *Ursula*, we are told, it was prophetically given her in her Baptism (God so ordering it, who *calls* whom he *predestinates*) because she should one Day choak the Devil, that * great *Bear*, as *David* did. Her Mothers name, the Visions tells us, was *Daria*. The name of her Father (whom the Breviary calls only a Prince of the *Brittons*) is diversly given us: In the Visions of S. *Elizabeth* he is called *Maurus*; by Others *Dionetus*. *Jacobus de Voragi.* calls him *Nothus*; but in the Cotton. MS. (a) he is called *Deonotus*, and so it is in her life in *Surius*. *Fuit in Brittaniæ partibus rex quidam Deonotus, tam vitâ quàm nomine;* which last

* *Quia exemplo David immanem ursum, sc. diabolum, quandoque suffocatura erat, Deo disponente (qui quos prædestinat, vocat) à parentibus illi in baptismate præsagum nomen Ursula inditum est. Vit. Ursula apud Surium. 21. Octob.*

(a) Bish. *Usher, ut supra. p. 618.*

words make it uncapable of a literal mistake for *Dionetus*: and so it is in the *Breviary* of the *Cistersians*, Printed at *Paris*, 1516.

| Deonoto fuit nata Placens cunctis, Deo grata, Ursula regalis: | By a Prince call'd Deonot Royal Ursula was begot, To God and Men most dear. |

| Cujus miræ speciei Plus mirandæ & fidei, Non erat æqualis. | Her face was wonderously fair Her faith more admirably rare In both she had no Peer. |

| Regi magno pulchra nimis Desponsatur, dum instatur Precibus & minis. | This over-fair ones Spouse was a great King: Who had woo'd her both by pray'rs and threatening. |

A very fit name, (whether his true one or no, it matters not) for one that reigned *God knows* when and where. For there was scarce a greater contest about what City it was (among 7) where *Homer* was born; than what Country it was (whether *England*, *Scotland*, or *Ireland*, be meant by *Brittany*) where he reigned. S. *Elizabeth* calls him the King *Britannia Scotica*; *Petrus de Natalibus*, the most Christian King of *Scotland*, and so the Verses in *Wicelius*, cited by Bish. *Usher*. One *Candidus Eblanius* (in his Catalogue of *Irish* Saints) stands up stoutly for his being a King of *Ireland*, so also does *Phil. Bebius*, who would have *Scotia* to be understood of *Ireland*, the like does *Crombachius* in his *Ursula Vindicata*. But our *Al-*

Verò similior eorum opinio esse videtur, qui illam Scotiæ majori seu Hyberniæ adjudicant. Bebius vit. Ursulæ apud Ribadeneir.

* *Alford. Annal. ad an.* 453. *p.* 590. &c. & *p.* 597.

ford * (and Mr. *Cressy* his Interpreter) has as stifly opposed this, showing by a great deal of Critical learning, and by proofs from History and Chronology, that *Ireland* never went under the name of *Britany*; that *Ireland* was Heathen long after this time (for they place this story as the *Breviary* does

does in the Year 237) and particularly infifts upon that of the *Roman Martyrologie,* concerning S. *Patrick*'s Preaching the Gofpel *firft of all* in *Ireland.* As for *Urfula*'s Spoufe; (who is called in the Leffon the Son of a King of *England*) his Father's Name, *Elizabeth*

In Hiberniâ Natalis S. Patricii Epifcopi & Confefforis, qui Primus ibidem Chriftum Evangelizavit. Roman. Martyrol. 17. Martii.

fays, was *Agrippinus :* The Son has *three* Names ; The Hiftorians call him *Conanus* (as we heard before) but the Revelations of *Elizabeth* and *Richard* call him *Holofernes,* though after Baptifm he was named *Etherius ;* and we are certified from the *Sepulchral Titles,* that he was *feven* years elder than *Urfula.* There is nothing more need be added, to explain the Leffon ; unlefs it be that paffage, of *her being divinely infpired,* to confent to the Treaty of Marriage, and to propofe thofe witty conditions. This was done, fayes *Capgrave,* by an Angel, that was fent from Heaven to perfwade her ; or in a Vifion, as it is in *Surius,* wherein by a Divine Revelation fhe was informed of the whole order of her Life, of the number of her Fellow-virgins, and of the glorious Crown of their Martyrdome.

Cafgr. vit. Urf. f. 316.

Leffon 2.

"Becaufe this affair was carried on by the Lord, the young
"Man agreed to all the Propofals, and perfwaded his Fa-
"ther to do the fame. And now this Spoufe of hers be-
"ing baptized, commanded to haften all things that were
"demanded, and pitcht upon the Virgins for *Urfula* his
"Spoufe. Then the Father of *Urfula* receiving the Vir-
"gin's Counfel, ordained that his Daughter fhould have
"Men for her Directors *, by whofe fuffrage fhe with the
"Virgins fhould be governed in Spirituals, and in Tempo-
"ral neceffities. Abundance of People came together from
"all Places to fee this wonderful fight, even Bifhops them-

* *Pater ordinavit quod vires, quorum folatio tam ipfa quàm ejus exercitus indigebat, in comitatu fuo haberet. Jac. de Vorag. de 11000 Virgin.*

"selves: Among whom was *Pantalus* Bishop of *Basil*; "who conducted them to *Rome*, and returning with them "from thence suffered Martyrdome: Also S. *Gerasina* the "Queen of *Sicily*, and the Sister of *Daria* Mother of *Ur-* "*sula*, when she was informed of this thing, went to them "with her *four* Daughters, and her young Son *Adrian*, "leaving her Kingdom in her Sons hand, and accompanied "them to Martyrdom.

NOTES.

This Lesson mentions the Collection of the Virgins, but the Revelations have formed them into an Army. The Dreamer *Richardus* tells us, that by the counsel of the Bishops that were with her, and God's direction, she marshalled them thus. She appointed 5 Virgins to be Heads over the whole Army, whose Names were these. 1. *Ursula* her self, the King's Daughter, who was the Head and Princess of them all. 2. *Pinnosa*, the Daughter of *Ludrencus*, a famous Duke, *Ursula*'s Unkle. 3. *Cordula*, the Daughter of Count *Quirinus*. 4. *Eleutheria*, the Daughter of Duke *Eusebius*, and of *Josippa*, S. *Ursula*'s Aunt. 5. *Florentia*, the Daughter of King *Ægidius*, who was Cousin-Germane to *Ursula*'s Father. Under these *Five*, she chose Eleven other Virgins, each of which was to govern a *Thousand*, whose Names are these: 1. *Jota*, the Daughter of King *Lucius*, she had *two* Sisters besides in the Company. 2. *Benigna*, the Daughter of an Illustrious Duke; she had *four* Sisters besides among them. 3. *Clementia*, the Daughter of a powerful *Count*. 4. *Sapientia*, the Daughter of Prince *Hermicus*, Unkle to *Ursula*. 5. *Carpophora*, the Daughter of a certain King, who was a good and religious Man. 6. *Columba*, the Daughter of King *Anitus*. 7. *Benedicta*, the Daughter of an Illustrious Prince. 8. *Odilia*, the Daughter of a certain *Count*, who had *two* Sisters with her, the one adult, the other a sucking Sister. 9. *Chelindris*, whose

Vid. Caprav. & Usher. lib. citat. p. 632.

whose Father was a Noble *Count*, her Mother *Ursula*'s Father's Aunt. 10. *Sibilia*, the Daughter of King *Firanus*. 11. *Lucia*, a Kings Daughter, and Kinswoman to the Spouse of S. *Ursula*.

[Here I cannot but take notice by the way, that Mr. *Cressy*, after he, in one place of his History, has railed against these *Revelations* concerning the 11000 Virgins, calling them *Dreams, the Inventions of vain and idle wits, which gain no belief to themselves, and disgrace truth reported by others, that deserve not to be confuted, but with indignation to be rejected and contemned:* Yet this very Mr. *Cr.* in another place, has martialed this Virgin-Army, just in the same order you here see it. He quotes indeed *Usuardus* his *Chronicon* for it, and talks of Martyrologies of *Canisius*, and of *England*; but these are all but *Blinds*, for they all had them, it's plain from these Revelations originally; and now when it serves his purpose (as indeed without the Revelations, the Reliques at *Colen* would want names) he has the conscience to say, *that it must be ascribed to a Miraculous Providence, or Revelation, that their Names have not utterly perished.* But sure there's all reason to debar him from making any advantage of them in one case, if he will not allow them to have any credit in others.]

Ch. Hist. l. 5. cap. 9.

Ch. Hist. l. 9. c. 21. & 23.

What is farther said in the Lesson concerning *Pantalus*, and other Bishops that came to them; S. *Elizabeth* pretends to explain it thus, from her Interpreter *Verena*, (one of these Virgins that appeared to her) "When we first begun "to meet together in our Country, the holy "fame of it was far and wide dispersed, and "many came together on every side to be- "hold us; It happened also, God so ordering it, that cer- "tain of the *Brittish* Bishops were joyned to us, and passing "over Sea in our Company came to *Rome* with us: In which "Journey, Bl. *Pantulus* Bishop of *Basil* was our associate, "and brought us to *Rome*, and was a Fellow-sufferer with "us. But *Richardus* is more particular, and tells us by

Eliz. Vision l. 4. cap. 2.

name of 5 *Brittish Bishops* that followed them. 1. *Willelmus*, Cousin-German to *Ursula*'s Father, and Brother to S. *James* (the forenamed Bishop of *Antioch*) and Bl. *Gerasina*. 2. *Columbanus*, the Son of S. *Alexandria*, an Illustrious Dutchess, the Sister of *Ursula*'s Mother. 3. *Twanus*, a very Aged Man, Unkle to *Ursula*'s Mother. 4. *Eleutherius*, Brother to *Count Eustace*. 5. *Lotharius*, Cousin-German to *Ursula*'s Spouse. It would be too tedious to give you all the rest of the Romantick story: I'le therefore only give you his account of the Eleven Kings, which he says by a Revelation from Heaven, he understood to have gone along with them. 1. *Olofernes*, the Spouse of S. *Ursula*. 2. *Oliverus*, the Son of the most Noble King *Oliver*, who was converted by the Virgin *Oliva* his Spouse, who was the Daughter of the great King *Cleopatrus*, *Ursula*'s Father's Unkle. 3. *Crophorus*, the Son of King *Pinnosus*, *Ursula*'s Kinsman, whose Wife *Cleopatra* was in the company too. 4. *Lucius*, the Father of *Jota*, *Ursula*'s Kinsman. 5. *Clodoneus*, who with his Queen *Blandina*, was converted by his Daughter, Dutchess *Eugenia*, and by her Husband Duke *Alexander*. 6. *Canutus*, who travelled, leaving his Kingdom to *Carolus* one of his Sons. 7. *Pipinus*, *Ursula*'s Cousin-German. 8. *Odulphus*, the said King *Pipin*'s Son. 9. *Anitus*, who followed his *two* Daughters, *Columba* and *Cordula*. 10. *Firanus*, who with his Wife *Sibilia*, followed his Illustrious Daughter *Sibilia*, and her *three* Sisters. 11. *Refridus*, King of *Denmark*, who was converted by his Wife *Oliva*, the Duke of *Saxonies* Daughter. It was very seasonably added here at the conclusion of this Catalogue of Kings, that the Relator of these things, *walked in the path of pure truth, and hated lying*; and therefore ingenuously acknowledges, that these Kings had but *Regna modica*; their Dominions were not very large. I believe their Territories were muchwhat of the bigness of *Gerasina*'s, (*mentioned in the Lesson*) as she was Queen of *Sicily*, which in that Age was no Kingdom at all. And some of them were Kings, (particularly *Pipin* and *Canutus*) just in the same sence, that the *Angli* and *Walliones* (of which Nations,

Nations, there were several, he says, among these Virgins) were a People, that is, they were to be such some Hundreds of Years after. *But to go on.*

Lesson 3.

"The Ships and Provisions being prepared, this most ho-
"ly Society, departing from *Brittany,* arrived at the City of
"*Colen.* And there it was revealed to S. *Ursula* by an An-
"gel from the Lord, that they should go to *Rome,* and from
"thence returning thither, she with her Spouse and all the
"Company, should come to glory by Martyrdome. Com-
"ing therefore from the City of *Colen* to *Basil* by Water,
"they went from thence to *Rome* a Foot. All which Com-
"pany were received with joy and honour by Pope *Ciriacus*
"and his Clergy, for he himself was of *Brittany,* and had
"some Kindred among the Virgins; and to him who was
"himself a Virgin, it was revealed, that he should obtain
"the reward of Martyrdome with them. When therefore
"they had stayed some while there at *Rome,* Pope *Ciriacus*
"caused some of them, that had not yet obtained the grace
"of Baptisme, to be baptized. And at length declaring
"his mind before all the Clergy, he renounced the Pope-
"dome, after he had governed the Church one Year and
"about *three* Months, being the 19*th.* in succession after *Pe-*
"*ter* the Apostle: which thing was taken ill by the Clergy,
"who knew not the Counsel of God, that leaving the Seat
"of S. *Peter,* he should go after that Multitude of Women.
"Therefore by common advice they chose another called
"*Antheros,* removing this *Ciriacus* out of the Catalogue of
"Bishops.

NOTES.

Before this glorious Company parted from *Brittany,* we are told that they spent *three* Years in pretty ludicrous exercises upon the Sea, which was hard by. Sometimes they imitated a Sea-fight, sometimes a Flight, and ran up and down from one *place*

Vit. Ursula apud Surium.

place to another, spending sometimes half, sometimes the whole Day in these pastimes; at which the King and Peers of the Realm were frequently present to behold them; and the common People laying business aside, attended these sports of the Virgins, and applauded them. In which there were *two* things very wonderful; that they were *preludes* to their *Martyrdome:* and that they ended in the *Conversion* of all the Virgins to the Faith. (if we believe the Legend:) Prayers and Fasting, one would guess, had been better preparatives for Martyrdome, than these sports and fooleries; onely we are to remember that this Church does its work by no common ways, and that fine Sights and Pageantry have no small place (and upon Women and Children may have no small effects) in the publick exercises of its Religion. There is nothing farther considerable that we are told of, before they set Sail for *Culen*, only that Heavenly Angels came often to give them visits, and to confirm them in their good purpose; and that evil Angels too were very busie among them, to perswade them to be lawfully married, to incite them to evil works, and to fulfill the desires of the Flesh; whom they did not hearken to. And now the Virgins by a Divine admonition are required to begin their Voyage, which they dispatcht in little time, in which the most remarkable passage I meet withall is this: *viz.* That the sucking Children, (of whom there was in the Company near *Five Hundred*) that used to be fed with Breast-milk, now lived without it; for they onely put their Fingers into their Mouths, and immediately they suckt from their very Fingers a Dew ministred to them from Heaven, by whose vertue they were sustained; neither did they ever in the whole journey * be-piss themselves, as the manner of Children is, (much less do worse) nor by their

Sidenotes:
Cum multa jucunditate celebrato per triennium hoc Martyrii præludio. Surius.
Richardus præmon. apud Capgrav. p. 317.
Nuptias eis suadere legitimas. Ibid.
Rich. præmonst. apud Capgr. p. 320.
* *Nec fordebant se madefacientes.* Ibid.

Devotions of the Roman Church. 137

their peevish crying disturb the Company: Troops of Angels presented themselves to them, and appeared *above* and *round about* them; insomuch that the little Infants that were carried in armes, admiring the Visions of Angels, and their unusual and shining Effigies, pointing with their Fingers into the Aire (*and at this sight no doubt they would leave sucking them*) testified their wonder by the pleasant noyses of *Ha, Ha.* (and it's hard methinks to forbear imitating them upon the report of it.) You need not wonder if they made a quick Voyage, when Angels thus attended them, though they went against the swift stream of the *Rhine*, for that which would have cost others above *Eight* Days time, they did it in *two* Days and an half, and came safe to *Colen*: but they stayed not there; for upon a new Vision to *Ursula* by an Angel, (which the Lesson mentions) that they must go to *Rome*, and commend themselves there to God, and his Bl. Mother, and to the Apostles, whose Bodies and Reliques rested there, with a promise by the Angel, that they should upon their return *Richard. præm. in Capgr. p.321.* to this City, there obtain the triumph of their blessed Combat, and be Martyr'd, which the Virgins were very desirous of (says *Surius*) they took Ship again, and in *three* days and a half more came to *Basil*: From this place they all set forward on foot to *Rome*; in which Journey, they mounted the *Alpes* and the Tops of high Mountains, without the least weariness, and they seemed all the while to walk upon plain ground; *Richard. Ibid.* they passed Rivers without Boat or Bridge; not one drop of Rain fell to incommode them in their passage all the way: the Infants lived upon their old Diet, sucking their fingers; and the other Virgins needed very little food, the grace of God inwardly comforting and sustaining them; which need not seem incredible (says the Dreamer) to him that reads the Saints lives, for he may find how S. *Maria* the *Ægyptian* was sustained *Seventeen* Years, only with *two* Loaves and a half of Bread.

The next thing we are to remark, is, that all this Company came

came safe and sound to *Rome*; where the Pope (*Ciriacus*) with his Cardinals and Clergy, Princes, Matrons and Virgins, Citizens and common People, with great joy, and a Noble Procession, worthily received them:

Richard. Ibid. p. 322, 323.

where while they stayed, some of them, (that were new Converts) were baptized, particularly, among the more Noble, S. *Lucia* and *Anastasia*, two Kings Daughters, and both of Kin to *Ursula*'s Spouse. And now they bethink themselves of their return to *Colen*, (after they had visited the holy Places at *Rome*, and paid their Devotions there.) And here comes in that passage, which has created much controversie and trouble to the *Romish* Writers, concerning Pope *Ciriacus*, his laying down his Office, to accompany them; which we are told, he was incited to do by a Vision of *three* Saints in white, promising him if he did so, an Eternal Crown of Martyrdome, and threatning that if he continued still at *Rome*, he should quickly dye. Whereupon (as S. *Elizabeth*'s visions inform us) "he re-
"signed the Popedome in the face of the whole Church, all
"Men crying out against it, and gain-saying it, especially
"the Cardinals, who looked upon it as a piece of madness
"for him to go after these fool-

Deliramentum arbitrabantur quod quasi post fatuitatem muliercularum declinaret.

"ish Women (*as indeed any one would have judged, that it was not gravely done of a Pope, to quit his Headship of the Universal Church, together with his Infallibility, to ramble up and down with a number of idle Girles, and as it were in the company of so many* 1000 *Gypsies*) "but,
"says she, they knew not the Divine admonition, which inci-
"ted him to do it, and therefore blotted his name in indig-
"nation out of the Catalogue of *Popes*; but in truth (says *Richard, her second*) his name is ever written before God in the Book of Life, among the precious Martyrs of Christ. That indeed will justly be doubted by a great many, who think they have reason to believe, that no such Person as this *Ciriacus* was ever in being, or at least possessed the Chair of S. *Peter*; among whom is *Baronius*, who smartly urges it

in

in these words. "Nor are those later Men to be regarded, "who after *Pontianus*, introduce one *Cyri-* "*acus* as Bishop of *Rome*, concerning whom "there is no mention at all made in the Series "of *Roman Bishops* described by the *Latines*, as in the Book "of the Popes (*libro de Rom. pontificibus*) or in *Optatus* "*Milevitanus*, S. *Austin*, *Cresconius*, or other *Index's* of "the *Vatican* Library; nor by the *Greeks*, as *Eusebius*, or "*Nicephorus* the *Chronographer*, or others: so that this O- "pinion deserves no more words to confute it, because it is "supported by no Reason, or Testimony of the Ancients, "but only fetched out of the fabulous Acts (*he means the* "*Revelations and Colen Tradition*) concerning the Martyr- "dom of S. *Ursula*, and her Companions. This is so shrew'd a Censure and Objection, that the *Colen* Jesuite *Bebius*, and others, are fain to make him *Pontianus* his *Vicar*, in the time of his banishment; but this *Vicarship* has no Authority to countenance it. I would therefore advise the *Colen* men to stand to their *Tradition*, and make much of *Revelations*, and oppose those excellent *Rithmes*, against all the other Men's *Reasons* and *Authorities*, which we are told may be read at their S. *Ursula*'s Church. At the entrance of the Church these.

Baron. Annal. ad an. 237. ſ. 11.

Bish. Usher. de primord. Eccl. Brit. p. 628.

Hæc est Basilica excellens honore,	This Church great honor does retain,
Ubi gens *Hunica* magno cum furore	Where by the Huns the Virgin train
Virgineos stravit choros.	Was barbarously slain.

Within the Church these Verses, to Pope Cyriacus.

Clemens *Ciriace* papatum renuis;	Mild Cyriack matters not the Papal Crown,
Ad nutum *Ursula* decedens strenuus	At Ursula's call he lays his Office down,
Triremibus ad *Ubios*.	And stoutly comes by Boat to Colen Town.

To

To Etherius, Ursula's Spouse.

Dive *Etherie* dignè fers annulum,	St. Etherius *worthily carries the Ring,*
Nobilis *Ursula* optans connubium	*All a gog to wed* Ursula, *fit for a King,*
Consummatum *Agrippinæ.*	*And at* Colen *concluded the thing.*

As for *Baronius*, Mr. *Cressy*, and such others, as think that *Cyriacus* his Name was never blotted out of the Catalogue of *Popes*, (judging that he was never in) let them remember, that it is not long since his Name was expunged out of a new *Roman* Edition of the *Decretals* (and why not heretofore, may a Man of *Colen* say, as well as of late?) In the Ancient Editions of the Sixth Book of the *Decretals of Boniface the eight*, in a gloss there, we find these words (*speaking of the Popes power to renounce the Papacy*, and lay his Office down:) "There is a certain example of this in Pope *Cyriacus*, concerning whom we read, that he suffered Martyrdome with *Ursula*, and the 11000 Virgins: For it is written of him, that it was revealed to him that he should receive the rewards of Martyrdom with those Virgins. Then gathering together the Clergy and the Cardinals, before them all he renounced his Dignity and Office, though all were unwilling, especially the Cardinals. But this *Cyriacus* is not named in the Catalogue of *Roman Popes*, because it was believed by the Cardinals, that he did forgoe the Papacy, not for Devotion sake, but for the Delights of the Virgins. But I leave them to scuffle it out among themselves, now that we have seen them ingaged; only I cannot chuse but think how blewly they of *Colen* would look, (if their opponents

Bishop Usher. Ibid. pag. 625.

Sexti Decretal. lib. 1. tit. 7. de renunciatione, cap. 1. Quoniam.

Propter delectamenta virginum papatum dimisisset.

ponents get the better of them) with their *three* silver Tombs *, gilt and richly adorned with Jewels, in which they pretend to keep the *three* Bodies of Pope *Cyriacus*, *S. Ursula*, and *her Spouse*; whose Heads also, put apart in their Gilt-Chamber, they *reverently* (we are told) secure under firm Lock and Key.

* *Asservatur in tribus argenteis deauratis gemmisque pretiosè vestitis ac summo Altari incorporatis tumbis tria corpora, viz. S. Cyriaci pontificis, S. Ursulæ, & S. Conani ejus sponsi, quem alii Ethereum nominari volunt: quorum capita, mediis argenteis statuis inclusa, in Aureâ camerâ seorsim, cum multis aliis primariis capitibus, reverenter sub firmâ clausurâ custodiuntur. Erhardus Winheim. in sacrar. Agrippinæ.*

Lesson 4.

"Whilst the aforesaid holy Company abode at *Rome*, two
" wicked *Gentile* Princes, *Maximus* and *Africanus*, fearing
" lest from so great a Multitude of the Faithful (to whom
" others also were joyned) the Christian Religion should be
" too much increased; and having learnt the Place whither
" they intended to go; they sent a message to *Julius* their
" Kinsman, Prince of the *Hunns*, that as soon as the Virgins
" were got to *Colen*, drawing his Forces thither, he should
" kill all that Multitude. Pope *Cyriacus* therefore going
" out of the City with the said Company of Virgins and
" many holy Bishops their Associates, took his Journey to-
" wards *Colen*. In the mean while *Ethereus* the Spouse of
" *Ursula*, his Mother being made a Christian, and his Father
" being dead, to whose Kingdom he succeeded, was admoni-
" shed by an Angel to go and meet his Spouse at *Colen*, and
" that there he should suffer Martyrdome with her. And
" now this young Person, being made a Christian, tasted so
" the Divine grace, that despising carnal marriages, he long-
" ed for those that were Celestial, and thought it most de-
" sirable for him to dye for Christ.

NOTES.

NOTES.

This Lesson is taken out of the Revelations of *Elizabeth* almost word for word. Wherein she cunningly endeavoured to make the slaughter of these Virgins agree with the known Names of that Age. Pope *Damasus*, or *Anastasius Bibliothecar.* (*in Libro pontificali*) says, that *Anterus* sate in the Chair when *Maximinus* and *Africanus* were *Consuls*, and suffered Martyrdome by one *Maximus* the *Præfect*; at which time *Julius Maximinus* was Emperour. In all probability she took occasion from hence to make this wild jumble of Names; and to tell us, that the slaughter of these Virgins was made by *Julius* Prince of the *Hunns*, by the perswasion of *Maximus* (*instead of Maximinus*) and *Africanus* two wicked Princes. But this is a foolish story, and many ways inconsistent both with History and Reason. For (as we shall note afterwards) the *Hunns* were of a Later date than this time, and no mention made in History of any *Julius*, as Prince of them; and *Maximinus* (as *Alford* shows) neither while he was *Consul*, or *Emperour*, ever saw *Rome*. But nothing can be more ridiculous, than to make such a number as this in such times of Persecution, either to come safely in such a Pilgrimage to *Rome*, or to go quietly away in such a Body from thence; especially when we must not confine the number precisely to a 11 Thousand; but are made to believe (if we will hearken to Traditions and Revelations) that there were many more. *Richard* the Dreamer, has reckoned up above 12000: In the Passion of the Ten Thousand Martyrs crucified at Mount *Ararath*, whose Chief Leader was S. *Achatius* (not *Achabius*, as *Bebius* cites it in the Life of *Ursula*, p.503. and Bish. *Usher* out of him) there we are told, that according to the *Colen* account, the number was above 14000, reckoning in many Men and Matrons, whose

See Bishop *Usher de primord.* p.623.

Alford. ad an. 238.

Apud Surium, ad Junii 22. p. 294.

help

Devotions of the Roman Church.

help the Virgins stood in need of. But it seems at *Colen* they vary their story: for *Guil. Caxton* (or whosoever was the Translator of the Golden Legend, Printed at *London*, 1512.) says, that he had it at *Colen*, that together with the Eleven Thousand Virgins, there suffered Fifteen Thousand Men, so then the Company is made 26000. But this is too little still, if we believe *Trithemius*, (cited by Mr. *Cr.*) who makes the *Eleven Thousand* Virgins to be all of Noble blood; but says, that besides these, there were *Threescore Thousand* Women of inferiour rank, partly Maids, and partly such as had been married; so then the Number is vast indeed, amounting to 71 Thousand [v], and one would think the Later *Popes* thought some of these accounts might be true; because in their corrected Breviaries and Martyrologies, they define no number of Virgins at all, but speak of *Ursula* and her Companions, not naming how many they were. But be this how it will, no old Wives Tale could ever be more foolish, than that passage in the pretended Revelations of *Elizabeth*, for the two Heathen Princes, *Maximus* and *Africanus*, to send a Message from *Rome*, to their Cousin *Julius*, to slay this Company at *Colen*, when they themselves had power to do it at *Rome*; for just at this time there was a Persecution against the Christians, by the Emperor *Maximinus*, (reckoned by S. *Augustine* and *Orosius*, sayes *Alford*, for the *Sixth* Persecution) who caused Pope *Pontianus*, who had before been banished by *Alexander*, now to be beaten to death with Clubs; who also the next Year after put *Anteros* his Successor (according to the Catalogue of *Popes*) to death; and now how in the middle, between these two, *Cyriacus* should be *Pope*, and

Bish. Usher, ut supra. p. 635.

Ch. Hist. l. 9. cap. 21.

---

* *Which if it were a true account, I pray what becomes of that which Mr. Cr. said, that it's no wonder, though Gildas or Bede never wrote any thing of them, who stood so thick as not easie to be overlookt? and what will he say for his Church, that by putting in only the 11000 Nobler Maids, would tempt one to doubt whether it thought that poor Maids and Widdows could ever make Martyrs?*

scape

scape with Life from this Tyrant; nay, which is more, that all things should be so peaceable, that so many Thousands should make this Progress without disturbance, and he with them, is not possible for a wise Man to conceive. As for the *Colen* Jesuite *Bebius*, he was asleep sure, when he wrote these words, (speaking of the Journey of these Virgins) "*Erat tunc Imperium Romanum pacatissimum, administrante illud Alexandro Severo, juris naturalis amantissimo principe:* i. e. The *Roman* Empire was in perfect peace, *Alexander Severus* governing it, &c. For according to many excellent Chronologers *, *Alexander Severus* was slain in the Year 235. according to *Baronius* (whom *Alford* follows) An. Dom. 237. but neither way can *Bebius* be helped in his account, for he tells us (*a little before*) that in the Spring of the Year, 237. these Virgins set out of *Brittany*; and all make the Persecution I spake of, wherein *Pontianus* was slain, to begin in the first Year of *Maximinus*, who was *Alexander's* Successor; that is, either two Years before, or the same Year that the Virgins, according to him, began their Voyage and Travels.

Vit. Ursula apud Ribaden. p. 502.

* *Petavius, Ration. Temp. Calvisius, Chronol. Labbe, in Indic. Imperat. in Apparat. ad Concil. &c.*

Lesson 5.

" *Etherius* resting satisfied in what the Angel informed
" him, God so ordering it, he with his Mother and Sister
" *Florentina*, and the Bishops, *Clemens* and *Marculus*, with
" a Neece, and many others, arrived at *Colen* one way; and
" *Ursula* with Pope *Cyriacus*, and the Eleven Thousand Vir-
" gins another way, at the same time. When they were
" Landed, the *Hunns* that then besieged *Colen*, fell upon
" them as so many ravening Wolves upon tame Sheep, and
" slaughtered all that Sacred Company, which willingly of-
" fered it self to death for Christ's sake, and by Martyrdom
" conveighed them to Heaven. When the *Hunns* had killed
" others of them, coming to *Ursula*, and being astonisht at
" her beauty, they brought her to their Prince alive; who
" being

" being inamoured with her Beauty, and comforting her for
" the flaughter of the Virgins, promifed to marry her, if fhe
" would confent; but fhe refufing the offer, the Tyrant in a
" rage directing an Arrow againft her, made her a Martyr.

NOTES.

THE *Colen* Tradition making the *Hunns* to be the Authors of this flaughter, *An.* 237, or 238, its defenders are fadly put to it to make this out; becaufe the *Hunns* were not known in that Age, but appeared long afterwards. I'le onely give the Reader *two* or *three* accounts of this difficulty out of the Jefuite *Bebius (in the place oft cited)* One is, that they were indeed the Souldiers of *Maximinus* that killed them, but becaufe *Maximinus* his Father was a *Goth*, and his Mother an *Alan*, therefore they are faid to be deftroyed by the *Hunns*, that came out of the *Gothifh* Nation. Another conjecture is, that the *Sunici* (an ancient People in *Germany*, by the River *Rhine*) were they that flaughtered them; and in following times (thefe being lefs known) the Tranfcribers of the ftory, put the word *Hunni*, (a People more known) inftead of *Sunici*. But there is another fancy ftill, which he feems to lay more ftrefs upon, that the *Hunns* in *Attila*'s time having deftroyed all before them, their Name was fo terrible in the after Age or two, (for he would have their ftory in *Surius* to be written between 6 and 700 Years after Chrift) that all things cruelly and barbaroufly acted, were faid to be done by the *Hunns:* which is fo clear a folution, that it's pitty any one fhould offer a word againft it. You may eafily imagine that *Urfula* the brave Leader of this Virgin-band, faid a great many things to incourage her Companions not to fear death; *Alford* has made a fhort fpeech for her in his Hiftory; but a much larger *Bonfinius* has given us for hers, (*Hift. Ungar. decad..*1. *lib.*5. put at the end of *Urfula*'s Life in *Ribadeneira*) where

Alford. Annal. Eccl. ad an. 453. *p.* 581.

at

at the end of her speech she urges this Argument, to encourage them to Martyrdom; because Christ had sent his *Vicar* * amongst them, (*viz. Ciriacus*) to absolve them, according to his Office and Power, from their sins, and to dye a Martyr with them.

* *Ut tutius Martyrium obeamus, nobis Vicarium suum delegavit, qui mentes nostras pro demandata potestate lustraret, ipseque nobiscum paria stipendia meritus in astra reduceretur.*

As for that which we are told at the end of this Lesson, that *Ursula* was shot to death with an Arrow, who can question the truth of it, when *Erhardus Winheim* (*in Sacrario Agrip.*) tells us, that he saw in the Gilt-Chamber at *Colen* the *very arrow* wherewith she was transfixed? where also he saw the fine *Ivory Coffers*, in which *Ursula* put the Reliques she brought with her from *Rome*, and the implements for adorning Women, which she used in her Journey; and there too, he says, he drank (*to his great comfort no doubt*) in one of those Water-pots, wherein Christ at *Cana* in *Galilee*, converted the Water into Wine.

Lesson 6.

" But there was among those Virgins one called *Cordula*,
" who being overcome by humane fear, remained that night
" in a Ship; but being comforted by God, the next day she
" discovered her self, and was slain by the *Barbarians*. Who
" after that appeared to a certain Person, and commanded
" that her *Festival* should be kept the Day following. All
" whose venerable Bones, happy *Colen* (which flourishes in
" singular grace by their merits) preserves honourably in a
" Church they built. These Virgins suffered about the Year
" of our Lord 237, in the Days of Pope *Anteros*, and of
" the Emperour *Maximian*.

NOTES.

THE *Roman* Church celebrates the Feast of S. *Cordula*, the Day after that of S. *Ursula*; and this Lesson gives the account of it, from a Vision of her self commanding it

should

Devotions of the Roman Church.   147

should be so. I see the Saints while they were upon Earth were very shy of seeking their own honour; but it seems by this story, that this is one of the imployments of Heaven, for glorified Saints to procure their own veneration, and to advance their Name among Men; which is a new and strange notion of Heaven, that it should improve its Inhabitants in self-love and poor regards of fame, things that they despised in their imperfect state, and counted it their imperfection at all to mind. But thus do these men disgrace the Saints they profess to worship, and affix such passions to them, which a good man here on Earth would be ashamed to own. To lye decently interred, is as much as any wise Man need take care of while he lives; but that the separate Souls of the Saints are *so far* concern'd about their Bodies, I can hardly think; much less that they matter who treads over their Graves: Yet upon such trifling errands, they send the Saints to visit this World; and S. *Walburg* (or *Walpurg*, as *Surius* calls her) is said to appear to *Prior Otgar*, and to make this foolish complaint; that *she was trod upon by dirty Feet*, (Servorum, *Surius* adds) *and press'd with vulgar steps*.

<small>Capgrav. vit S. Walburg. p. 253. & Surius 1 Maii. p. 12.</small>

It happened once that while *Rome* was in a great Tumult, no Divine Offices were performed either by Night or Day, on the Festival of the great Apostle S. *Peter* in his own Church: they bring him in now,

<small>Baronius ad an. 1087. p. 586.</small>

appearing like one discontented, to want the great honour he used to have at *Rome*, and seeking to have an equal share with other great Saints in other places; for thus *Baronius* relates, "That at that time certain Pilgrims going to pay
" their devotions at the Monastery of S. *Benet*, they met an
" old Man in Canonical Habit: They asked him who he
" was; He answered, I am the Apostle *Peter*; they deman-
" ded whither he was going; He told them, to Brother
" *Benedict*, that I may celebrate the Day of my Passion with
" him; for I cannot stay at *Rome*, my Church there being
" tossed with many Tempests: which thing when they told
" afterwards

"afterwards to the *Friers*, they appointed that S. *Peter's*
"Day should be kept with no less Solemnity than S. *Benet's*
was: (for it seems before this, his Day was not in any great
regard among them.)

    A *Prior* that denied to admit the singing of S. *Nicholas*
his History, in his Church, upon that Saints day, because it
was a new thing: S. *Nicholas* appeared terribly to him in
the Morning, drew him out of his Bed by
the Hair, dashed him against the Pavement,
and beginning the *Antiphona, O Pastor a-
terne*, he sung it morosely to the end, whipping him with
terrible lashes of a Rod he had in his hand, and so left him
half dead; who, I suppose, did never whilst he lived, forget
S. *Nicholas*, or the Lesson he taught him. It's pretty to
observe what Originals some of the great Festivals, in honour of the Bl. *Virgin*, had; even none but such idle Tales of
Visions and Voices, as this of *Cordula*. To mention onely
two; that of her *Conception*, and of her *Nativity*.

Durand. Rational.
l. 7. c. 39.

    The occasion of the first, we are told, was this. "In the
"days of *Charles* King of *France*,
"there was a Clerk a Kinsman of
"his, a great Lover of the Bl. *Vir-*
"*gin*, and one who daily read her *Hours* devoutly, who by
"the advice of his Parents, consenting to marry with a fair
"and noble Maid, and receiving the Nuptial Benediction
"from the Priest, after Mass was ended, he remembred that
"he had not read that day the Ladies Hours; wherefore
"making all go out of the Church, and sending his Spouse
"home, he read the Ladies Hours hard by the Altar; and
"when he repeated that Antiphona, *Thou art fair and come-*
"*ly, O Daughter of Jerusalem*, suddenly the *Bl. Virgin* ap-
"peared between two Angels, with Christ in her Armes,
"saying to him; If I be so fair and comely, wherefore is it
"that thou leavest me, and takest another Spouse? Am not
"I fairer than she is? Hast thou seen any so fair? He made
"answer, O my Lady, thy brightness excells all the beauty
"of the World, thou art elevated above the Quires of An-
"gels,

Dauroutii Catechis. Historial.
Tom. 2. p. 809.

Devotions of the Roman Church.

"gels, What wouldſt thou have me to do? She anſwered,
"If thou wilt forgoe thy Carnal Spouſe for my Love, thou
"ſhalt have me for thy Spouſe in the Celeſtial Kingdome;
"and if thou wilt ſolemnly celebrate the Feaſt of my Con-
"ception Yearly, upon the 6*th.* of the *Ides* of *December,*
"and Preach the Celebration of it, thou ſhalt be crowned
"with me in the Kingdom of my Son; after which words,
"the Bleſſed Mother of Chriſt vaniſhed. The Clerk refu-
"ſing to return home, became a *Monk* in another Country,
"and after a ſhort ſpace of time, by the merits of the Vir-
"gin, he was made the *Patriark* of *Aquilegia*, and care-
"fully celebrated the Feaſt of her Conception, and ordain-
"ed it to be kept Yearly.

The other Feaſt of her *Nativity*, ſays *Beleth*, was occaſi-
oned thus. "On a time when a certain pi- *Johan. Beleth de*
"ous Man was praying by Night, he heard *Divin.offic.c.*149.
"the Angels ſinging in Heaven: This he
"heard many Years always on the ſame Night: Wherefore
"he prayed to the Lord, that he would reveal to him, what
"the meaning of this ſhould be. To whom it was declared,
"that the Angels did rejoyce in Heaven, and as it were kept
"a Feſtival, becauſe on that Night the Bl. *Virgin* was born.
"This thing that the Man had heard, he relates it to the
"*Pope*, who when he underſtood that he was a holy Man,
"and of great Authority, and believing that he ſpake the
"truth, he appointed that this Feaſt ſhould be obſerved
"throughout all the Chriſtian World.

Neither need we fear, when Days are thus ſet apart in devotion to the Saints, eſpecially when they themſelves deſire
it; that God will be wanting by as miraculous ways to
countenance them; rewarding the obſervers, and puniſhing
the Prophaners of ſuch days. For when we are told, that
a Man of great Devotion to the Saints, and particularly to
the Feaſt of *All-Saints*, preparing himſelf
for it a Week before-hand, by Faſtings and *Dsurontias et*
Penances, and keeping it ſolemnly *eight* Days *ſupra. p.* 8 0.
together, when ſuch a Perſon ſhall dye upon *All-Saints* day,

L 3

as he did; Can any one doubt of his going to Heaven? especially when he appeared to a Religious man, after his Death, in a Dream, telling him that he was now associated to the Colledge of Saints? Will any Day-labourer hereafter grumble to desist from his work, being called to Devotion upon a Saints day, when he remembers the story of the *Mower*, who when the *Bell* tolled to *Vespers*, on the *Vigil* of a Saint, went out of the Field, and left his work, and was afterwards derided by his Fellow-labourers, because he was much behind-hand with them? but he was well rewarded for his Devotion, for he found, when he begun his mowing again, a great Piece of Gold in the Grass, which had this wonderful Inscription upon it. *The hand of God made me, and bestowed me for a gift upon a poor man, who did not profane the Saints day.* Will it not shame any ones negligence in this kind, when he is told, that upon S. *Regulus* his Anniversary, the *Harts*, and *Fawnes*, and *Kids*, laying aside their wildness, and mixing themselves freely among the People, went with a slow pace to his Grave, and fell down prostrate on the ground, expecting the Solemnities of the *Mass*? Was it not easie to understand, that God would have S. *Colman*'s day honoured, and the *Vigils* of it kept with Solemn Fasting, when he reads, how that upon his *Vigil*, one that venerated this Saint, could cut no Meat at a Nobleman's Table, but what sprung out blood? and that when the Thrashers, not being contented with *Lenten*-fare, at that time, had a mind to eat *White-meats* *, those also were all changed into blood? When he that was Brewing Ale upon S. *Ledger*'s day, and the Fire would not burn as it was wont, but the Wood blaz'd out in a moment like Straw; when the Liquor would not run freely, and that which did, was bitter and good for nothing; when the Plows upon that Day were broken, and the Oxen cast off their Yokes, it was pretty easie to collect, that Men should give over

Id. Ibid. p. 819.

Act. Sanct. Bolland. ad Mart. 30. p. 825.

Colganus vit. Colmani. 3. Feb. p. 247.

* *Lacticinia.*

Act. Sanct. Bolland. 26. Mart. p. 356.

over working, and keep his Festival; and the like must be concluded for S. *Benedict*'s day, when we are told, that a Husbandman that was plowing upon it, his Hands clave to the Plow-staves, and he could by no means release them, till he had vowed to the *Saint* not to prophane his Festival any more. I know not what *other Saints* have directed to be done, by way of Devotion, for their honour; but one of these Virgins was so kind, we are told, as to appear to a Religious man, who much venerated them, acquainting him with this secret, when he was languishing and infirm; If, said she, thou wilt for our love and honour, repeat the *Lords Prayer* Eleven Thousand times, thou shalt have our company to protect and solace thee in the hour of Death (*this is the very Story, no doubt, the Antiphona*, at the beginning, harps upon. *In vita me defendite; in morte vos ostendite*, &c.) He went presently to work with his *Pater noster's*, and fulfilled his task; and then immediately sent for the *Abbot* to give him Unction; which when it was over, he cryed out, that every one should quit the Room, and give place to the holy Virgins that were coming. The *Abbot* asked him the meaning of this, and the sick Man told him in order the Virgins promise; so all withdrawing for the present, and returning again a little after, they found that he was gone to Heaven.

Item ad 21 Mart. p. 339.

Apud Catgrav. fol. 326.

As for that which the Lesson says, that *Colen* preserves their venerable Bones, and is happy and flourishing by their merits; I believe indeed, *this fiction* has been many a Thousand Pound in their way; and that they have a mighty advantage of other places, in these Reliques, by reason of the *numerousness* of them; for they are good chaffer at all times: What belong'd to *Ursula* alone; her Ring, her Dressing-box, and all that was contained therein, might furnish a pretty Pedlers Stall; and if People should grow weary, and look upon these as stale commodities; it's but opening a *fresh Stone Chest*, telling the People, Here you have the bones of the admirable *Gerasina, Queen of Sicily,* King *Quintian's*

Elizabeth.Vision. tian's Wife, *Sister* to *Dorotheus,* King of Greece, and *Ursula's* own *Aunt*: or, showing a Miraculous *Finger* of one of those Children, that never whimpered after its Nurses milk, but lived wholly upon Finger-juice, as they say, *Bears* do by sucking their Toes; I warrant you, this will toll in fresh Customers, and every one will be ready to give handsel. *Colen,* moreover, has their *blood* to shew, as well as their *bones*; a collection of which they have in a Well of SS. *Machabees* Church: but I would have the *Colen* faith shewn for the greatest Miracle of all; that they can venerate this, and never once question, whether the Priests may not have played such tricks with this blood, as they did at *Hales* in *Glocestershire,* with the blood pretended to be Christ's, brought from *Jerusalem,* which was proved to be the blood of a *Duck,* every Week renewed by the Priests, who kept this secret between them.

Ph Bibius vit. Ursul. p. 504.

L. Herberts Henry 8. p. 432.

But to conclude this Romance. These Virgins suffered about the Year 237, says this Lesson; which is, in effect, to give the lye to the Writings of *Popes* and Kings, and to the Tradition of the whole *English* Nation, which all have agreed to call S. *Alban* the *British Protomartyr*; but *he* dyed either at the end of this Age, or beginning of the next; so that here are 11000 *Brittish Martyrs* before him. There is nothing now remains, but to know (if it be possible) what kind of reception these Martyr'd Virgins met with, when they came to Heaven; It was very great and honourable.

Richard. præm. apud Capgr. p. 324.

They were first of all conducted thither by Multitude of holy Virgins and Armies of Matrons, who went next to them: All the several orders of Angels, sent Thousands of their Companions to meet them, except only the *Thrones,* who sent but a very few, (not for want of civility, you may be sure towards them, but) because they are so confirmed in the Presence of God, that they cannot easily be separated from him: Then Heaven being opened, and they introduced, almost all the

Saints

Saints that remained in Heaven came to welcome them, brought them with singing and jubilation into the Presence of Christ, and his glorious Mother; where they were adorned with white stoles and glittering Crowns; placed in a Mansion by themselves, separated from the rest of the Virgins; and on one side of them, the Matrons that accompanied them had their appartment; where they for ever rejoyce.

De S. Katherina, Virgine & Mart. Alexandrina.

Of S. Catherine of Alexandria, *Virgin and Martyr.*

Missal. Rom. de S. Kather. Paris. 1520.

VOX de cœlis *Katherinæ* redditur; veni sponsa gloriosa, veni sanctissima virgo, accipe præmium tui certaminis inter choros Angelorum.

A *Voice from Heaven came to* Katherine; (saying) *Come O glorious Spouse come most holy Virgin, receive the reward of thy combat among the Quire of Angels.*

Horæ sec. us. Roman.   Antiph.

Antiph.

VIrgo sancta *Catherina*, *Græciæ* gemma, urbe *Alexandrina, Costi* regis erat filia.

Vers. Ora pro nobis beata *Catherina*.

Resp. Ut digni efficiamur promissionibus Christi.

THe holy Virgin Katherine, *the Jewel of* Greece, *of the City of* Alexandria, *was the Daughter of King* Costus.

Vers. *Pray for us S.* Katherine.

Ans. *That we may be made worthy of the promises of Christ.*

Orem.

Oremus. — Let us Pray.

Briv. Rom. Antiq. & reformat.

Deus qui dedisti legem Moysi in summitate montis *Sinai*, & in eodem loco, per sanctos Angelos tuos, corpus *Beatæ Catharinæ* Virginis & Martyris tuæ, mirabiliter collocasti; tribue quæsumus, ut ejus meritis & intercessione, ad montem, qui Christus est, valeamus pervenire.

Per Dominum.

God, who gavest the Law to Moses on the top of Mount Sinai; and who on the same place, by thy holy Angels, didst wonderfully place the body of S. Katherine thy Virgin & Martyr; Grant, we beseech thee, that by her merits & intercession, we may be able to arrive at the Mount, which is Christ.

Through our Lord, &c.

Missal. Rom. ubi prius.

Percussa gladio dat lac pro sanguine collo,
Quam manus Angelica sepelivit vertice Syna.
Membris virgineis olei fluit unda salubris.

The Sword that from her neck the head did chop,
Milk from the wound, instead of blood, did bring;
By Angels bury'd on Mount Sina's top,
From Virgin Limbs a Soveraign oyl did spring.

Post Communionem. — After the Communion.

Ibid. Sumptis Domine salutis æternæ mysteriis, suppliciter deprecamur, ut sicut liquor, qui de membris *Beatæ Katherinæ* virginis & Martyris jugiter manat, & languidorum corpora

Lord, after the receiving the mysteries of eternal salvation, we humbly pray thee, that as the Liquor which continually flowed from the Limbs of S. Katherine Virgin & Martyr,

Devotions of the Roman Church.

sanat, sic ejus oratio cunctas à nobis iniquitates expellat.

Per Dominum.

tyr, did heal languishing bodies, so her Prayer may expell out of us all iniquities.

Through our Lord, &c.

In the *Sarisbury Missal*, at the end of a long *Sequence*, they pray thus to her.

Virgo sidus honestatis,
Dux & decus probitatis,
Christi reos majestatis
Christo reconcilia.

Vas virtutum, via morum,
Flos odoris, odor florum,
Nos tuere, nos cœlorum
Transfer ad palatia.

Virgin, who art the Star of honesty,
Of Probity the ornament and guide;
Though we offended have Christ's Majesty,
Now make us friends to him we crucify'd.

Vessel of vertues, wand'ring life's best way,
Thou flower of smell, sweetest of flowers that spring,
Defend us; and when Natures debt we pay,
Translate us to the Palace of Heav'ns King.

Neither are those rare Devotions to be forgotten which are mentioned by *Chemnitius*, in his *Examen Concil. Tridentini*, out of the *Horæ B. Virginis sec. ordinarium Eccles. Hildensheimensis.*

Ave virgo dei digna;
Christo prece me consigna,
Preces audi, præsta votum,

Cath'rine GOD's worthy Virgin, hail;
May thy Pray'rs to Christ consign me,
Hear me and let my vows prevail,

Cor

Cor in bono fac immotum,
Confer mihi cor contritum,
Rege visum & auditum,
Rege gustum & olfactum,
Virgo sancta, rege tactum:
Ut in cunctis, te regente,
Vivam Deo pura mente.
O beata Catharina,
Babylonis de sentina
Tutum mihi fer ducatum,
Plasmatorem fac placatum:
Esto mihi consolatrix,
Pro me sis interpellatrix;
Christum pro me interpella,
Salva mortis de procella;
Superare fac me mundum,
Ne demergar in profundum;
Ne me sinas naufragari
In peccatis in hoc mari:
Visita tu me infirmum,
Et in bonis fac me firmum:
Agonista Dei fortis,
Esto præsens in hora mortis.
Decumbentem fove, leva,
Et de morte solve sævâ;
Ut resurgam novus homo,

To good immovably incline me,
Bestow on me a heart contrite,
Govern my smelling & my tast,
Govern my hearing & my sight,
And guide my touch, O Virgin chast.
That I, when thou dost rule my Soul,
May live to God with purest mind.
Safe out of Babels sink so foul
Bring me, and make my Maker kind.
Be thou my comforter in need,
And interpose thy prayrs sweet breath,
For me with Jesus intercede,
And save me from the storm of death.
Let not the world o're me prevail
To sink me in th' Abyss profound,
Or shipwrackt be, while here I sail,
And in this Sea of sins be drown'd.
Visit me in my feeble state,
To all good actions me impowr,
Since conquests on thy valour wait,
Stand by me at my latest hour.
Ease and refresh me in all sickness,
Dissolve death's bands, that shows no pity;
That rising in another likeness

Civis

Devotions of the Roman Church.

Civis in cœlesti domo:
Duplex mors ne me infestet,
Jesus Christus illud præstet,
Tua prece exoratus.
Idem pater, idem natus,
Idem utriusque flamen,
Qui vivit & regnat. *Amen.*

I may be own'd i'th' Heav'nly City.
Christ Jesus grant to thy request,
No second death may me infest,
O Father, Son and holy Spirit,
In substance One, of equal merit,
To praise this God let all things sway men,
Who lives and raigns for ever.
Amen.

All these wonderous Stories and Prayers, concerning S. *Catherine*, cannot well be understood, without the help of the *Roman Breviary*, but the Lessons being too tedious to set down at length, I'le only give the Reader the summe of them.

Brev. Roman. Antiq. ad Novemb. 25.

Lesson I.

In the Raign of *Maxentius Cæsar*, there was in *Alexandria*, a beautiful Maid, Twenty two Years old, called *Catherine*, the only Daughter of King *Costus*, one who was very Religious and very Learned, both in Divine and Humane Philosophy, and skilful in the Languages of several Nations, living, after her Fathers death, in his Palace, seeking only to be espoused to Christ, and bestowing all to the poor, save what was necessary to the maintenance of her Self and Family. [Neither must that be omitted which *Ribadeneira* mentions out of *Petrus de Natalibus*; (and I wonder how it came to be left out of this Lesson) that before S. *Catherine* was baptized, she saw one Night in a Vision the Bl. Virgin with Christ in her Arms, who offering *Katherine* to her Son, he turned his face from her, as if he abominated her, and denied her to be fair, that was not yet baptized.

Ribadeneira flos Sanctor. in vit. S. Cath. p. 364.

Where-

Whereupon *Katherine* awaking, perceiving what she wanted, to make her acceptable to Christ, was baptized. Then Christ appeared again to her in the same form as before, and espoused her to himself before his Mother and a numerous company of Heavenly Spirits, and gave her a Ring as a pledg of his espousing her, which S. *Katherine*, awaking, found upon her Finger.]

Less. 2. *Maxentius* coming to *Alexandria*, commanded all Persons to offer Sacrifices to the Gods. This Virgin being troubled to see many Christians, through fear, not daring to confess Christ, boldly speaking to the Emperour, discoursed to him against his false Gods, and concerning the Knowledge of the true God the Creator of all things; who being moved by her reasoning, and more amazed at her beauty, commanded her to be carried into his Palace.

Less. 3. Where upon discourse with her, finding himself unable to maintain an Argument against her, he caused 50 Philosophers to be assembled, to dispute with her: Who being incouraged by an Angel to undertake them all, she did so; and was too hard for them in disputation: upon which the Emperour, in great indignation, commanded them all to be burnt.

Less. 4. Who as they were led to Execution, humbled themselves before the Virgin, confessing their sins in contradicting her sacred admonitions, and professing themselves to be Christians, signed themselves with the Cross, and entered the Fire; but God miraculously preserved their Bodies untouch't, as he did the *Three Children*, and received their Souls. Then the Emperour attempted her by flatteries, and large promises of making her a *Queen*; but she resisting them all, he commanded her to be stripped of her cloths and chastized with Scorpions, and to be shut up in a dark Prison 12 days without any food: but she was comforted by the visit of an Angel, and a white *Dove* brought her provisions to sustain her.

Less. 5. The *Queen* mean-while, pittying the miseries she was condemned to, by means of *Porphyrius* (the Chief Commander

Devotions of the Roman **Church.**

mander of the *Militia*) who bribed the Guards, she with *Porphyry* give S. *Katherine* a visit in the Prison, and beheld her there shining with inestimable brightness, and upon discourse she converted them both to Christ.

Les. 6. After this, the Emperour caused *four* Wheels to be prepared stuck with sharp Irons, (as we see in the Pictures of the *Catherine Wheel*) two of which were to turn one way, and the other two the contrary way, and so tear her flesh in pieces: but when she was brought forth thus to be punisht, upon her prayer, an Angel descending from Heaven, broke the Wheels in pieces, and slew 4000 of the Heathens.

Les. 7. & 8. All which the *Queen* beholding, and desiring her Husband to take notice, how powerful the God of the Christians was, He in great indignation to see her made a Christian, commanded her Breasts to be torn off with Iron Hooks; which she, being heartned by S. *Katherine*, chearfully underwent, and both *She* and *Porphyry* were beheaded.

Les. 9. Then when the Emperour found all means unsuccessful to move *Katherine*, he commanded her also to be beheaded; who coming to the place, and obtaining respite to make her prayers to God, she said thus. O Lord Jesu Christ, I desire of Thee, that all Christians, who in any tribulation seeking my Patronage, cry to Thee, that thou who art blessed for ever, wouldst hear them. Then a Voice coming from Heaven, said, Thy Prayer is heard; and so her Head was struck off, on the 25 of *November*.

Immediately, in token of her pure Virginity, instead of Blood, Milk flowed from her Body upon the Earth abundantly. Her Body was carried by Angels, and placed on Mount *Sinai*, where many Miracles are wrought, upon the Invocation of this Saint. For from her Grave a Fountain of Oyl perpetually flows forth, with which the Bodies of infirm People being anointed, to their great joy they are restored to soundness.

[*So far the Lessons.*]

This

This also is all told in several *Prosa's* of the *Roman Missal* forenamed, of which I'le only set down one.

COrdis oris digna laude *Catharina* virgo gaude, Summæ consors gloriæ.	O VIrgin Catherin *rejoyce*, Worthy all praise of heart and voice, Consort of glory high:
Gaude quod ad viam lucis Excœcatos tu reducis Fumo Philosophiæ.	Thou didst to th'way of light revoke Those that had lost their sight, through smoke Of vain Philosophy.
Gaude dulcis *Catharina*, Spreto rege fit Regina Per te fide stabilis:	By thee sweet Catherine, the Queen No ways regarding th'Emperours spleen In Christian faith was stable:
Mortem subit nec tristatur, Et cum ipsa decollatur *Porphyrius* nobilis.	Who bravely dy'd without all dread, And Porphyry with her his head To lose thou didst inable.
Non te terrent flammæ, rotæ, Nec evellit à Christo te Rex prece nec pretio.	Neither Flames nor Wheels do fright thee, Nor the King from Christ invite thee Either by gifts or prayer.
Lac effudit pro cruore Ægros sanat à languore Olei profusio.	Pure Milk from thee for blood does spring; For oyl that flows and health does bring The sick to thee repair.
In supremo *Sina* montis Tu sepulta, veri fontis Quo frueris poculo.	Thou buried ly'st on Sina's Mountain There of all joys from the true Fountain Delicious draughts thou hast.

Ut

Ut nos potes Christum ores	To Christ for us less-worthy
Et corónet nos minores	pray,
Hoc finito seculo.	That we may tast those joys,
Amen.	and may
	Be crown'd, when life is past.

NOTES.

ONE that reads this Formal story of a Saint, whose life is placed about the Year 300 after Christ, might well expect that some of the ancient Writers should have given us a fair account of a History so famous, and whose circumstances, if they were true, are highly remarkable. But alas! *Baronius* has spoiled all this expectation, where he complains that they were pretermitted by *Eusebius*; and, which is worse, that her *Acts* were written largely by an uncertain Author, but less faithfully than was meet; and gravely adds, *Melius consulitur Ecclesiastica veritati, &c.* "They provide better for the "truth of Ecclesiastical History, who pass over in silence "things that are uncertain, than such as tell any lye, though "never so specious, and mixed with some truths: for the "mind rests satisfied in those few truths, and by probable "conjectures, leaning upon truth, can conceive and medi- "tate, and contemplate the rest: But in the other case, the "mind of the Reader being once offended with a lye "(though but a little one) becomes doubtful and wavering, "and knows not where to fix a sure footing, but having once "stumbled upon a lye, suspects even truths themselves.

Baron. ad an. 307. sec. 33.

A very observable *Memorandum* this is for Protestants, who may therefore the better be excused, having met so often in the lives of their Saints, not little but loud untruths, if they be very cautious what they assent to, (and much more when it comes to be a ground of their Prayers,) especially when the late Author of *Sure-footing*, has so horribly miscarried in his Attempt to establish them by Tradition. I think this of S. *Catherine* of *Alexandria*, is as remarkable an Instance as any; which may well be looked upon, from the beginning to the end, as a *Fiction*.

We need not go much farther than to their own *Cassander* to prove it; who shews, that the very Name of *Catherine* was not known to the *Latines* above 300 Years since at most; nor known to the *Greeks* (from whom the *Latines* derived the veneration of her) much sooner. *Eusebius* that writ diligently the affairs of *Alexandria*, and lived about the same time that her Acts are recorded, says nothing of her, nor *Nicephorus* who lived after that, nor any of the *Greek* or *Latin* *Ecclesiastical Historians*. All the *Martyrologies, Kalendaries, Ecclesiastical Offices* of any Antiquity, are wholly silent in this matter. Even *Aldelm* the Bishop of *Sarisbury* in the Books he writ on set purpose in praise of the famous Virgins of both Sexes, has passed her over; which he could not have done, if her fame had either been so great as now, or her Name known: neither is she to be met with in S. *Jerome's Kalendar*, or in *Bede's Martyrologie*.

Cassandri opera p. 278.

Besides, the truth of History contradicts what is told of her: especially when she is said to be put to death by *Maxentius* at *Alexandria*, whereas he passed the time of his whole Reign, or Tyranny, at *Rome*. She is said to be a *Kings* Daughter, whereas *Alexandria*, and all *Egypt*, from the time of *Augustus* his Victory at *Actium*, was reduced into a *Province*.

The story of her Father *Costus*, how he was born at *Constance*, a City of *Germany*, and warred under the King of *Alexandria*, and afterwards when the King dyed, was chosen to be King in his room; that he was called *Costus*, because he came from *Constance*, which in the *German* Tongue is called *Costnitz*; these (says he) are all so absurd, that they deserve no Confutation. See farther what *Cassander* adds concerning the deriving of her Name and Worship to the *Latines*, out of a certain Book, *De ortu S. Catharinæ*; and that S. *Catherine* was first put into the *Martyrologie*, by Pope *John* the XXII. who lived about the Year 1316.

As for the pretences of *Baronius*, for the countenancing of her from *Eusebius*, and his *Æcatharina* which he findes in the *Greek Menologies*, they have been all so shamefully baffled by our *Joh.* * *Reinoldus*, and so poorly defended by (a) *Serarius*; that it had been wiselyer ordered a great deal, to have put her with S. *George* and S. *Christopher*, among the *Symbolical Saints*, (as *Reynolds* advised) for then indeed it would have run well. S. *Catherine* would then (as he says) have represented the *Church*, the Daughter of the King of Heaven, living in Earth, as in *Egypt*, opposed by the powerful and wise Men of the World, but conquering them, though passing through many afflictions, and at length conveighed by Angels to Heaven after death.

Baron. ad Rom. Martyrol. Nov. 25.

* *Reinold. l. 1. de Rom. Eccles. Idolols. c. 5.*

(a) *Serar. in Litaneut. 2.*

Now let us farther observe, what work they have made since the *Council of Trent*, in Reforming the *Roman Breviary*, as to this Legend of S. *Katherine*; from whence we may better conjecture, how rarely *Popes* are wont to reform things amiss. In the *Breviary* of *Pius* the V. Printed at *Antwerp*, 1580. the old Prayer (*Deus qui dedisti legem*, &c.) is still retained, and all the substance of the Legend, though not made so large; only the name of King *Costus* is left out, the *Queen* is now named *Faustina*, *Katherines* prodigious Learning is determined to be at 18 Years of Age; one Wheel is said to be prepared for her torments instead of four; the 4000 slain by the Angel, the Milk and Oyl flowing after her Death, and the voice from Heaven, are left out: And as in other Lives, the Names of the Authors are set down usually, at the beginning, out of which they are taken; so here is prefixed, *Eusebius*, *lib. 7. c. 26.* That which has been done since that time by succeeding *Popes*, is this; That in the present *Breviaries*, the quotation of *Eusebius*, which was both false, and nothing to the purpose, is omitted; (which, by the way, I observe is now generally practised in most of the Lives of the Saints; the Authors are not quoted out of which they are taken, and it has this cunning in it, that now the falsities cannot so easily be discovered) now also, after the diligence and observations of *Baronius* upon the *Martyrologie*, in every place, instead of *Maxentius*, is put, the Emperour *Maximinus*; the Name of *Faustina* is omitted; the number of Philosophers not determined to be 50 as before: but instead of it is put *many Philosophers*: and yet all the circumstances of the story, as it is in the old *Breviary*, have the same Authority of Tradition, and long usage in the Church; which, in the judgment of Mr. *Sergeant*, and his Brethren of the Scientifical way, is a hundred times more Infallible than any *Pope*. And for my part, I look upon the Milk and Oyl as the most pretious part of the story; nor can I altogether excuse the *Pope* from rashness, in taking away *three* of the Wheels, for who knows what mystery may be in them? However, this good use may be made of these *two* great Examples, the *Pope* and *Baronius*, to believe as much of any Legend, as every Man thinks fit.

Now though these alterations signifie not much, yet in one particular, these *Popes* may shame Mr. *Cressy*, if he be capable of it: *viz.* In their leaving out the miraculous attestation of her chastity, the Milk when her Head was cut off streaming from her Body instead of Blood.

If Mr. *Cr.* had been of the Council, he would by no means, I dare say, have consented to this omission: for he has, in his Church-History, commended some for living like *Virgins*, and others for preserving even their Virginity, in a state of Marriage. "Thus *Ethelfleda*, he says, was of such

Ch. Hist. l. 30. cap. 8.
"chastity, that even in Marriage she lived as a "single Woman, abstaining from the use of it. "For having at the beginning of her Marri-
"age, had experience of the pains and incommodities of
"Child-bearing, she ever after abstained from her Husbands
"embraces, protesting that it was unbecoming the Daughter
"of a King, to admit a sensual pleasure, attended not long
"after with so great incommodities. And again,
Ibid. cap. 14. *Ethelfleda* for the space of 40 Years after the
"Birth

Devotions of the Roman Church. 165

"Birth of *Alwina* her only Child, always refused the embraces of her Husband.

Such another story, *Surius* affords us, concerning S. *Matrona* of *Perga*, who after her Marriage, and the having had one onely Child, resolved, for her greater freedome in serving God, to forsake her Husband; being encouraged to it by this Vision: A certain Man seemed to run after her, and she to fly away from him, and hardly escaped, being saved by certain *Monks*: which she interpreted in this sence, that she must take upon her the habit of a *Monk*, to escape her Husband: This she did by feigning her self to be an *Eunuch*, and changing her Name to *Babyla*: She had like to have been discovered by a *Monk*, who observed her Ears to have been bored through, where Jewels had heretofore hung. But the holy *Abbot Bassianus*, had it revealed to him by a Vision, that she was a Woman in Mans habit, and charged her with it: he proposed also a hard Question to her, how she could satisfie her self, to have offered her mouth securely, to receive the * salutation of peace from the *Friers*. Her answer was, that she looked upon those to whom she offered her self, to be as uncapable of any bad impressions as the Angels. (and I suppose if one of them had embraced her, she would have interpreted it according to the Gloss, that the *Frier* did this, hereby to (a) give her his Benediction.) And against the Objection, why she did not in prosecution of her design go into a *Nunnery* rather among Women; she defended her self by her Vision, and that in this Habit she might the better be concealed from her Husband; and so she still remained there. I'le add but one passage more, to show how finely they make these

Surius Tom.6. ad Nov. 8. ex Metaphraste.

* This refers to the custome of giving the kiss of peace mutually; which *Polydore Virgil* explains, *De inventor. rerum, lib. 5 cap. 11. Finito canone, dicitur pax Domini; hic osculum pacis datur inter sacerdotes mutuò, quod Innocentii primi inventum est.*

(a) *Si ergo Clericus amplectitur mulierem, interpretabitur quod causa benedicendi eam hoc faciat. Causa 11. qu.3. ca. Absit. in glossa.*

these foolish perswasions, about Religion, work. When S. *Matrona*'s Husband after this pursued her, having learnt how she had concealed her self; she fled again from him, and hid her self in an Idols Temple at *Beritus*, chusing rather to fall among Devils, or wild Beasts, than to be taken by her Husband: and an excellent Reason is given of it. For if *they* should light upon her, they would only hurt her Body; But if *her Husband* should take her, he would be more pernicious to her than Devils, or wild Beasts, as one that could hurt her Soul * together with her Body, drawing her again to the World, and challenging her for his Wife.

* *Ut qui possit cum corpore animam lædere, eam rursus trahens ad mundum, & tanquam suam uxorem vendicans.* Ibid.

But a more famous Instance of this abstinence, countenanced even by Miracles, is given us by Mr. *Cr.* in *Ethelreda* (or *Saint Audrey*) who in obedience to her Parents consented to marry Prince *Tombert*, though she before had fixed all her affections on *Christ* alone, and her desire was to confine her self to a Cloyster. And now her next design (and a worthy one it was) is to obtain of her Husband a permission to preserve the integrity of her Body; and to that end spared no Prayers nor Praises of Virginal Purity; and her Husband admiring her Angelical chastity, he gave her hope of a compliance with her desires: But not long after, reason being overcome with the violence of (*a*) corrupt nature, he yielded to his own desires, and required of her that right which the Laws of Marriage allowed him. [and which, if S. *Paul*'s discourse be not foolish with these men, she could not without injustice, deny him, 1 *Cor.* 7. Where speaking of the ὀφειλομένη εὔνοια, he says, ἀποδότω ὁμοίως καὶ ἡ γυνὴ τῷ ἀνδρί· ἡ γυνὴ τοῦ ἰδίου σώματος οὐκ ἐξουσιάζει, ἀλλ᾽ ὁ ἀνήρ — μὴ ἀποστερεῖτε ἀλλήλους, εἰ μή τι ἂν ἐκ συμφώνου πρὸς καιρὸν, &c.] But when he came to extort her consent to his impatient desires (now

(*a*) An excellent comment this is, upon τίμιος ὁ γάμος ἐν πᾶσι, καὶ ἡ κοίτη ἀμίαντος. Heb. 13. 4.

θεὸς ἀπὸ μηχανῆς, *to save the Virgin*) God prevented him, for he found the holy Virgin encompaſſed with a wonderful Light, and a Celeſtial Flame, which dazeled his Eyes, and conſumed the Fire of Luſt burning in his boſome; and ſo he continued for *Seven*, or *Eight* Years without touching her, till he dyed. And now, as if all this were too little to celebrate the fame of this Virgin, Mr. *Cr.* brings a ſecond Scene of her upon the Stage.

For, after Prince *Tombert*'s death, *Egfrid* the Heir of the *Northumbrian Kingdome*, invited by the fame of her ſanctity and perfections, [*and if this, that has been related, was part of her holy fame, it was indeed a great temptation to court her for a Wife*] demanded her in Marriage, and by the preſſing importunity of her Parents, and the *Nobles* of the *Eaſt-angles*, her reſiſtance was conquered: ſo that once more for the common good, [*and you may well imagine what great good to the publick, was to be expected from her marriage*] ſhe was compelled to ſubmit her ſelf to a new ſervitude. And now ſhe uſes her former Arts with this *Prince Egfrid* alſo, that there might be a conjunction of minds only, with a ſeparation of Bodies; and ſo ſucceſsful they were, that they lived together *Twelve* Years without any prejudice of S. *Etheldred*'s Virginity, and converſed together, as if they had been diveſted of their Bodies. After which, all attempts proving in vain to change his Wives purpoſe, he gave her Liberty to enter into a *Monaſtery*: But afterwards, repenting of his indulgence, he came by force to take her out thence: who upon notice of it, fled with two Virgins up a high Hill, whither he purſued her: but Almighty God, to preſerve his Servants, had encompaſſed the Hill with deep Waters from the Sea, which the King could not paſs; and there Tradition informs us, that they were ſuſtained by God *Seven* Days on the Mountain, without any corporal food; and travelling from thence, on a Night, laying her ſelf down in a commodious ſhade to ſleep; ſhe found when ſhe awaked, that her * Staff, which ſhe had faſtned in

---

* *Let Mr.* Cr. *remember S.* Patrick's *Staff, and tell me, whether this ſtory be not as credible as this.*

the ground at her head, had taken Root, and began to flourish with Leaves, and in succeeding times it became a very large and tall Tree, and continues to this day (says the *Hist. Eliens.*) called *Etheldred-Stow*, or *Etheldred*'s rest. When she was dead, (says *Bede*) the flesh of this Saint, a long time after she was buried, could not be corrupted, which was a sign (says he) that whilest she was alive, she remained uncorrupted by humane touches. But what is this number of Years to the Body of such a Virgin? Mr. *Cressy* has found Vouchers, that almost 500 Years after this, (in the Year 1106, and her Life is placed in the Year 660) She and her Sister *Withburga*, being both taken up to be buried more magnificently, the Miracle of her Incorruption was publickly manifested. And concerning *Withburga*, *Capgrave* comes in with his Spring of pure Water (which he scarce ever fails to tell us of) that issued from the place where she had been first buried, and cured many Diseases. And for a farewell, *Capgrave* adds, That one of the *Monks* adventuring to touch her Body, a lively blush coloured her Cheeks, as if she still had breath in her: To which Mr. *Cr.* subjoyns in a different Character, *Her dead Body expressing the same shamefastness, which her self would have done when alive.* And indeed I can almost believe that the dead Body of this Virgin, might blush as soon as the tellers of this story. Mr. *Cr.* is too old now, to have any of this colour in his Face; and the other *Miracle-monger*, I believe, never had so much grace in all his life, as to feel the very *motus primo-primos* to any such thing. However I have done my part to make Mr. *Cr.* ashamed, by showing him the Example of several *Popes*, who all have consented to blot out the foolish story of S. *Katherine*'s Milk, and if they had been so good natur'd, might have done the same to the translation of her Body from Mount *Sinai*, and the rest; for all depends upon their pleasure,

(a) *The* Roman *Martyrologie,* Jun. 23. *says, the body of* Ediltrudis (*so she is there called*) *was found uncorrupt undecim post annis: The Breviary of* Sarum *sayes,* Sexdecim annis.

Ch Hist. l. 16. cap. 6.

pleasure, and Antiquity countenances one no more than the other. They were ashamed of the unlikely change of blood into milk, though it was to attest the snow-white chastity of a Virgin (*in signum nivei pudoris*, was the phrase in the old *Breviary*.) But here we must be ingaged to believe, I know not how many Miracles one after another, while she was alive, and when she was dead, only to testifie to the World, that S. *Audrey* was true to a wicked and superstitious resolution, against the sense, not of the sensual (as he phrases it) but of all sober Man-kind, and against the Faith and Covenants of Marriage, though no less with him than a Sacrament. *To the present sensual Age, this may seem incredible. Cres. ubi supra.* I would ask him, if either of her Husbands should have taken that Counsel, which they falsly Father upon *Luther*, *Si non vult uxor, veniat ancilla*; or when *Egfrid* upon her going into the Monastery, took (as Mr. *Cr.* says) *Ermenburga* to Wife, whether the guilt of such supposed Fornication, or of this Adultery, did not in great measure lye at her Door, for withholding the *debitum conjugale*, notwithstanding all her superstitious veneration of Virginity? and whether she did not better deserve to be served as that Man was, who for leaving his Wives Bed, and withholding this *debitum*, though it was onely in the time of *Lent*, yet was severely chid for it by S. *Henry* the *Hermit*, and as a *Capgrave in vit. S. Henrici.* punishment of his presumption, found himself one Night when he awaked, laid naked in a stinking Stable, under the Horses feet? The truth is, I wonder that when so many Miracles are pretended to save her Virginity, that no body, to free her from this blame, would coine one such wonder for her Husband, as they report concerning S. *Thomas* of *Aquin*; who in his Youth praying with bended Knees before the sign of the Cross, and there falling asleep, he seemed in his sleep to feel his *Rom. Breviar. 7 Martii. lec. 4.* Loines fast bound by *Angels* *, from which time forward,

* *We are told in the Life of S. Severus, that he had a Wife, before he was a Bishop, but after that, he did not use her, but she was turned into a Sister, because of that thundring command of our Saviour,* Sint vestri Lumbi præcincti. *Bolland.* 1 *Febr. in vit. S. veri. p.* 86. Omni

Omni libidinis sensu caruit, He never had any lustful inclinations more; or such a one as they tell of *Father Elias,* who being vexed with fleshly temptations, upon his fasting and prayer, *three* Angels appeared to him in a Dream, one held his Hands, another held his Feet, and the third seemed with a Rasor to geld him, and from that time, *Nec pristinæ tentationis scintillam sensit,* He never felt any spark of the old temptation: but the case was quite otherwise (as you heard) with *Egfrid.*

<small>Dauroutii Flores Exemplor. Tom. 2. pag. 214. Capgrave. fol. 38.</small>

Let the *Roman Church* therefore praise such examples of the Saints, as that of *Alexius*; who the first Night of his Marriage, for his singular love to Christ, left his Spouse untouched, and undertook a Pilgrimage to visit the famous Churches of the World. Let Mr. *Cr.* boast as much as he pleases, of the Examples of Princes, that have vowed abstinence after Marriage. Let him vent his Gall against the Reformation, as indulging the Flesh (who I am sure in their Principles allow no more in this particular, than the Scriptures do, nor condemn any thing which that does not) I shall not at all stick to assert, that it is a true Reformation of foolish and impious Opinions in the Church of God, to forbid living in such hatred of the Flesh(*I use his own phrase*) as this Virgin in her circumstances unlawfully practised, and he as foolishly applauds. It may be he is much taken with that, which Pope *Siricius* urged upon the Clergy, as worthy, chast and honest, that the Priests and Levites should not company with their Wives, because of their daily necessary imployment in Divine Ministrations; and because that *they that are in the Flesh, cannot please God, but ye* (says he) *are not now in the Flesh, but in the Spirit.* Indeed an admirable application of Scripture, and worthy of a *Pope!* which may be matched with a sutable story of the *Monks* inventing, how

<small>Rom. Brev. 17 July. Lef. 3. Alexius propter eximium Jesu Christi amorem, primâ nocte nuptiarum, relinquens intactam sponsam &c.</small>

<small>Ch. Hist. l. 10. c. 1.</small>

<small>Epist. 3. inter Concil. Labbe. Tom. 2. p. 1029.</small>

how a married Priest, having Bedded with his Wife over Night, the next day when he came to receive the *Sacred Mysteries*, he saw the Particle of the Body of Christ, which he had put in the *Capgrave vit. S. Cuthbert. f. 76.* Cup, changed into a horrid form, of the colour of Pitch rather than of Bread and Wine, and the tast as bitter as Gall, which made him confess his fault to the Bishop, and resolve to live more chastly and religiously afterward : (that is, I suppose, to forsake his Wife and fornicate.) For the course which they tell us, S. *Lewis* took before he companied with his *Queen*, to pray three Days and three Nights together ; *Martyrol. Francisc. ad 25 Aug. p. 367.* even this would not have sufficed, to sanctifie the Marriage-Bed to a Priest. As for Mr. *Cressy*'s flurt against *Luther*'s Marriage, (at the end of the Chapter) it only tempts me to question, whether possibly he may not be of *Cardinal Campegius* his mind, *Ch. Hist. l. 10. c. 1. in fine.* who, as *Sleiden* * informs us, declared that it was a greater sin for Priests to marry, than to keep many Whores. But as sensual as he would insinuate the Reformation to be, I would fain have him tell us of any one in it, that ever appeared to justifie that ** Sleidan. Comment. lib. 4. Quòd sacerdotes fiant maritos, multo esse gravius peccatum, quàm si plurimas domi meretrices alant, &c.* which *Johannes à Casa*, the *Pope*'s Legat and Arch-Bishop of *Beneventum*, did ; (and one who gloried too, no doubt, that he was never married, as *Luther* was) who wrote a Book in defence of that sin, for which God destroyed *Sodom*. Let him show among us any such Legal exemption for the encouraging of Fornication, as that in their Canon Law. *Sleidan. Comment. lib. 21. pag. 652.* He that has no Wife, but a Concubine instead of a wife, let him not be driven from the Communion. *Decreti distinct. 34. ca. 4. Is qui non habet uxorem ; & pro uxore concubinam habet, à communione non repellatur.* Let him show any such impure Doctrine among us, as that

Gloss

Decreti distinc. 34. ca. 16. Vidua est: where the Gloss says. *Meretrix est, quæ admiserit plures, quàm viginti tria hominum millia.*

Gloss on the Canon Law. *She is a Whore, that has had to do with more than Three and Twenty Thousand Men.* I desire Mr. *Cr.* also, to parallel in the impure Reformation, the story that is related by *Matthew Paris*; how when Pope *Innocent* IV. was taking his leave of *Lyons* in *France*, Cardinal *Hugo* made a farewell Sermon; wherein,

Matth. Paris ad an. 1251. p. 819. Amici, magnam fecimus, postquam in hanc urbem venimus, utilitatem & eleemosynam; quando enim primùm huc venimus, tria vel quatuor prostibula invenimus; sed nunc recedentes, unum solum relinquimus, verùm ipsum durat continuatim, ab Orientali porta civitatis, usque ad Occidentalem.

after he had saluted the Town in the Name of the *Pope* and his whole Court, he added this Speech. " Friends, we " have brought much " profit, and done an
" act of great Charity to this City; for when we first came
" hither, we found *three* or *four* Whore-houses; but now,
" at our departure, we leave only one; but that one ex-
" tends it self all along from the *Eastern* to the *Western*
" Gate of the City.

Luther is a carnal Man for marrying a Wife; but here are your spiritual Men, the *Pope* and his Attendants; who by this Cardinal's confession in a publick Sermon, had debauched a whole City, and turn'd it into a Stews; and yet, I doubt not, but after all this, modest Mr. *Cressy* will wipe his mouth, and in his next Book, rail against the carnal Protestants, with as good a grace as ever. If any one suspect this Sermon of the Cardinals at *Lyons*, as a *light Frolique*, or expressing only the *corrupt practices* of that Church at that time; he may do well to consult the *Decretals* *, and there he will find, but a few Years before, an Epistle of Pope

* *Decretal. Gregor. l. 1. Tit. 20. ca. 6. Sanè postulasti per sedem Apostolicam edoceri, si Presbyteri, plures concubinas habentes, bigami censeantur; ad quod duximus respondendum, quod cùm irregularitatem non incurrerint Bigamiæ, cum eis tanquam simplici fornicatione notatis, quoad executionem sacerdotalis officii poteris dispensare.*

Innocent

Innocent III. to an Arch-Bishop of *Lyons*, and his *Legate*, where he may be satisfied, that the *Opinion* also of that Church, was more favourable to the Whoredome than to the Marriage of Clergy-men. "Thou desirest to be instructed, whether Priests keeping many Concubines, are to be reckoned among the *Bigames*; [i.e. *those that had been twice married, who were thereupon uncapable of Orders:*] to which we have thought fit to answer, that since these have not incurred the irregularity of *Bigamy*, thou mayst dispense with them, as to the exercise of the Priestly Office, as with those that are noted only with the crime of simple Fornication. Where you see that second Marriage of Priests, is by this *Pope* accounted a more heinous crime than the having many Whores. Nay even *Adultery*, as well as *Fornication*, passed among them for lesser sins, as appears by the *Decretal*, where we find that Pope *Alexander* III. orders, that Clergy-men that were convicted of a crime before a *Decretal.l.2.Tit.1.ca.4.* Secular Judge, are not thereupon to be condemned by the *Bishop*, but must be again convicted before him, and punished by him (without sending him back to the secular Judg) or deposed, unless he dispense with him; and then he adds, *De adulteriis verò & aliis criminibus quæ sunt minora, potest Episcopus cum celericis post peractam pœnitentiam dispensare.* i.e. "But for Adulteries and other Crimes which are lesser, the Bishop may dispense with Clergy-men, after they have undergone their Penance. The story of Cardinal *Joh. Cremensis* is sufficiently known from our Historians; who came into *England* in *Henry* the First's time, to divorce the Clergy from their Wives, and made a *Canon* in a Council at *London*, that Clergy-men should have no society with their Wives or Concubines, or any other Women, save those that could not be suspected; but after he had made a fierce declamation, to this purpose, in the Synod; the very Night following, the Cardinal was found in Bed with a Whore. *Baronius* indeed would fain deny this story, by supposing that *Roger Hoveden* and *Matth. Westmonaster*, had it from *Hen. Huntingdon*, the firſt Writer of it, and that he was a favourer of the married Clergy; And, what then? perhaps one reaſon why he was ſo, was by ſeeing the baſeneſs and wickedneſs of the contrary Zealots. But *Matth. Paris* has told the ſame thing of him, and ſays, that *Res notiſſima negari non potuit* : i. e. *It was ſo known a thing, it could not be denyed:* and after ſo many witneſſes that aſſert it, I think the beſt way to have brought him off, would have been, to have told us that he tryed S. *Colman*'s Girdle, and it met about him exactly; whoſe vertue is known to be ſuch, that he that preſerves his Virginity, though he be never ſo corpulent, it will upon tryal compaſs his body ; but he that has violated his Chaſtity, though he be never ſo ſlender and lean, can never gird himſelf with it. I ſhall only add this, that *the Romiſh Writers*, do not upon any argument want a convenient *confidence*, but in this Controverſie about Marriage and Virginity, they are *impudent* even to admiration.

Baron. ad an. 1125. p. 164.

Matth. Paris ad an. 1125. p. 70.

Colganus de S. Colmano. 3 Febr. p. 246.

I Might alſo here ſubjoyn another of their Saints, who is placed in the *Roman Kalendar*, upon the 13 of *Auguſt*; to wit, *Hippolytus*, (the *Souldier*, not the *Presbyter*) who may well be ranked among the Fabulous ones. The Legend concerning his ſuffering under *Decius* the Emperour, who condemned him to be tyed to wild Horſes, and ſo drawn to death, ſeems to be taken from the Fables of the Poets, concerning *Hippolytus* * (one of the ſame name) the Son of *Theſeus*, who loſt his Life in the ſame manner. The Acts of S. *Laurence*, out of which his ſtory is taken, by the confeſſion

---

* *Vid. Euripid. in Phædra. Senec. in Hippolyto. Ovid Metamorph. l. 15. & Faſtor. l. 3. & Faſtor. l. 5.*
Hippolyte infelix, velles coluiſſe Dionen,
Cùm conſternatis diripererís equis.

of *Baronius* (a) contain in them many things *Apocryphal*, & contrary to truth. In the *Old Breviaries*, the Lessons make *Decius* the Emperour, after the death of S. *Laurence*, to hear his cause as a Judge, and to deliver him to *Valerian* the Prefect, to inflict the aforesaid punishment on him; whereas S. *Laurence* himself suffered under *Valerian*, seven or eight Years after *Decius* his death, as *Baronius*, in the forenamed place, confesses. The inquisitive Reader may more fully satisfie himself, by consulting herein *Joh. Raynolds de Rom. Ecclef. Idololat. L. 1. cap. 5. sec. 23.* to whom I refer him, without adding any more about him, only this; that though his Body might have been torn into *Forty* Pieces while he was dragged along with the wild Horses; yet, we are told by *Surius*, that *Colen* has got the Body of *Hippolytus*, (and I do not read that it wants there any one part) and it lies in the Church of S. *Ursula*: a very convenient place, where it is joyned to very sutable company; and where, if it had been as much for their interest, we might have met with the Body of the Son of *Theseus* also.

(a) *Baron. ad Roman. Martyrolog.* 10 *August.*

Surius vit. S. Laurentii. 10 *August. in fine.*

AND now after I have given this account of so many of their Fabulous Saints, and the many Fabulous reasons of worshiping the true ones; I cannot but give them joy, before I part with this Subject, of that mighty comfort and satisfaction, which such Devotions are able to afford them, and of the vast advantages *they* have of *us* in this regard.

Oh how joyful, and how becoming the Devotions of Christians it is, to sing a *Hymn* in praise of a Virgins beard; and to celebrate the fame of a man, that walked *two* Miles with his Head off? How pleasingly, in a devout fancy, does the Saviour of the World, sit mounted upon the back of a tall Gyant, while he carries him safely over a dangerous River? And who can entertain a doubt against the Resurrection,

rection, who contemplates in his mind the *seven* Sleepers in their Cave, taking a comfortable nap of above three hundred Years long, and then waking as young and fresh, as when they lay down; and thinking, that only one common Night of time had passed over their Heads? What man dares open his mouth to plead for Idolatry, after *Longinus* his glorious confutation of it? —— *Who then, without all doubt, Spake to good purpose, when his tongue was out.*

See 2d. Lesson of Longinus.

Alas! what would have become of our Christianity, if these *Traditions* and *Revelations* did not back and support it? How dully would Religion have been conducted, as the Courtships of those Lovers are, that eat and drink as other Men do, which now by vertue of these *Spiritual Romances*, may live almost in perpetual rapture and extasie; be maintained I know not how long, by a sweet glance from one of these Saints in a Vision; be carried almost up to Heaven, by a sight of one of the *Feathers* that fell out of the Wing of *Michael the Arch-Angel*, and kiss it with a greater transport, than ever Romantick Lover did the fallen Glove of his *Mistress*? need no other Physick in sickness, though one lay gasping, as if he was taking his last breath, save onely that of S. *Gilbert* *, a little breast-milk from the fair pap of the Blessed Virgin; and one that is troubled with imaginations of being deserted by Jesus, may with that wise *Nun* seek him up and

* *S. Gylbert on a time was near dead of the Quency, and when his throat was so great, that he might not take breath, our Lady came to him and said:* Gilbert *my Servant, it were evil do, that thy throat should suffer penance, that hath so often times gladded me with joyes; and anon she took her fair pappe, and milked on his throat, and went her way, and anon therewith he was who'e, and thanked our Lady ever after. Festivale f. 95.*

Cæsarius in Dialog. distinc.6. cap.31, 32.

down the House, and find him in a hole of the Wall; or as another weeping sadly in a like distress, having lost her wooden Crucifix, heard *Christ*'s voice, saying to her, Weep not, Daughter, for I lye in a Bag under thy Bed-straw; and

Devotions of the Roman Church.

no Body, without such a voice, would have lookt for him there. We poor Protestants thought we were well provided for by the mercy of God, after we had offended him by our sins, when we heard how pleasing to God the Sacrifice of his dear Son was, when he dyed upon the Cross, and that we should have this compassionate Saviour to be our Judge. But alas! these Men have discovered another spring of comfort and way of pardon, that we never thought of, nor God ever told the former World of, till these blessed Revelations came in vogue. We hear now of a *Queen* as well as of a *King* of Heaven, and of a *Mother*, as well as a *Father* of mercy; and what may we not now expect from this *Patroness*? If Prayers to *Christ* himself be not speedily answered, here is a new course may be taken, even that which the tempted *Monk* took, who said to him. "*Truly Lord, if thou dost not deliver me from this temptation, I'le complain of thee to thy Mother*: *Cæsar. Dialog. distinc.6.c.30.* This we should judge to be intolerable pride and sawciness; but, says the Relator, "Our "Lord the Teacher of humility, and lover of simplicity, as "if he feared to be accused before his Mother, prevented "his complaint, by mitigating his temptation. The name of a Judge, *that* carries terror in the face of it; but oh! the sweetness of these Mothers breasts. Is it not pitty, that any should call that Blasphemy, which *Carolus Scribanius**, being heated not so much with Poetick rapture, as with Devotion to the Bl. Virgin, sang in her praises, in the words that follow; though they seem indeed to prefer her before our Saviour?

* *In Amphitheatro honoris.*

HÆreo lac inter meditans, interque cruorem,	IN doubtful thought whether to chuse,
Inter delicias uberis & lateris.	The Virgin's Milk, or Saviour's Blood,
Et dico, si fortè oculos super ubera tendo,	Upon the sweets of both I muse, And both do seem delicious food.

N

Diva parens mammæ gaudia
   posco tuæ.
Sed dico, si deinde oculos in
   vulnera verto,
O Jesu lateris Gaudia malo
   tui.
Rem scio, prensabo, si fas erit,
   ubera dextrâ,
Lævâ prensabo vulnera, si
   dabitur.
Lac matris miscere volo cum
   sanguine Nati,
Non possum Antidoto nobili-
   ore frui, &c.

If to her Sacred Breasts I
   guide
Mine Eyes, those sweets I
   longing crave;
But if to Jesus wounded side
I look, those joys I h'd rather
   have.
I'le doubt no more; with my
   right hand
The Virgins breasts I'le gently
   press,
My left (without a counter-
   mand)
To Jesus wounds shall do no
   less.
I'le mix the Mother's Milk
   with the Son's Blood,
No other Antidote is half so
   good.

   There is also another advantage, which they of the Church of *Rome* clearly have of us; that, as they have ordered the matter, their way of Devotion, may be as well exercised, and as comfortably, when a Man is asleep, as when he is awake; nay, what if I say better, and more to a Man's content? For there is a certain scurvy troublesome thing called *Reason*, which is wont uncivilly at other times, to disturb the pleasing Visitations of those *Imaginary and Chimerical Saints*, and to blaspheme the raised and rapturous fancies of the *true ones*: but in Dreams of the Night, when reason is laid asleep, then is the season to entertain sweet communion with them. And now the Soul may take an easie flight, and advance as high as the Mountain, to whose top S. *Katherine* was conveighed by Angels: That grace which before was as hard to be discerned as an invisible Hair, may now as plainly be perceived, as the downy * Beard

   * *I hope the Catholick Reader will pardon me, if I am mistaken in the description of her beard, having never consulted their best Books about her, I mean her Pictures, wherein, possibly, she may be represented with great Whiskers.*

that covered so gracefully the Lip and Chin of S. *Wilgefortis*. And those cross-grain'd and knotty Vices, that had before blunted the edge of all the keenest Sermons of Religion, may in one Night, without feeling any pain at all, be quickly hewen down and destroyed, by the powerful Arm and Axe of the Blessed Carpenter *Joseph*. It was no doubt, at one of these happy seasons of Revelation, "That the Woman that "was defouled in Lechery (to give you the words of the "*Festivale*) after fell into despair, thinking "of *Christ*'s doom, and the horrible pains of "Hell; but she bethought her, how that Children, be they "never so wroth, and shew never so great vengeance, how "lightly they will cease and forgive; wherefore this Wo- "man cryed to *Christ*, praying him for *his Childhood* to "have mercy upon her, and anon she heard a voice on high "in the Aire, which said, Thy Trespass is forgiven Thee. And I would fain known, what Protestant ever had the wit, to make use of so melting a Topick, to move the great God to forgiveness? Alas! how weak and feeble would *our* Moral Arguments be, to prevail with a sinner inflamed with unchast desires, to sleight that temptation, which offers them present satisfaction? but in this Church we hear of a *lascivious Nun*, going upon such an appointed meeting out of her *Convent*, that was stopt at every Door she try'd to go out at, by a *Crucifix* that opposed her passage; who thereupon falling down before the Image of the Bl. Virgin to beg her pardon, the Image struck her a good Box on the Ear, saying; *Whither, fool, would you go? get you into your lodging*: and the effect was quick and powerful; she was preserved from the sin, and never tempted any more: Here is sudden dispatch; One Box o'th' Ear, doing that which a long course of Prayer and Fasting and Mortification, perhaps would scarce have effected. Neither does this compassionate Lady always deal with so much severity, or testifie so much displeasure, as this Example seems to express. Sometimes she has sweetly courted sin-

Festiv. fol. 69.

Cæsarius Dialog. dist. 7. cap. 33. & Gononi Chronicon, p. 14.

ners, and done the fame in a more living way. That Man found it fo, who having very bad inclinations towards his Mafter's Wife; the Bl. Virgin appeared to him, as he was going on Horfeback from a Church, where he had been paying her fome Devotions; fhe laid hold on his Bridle, and afked him, whether he liked her Countenance? he anfwered that he never faw any one fairer: Then replyed fhe, would it fuffice thee, if thou couldeft have me for thy Wife? Any King, quoth he, might be judged happy in fo fair a Confort. The Bl. Virgin made Anfwer; then I will be thy Wife, come near and kifs me: And fhe compelled him, and faid: This is an earneft of our Nuptials, which fhall be confummated fuch a Day in the prefence of my Son: by which expreffion he knew that fhe was the Mother of our Lord; and from that Hour he was perfectly delivered from the aforefaid temptation. Here is a comfortable way, by a chaft Kifs of the Bl. Virgin, to be rid for ever of unchaft thoughts.

Cafar. ibid. cap. 32.

This gives me alfo farther occafion, to congratulate thofe great finners, who finding no comfort in our fullen way, where, after Men have finned, ferious thoughts and hearty forrow, and unfained repentance are indifpenfably required, before we can promife them the forgivenefs of their fins, have fled into the bofome of Holy Church. Thofe Men had a bleffed time of it, you'l fay, who once found it as eafie to be made good, as to drink; as thofe Souldiers did, who upon drinking S. *Bernard's Ale*, which he called the *Potion of Souls*, were immediately converted; fuch powerful Liquor I think the Church does not now pretend to have; but however, if it be now as kind and good natur'd as heretofore, the fame Revelations that have created Saints out of nothing, may alfo bid fair to make fuch finners happy after Death, whofe good actions were next door to nothing while they lived. For are not thefe three (to name no more) comfortable ftories, that heretofore were preached to the People?

Vita S. Bernardi, (inter ejus opera) lib. 1. cap. 11.

"A

Devotions of the Roman Church.

"A Woman of evil living dyed, who had never *Festivals,* "done a good deed in her Life, but only found a *fol. 81.* "Candle to burn before our Lady: when she was "dead, *Fiendes* came to her, and took her Soul; and when "they were going, there came *two* Angels and rebuked the "Fiends, why they were so bold to take the Soul without "doom; then said they, there needeth none, she did never "a good deed. Then said they, take and bring the Soul "before our Lady, and so they did. But when it was found "that she did never a good deed, she must needs go to Hell: "Then said our Lady, she found a Candle brennyng before "me, and was ever her will while she lived, and therefore I "will be kind to her, as she was to me, and bad an Angel "take a great Serge (*Torch*) and light it, and set it before "her in Hell; and our Lady charged and commanded, that "there should no Fiend come there-nye, but let it stand "brennyng for evermore, to comfort all that been in Hell: "Then said the Fiends, they had lever leve the Soul, than "do so: Then bad our Lady take the Soul, and bear it to "the Body again, and so they did: and when she was alive, "she bethought her on her streight doom there as she was, "and went and shrove her to a Priest, and lived long after, "and she amended her life, and was ever after a good Wo-"man, and an holy.

Neither is this second, any whit short of the former, which the same Book gives us. "A wicked *Festiv. fol. 131.* "Emperour dying, a Legion of Fiends went "to fetch his Soul, and coming by a Hermits Cell, made a "great noise; who opening a Window, asked one of them "that came behind, in the name of God, what they were: "He said, Fiends that were sent to the Emperour that was "dead, to look if they might have him for their reward: "Then the Hermit commanded him to come again to him, "to know how he sped; and he did so, and said; his sins "were laid in the Balance, and he was nye overcomen; then "came the brennynge Deken Laurence, and laid a great Pot "in the Balance, and it drew up all together: This Pot was

"a great Chalice, that the Emperour made to worship S.
"Laurence withall. [The *Reader* may see a story just
like this, of one good work of a Priest, laid in the Balance
against a Multitude of his sins, and weighing
them all down, in the Life of S. *Henry* the
Hermit, in *Capgrave*.] Is not that also very comfortable,
which the same pious Book in another place gives us?

Capgr. fol. 78.

"S. *Brandon*, as he sailed on the Sea, saw
"*Judas* sit upon a Stone, and a Cloth hang-
"ing before him that lay in the Water, and often bette him
"in the face, and he asked him in God's Name what he was.
"He answered, I am *Judas*, God's Traytor, that have this
"place of God's great grace and courtesie; for it refresh-
"eth me of the great heat I suffer within me, and for no
"merit that ever I did deserve. Then said S. *Brandon*,
"why hast thou that Stone under thee, and wherefore doth
"that beat thee on the face? Then said he, I laid this Stone
"in an High-way, thereas the common People should go,
"and they were eased thereby, and this is the cause that
"I am eased thereby now: This Cloth was not mine own
"that doth me this refreshing now; but and if it had been
"mine own, it should have refreshed me much the more,
"for I gave it unto a poor Man: Then said *Brandon*, how
"long hast thou this ease and refreshing: Then said he,
"every Saturday from Even-song till Even-song on the Mor-
"row be done, and from *Christmas day* till the *Twelfth day*;
"& from *Easter-day* till *Whit-Sunday*; and on our *Ladies As-
"sumption* and *Candlemass-day*. Then *Brandon* thanked God,
"that he is so merciful and gracious in all things. And is it
not a consideration full of comfort, that the Charity even of
Judas, in giving a poor Man what was not his own, should
meet with such a reward? That his reward would have been
much greater, had it been his own, is an Argument to Men
to be just, as well as charitable; but that he was rewarded
however, seems to me, to be a good gracious encouragement
to filching and stealing, in order to Charity.

Festiva'. fol. 92.

But now, to be just on all sides, I cannot but observe one
thing

thing farther, wherein apparently they have the disadvantage (I do not say of *our Church*, but) of *our Enthusiasts*. For the Devotions and Belief of *our Men* are agreeable, and all of a piece, that is, raised and improved non-sence and folly: But alas! *among them,* the Mantle of those *Elijah's* that made the Lessons on their Saints, never fell into the hands of the Makers of their Prayers, nor any jot of their Spirit seems to be upon them. For it's plain, there can be nothing more luscious food, than what is presented to us in the Legend, but the Prayers that should spiritually improve them, are generally very dull and insipid. For, to instance in S. *Katherine*; was there ever a more dull descant upon such a Subject, as her being carried by Angels to be buried on the top of Mount *Sinai,* than to pray, *that we, by her Merits and Intercession, may come to the Mount, which is Christ?* And could the Romance of S. *Denys,* raise their requests to no higher a strain, than such general desires, *that we may imitate him, by despising prosperity, and not fearing adversity?* Or that, of *Hippolytus* his being drawn to death by wild Horses, than, *that his venerable solemnity may increase both Devotion and Salvation?* If *our* Men had been in their place, and had felt their Devotions flagging and sinking in this manner; we should have heard, to be sure, of *their* keeping Days, to humble themselves for the loss of such *pretious opportunities,* and for not thriving under such *fatning dispensations,* bewailing their unthankfulness for *Katherine mercies,* and *Christopher mercies,* and bemoaning their barrenness under them.

De S. *Thomæ* Archiep. Cantuar.

Of S. *Thomas* A. Bishop of Canterbury.

Antiphona.

Hora sec.
us. Sarum.

TU per *Thomæ* sanguinem quem pro te impendit,
Fac nos Christe scandere quo *Thomas* ascendit.

Vers. Gloria & honore coronasti eum domine.

Resp. Et constituisti enm super opera manuum tuarum.

BY that same blood Thomas *for thee expended,*
Christ *raise us thither, whither he's ascended.*

Vers. *With glory and honour, thou hast crowned him, O Lord.*

Ans. *And hast placed him over the works of thine hand.*

Oremus.

Ibid. & Brev.
Rom. 29 Decem.

DEus, pro cujus Ecclesia gloriosus Martyr & Pontifex *Thomas* gladiis impiorum occubuit, præsta quæsumus, ut omnes qui ejus implorant. auxilium, petitionis suæ salutarem consequantur effectum.

Per Christum, &c.

Let us Pray.

O God, for whose Church the glorious Martyr and Bishop Thomas was slain by the Swords of wicked Men; grant we beseech thee, that all they who implore his help, may obtain the saving effect of their Petitions.

Through Christ, &c.

Brev. Sarum in
Translat. Thomæ
7. Julii.

DEus, qui nobis Translationem B. *Thomæ* Mar-

O God, who givest us leave to celebrate the tyris

tyris tui atque Pontificis celebrare concedis; te supplices exoramus, ut ejus meritis & precibus à vitiis ad virtutes, & à carcere transferamur ad regnum.

Translation of S. Thomas thy Martyr and Bishop, we humbly beseech thee, that by his Merits and Prayers, we may be translated from vice to vertues, & from the Prison to the Kingdom.

Ibid. JEsu Christe per *Thomæ* vulnera
Quæ nos ligant relaxa scelera,
Ne captivos ferant ad infera,
Hostis, mundus, vel carnis opera.
Per te *Thoma*, post lævæ munera
Amplexatur nos Dei dextera.

BY blest S. Thomas *wounds*
O Jesu please,
Sins cruel Chains which bind
us to release;
Lest World, or Flesh, or Devil our sworn Foe,
Hurry our Captive Souls to
Hell below,
Let Gifts of God's left hand,
O Thomas, *grace us*,
And then, by thee, may his
right hand embrace us.

Ibid. NOvis fulget *Tho-*
*Lec.*8. *mas* miraculis,
Membris donat castratos masculis,
Ornat visu privatos oculis,
Mundat lepræ consperos maculis,
Solvit mortis ligatos vinculis.

NEW *Miracles make*
Thomas *shine*,
The Gelt with Members masculine
By him are blest; the blind
with Eyes,
He the foul Lepers purifies,
And the hard Knot of death
unties.

NOTES.

THE *Breviary* of *Sarum*, in the First Lesson on the Translation of *Thomas*, says, "That *Pope Honorius* III. "granted such Indulgences, to those that came Yearly to
" solemnize

"solemnize his Translation, as we never remember any "*Popes* in former times to have afforded. Which seems to me to give great suspicion, that *Thomas* was more the *Pope's* Martyr than *Christ's*: for else, he might have found fitter occasions for these liberal grants, from those many famous Sufferers for *Christ*, who made a more glorious confession of him, than ever *Thomas* did.

But to make the evidence of this undoubted, and to show in this instance, not only the Absurdity, but Impiety of the foregoing Devotions, it will be requisite to give as short an Account of his story as I can; by presenting the Reader (out of their own Authors, especially *Baronius*) with the first occasion of the Quarrel betwixt him and his Prince; to what height the Contest was afterward carried; the many Mediations for agreement, and the cause of their being unsuccessful; and the Conclusion of all in the death of this Prelate, whom (as the Prayer told us) they would make a glorious Martyr. And when all this is done, we shall find, I believe, more of a *Rebel* in him than a *Saint*, and see the most extravagant abuse in the *Pope*, of a pretended power to Canonize, that ever was. For the first:

1. The occasion of the Quarrel.

1. The occasion of the Quarrel between him and *King Henry the Second*; *Neubrigensis*, who lived at this very time, tells us expresly, that the Contest between them arose *Super prærogativa Ordinis Clericalis*, about the Prerogatives of Clergy-men. For the King being busied about the Affairs of the Realm, and commanding Malefactors, without any difference, to be extirpated, it was intimated to him by the Judges, that many Thefts, Rapines, Homicides, against the publick Discipline, were committed by the Clergy, whom the vigour of Common Laws was not permitted to reach. *Baronius* acknowledges, that a Priest that had committed Murder, was thrust into a Monastery, after he was degraded, but *Thomas* would not deliver him to the Secular Courts. But *Neubrigensis* says, that it was declared to the

Neubrig. de reb. Angl. l.2. cap.16.

Baron. Ann. il. ad An.1163. p.482.

the King, that more than a Hundred Murders were committed by the Clergy of *England*. Thus also the rise of the Quarrel is represented by the Bishops and Clergy of the Province of *Canterbury*, in their Letters to the *Pope*. "That the King finding the Peace of his Kingdom much molested, by the outragious excesses of some insolent Clerks, he referred their Crimes to the Bishops, the Judges of the Church, that one Sword might assist another; but the Bishops persisted in this judgment, that Murder, and any other like Crime, should only be punisht in the Clergy by Degradation; the King on the other side being of Opinion, that this punishment did not condignly answer the Offence; neither was it sufficient provision for maintaining Peace, if a *Reader*, or *Acoluthus*, killing a Man famous for Religion or Dignity, should escape only with the loss of his Order. Now I dare appeal to any honest *Turk* or *Heathen*, whether in this first occasion of contending, the King had not apparently more of the zeal of a Saint in him, than the Arch-Bishop. For did ever any Saint before this, put in for an exemption of any Men from Death in the case of Murder? Can there be any pretence that their punishment should be less than that of others, who committing the same enormous Crimes, yet deserve less favour, because they must needs sin with greater malice, and by the example of their Vices do greater mischief? *If I have spoken evil*, says our Saviour himself, *bear witness of the evil*. He was only concerned, that he might not be smitten when he was innocent; but if any plain proof, either of his saying, or doing wickedly, could have been brought against him, no doubt he would have made no exception against any Legal Court that had tryed him, though it had been any other than that of *Caiaphas*. I once read indeed of an Apostle of his that appealed to *Cæsar*, but of none in any case that ever appealed from him. And I dare say, no true Martyr among the Primitive Bishops, would have desired for any Priest under him, that had been

Neubrig. Ibid.

Baron. ad an. 1167. p. 546.

Joh. 18. 23.

clericum, aut bonum Chri-stianum decuit. Stapleton de 3 Thomis. p. 26.

chief of such exemptions, when he expresses himself thus. "The Bi-
"shops whilst they are watchful ra-
"ther to defend the Liberties and Dignities of the Clergy,
"than to correct and cut off their Vices, think they do God
"and the Church good service, when they defend the wick-
"ed Clergy against the publick Discipline, whom accord-

Neubrig. loc. citat.
"ing to the Duty of their Office, they have
"either no mind or neglect to restrain with
"the vigour of Canonical censure; whence it comes to
"pass, that Clergy-men, who being called into the Lord's
"Lot, ought in Life and Doctrine to shine upon Earth, as
"Stars placed in the Firmament of Heaven, taking Licence
"and Liberty, through impunity, to do whatsoever they
"please, reverence neither God, whose Judgment seems to
"linger, nor Men that are in Authority; when the Episco-
"pal care about them languishes, and the Prerogative of
"their Holy Order shall exempt them from Secular Ju-
"risdiction.

2. To what height the Quarrel was carried.

2. Proceed we to show, to what height the Contest was carried, after this beginning. The King being vexed at these
Reports, demands of the Arch-Bishop, that such of the

Baron. Ibid. p. 482.
wicked Clergy, after the inflicting Canonical
Penance, might be delivered to the Secular
Court; which he refused to grant: where-
upon the King, being very angry, asked him, and the rest of
the Prelates, whether they would observe his Regal Customes, observed by Arch-Bishops and Bishops, private and
priviledged Persons, in his Grand-father's time: to which
Thomas answered, that he would, *Salvo ordine suo*, saving
his Order; only *Hilary* Bishop of *Chichester* said, he would
observe

observe them, *bona fide*, without that reservation. The King told *Thomas* that his Answer was captious, and required him to promise absolutely without any addition, which he refused. The *Pope*, being advertized of all these proceedings by *Thomas*, wrote Letters to the Bishops, that by vertue of their Canonical obedience to the See of *Rome*, they should not attempt any thing against the Ecclesiastical Liberty, nor engage themselves in any Promise or Oath, save that which Bishops use to make to their Kings; and that if they had promised any thing of that kind to him, they should not observe but revoke it, and reconcile themselves to God and the Church.

After this was a Meeting at *Clarendon* of the King, Bishops, and Lords of the Realm, where the Ancient Customes were produced, and *Thomas* having made a promise at *Oxford*, to change the words that offended the King, was then challenged with his promise, which at first he refused to perform; but after by the vehement urging of some Bishops and Nobles, that he would not too stifly oppose the King, declaring the danger of it, he was perswaded to give his consent, *Bona fide*, to observe the Regal Customes, and swore to it as the rest did; but yet refused to set his Seal to it. This Oath very much troubled him after the taking of it, being sensible how the Ecclesiastical Liberties were invaded by it, and he resolves, as his Penance, to desist from the Exercise of his Priestly Office. But the *Pope* quickly absolves him from his Oath, requiring Him not to forbear Celebrating Mass upon this account. *Baron. ad an. 1164.*

But the King, upon his Refusal to Seal the Writing, was more incensed, sought by his Messengers to the *Pope* to hinder him from being his Legat, which usually was bestowed upon the *Arch-Bishop* of *Canterbury*, and to confer it on the *Arch-Bishop* of *York*, and to perswade the *Pope* to confirm the Customes of *Clarendon*. The *Pope* grants his request as to the *Arch-Bishop* of *York*, but refuses to confirm the other: and writes to *Thomas* to behave *Bar. Ib. p. 488.*

have himself prudently, and discreetly, and yieldingly to the King, and to do all to sweeten him, and regain his favour, that was consistent with the honesty of his Ecclesiastical Order. But the next news we hear of him is, *pag.* 490. that he is endeavouring to fly into *France* without his leave, though driven back at Sea by cross Winds. He is summoned to a *Parliament* at *Northampton*, by the King: There in the Morning before the Meeting, he caused the Mass to begin with the words proper to S. *Steven's* Day, (though it was not his day) *Princes sate, and spake against me, &c.* [a good beginning to sweeten the King] When he was called to give his answer to the charges against him, he declined the judgment of the Court, appealed to the *Pope*, and so departed; who as he withdrew, was followed with the cries of those that called him *Traytor*. The Bishop of *Chichester* told him plainly, *You were sometimes our Arch-Bishop, whom we were bound to obey; but, because you have sworn Fidelity to our Lord the King, and to keep the Customes which he requires, and you endeavour to destroy them, though tending to his Worldly Dignity and Honour; we therefore pronounce you guilty of Perjury, and we are not bound any longer to obey a Perjured Arch-Bishop.*

Thomas, after this, presently hies over into *Flanders*, and the King seizes on his Revenues, and made severe Laws against all Persons that should hold any correspondence with him, or receive any Letters of Interdict from him; all which the *Pope* by his contrary Letters did abrogate: As he did also most of those Customes established at *Clarendon*, which when *Thomas* appeared at *Rome*, were produced and read before the *Pope* in the Consistory: They *p.* 499. were 16. in Number, some of which he tolerated, but said none of them were good: those which he condemned, were these that follow; (which I think no body besides the *Pope* can find fault with: but no wonder that he did, when they plainly checkt his growing Usurpations over the Rights of our Princes.)

1. Contro-

1. Controversies concerning the advowson and presentation of Churches, shall be heard and determined in the *King*'s Court.

2. Clerks cited and accused upon any Cause, being summoned to the King's Court, shall appear and answer before the said Court; so as the *Kings Bench* shall send into the Court of H. Church, to see upon what ground the cause shall be there handled, and if the Clerk be convicted, or do confess, the Church ought not any longer to defend him.

3. Arch-Bishops, Bishops, and other Persons of the Kingdome, shall not depart the Realm without the King's leave; and if they will depart, they shall give security, if the King demands it, that neither in their going, staying, or coming back, they will seek the hurt or Damage of the King or his Kingdomes.

4. No Man that holds of the King *in capite*, nor any of his Houshold-servants shall be excommunicated, or their Lands interdicted, unless the King or his Chief Justice be made acquainted with it, that he may determine right concerning him; whereby such things as belong to the *King*'s Court, may there be determined; and what belongs to the Ecclesiastical Court, may be returned thither, and there ended.

5. Touching Appeals, Men ought to proceed from the Arch-Deacon to the Bishop, from the Bishop to the Arch-Bishop, and from him, if he fail to execute Justice, to the King in the last place, that by his commandment the Controversie may be determined in the Arch-Bishops Court; so as they shall not proceed any farther, without the *King*'s assent.

6. Any Person of City, Castle, Burrough, or the King's Demesne Mannor, being cited by the Arch-Deacon or Bishop for any crime wherein he is bound to answer him, and will not satisfie him upon the citations, it shall be lawful to subject him to interdiction, but not to excommunicate him, before the King's Chief Officer of the Place be acquainted with it, that he may adjudge the Offender to make satisfaction,

ction, wherein if the *King*'s Officer be defaulty, he shall fall into the *King*'s mercy, and then the Bishop may after punish the accused with Ecclesiastical censures.

7. When an Arch-Bishoprick, Bishoprick, Abbacy, or Priory of the King's Dominions shall fall void, it ought to be in his Majesties hand, and he shall receive all those Rents and Revenues, as those of his own Royal Demeans; and when the time cometh to take care to fill the Church, the King ought to Summon the Chief Persons of the Church, and the Election ought to be made in his Chappel by his Royal assent, and by the Counsel of such Persons belonging to His Majesty, whom he shall call about that affair; and there the Person Elected, shall do his homage and fealty to our Lord the King, as his Liege Lord, of Life member and earthly honor, saving his Order, before he be consecrated.

8. Pleas about Debts, which are grounded upon Oath, as well as those which are without Oath, shall be handled in the *King*'s Court.

These are the most material Articles he condemned, to omit the rest.

The next Day *Thomas* resigned up his Arch-Bishoprick to the *Pope*, acknowledging his entrance into it not to have been Canonical, but by intrusion, and the *Pope* restored him again to it.

Ibid. pag. 502. The King also publishes new Constitutions in *Normandy*, the summ of them was: To punish them as Traytors, who carried into *England* the *Pope*'s or the Arch-Bishop's *Mandate*, containing the *Interdict of Christianity*. To imprison those Clerks that passed the Seas, or returned into *England* without the *King*'s, or his Justices Letters. That none should appeal to the *Pope*, or Arch-Bishop. That no Plea be held by their command, nor their *Mandates* be received in *England*, nor any *Mandate* of Clerk or Layman be carried to them, upon pain of Imprisonment. That if any defended their Sentences of Interdiction, they and their whole Kindred should be banished, and their Chattels confiscated. That Clerks that had Rents

in

in *England*, and did not return into *England* to their Rents within three Moneths time, their Rents should be seized into the King's hand. That *Peter's Pence* should not be paid to the See of *Rome*, but be gathered and disbursed at the King's commandment, &c.

Thus we see matters carried very high, but the heats were still increased, when the *Pope*, the better to raise *Thomas* above his adversaries, and humble them, made him *Legat* over all *England*, excepting only the Province of *York*, and required by his *Mandate* delivered to the Bishop of *London*, that those who had received by the *King*'s Commandment the Revenues of the Church of *Canterbury*, should within 2 Moneths make restitution, or be anathematized; and that *Peter's Pence* should be gathered, and delivered to such as he should appoint.

Baron. ad an. 1167. p. 536, &c.

And here it may not be amiss, before I proceed farther, to observe, how much Pride and strange Insolence *Thomas* expressed in this quarrel; (much of which was the effect of his own temper, but more increased by the *Popes* forward backing of him, and animating him against his Prince) which appears by his own Letters, and the account others give of him.

In his Letter to the King, he speaks with such sawciness, as is unbecoming a *Subject*, and such silly reasoning, as is unworthy a *Divine*:

Baron. ad an. 1166. p. 524.

" Expecting I have expected, that the Lord would look up-
" on you, and that being converted, you would do Penance,
" departing from your perverse ways (a humble style for a
" subject)—— Bishops, whatsoever they are, though as Men
" they do amiss, yet if they fall not from the Faith, they nei-
" ther can, nor ought to be censured by the secular power.
" ————Who maketh question, but that Christ's Priests are
" the Masters and Fathers of Kings and Princes, and all the
" faithful; that it is a point of madness for a Son, or Scho-
" lar to endeavour to subject his Father or Master to him,
" and with unjust obligations to reduce him under his rule,
" by

" by whom he ought to believe that he may be bound and
" loosed (*), not only on Earth, but in Heaven also: (*a learned argument! as if Alexander had nothing to do to order Aristotle, if he had been a Traytor, because he was his Master*) —— " Yield therefore speedily with all humility,
" and all manner of satisfaction. It is written (**) that
" none ought to judge the Priests but the Church, nor doth
" it belong to Temporal Laws to sentence them. Christian
" Princes were wont to obey the Orders of the Church,
" not to advance their power before them, to humble their
" Heads to the Bishops, not to judge them, &c.

(*) These are the words of Pope *Greg*.VII. a great Oracle no doubt with *Thomas*, which are cited, Decret. distinc. 96. c. 9. *Quis dubitet*. and just such a doughty argument, of another *Pope* you find in the same Distinc. c. 7. *Satis evidenter ostenditur à seculari potestate nec ligari prorsus nec solvi posse pontificem, quem constat à pio principe Constantino Deum appellatum, nec posse Deum ab hominibus judicari manifestum est*: which words, if he spake any such (as may well be doubted, since *Eusebius* says nothing of it, who was present in that Council where they are pretended to be spoken) are falsly attributed to the *Pope*, since the Gloss confesses that he spoke them to all the Clergy, *Omnes clericos deos appellasse*, and adds, *Secundum hanc rationem nec ab Episcopo possent judicari Clerici*.

(**) A fine Saint this is, who quotes the words of Pope *Gelasius*, (Decret. distinc. 96. c. 12.) as if they were Scripture; he may deserve to be called the *Pope's* Martyr, whose sayings are as sacred with him as the *Bible*.

*Ibid.p.*537. And in his Letters to the Bishops of his Province, he begins thus. " Most Beloved Bre-
" thren, Why rise ye not with me against the Malignants?
" Why stand ye not with me against the Workers of Ini-
" quity? —— *He tells them*, that he had enough, and too
" much forborn the King of *England*; —— That having
" indeavoured to recall him from his perverse purpose, it
" was now dangerous and intolerable to leave his, and his
" Officers great excesses against the Church of God and Ec-
" clesiastical Persons (*a*) unpunished; after Invocation

(*a*) In a Letter to the Bishop of *Hereford*, he had the insolence to say, *That Christ was again judged before the Tribunal of a Prince*: reflecting upon the charges laid against him; *Baron.Ibid. p.*509.

" therefore

Devotions of the Roman Church. 195

"therefore of the Holy Ghost, he condemns and declares
"void the Customes of *Clarendon*, and excommunicates all
"Observers, Counsellors, Assistants, and Defenders of the
"same, and absolves the Bishops from the promise they had
"made to observe them, and excommunicates several Per-
"sons by name, and writes Letters to the *Pope*, to certifie
"him what he had done, wherein he complains of the King,
"that he grew worse and worse, and threatens that he would
"shortly pronounce against him the sentence of excommu-
"nication; *telling the Pope*, We have not yet pronounced
"our sentence against the King's Person, but are likely to
"do it, unless he repent, and by what we have done embra-
"ceth Discipline.

In his Letters to *William* Cardinal of *Papia*, (who with *Oddo* were sent as *Legats* to compose matters) he tells him, "That all Mens *Baron. ad an. 1168. p. 562.*
"eyes were upon them, expecting the conclusion of this ne-
"gotiation, according to which, *the insolency of Princes will
"exalt its horns, or (as it deserves) be suppressed*, and would
"to God, by your coming, it may rather sustain *loss* than re-
"cover *strength*.

In another to the *Pope*, he complains of the *Bishops*, that they gave Horns to the *sin- Ibid. pag. 572.* ner, meaning the *King*.

All which expressions do tell us, that *Thomas* was a Man after the *Pope's* own heart, the fittest Instrument he could ever meet with by his pride and stubbornness, to carry on his design of bringing the power of the *Empire*, and the Kingdomes about him under the slavery of the *Papacy*. And therefore we need not marvel, that when upon his resignation of his Arch-Bishoprick to the *Pope*, some of the Cardinals were of opinion, that by the Election of another Bishop the King might be appeased, and *Tho- Baron. ad an. 1664.* mas otherwise provided for; the *Pope* rather *pag. 501.* chose to follow *their* Counsels, who told him, that if *Thomas* his cause were maintained, he would be a pattern to others in like case for *resisting Princes* (a fine design for *the pretended Vicar of Christ to drive on*) but if he were suffered to fall, all other Bishops would fall after him, and none for the future dare to *resist the power of wilful Princes*, whereby the state of the Catholick Church would stagger, and *the Pope's Authority perish*.

And now he having given us such an abundant discovery of his own temper, we may the better credit the reports of others concerning him, which I shall now produce.

The Bishops that came on an Embassy to *Rome*, accuse *Thomas* before the *Pope* of immoderation and imprudence, and adhering too much to his own Counsels, his disturbing the Tranquillity of the Church, and devotion towards the King.

<sub>Baron.
Ibid.p.498.</sub>

The Bishops and Clergy of his own Province in their Letters, both to him and the *Pope*, make the like complaints. In those to him they tell him, That they had great hopes, when they heard that he gave himself to Reading, Prayers and Fasting, &c. That things would tend to a peaceable reconciliation; but their hopes were dashed, when they heard he had sent a commination, wherein, passing by all salutation, he rigorously menaced Interdiction or Excommunication to be pronounced against him.——"*They desire him*, that setting threatnings "aside, he would imbrace patience and humility, that he "would commend his cause to the Divine clemency, and "himself to the grace and mercy of his Soveraign. *They put* "*him in mind* of the favours the King had conferred on him; "the troubles the Church now groaned under; the possibi- "lity, that by his bitter provocations the King might revolt "from the *Pope*; *They tell him*, they will not say, the King "has never offended, but confidently pronounce that he is "ready to give satisfaction to his Holiness. In their Letters to the *Pope*, they excuse the King, that not out of any Ambitious ends, or designs to oppress the Churches Liberties, but for making a firm peace, he had searched and produced the Cu- stomes and Dignities of his Kingdom, "which had been "anciently

Ibid.p.541.

Ibid.p.547.

Devotions of the Roman Church. 197

"anciently obferved, and quietly fubmitted to, by Perfons
"Ecclefiaftical in the Reigns of former Kings.——If there
"were any thing contained in them dangerous to his Soul,
"or ignominious to the Church, he has facredly promifed
"to Reform the fame by the Advice and Counfel of the
"Church of his Kingdome. That thefe Contentions had
"been long fince quieted, had it not been for the bitter pro-
"vocations of the Arch-Bifhop, who had threatned the King
"with terrible Letters, unbecoming the Devotion of a Fa-
"ther, and not favouring at all of the meeknefs of a Bifhop;
"who had excommunicated fome of his *Majefties* Liege-
"men and Intimates, the Chief Peers of the Realm, by whom
"the Counfels and Affairs of the Kingdome were managed,
"and this without citing them, or hearing their Defence;
"they inftance in the Bifhop of *Salisbury*, whom abfent and
"unconvicted, he had fufpended from his Office, which
"they call a prepofterous and diforderly way of proceed-
"ing, &c.

3. Let us now fee the 3d. thing I mentioned, *viz.* The many Medi-ations for agreement, and the caufe why they were unfuccefsful. *Mediations for agreement, and what made them unfuccefsful.*

In the Year 1165. there went feveral Meffen-gers betwixt the *King* and the *Pope*, and they had agreed a Meeting, but *Thomas* perfwaded the *Pope* not to do it, unlefs he were prefent, infinuating to the *Pope* the *King*'s cunning and fubtilty, which he was beft acquain-ted with; but the King (knowing the fury of his Spirit) would not confent to a Parlee in his prefence, and fo the ap-pointment came to nothing. *Baron. ad an. 1165.*

I mentioned before *two* Cardinals, *William* and *Oddo*, who were fent by the *Pope* to compofe matters betwixt the *King* and Arch-Bifhop. It may be worth the while to take notice of the report they made to the *Pope*, after they had examined matters. They tell him, that they found the Controverfie betwixt the *King* and *Thomas* aggravated to a greater height *Baron. ad an. 1168.* *Ibid. p. 568.*

O 5   than

than they could have wished. That the *King*, and better part of his Followers affirmed, they had evident demonstrations, that *Thomas* had incensed the King of *France* against him, and induced his Cosin, the *Earl of Flanders*, to fall out with him, and raise the most powerful War he could against him. That the King offered, that if any Customes were added in his time, contrary to the Ecclesiastical Laws, he would submit them to his Holiness, at his pleasure to be cancelled.

That they had appointed a Conference, and he somewhile put it off, and at last would meet in no place, but where himself appointed. That when he came at last to a Conference, and they exhorted him to behave himself humbly to the *King*, who had been his singular Benefactor, he answered, that he had sufficiently humbled himself to the *King*, saving his honour to God, the Liberty of the Church, the reputation of his own Person, the possessions of the Churches, and saving the justice due to him and his.——— We demanded whether he would submit himself to our judgment, as the *King* and Bishops had before promised *they* would do; to which he replyed, that he had received no command from you to that purpose, but if *he* and *his* might first be restored, he would then proceed herein, according as he should be commanded by the Apostolick Sea; and so (say they) the Conference ended, since his words neither tended *to judgment nor agreement*, neither would he by any means enter into the matter; and we by your Authority absolutely forbad the Arch-Bishop (in regard he was restrained by your Letters; and because they solemnly appealed) that he should not attempt any thing to the grievance of the Kingdome, Persons or Churches of the Realm.

But we have a far better account from *Oddo*, concerning the *King*, of his inclinations to peace, and condescentions in order to it. For when this Cardinal before he departed, seriously dealt with the *King*, that he would be reconciled to the Arch-Bishop; The *King* answered him, That for the love he bore to the *Pope* and Cardi-

Ibid. pag. 579.

Devotions of the Roman Church.   199

Cardinals, he would permit the Arch-Bishop to return to his See in peace, and dispose of his Church, and what belonged to it : and because there had been long contests about the Customes, he said that he and his Children would be contented with those, which it should be made apparent his Ancestors enjoyed, by the Oaths of 100 *English*-men, a 100 *Normans*, and 100 Persons of *Anjou*, and other Places belonging to him : That if this condition displeased the Arch-Bishop, he said he was ready to stand to the Arbitration both of the Bishops of *England*, and those Beyond-Sea, *viz.* of *Roan, Bayon,* and *Cenoman.* And if this did not suffice, he would submit to the judgment of the *Pope*, with this reservation, that he would not impeach his Childrens right, for during his own life he was contented, the *Pope* should abrogate what he pleased. That he being farther asked what restitution he would make to the Arch-Bishop and his Adherents, which was due and required of him ; his answer was (swearing with many and exquisite Oaths) that what he had received, he had bestowed it onely on the Churches, and the Poor.

The same Year the King of *France* interposed as a Mediator, and procures a conference betwixt the *King* and *Thomas* in his Presence. Where *Thomas* fell down at the *King*'s Feet, saying, I commit the whole cause, whence the difference has risen between us, to your discretion, *saving the honour of God :* Which last words the King was offended with, and said to the King of *France,* "Mark, my Lord, this Man, whatsoever shall dis-
"please him, he will say it is contrary to the honor of God,
"whereby he will challenge not only his own, but what be-
"longs to me ; but that it may appear that I oppose neither
"God's honour, nor his, I make this offer. There have
"been many Kings of *England* before me, of greater or
"lesser Authority than my self ; and there have been before
"him, many great and holy men Arch-Bishops of *Canter-*
"*bury* ; whatsoever the more eminent and vertuous of his
"Predecessors, have done to the least of my Predecessors,

Ibid. pag. 585.

let him do to me, and I shall rest satisfied. Whereupon followed an acclamation on all sides; The *King* has sufficiently humbled himself. The King of *France* added; My Lord Arch-Bishop, will you be greater than holy men, Will you be better than *Peter*? What Question make you? (for he remained a while silent) Lo peace is even at the Door. The *Peers* of both Kingdomes were so little satisfied with the return he made, that they were all against him; and imputed the want of peace to his arrogance; one *Earl* openly protesting, that since the Arch-Bishop resisted the Counsel and determination of both Kingdomes, he was not worthy hereafter of the assistance of either; so both Kings took Horse without saluting the Arch-Bishop; and the Courtiers that were Mediators for peace, at their departure charged him to his face, that he was ever proud, high-minded, wise in his own eyes, a follower of his own will and opinion; adding, that it was a great mischief & damage to the *Church*, that he was ever made a Governor of it.

Biron. al an. 1169.
The next Year the *Pope* sent *two* other *Nuncio's*, *Gratian* and *Vivian*, upon the same pretences of making peace and agreement. (That is, to try again whether the King would be brought to condescend to part with his ancient Rights, for if you observe it, there is no dispute all along whether they had been his Rights or no, but the *Pope* and *Thomas* would either perswade or threaten him out of them, and on their part offer nothing at all towards peace upon any other termes.) These *two* had an ample Commission to exercise Ecclesiastical severity on the *King* himself, or *Kingdome*, or any part of the Realm, as should be expedient for the Church. They had a conference with the *King*, from which he went very angry, grievously complaining of the *Pope*, that he would not yield to him in any thing, and swore that he would take another course. To whom *Gratian* replied; *Threaten not, my Lord, for we fear no threats, for we belong to such a Court, which hath been accustomed to rule over Emperours and Kings.* Many Conferences they had, but all came to nothing,

p.591.

nothing, for the *Nuncio's* would not admit this clause, (which he would have inserted in the agreement) *saving the dignity of his Kingdome*; and the King would not agree without it. And now the *Pope* begins to thunder and lighten. For this Year he denounces the Sentence of p. 598. Excommunication against all such as received *Investitures*, or any *Ecclesiastical Benefices* from the hands of Laymen, unless within 40 Days they resigned such Benefices and the Profits of them, into their hands to whom they did appertain: And by *two* other Nuncio's, *Simon* Prior of *Gods-Mount*, and *Bernard de Corilo*, he sends his Comminatory Letters, telling him that he resolves no longer to tolerate the hardness of his heart against justice, and the *Pope's* safety, nor to shut up any longer the mouth of the *A. Bishop*, but freely permit him to execute his Office, and with the Sword of Ecclesiastical Severity, to revenge the injuries offered himself and his Church. This Embassy came also to nothing, because *Thomas* still used the old reservations of *The Honour of God*, and *Saving his Order*, and the *King* stood upon it, to have him observe, what his Predecessors had paid to former *Kings*.

The next Year was the last of the *Pope's* Treating about *Thomas* with the *King*; if I may call it *Treating*, and not rather *sending commands* to him, Biron. ad an. by the Arch-Bishop of *Roan*, the Bishop of 1170. p. 606. *Nivers*, and the Bishop of *Senon*, his three *Legats*. The demands they were to make were such as these. That *Thomas* should return to his Church, and receive back all the Possessions taken away from it; that those that had been exiled for his sake, should be restored to their own; that the *King* should grant *Thomas* a full peace in a holy Kiss; and should abolish the wicked Customes, contrary to the Churches Liberty, &c. which things were to be performed in *Forty* Days time, and if within that time matters were not agreed, they should presently interdict the Province on this side the Seas, where the *King* then remained.

But while these things were transacting, another angry
difference

difference arofe. For the *King* declaring that he would have his *Son* crowned in his life-time, and that it fhould be performed in *Thomas* his abfence by the *Arch-Bifhop* of *York*; the *Pope* fent Letters to that *Arch-Bifhop*, and to the reft of the *Bifhops*, requiring them, upon the peril of lofing their Office and Order, not to Crown or Anoint him, while *Thomas* was in Exile; becaufe that Office only belonged to the *See* of *Canterbury*. *Thomas* alfo writ over his Letters forbidding the fame. Upon which the King was fo moved, that he caufed the Bifhops to take an Oath, not to obey the Conftitutions of the *Pope* and *Arch-Bifhop*, forbidding the fame. Thus the young *King* was crowned by the *Arch-Bifhop* of *York*, other Bifhops affifting him; and prefently after, the faid *Arch-Bifhop* and the reft, were by the *Pope* fufpended from the execution of their Epifcopal Function; and the *Pope* fent threatning Letters to the *King* to tell him, that if the Peace betwixt him and *Thomas* was not concluded in the prefixed time, he muft then expect the fame fentence, which he had pronounced againft *Frederick* the *Emperour*: which fo ftartled him, that he promifed his *Legate* to perform what the *Pope* commanded. But before the *Treaty* began with the *Legats*, *Thomas* rarely prepared them how to proceed with the *King*. He tells them, "that they could not eafily difcover the manifold deceipts of that pro-"digy, and therefore whatfoever the *King* fays, "whatfoever fhape he puts on, they ought to fufpect all as "full of deceipt, unlefs approved by his deeds: for if he "perceive that he can corrupt you with promifes, or terri-"fie you with threats, he will fcorn and contemn you; but "if he fee that he cannot bend you from your purpofe, he "will counterfeit fury; firft he will fwear, then forfwear, "and change fhapes as *Proteus* did, and at laft come to him-"felf; and then unlefs it be your fault, thenceforward you "fhall always be a *God to Pharaoh*.

Baron.ibid. p. 614.

Baron.ib. p. 615.

And now the Conference begins with the *Legats*, who brought *Thomas* along with them; and after many debates, the

the *King* with a pleasing Countenance granted *Thomas* his peace, patiently heard his reproofs, not insisting upon the *Customes*. And *Thomas* himself says, that when he alighted from his Horse to humble himself at the *King*'s feet, he catching the Stirrup (*) of *Thomas* his Horse, inforced him to get up again. He also wrote into *England* to the young *King* concerning the peace, and required him to restore *Thomas*, and those that belonged to him to all their Possessions.

(*) *Matth. Paris* says, the *King* held his Bridle twice: *Cum autem Rex & Archiepiscopus in partem secessissent, bisque descendissent & bis equos ascendissent, bis habenam Archiepiscopi Rex tenuit, quum equum ascendisset.* ad an. 1170. p.g. 122.

And now before I come to the last particular, concerning the *Death of Thomas*, I shall a little stop the *Reader* so long, till I make a short reflexion upon the *Insolency* of this *pretended Head* of the Church; so I may well call this *Pope*, because such a power over Kings and Emperours as he challenged and exercised, was in it self plainly an Usurpation, having not the least countenance from Christ's example (*whose Vicar he pretends to be*) who always refused worldly *Rule* when it was offered him, but never once resisted the *Rulers* of the World; nor from any grant of his to S. *Peter*, or any of his *Successors*, establishing any *Temporal Monarchy* in the Church. But besides this, I add farther, that this *Rowland* (call'd *Alexander* III.) who was the abetter of *Thomas* in resisting his lawful Soveraign, was himself an *Usurper* of the Popedome, and that *Octavian* (call'd *Victor*) was the right Pope. For it was decreed by the *Roman Council* under *Adrian* I. *An. Do.* 774. that *Charles* should have power to choose the Pope, and order the *Apostolick See*, and that Arch-Bishops and Bishops should receive investiture from him. Which thing was also, after *Adrian*'s example, afterwards confirmed to the Emperour *Otho*, and to his Suc-

A short account of the Progress of the Pope's power.

Decret. part. 1. distinc. 63. cap. Hadrianus.

Decret. Ibid. ca. 23. in Synodo.

cessors

cessors for ever, in another *Roman Synod* by Pope *Leo* VIII. Now according to this Rule of their own Canon Law, the *Emperour*, together with a *Council* held at *Papia* (*an.*1160) did declare *Victor* to be *Pope*, against *Alexander*, who pretended to it. Yet this *Intruder* is he, who claims a Jurisdiction over our King, and exempts the Clergy from his known Laws and Customes of his Realm,

Baron. ad an. 1160.

and whose *Legat* (as you heard) told him, that they belonged to such a Court, as was accustomed to rule over Emperours and Kings. But a *Legat* of his Predecessor, (if it was not *Rowland* himself, for he was one of the *Legates*) had like to have lost his Life for asking this saucy Question, *From whom had Frederick the Empire, if not from our Lord the Pope?* For *Count Otto* had dispatcht him with his Sword for this insolence,

Baron. Annal. ad an. 1157.

if the *Emperour* had not interposed; and when the *Pope* himself had told him of the benefits bestowed on him, having conferred on him the *fulness of Dignity and Honour, and the Imperial Crown*; *Frederick* in his Letters answers, that the *Empire* was his from *God alone*, by the Election of *Princes*, and it was a lye, to say that his Crown was a *Benefit* or *Donation* from the *Pope*. The *Pope*'s return was very sneaking, and not like one *accustomed to rule over Emperours*, for he tells him, that by

Baron. ad an. 1158. *p.*408.

Beneficium, he meant not *feudum* but *bonum factum,* and that the word *contulimus* (which he had used concerning his Crown) signified no more than *imposuimus*; plainly granting that he could not challenge the right of making him *Emperour*, nor that he held the *Empire* in *Fee* of him: When the same *Pope* also a while after, quarrelled with him, for not giving due reverence to S. *Peter*,

Baron. ad an. 1159. *p.* 412.

and the holy Church of *Rome*, because, forsooth, the *Emperour* in his Letters had set his own Name before the *Pope*'s, which he interpreted as a piece of insolence, if not arrogance: The *Emperour* defends himself, and asks him, "Whether Pope *Silvester* in *Constan-*
"*tine*'s time, was noted for having any *Regalities*?" Indeed,
"says

"says he, by his pious grants, Liberty and Peace was resto-
"red to the Church : but whatsoever your Papacy has, it
"obtained it by the *Donation of Princes*. And indeed we
may know by the Language of the *Popes* of old, that the
Emperours, not *they*, were the Rulers. *If your piety will
vouchsafe to yield to our suggestion and supplication*, was the
style of Pope *Leo* I. to *Theodosius*. Nei-
ther did *Gregory* the *Great* hector *Mau-*   *Leo* I. *Epist. 9. inter
ritius*, though he had made a Law which   *Labbei Concil.Tom.3.
he did not like, (against receiving Soul-   p.1304. an.do.449.*
diers into Monasteries, till they were dis-   *Gregor. 1. Epist. 62.
charged from the Wars) and command-   Lib.2. in Tom.5. Con-
ed the *Pope* to publish it; his Letter runs   cil. Labbe. p.1133.*
thus. *As for me who speak these things to my Lords,
what am I but dust and a worm* —— *He is guilty before Almighty God, who is not pure in all that he says or does to the
Most Serene Lords*, (*i.e.* the Emperours) he calls himself,
the unworthy Servant of his Piety; after this, he tells him
that he did not look upon this Law as agreeable to the will
of Almighty God, yet, says he, *I being subject to command,
have conveyed it through several parts of the Earth; both
ways therefore I have done my duty, having both yielded obedience to the Emperour, and also on Gods behalf I have declared my opinion.* The style of Pope *Adrian* I. also is far
from commanding, when in his Letters
to *Constantine* and *Irene*, he pleads for   *Epistola inserta Concil.
the restoring of Images. I offer to   Nicen 2. Act.2. vid.Con-
Your Serene Majesties the Testimonies   cil.Labbe. Tom.7. p.115.*
of the Scriptures and Fathers with all humility. *Beseeching
your clemency with a great fervour of mind, as present upon
my bended Knees, and rolling my self at your
footsteps, I intreat you*, &c. [Whence, by   Τοῖς ἡμετέροις
the way, I suppose we may safely conclude   ἴχνεσι κυλινδό-
that the Ceremony of kissing the *Pope*'s feet   μενΘ ἱκετεύω.
by Kings and Emperours, was not yet come into fashion; a
practice derived from that Monster of Men *Caligula*, who,
as *Seneca* tells us, when he gave *Pompeius Pennus* his Life,
stretched

stretched out to him his left foot to kiss; against which *that Philosopher* so severely declames, for changing thus the manners of a free City, into a *Persian* slavery. But our *Thomas* his Master, *Alexander* III. was not at all shy to receive the honour, nor afraid of the Blasphemy that once attended it: For *Baronius* relates, that when he came to *Mompelier*, a *Prince* of the *Saracens* coming before him, kissed his feet; and kneeling down and bowing his head, adored the *Pope*, as the *Holy and Pious God of the Christians*; they that stood by and saw this, wondered greatly, and they repeated among themselves that of the Prophet, *All the Kings of the Earth shall worship him, and all Nations shall serve him*.] My last instance shall be in Pope *Agatho*, who being required by the *Emperour* to send *three* choice Persons to the *Synod* of *Constantinople* : The Pope answers thus, *According to the most pious Command of your* * *Mansuetude to be protected of God, according to the obedience we owe, with humble devotion of heart, we have taken care, &c.* Afterwards in the same Epistle, *This, your* * *Imperial benignity has exhorted me to by your mild command, and our smalness has obediently fulfilled your command.* Alas poor Men! they little dream'd, while they spoke thus humbly, of any such Superiority over the Monarchs of the Earth, as their Successors have since claimed; they talk'd, as if they *borrowed* all their power; and therefore often desire *Emperours* to command a Council to be called in such a place, or to do such kindnesses for them : this lowly courting of their favour plainly argues, that if the comparison of the *two Luminaries*

Senec. de benefic. l. 2. c. 12. Invenit aliquid infra genua quo libertatem detruderet, non bene est civitatem calcare?

Baron. ad an. 1162. p. 465.

Concil. Constantinop. 3. Act. 4. Epist. 1. Concil. Labbe. Tom. 6. p. 634, 635.

* *A deo protegenda mansuetudinis vestra.*

* The Latine I am forced to put in the Margin, that every one may translate it better for himself. *Hoc Imperialis vestra benignitas, clementer jubens hortata est, & nostra pusillitas quod jussum est obsequenter implevit.*

Luminaries had been made in their days, they could have been contented with the place of the Moon in the Firmament, and not with *Innocent* the III.(*), have asserted themselves to be the Greater Light of the two. How undeservedly alas! did *Gregory* and *Leo* (the first of each Name) bear the Title of *Great*: Let it rather be given to our *Alexander*; who bravely trod upon the Neck of *Frederick* at *Venice* (whatsoever *Baronius* pleads to the contrary*, when so many good Authors attest it) adding those words of the Psalm, *Super aspidem & basiliscum, &c. Thou shalt tread upon the Lion and Adder, the young Lion and the Dragon shalt thou trample under Feet*: Give it to *Cœlestine* I. who sitting in his Pontifical Chair, and holding the Imperial Crown between his Feet, the Emperour bending down his Head, received the Crown from the Feet of this Pope; who immediately kicked it off with his Foot, and cast it to the ground; hereby giving him to understand, (as *Baronius* adds) that the Pope could at his pleasure give, keep, preserve, or take away the Empire, if he saw cause: and if the gloss upon the Canon speak his sence, a small cause will serve the turn to lay him aside: For asking this Question: For what fault may an Emperour be deposed? The answer is, *For any, if he be incorrigible, and therefore he may be deposed, if he be less profitable*. The World you see is finely mended with these Men; and such poor Kings as ours, must not take it ill, if now they be called the *Pope*'s Vassals and Slaves *, and be used so; be whipt and beaten for their faults, as we shall see our K. *Henry* was. If any of them should be so hardy, as not to tremble at his terrible sentence of Excommunication, he has other ways to humble them; (unknown to the former Popes I mentioned) for every King ought to think

(*) *Decret. l.1. tit. 33. c. 6.*

* *Baron. ad an. 1177. p. 704.*

Ps. 91. 13.

Baron. ad an. 1191. p. 810.

Gloss. in Decret. distinc. 40. cap. 6. si papa.

* *M. Paris ad an. 1253. p. 872. Nonne Rex Anglorum noster est Vassallus, & ut plus dicam mancipium?*

think it honourable to be his Executioner; and though his own Ambition do not tempt him, nor any injuries against himself provoke him, to invade the Dominions of his neighbour Prince; yet the Pope can oblige him to it, as *Innocent* the III. did *Philip* of *France*, to expell K. *John* out of his Kingdome, by bidding him, *In remissionem suorum peccaminum hunc laborem assumere*, as *M. Paris* tells us, *Undertake it for the remission of his sins.* [A pretty way, by committing new sins, to get pardon for his old ones] And we need not wonder at any of these things; for *Erasmus* tells us in his days, these were Moot Points, and disputed *Pro* & *Con* in the Schools;

M. Paris ad an. 1212. *pag.* 232.

"Whether the *Pope* could abrogate that, "which was decreed by the *Apostles* wri-"tings, or determine that which was con-

Eras. Annot. N. Test. in 1 *Tim.* 1. *v.* 6.

"trary to the Evangelical Doctrine, or make a new Article "in the Creed. Whether he has greater power than S. *Pe-*"*ter*, or only equal. Whether he can command Angels. "Whether he can wholly take away Purgatory. Whether "he be a meer Man, or as God, participates both Natures "with Christ: Whether he be not more merciful than "Christ was, since we do not read that he ever recalled any "from the pains of Purgatory, *&c.* He spake this sence very plainly, who called the *Pope* the *Worlds wonder* *; and added,

* *Cited in the gloss upon the Præmium of the Clementines.*

Nec Deus es nec homo, sed Neuter es inter utrumque.

That is,

To call thee God, or Man, I'm loth,
Thou'rt something Neither *between both.*

It may be some may look upon much of this I have now said, as the flattering expressions only of foolish Parasites; who always fawn upon those that have got Power into
their

their hands; like that profane interpretation a Jesuite gives of our Saviour's words, *Seek ye first the Kingdom of God, &c.* The Church, *says he,* has studiously preserved God's Kingdom, and it has fallen out happily, that she has found that Oracle verified, *Seek ye first, &c. and all these things shall be added unto you.* For God has also bestowed upon her the Kingdomes of the World. But, believe it, the *Popes* have given sufficient occasion for them, if we consider either what they challenge to themselves, when they show the greatest respect to Princes; or the Ceremonies of state and honour, which by setled practice is used towards themselves. One of the greatest respects they show to Princes, is the presenting them with a consecrated Sword: which when it is done, by Pope *Sixtus* the IV.th's order, these words are said: *This pontifical Sword denotes the highest temporal power, conferred by Christ upon the Pope his Vicar on Earth; according to that, All power is given to me in Heaven and in Earth; and in another place, He shall reign from Sea to Sea, and from the River to the ends of the Earth.* The Ceremonies also of the *Popes State,* are such as plainly speak the same. "When the *Pope* makes a Feast, if a *King* "be present, he sits at the Table below the "First *Cardinal Bishop.* The *Emperour* or "*King* bring in Water to wash the *Pope's* "hands. The most noble Prince carries the "first Dish, whether he be the *Emperour,* or "a *King.* When the *Emperour* comes to *Rome* to "be crowned, as soon as he comes in sight of the "*Pope,* uncovering his Head, he venerates him, his Knee "touching the ground; when he approaches farther to the "steps of his Seat, he bends the Knee; and after this he "comes to the *Pope's* feet, and devoutly kisses them in re- "verence to our Saviour: the *Pope* chearfully looking up- "on the Emperour, receives Him to kiss his Hand and "Mouth. Then the *Emperour* again bending the Knee of-

Silvester Petra Sancta adv. Molinei Epist. cap. 8.

Sacrar. Ceremoniar. lib. 1. sec. 7. f. 36.

Sacr. Ceremon. lib. 1. f. 19.

Ibid. f. 20.

f. 22.

"fers

"fers a Summe of Gold, at the *Pope*'s Feet. An *Empress*
"is admitted to kiss his Feet and Hand; a *King* to kiss his
"Hand and Mouth; all other Prelates and Nobles belong-
"ing to the *Emperour* to kiss his Foot only. (Quite contrary to what was practised of old, for when *Charles* was
crowned by *Leo* III. *Baronius* acknowledges that the *Pope*
met him at *Numentum*, and there received him with great
veneration: but several other Historians tell us, that *Leo*
crowned and *adored Charles* the *Great*.) "The

<small>*Uspergensis, Trithemius*, &c *ad an*. 801.</small>
"*Pope* gives reverence to no Mortal Man, by
"manifest rising up from his Seat, or by
"bowing his Head, or uncovering it: indeed,
"after he has received the *Roman Emperour* to the kiss of

<small>*Sacr. Cerem. l. 3. sec.* 1. *cap.* 2.</small>
"his Foot and Hand sitting, he rises a little,
"receiving him graciously to the kiss of his
"Mouth, with a mutual embrace of charity:
"and he does sometimes the same to *great Kings*; but all
"other Princes and Prelates, he receives them to kiss his
"Mouth, not rising up, but sitting.

"When the *Pope* is going to be crowned, the Lay-person

<small>*Sacr. Cerem. l.*1. *sec.*2. *f.*12.</small>
"that is the most Noble, though it be the
"*Emperour*, or a *King*, carries up the train
"of his Garment. (*Pluvialis*) After this,
"when he goes the Procession, and gets on Horseback,

<small>*Ibid. fol.*17.</small>
"the Chief Prince that is present, though he be
"King or Emperour, holds the Stirrup of the
"*Pope*'s Horse, and leads his Horse by the Bridle a little
"way. If there be *two* Kings present, the greater holds
"the Bridle on the right side, the Lesser on the left. But
"if the *Pope* does not go on Horseback, but in a Chair, four
"of the chiefest Princes, although the Emperour be among
"them, ought to carry the Chair, with the *Pope* in it, a little
"way, in honour of our Saviour *Jesus Christ*. This stale
pretence of the *Honour of Christ* (which our *Thomas* wore
thread-bare) is extreamly absurd here, and it had been
more agreeable to have said, *in contempt of him*: For
the *Ceremonial* tells us a little before, that in this Procession,

𝔇𝔢𝔳𝔬𝔱𝔦𝔬𝔫𝔰 𝔬𝔣 𝔱𝔥𝔢 Roman 𝔆𝔥𝔲𝔯𝔠𝔥.

cession, the Sacrament is carried upon a white Horse, having at his Neck a well sounding Bell, which Horse is led by a Servant of the Sacrist. If this be done in honor of our Saviour, Why does not the Emperour or King rather lead that Horse by the Bridle, upon which (according to their opinion) our Saviour himself sits? A *Servant* of the *Pope's Servant* leads this Horse, and *Emperours* must lead the *Popes*; nay, upon the shoulders of *Kings* he must be carried, when *Christ* can have only a *Beast* to carry him: This is well contrived for the Honour of *Christ*, and is just such honour as was done him by their S. *Lewes* the *French King*; who was contented to leave the *Eucharist* (that is, his Saviour) with the *Sultan* for a pledge, till he redeemed it, by paying his ransome; according to those Verses of the Epigram.

Ibid. f. 16. Ducitur per familiarem Sacristæ equin album, mansuetum, ornatus, portans Sacramentum, habens ad collum tintinnabulum bene sinniens.

Vid. Martyrolog. Franciscan. ad 25 Aug. p. 372.

Accepit pignus Victor Saladinus Iesu,
Redderet ut regnis, te Ludovice, tuis.

That is,

Lewis *the Saint, when Prisoner he was ta'ne,*
His Liberty and Kingdomes to regain,
By the Victorious Saladine *was drawn,*
To leave in's hand his Saviour for a pawn.

And as ridiculously altogether does that humility look, which the *Pope* affects, in all the state of his Coronation. For when the *Pope* comes to the *Lateran Church*, he is led to the Marble Seat, before the Principal Gate on the left hand, which Seat is called *Stercoraria* *,

Ibid. fol. 17.

---

* See Platina's *conjecture of the name, in the Life of* Joh. 8. *Sentio sedem illam, &c.*

P 2   there

there they make the *Pope* fit down, or rather he fits in a lying posture; then the *Cardinals* approaching honourably, raise him up, saying, *He raiseth the poor out of the Dust, and the needy from the Dunghill, that he may sit with Princes*, &c. The *Pope* also takes a handful of Money (it must be all brass Coine, by reason of what follows) and he throws it among the People, saying, *Silver and Gold have I none, but such as I have give I to thee.* Which last, is the most profane and lewd personating an Apostle imaginable, by him that has much *Money* as every one knows, but can work no *Miracles*, as he did that spoke those words.

Thus I have represented the slavish Homage, usurped Power, and insolent State, the Later *Popes* have challenged, which *Thomas* did so stifly maintain, and our *King Henry* for a time resist, though not with that success the cause deserved. I will only, for a Conclusion of this Digression, show, that what the King contested in the case of *Appeals, Homage, Investitures, Collation of Benefices,* and the like, was but the same that other Kings before and after him did, who had due care to secure their own and their Subjects good, by opposing the unjust Oppressions of the *Roman See*.

Gregory the VII. was the first great troubler of the Christian World, by a new sort of Excommunications, in which he pretended to deprive *Henry* IV. of all Imperial administration, and to absolve his Subjects from that Oath, *Quo fidem veris regibus præstare consueverunt,* (as *Platina* speaks) whereby they used to assure their fidelity and allegiance to true Kings: As if when he had pronounced his words of Excommunication, all *Kingship* miraculously vanished, just as the *Elements* do, after the words of Consecration; well might he that thus practised upon Kings, say (what *M. Paris* tells us he confessed to his Cardinals when he came to dye) that he had grievously sinned in his Pastoral Charge, and by the instigation of the Devil, had raised the anger and hatred of God against Mankind. This *Pope* demanded *Fealty* of *William* the Conquerour,

Vid. Platinam in vit. Greg. 7.

M. Paris ad an. 1086. p. 13.

rour, and the *Moneys* that were used to be paid to the *Pope*. K. *William* granted the *Moneys*, but the *Homage* he peremptorily denyed. *Fidelitatem facere nolui nec volo.* Fealty he neither had nor would grant him, because, says he, "*I neither promised it my self, nor do I find that my Predecessors have done that to your Predecessors*; The money he speaks of, is no doubt, that which was called *Peter's pence*, and was a voluntary *gift*, not any sign of *Homage*, and therefore *Hoveden* sayes expresly, *This Penny is the King's Almes*. And *M. Paris* tells us that K. *Offa* gave it, to maintain a School of *English*-men that flourished at *Rome* *, and to encourage those that came thither. In the Controversie, after this, betwixt *Anselme* and K. *Rufus*, about appeals to the *Pope*, the *King* was angry at the mention of the *Pope's* name, and told him that *no Arch-Bishop or Bishop of his Kingdom was subject to the Roman Court or Pope*. And urged this, that *he had all the Liberties in his Kingdom, which the Emperour challenged in the Empire*, and mentions it as a known case, that the *Emperour* had power to nominate whom he pleased to be *Pope*; and therefore *Anselme* was accused by him as a *Traytor* for seeking to appeal to him, to which, says *Paris*, most of the Bishops agreed. He that has a mind to see this Controversie about *Homage*, menaged betwixt the *Pope* and the *French*, may consult *Marca de Concord. Sacerdotii & Imperii, lib. 6. cap.* 33. Especially the Contentions betwixt *Boniface* the VIII. and *Philip* the *Fair*. But that which he (I suppose) durst not mention concerning that King, but is told us by many others, shows with what scorn the Propositions of owning the *Pope's* Soveraignty were entertained by him. For when *Boniface* told him in his Letter, that he was *sub-*

Inter Epistolas Lanfranc. in Biblioth. Cotton.

Denarius hic Eleemosyna Regis est. Hoveden. Annal. part. 2 in Hen. 2. pag. 343.

* *M. Paris, in vit. Offæ 2. p. 29.*

Matth. Paris ad an. 1094. p. 19.

Quòd ipse omnes libertates haberet in regno suo, quas Imperator vendicabat in imperio. Ibid.

ject to him in *Spirituals* and *Temporals*, that the *Collation* of *Benefices* and *Prebends* did not belong to him nor their profits in their vacancy, and that whosoever thought otherwise he reputed them Fools, &c. The King's answer to this was very smart, which begins thus. *Let your Great Foolishness (instead of Holiness) know, that in Temporal matters we are subject to none*: and goes on to tell him, that the *Collation* of *Benefices*, and their profits in their vacancy did belong to him, and those that were of another mind he accounted *Fatuos & Dementes*, Fools and Madmen.

Sciat tua Maxima Fatuitas, in temporalibus nos alicui non subess. Apud Nich. Gillium in Philip. Pulchr. citat. à plurimis scriptor. v. Catalog. T.st. verit. p. 1687.

It would be too long, to discourse farther about *Collation of Benefices*, and *Reservations of Prebends*, which the Pope used to bestow upon strangers. How *France* complained of them to *Lewes* IX. and how thereupon he restored to the *Bishops* their Canonical Right, and prohibited the exactions herein of the *Roman Court*, the *Reader* may consult the Learned *Marca, de Concord. Sac. & Imp. l.* 4. *cap.* 9. who adds, "To this most glorious King is owing the first resti-"tution of Liberty *, which by his Edict after the change "of Discipline in the *Collation of Benefices*, he procured in "the Year 1268. under which one head were contained al-"most all the Contentions between the Bishops and the *Ro-*"*man* Court. In this Author you may see the Constitution of *Charles* VII. and other Kings, against all strangers, having any Benefices in *France*. See also *Lib.*4. *Cap.* 12. *Sec.* 5, 6.

* The Liberties our *Tomas* so much talked of, were not Liberties of the Church, but inslaving it and the Kingdom to the *Pope*.

As for *England*, I refer the *Reader* to that remarkable Epistle of *Rob. Grosthead*, Bishop of *Lincoln*, in *Math. Paris*, *ad An.* 1253. *pag.* 870. where you find him vehemently opposing the Pope in his Claim of Conferring Benefices.

I'le only add, that this Bishop (as the same Author informs us) us) made up an exact and punctual Accompt of the profits that strangers carried away by these grants of the *Pope*, and *Math Paris ad an. 1152. p. 859.* it was found that the Summ came to above 70 Thousand Marks, and that the meer Revenue of the King by computation did not arise to the Third part of it.

But it is more than time to come to the Fourth and Last Head.

4. Concerning *Thomas* his Death. We left all things in appearance fairly agreed betwixt the King and Him, and promising peace: but *4. The Death of Thomas.* all was quickly disturbed by new Quarrels; For the *Pope* upon the desire of *Thomas*, sends Letters to suspend the *Arch-Bishop* of *York*, and to excommunicate the rest that had a hand in the Young King's Coronation, as also such as detaining the possessions of the Church, would not restore them, unless within *Fifteen* Days they made full satisfaction; which Letters he sent over before him.

And now *Thomas* went over into *England*, and when he came to *Canterbury*, the King's *Baron. Ibid. p. 623.* Officers came and demanded in his Name to take off from the Bishops their excommunication (for it's altogether an unlikely story which *Thomas* told them, that what he did, was done *Ipsius Regis consilio & voluntate*, by his counsel and will, when he *Ibid. p. 621.* had employed them to Crown his Son.) This *Thomas* refused to do, unless they would take an Oath to obey the Commandments of the *Pope*; which they would not submit to, saying that such an Oath was not to be taken without the *King's consent*, because it was contrary to the Princes Dignity, and the Customes of the Kingdom.

Thus they parted, and the Bishops went over Sea to the King to acquaint him herewith. [These are Saint-like qualities indeed, for one that had suffered 7 Years banishment, to have learnt no better to temper his passions by his afflictions, but immediately to seek his private revenge, after his peaceable restitution to his Church; for *M. Paris* tells us, that even upon *Christmas* day, after he had preached to the People, he solemnly excommunicated one *Robert Broc*, who had cut off the Tayl of one of his Horses that carried his provisions.] The *King*, upon hearing these complaints, was so incensed, that he broke out into passionate words, expressing his wonder, that none did revenge him of one Priest, who so disturbed his Person and Kingdom, and sought to deprive and disinherit him of his dignities: Which speeches being heard by *Four* Knights (*Will. Tracy, Hugh Morvill, Richard Breton*, and *Reginald Fitz-Urse*) they interpreting his words in the worst sence, presently posted over into *England*, and slew *Thomas* in his own Church, whose dying words were these: *I commend to God, our Bl. Lady, with the Saints Patrons of this Church and S. Denis, my self and the Cause of the Church.* Though the King seemed to give occasion to his Murder by his speeches, yet he protested, as Almighty God should judg his Soul, that it was neither acted by his will or consent, nor wrought by any devising of his, and humbly submitted to any penance the Church should enjoyn him. The condition of the King's Absolution was, the granting away all that he contended for all this while, and giving the *Pope* more power in *England* than he had before: For these were the termes. To maintain 200 Knights in the *Holy Land*, for a whole Year, giving each *Knight* 300 Crowns. To abolish the Statutes of *Clarendon*. To restore to the Church of *Canterbury*, and to all *Thomas* his friends, all their possessions. And if the *Pope* required it, to go into *Spain* to free that Land from the *Pagans*; to all which he agreed, and both he and his Son swore to the *Legates*. But besides all this, he crossed into *England*, and underwent such a penance at *Thomas* his Tomb, after his Canonization, as became no *King* to undergo, nor any thing, but the insolency of *Monks* to inflict. For as soon as he came within sight of the *Cathedral*, where he was buried, stripping himself naked, save only

M. Paris ad an.
1171. *p.* 124.

Baron. ad an.
1172. *p.* 636.

Baron. ad an.
1174. *p.* 652.

ly

ly that he had one sorry Coat on, he went his pilgrimage bare-foot in the sight of all the people, through the dirty ways and streets; and continued all that Day, and the Night following watching and fasting at *Thomas*'s Tomb: Then the Convent being called the next Day together, he received more than double the stripes that S. *Paul* did from the *Jews*; for he received upon his naked Body *Eighty Three* Lashes from the *Monks*, and beside was *Five* times flasht by the Bishops that were present *: and returned *bare-foot* the Day following, without receiving any sustenance.

Quinquies ab Episcopis cæsus.

* But *Ribadeneira* has much increased the number of his stripes, for he says in his life, that there were more than 80 Bishops and Monks present, and every one of them gave him *three* Lashes, and he was lashed by them distinctly *five* times. Ribaden. Flos Sanctorum, pag. 640.

Matth. Paris says, *A singulis viris religiosis, quorum multitudo magna convenerat, ictus ternos vel quinos excepit.* p. 130.

Harpsfield says, *Virgâ ab Episcopis quinquies, à singulis monachis (quorum numerus erat supra octoginta) ter cæsus est.* Hist. Anglic. p. 337.

Thus we have given an account of this *Canonized Prelate*; the summ of whose Merits living and dying was this, That he zealously asserted the *Liberties* of the *Church*; But if you ask farther what those *Liberties* were; we shall find them to be much of the same nature with those *Liberties* that the Pope challenges for himself in the *Decretal*. *If the Pope be negligent of his own or others salvation——though he lead innumerable people by droves with him to hell, yet no mortal man presumes to reprehend his faults; because he is the Judge of all men, and to be judged of none, unless he be found to deviate from the Faith.* These are *Liberties*, which no old Saints I am sure ever contended for; but you see the *Pope* has enlarged the Charter to the Saints of his own making; and one of his greatest Champions has made all sure, when he tells us; *If the Pope should erre by enjoyning the practice of Vices, or prohibiting Vertues, the Church is bound to believe*

Decret. 1 Part. distinc. 40. c. 6. Si papa sua.

Bellarm. l. 4. de Rom. pontif. cap. 5. in fine.

those

those *Vices to be good, and Vertues evil, unless she will sin against conscience.* In this way (and none else that I know of) *Thomas* may be a *Saint*, but we must *put out our eyes*, before we can believe it.

And if we have no evidence of his *Saintship*, we are then at a loss to understand how he comes to be a *Martyr:* his being murdered in his own Church will not do it, without the other; for how many greater Persons than he have come to untimely ends, that yet were never put into any *Martyrologie?* We have no concern to excuse or defend the murdering zeal of private persons, but desire that such practices, as these upon *him*, may be for ever detested, though designed to never so good an end. But we know there have been Popes, that have excused such practices upon *excommunicated* persons (who yet many of them had far more to show for their being Saints, than *excommunicating Thomas*) witness Pope *Urban* the II. who in an Epistle, says, *Non enim eos homicidas arbitramur,*&c. *We do not think those to be homicides, who burning with zeal towards their Catholick Mother, against the Excommunicate, have happened to kill some of them.* Let *them* have the brand of *barbarous murderers* that killed him, but still I can see nothing of a *Martyr in him:* The words he used at his death, have more in them, that looks like a confession of his Faith, than hitherto I remember to have met with in his story; but this commending of himself to the P*atron Saints* of *Canterbury* Church, to the *Virgin Mary*, and S. *Denis*, tell us how he was abused by superstition, more than that he had a true understanding of Religion. I think, considering his former behaviour to his Prince, such a confession would have better fitted his Mouth, as *Radolphus* made when he was a dying, who lifting up his wounded hand, spake thus to those about him. (*) *With this hand I swore to my Lord Henry*

Decret. part. 2. cauſ. 23. qu. 5. c. 47.

(*) *Baronius* himself confesses that *Vspergensis, Sigebertus,* and others report, that he repented, at his death, of his rebellion against *Henry*, and confessed that by God's just judgment his right hand, with which he swore to the Emperour, was cut off. *Baron. ad an.* 1080. *p.* 541. (the

(the Emperour) *that I would not hurt him, nor lay trains against his honour, but the Popes commands brought me to this, that violating my Oath, I usurped undue honours to my self*; and so presently dyed. If *Thomas* had expressed more of such like *penitence*, and less *confidence*, he would have looked more Martyr-like, unless he had suffered in a better cause ; but all things considered, I think it would not be more profane or ridiculous, for a Man to pray, that he might *ride to Heaven* upon *Father Garnet's* fabulous *Straw*, than to pray, to be able to *ascend thither* by *Thomas's* blood, which was, as you heard, a piece of their Devotions to him. It is very observable, what *Cæsarius* the Monk, who lived a few Years after his death, has told us, that after he was slain, there were presently hot disputations concerning him ; some saying he was damned, as being a betrayer of the *Kingdom* ; others that he dyed a Martyr, for defending the *Church*. This question was canvased, says he, among the *Masters* at *Paris* : " *Master Rogerus* swore, that he was worthy of death, but not of such " a death ; judging the *constancy* of the blessed Man to be " *contumacy* ; but *Peter Cantor* swore on the contrary, that " he was a *Martyr* worthy of God, having been killed for " the defence of the *Churches Liberty* ; but, says *Cæsarius*, " *Christ* solved all the doubt, when he glorified him with " many and great signs ; that is, after his *Death*, for he says before, that he shone with no Miracles in his *persecutions*. Thus we are referred to Miracles, the last refuge, and surest defence of any desperate cause in this Church ; and now let the probabilities be never so great to the contrary, let the Saintship of a Person, with never so good reason be questioned, if the *Pope* once think fit to make him a subject of peoples veneration, I'le warrant the *Monks* will fit him with all sorts of wonders to countenance both *his canonization*, and the *peoples devotion*. And they were not wanting here in *Thomas* his case, which come now, for a Conclusion, to be considered.

Helmoldus Chron. Sclavon.

Cæsarii Dialog. distinc. 8. c. 69.

A

A while after his death the World begins to ring with the noise of his Miracles; so that *Petrus Blesensis* writes, that *England* need not envy the *Indies*; they had their *Thomas* the *Apostle*; we have *Thomas* the *Martyr*; he shall suffice *me*, who has the *name* of an *Apostle*, and does *imitate him* in *Miracles*, or overcome him. Now we are told, that *by his merits God raised the dead, gave sight to the blind, hearing to the deaf, and feet to the lame, cleansed Lepers, healed the infirm, and freed those that were possed with Devils*: but these are common Themes, and it's a hard thing to find any Saint almost in this Church, of whom the same has not been said, when they came to be canonized. I'le present therefore the *Reader* with some rare and extraordinary particulars, which I find are related concerning him, both in his *life-time*, and after his *death*, by which he may judge concerning this proof of his *Saintship*.

Concerning the Miracles ascribed to Thomas.
Baron. ad an. 1173. p. 642.
Idem Ibid. p. 644.

Thomas, we are told, from his Youth had vowed his chastity to the *Bl. Virgin*; and being, on a time, among some of his Companions, (before he was Arch-Bishop) he heard them boasting of their *Mistresses*, and the *special presents* they had received from them. *Thomas* told them, that they vapoured foolishly, for he had a *Mistress* that far excelled all theirs; who had bestowed such a present on him, that they never saw any thing like it. All this he intended in a *Spiritual sence*; but, they urging vehemently that he would show them what he talked of; he ran to the Church, and prayed the *Bl. Virgin* to pardon the presumptuous word he had spoken of her. To whom she appeared in a Vision, and incouragingly told him, that he did well to cry up the excellency of his *Mistress*; and she gave him a very fine and very little Box; which his Companions snatcht out of his hand, and opening, saw something of a purple colour, and taking it out, beheld a wonderfully fine *Casula*. (a Garment which the Priests wear.) This story came to the Ears of the Arch-

Gononi Chronicon SS. Dei para, p. 177.

Devotions of the Roman Church.

Arch-Bishop of *Canterbury*, who sent for *Thomas* and learnt of him the truth of it, whereupon he secretly determined in his mind to make him his *Successor*. But this favour of the Virgins in the present of a *new Garment*, was not so wonderful, as another we are told of, that concerned an *old one*. For when he was *Arch-Bishop*, he used to wear a Hair-shirt next his skin on *Saturdays*, (a Day dedicated to the *Bl. Virgin*) which being rent, *Wickman* tells us that the Bl. Virgin *held his shirt*, whilst he *stitched it*; but *Gononius* reports it thus. There was an *English* Priest, that daily said the Mass of the Bl. Virgin, because he had not skill to say any other; who being accused, was suspended by *Thomas* from his Office, for his want of skill: *Thomas* on a time had hidden his Hair-shirt under his Bed, that at a convenient season he might secretly sow it: the Bl. Virgin appeared to the aforesaid Priest, and commanded him to go to *Thomas*, and tell him, that the Mother of God had granted leave to the Priest, that daily celebrated her Mass, and was suspended, to officiate again; by this token, that she, for whose Love he said Mass, had sowed his Hair-shirt that lay in such a place, and had left the red Hair with which she sowed it. *Thomas* hearing this, was amazed, and found it so as the Priest related, and gave him power hereupon again to officiate.

Gonon. Ibid. p. 176. & Wickman's Sabbatismus Marianus. p. 73.

Besides, the *English Legend* in his Life relates, that when he was at *Rome*, upon a Fasting-day, a Fowl being provided for his Dinner, because no Fish could be bought, the *Capon* was miraculously turned into a *Carp*. (rather than the holy Man should break the Orders of the Church.) It may be perhaps a farther strengthning to our Faith in this matter, to observe that the *Irish* Saints have been very notable at these *Conversions*. S. *Riocc* entertained S. *Ædus* the Bishop, and set a great Supper of Flesh before him: But the Bishop would not eat *Flesh*, but blessing the Meat, it was turned into *Bread*, and *Fish*, and *Honey*. And in the Life of S. *Moedoc*,

Colganus ad 6 Febr. in vit. S. Riochi. p. 268.

Moedoc, we are told, that when S. *Molua* had killed a fat Calf for to receive him, hearing that S. *Moedoc* did not eat flesh, he blessed 8 Pieces of Flesh, and they became 8 Fishes; but the Bishop knowing by inspiration how they were made Fishes, he blessed them again, and they were turned again into 8 pieces of flesh: which S. *Molua* seeing was displeased, for he had no other Fishes in his Monastery; and therefore before them all he blessed them again, and they became 8 Fishes the 2*d.* time: and here this pretty contest ceased, and for the Honour of S. *Molua*, he was contented to feed upon them, though I warrant you he could have held play with him longer in these changes. But to return to our *Thomas. Polydore Virgil* has told us a remarkable story how God miraculously vindicated *Thomas* against his Enemies in his life-time. "For, says he, *Thomas* being
" accounted the King's enemy, began to be so contemned,
" and hated by the common people, that coming to a Town
" called *Strode*, the Inhabitants of that place minding to put
" an affront upon this good despised Father, presumed to cut
" off his Horses Tayl which he rode upon: but hereby they
" brought a perpetual reproach upon themselves, for after-
" wards it so fell out, by the pleasure of God, that all the
" race of those Men, that committed this fact, were born
" with Tayles, like brute Beasts. (whence the Proverb comes
" of *Kentish Longtailes*.) But this note of infamy is long since
" worn off, together with that generation of Men that so
" sinned; (which was cunningly put in, to save the credit of a lewd Fable.)

Colganus, Act. Sanct. Hibern. ad Jan. 31. *p.*221.

Polyd. Virgil Angl. Histor. lib. 13.

These you will say are pretty fair attestations of his Saintship, in the way of Miracle, *while he lived*; but are nothing to what we are told of the wonders that proclaimed his fame *after his death.* The first sort, I shall mention, are those that were shown upon his Murderers.

Hoveden. Histor. p. 299.

Hoveden tells us that all men shunned their company, and none would eat or drink

drink with them; they cast the fragments of their Meat to the Dogs, and when they had tasted them, they would eat no more of them: so manifest was God's vengeance, that they who contemned the Lord's anointed, were contemned even by Dogs.

S. *Antoninus* says, that of those who killed him, some with their Teeth gnawed off their own Fingers by pieces, others had their Bodies flowing with corrupt matter, others were dissolved by the Palsie, and others miserably dyed of madness: (though any body else, besides this *Canoniz'd Historian*, would wonder, how these *Four* sorts of Judgments could destroy above one a piece, when there were but four Men to be destroyed by them.) *Antoninus Hist. Tom. 2. p. 736.*

As for *Thomas* himself, if *Visions* and *Revelations*, and *lying Miracles* can do him any kindness; there are good store prest in his service; A little before he returned out of banishment, it was revealed to him, that a few days after his return he should go to Heaven, by dying a Martyr; and we are told, that while he was praying at the Monastery of *Pontiniac*, he heard a voice from Heaven, saying, *O Thomas, Thomas, my Church shall be glorified in thy blood*. *Antoninus Ibid.* *Harpsfield Hist. Eccl. Angl. f. 334.* A certain young Man being under an infirmity, his Soul went out of his Body and returned again; and he said that he had been rapt into Heaven, and saw an empty Seat mightily adorned, placed among the Apostles; and when he asked for whom that magnificent Seat was prepared; an Angel answered, it was reserved for a certain great Priest of the *English Nation*; which was understood of S. *Thomas*. *Heraclius* also, the Patriarch of *Jerusalem*, coming into *England*, related this Vision. "A certain "Frier was sick to death in a Monastery "of the Holy Land, the Abbot desired "him to certifie him of his state after death, which he pro- "mised, and dyed. A few days after he appeared to the "Abbot, and told him that he enjoyed the Vision of God, and *Capgrave in the Life of Thomas, f. 292.*

"and that you may not doubt of my happiness, know, sayes
"he, that when I was carried by Angels into Heaven, there
"came a great Man with an unspeakably admirable procef-
"sion following him, of Angels, Patriarchs, Prophets and
"Apostles, &c. This Man stood before the Lord as a Mar-
"tyr, all his Head being torn, and the blood seeming to di-
"still from the clefts of his wounds. To whom the Lord
"said: O *Thomas*, thus it becometh thee to enter into the
"Court of thy Lord; and added, I will give no less glory
"to thee, than that I have bestowed on *Peter*: and the Lord
"took a mighty Golden Crown and put it upon his wound-
"ed Head. The *Frier* added, know for certain, that *Tho-*
"*mas* of *Canterbury* is slain about this time, mark my words
"and observe the time: and so he vanished. This the *Ab-*
"*bot* told to the *Patriarch*, who related it in *England*. As
soon as *Thomas* was slain, the Monks shut their Gates, and perswaded the people that the Bells rung of themselves. Before he was buried, as he lay in the Quire upon the Bier, in the Morning lifting up his right hand, he gave his Benediction to the Monks. They made a great stir about the Water of an adjoyning Well, which they said appeared bloody by Miracle: which I suppose is that which the *Sarisbury Breviary* refers to in their Rithmes,

Lord Herbert Henry 8. p. 438.

Hoveden Hist. p. 299.

Lord Herbert Ibid.

Brev. Sar. Lec. 9. in Transf. Thomæ Jul. 7.

*Aqua Thomæ quinquies varians colorem
In lac semel transiit, quater in cruorem.
Ad Thomæ memoriam quater lux descendit,
Et in sancti gloriam cereos accendit.*

That is,

*Five times his Water changed colour quite,
Four times blood-red, and once not Milk more white;
And that S. Thomas fame might never dwindle,
Four times did Light descend, and Torches kindle.*

As

Devotions of the Roman Church.

As for the Reliques of *Thomas*, they have done mighty feats; for a Monastery of S. *Martin* in *Arthoise*, having got his *Rochet*, and part of his *Hair-shirt*, (with his blood sprinkled upon them, so as never to be washed out) his *Ring*, and some other things; they have upon Record a Catalogue of 67 Miracles wrought by them; nay, some that had visited his famed Reliques at *Canterbury*, and found no benefit by them, had relief here at this Monastery. *Stapleton de 3 Thomis, p. 108, 109.*

The worst is, that there is some reason, one would think, to question those wonderful relations, (of Miracles wrought by his Reliques) as forgeries, since there was so plain a cheat about his Reliques; for the most sacred of them was so apparently. A piece of his *Crown* that was pared off by his Murderers, was pretended to be kept as a Relique in the Church of *Canterbury* in one place, and *Erasmus* says that the whole face of *Thomas* being set in Gold, was kept in a Chappel behind the high Altar, and they told him that the rest of his body lay in his shrine; but when *Henry* VIII. caused his shrine to be defaced, they found an intire body compleat within the same, says *Lambert*, as some alive then present can testifie. But be that how it will, we are come to this fine pass at last, that *Cæsarius* has pleaded, that even the pretended, but false Reliques of *this Saint* can work Miracles. *Colloq. Peregrin, religionis ergo.*

Lambert peramb. of Kent. p. 248.

Cæsarius Dialog. dist. 8. c. 70.

" For, says he, a certain Souldier, a great lo-
" ver of *Thomas*, was inquiring every where
" how he might get any of his Reliques; which a crafty
" Priest hearing, at whose house he sojourned, said to him;
" I have by me a Bridle which S. *Thomas* long used; which
" the Souldier hearing, gave him the Money he asked for it,
" and received the Bridle with much devotion. And God,
" to whom nothing is impossible, willing to reward the
" faith of the Souldier, vouchsafed to work many Miracles
" by that Bridle in honour of his Martyr; which the Soul-
"dier considering, built a Church in honour of *Thomas*,
" and

"and instead of *Reliques*, put therein this *Bridle* of the "cheating Priest.

And now who is there, after all this, but will expect, that mighty wonders should be told us were wrought for the relief of those, who in their distresses did invoke him? Of this kind *two* or *three* Instances will serve for a Conclusion of my Discourse about him.

"There was a Bird, says the *Festivale*, that was taught to "speak, and could say S. *Thomas*; it hap- "pened that this Bird sitting out of his Cage, "a Spar-hauke seized on it, and was ready "to kill it; but the Bird crying, St. *Thomas* "help, the Spar-hauke fell down dead; *His inference is* "*very strong*, that if he heard the Bird of his grete grace, "moch more will he here a christen Man or Woman, that "cry to him for help and succor. King *Lewis* of *France*, you'l say, was extraordinarily heard, who coming over, to offer at his Tomb at *Canterbury*, and praying for a safe passage, he obtained (*I suppose by some voice that assured him*) that neither he, nor any other from thenceforth, that crossed the Seas between *Dover* and *Withsand*, should suffer any loss or shipwrack. (*Credat Judæus apella*.)

Festiv. fol. 80. & Antoninus loc. citat. p. 707.

Lambert's peramb. of Kent. p. 143.

But the finest contrivance, methinks, is that wonder for a special Friend of *Thomas*, who being under an infirmity, came to the Tomb of the Saint, to pray for the recovery of his health, which, says the story, he received to the full. But being returned home, he thought within himself, that perhaps that infirmity was inflicted on him for his salvation, and was for the greater profit of his Soul, than health was; and therefore returning to the Sepulchre of the Saint, he prayed, that what should most conduce to his salvation, whether sickness or health, that *Thomas* would obtain it for him of the Lord. Whereupon his infirmity returned again upon him. And it was very friendly done of him, to impute the return of his distemper, to the Saint's foresight of the danger of his continuing

Antoninus ibid.

Devotions of the Roman **Church.** 227

in perfect health. Some there were also, whom S. *Thomas* would not cure, in civility to other Saints. (though you may be sure he could have done it himself.) So *Capgrave* tells us, that a Clerk, having been troubled with vomiting, and a Bloody Flux, and a pain in his Eyes, that he was almost blind; this Man *Fifteen* Days together had implored the Martyrs help at *Canterbury*: To whom *Thomas* at last appeared; and bid him rise quickly, and go to *Durham* to S. *Cuthbert*, and by his merits he should obtain mercy and health. For (said he) I will have my languishing Patients and Servants go to him for Cure, and his come to me; and the first day he came thither he was cured. It's very observable, that this Clerk had served *Thomas* before his exile, and so could less take it ill, to be sent on his errand so long a journey. But the most shameful fiction is that which is told us in the History of the Monk of *Canterbury*, *De miraculis Thomæ*; concerning one *Eilwardus*, who, in his Drink, broke into a Man's House, and stole some of his Goods, who laid such an action of Felony against him, that he was condemned to have his Eyes put out, and his Privities to be cut off, which sentence was executed upon him; and he being in danger of Death by bleeding, was counselled to pray to S. *Thomas*; in the Night he had a Vision of one in white Apparel, who bid him watch and pray, and put his trust in *God*, and *our Lady*, and holy S. *Thomas*; The next Day the Man rubbing his Eyes, (to be sure he did his forehead that wrote it) they were restored; and a little after rubbing the other place, his *Pendenda* (as he calls them) were also restored, *Principio quidem valde parva, sed in majus proficientia*, very small at the first, but growing still greater, which he permitted every one to feel that would.

Capgr. it. S. Cuthbert. fol. 78.

V. For Martyr. Tom. I.; 293.

This very story, no doubt, is that which the Verses at the beginning refer to, *Membris donat castratos, &c.* And which the old *Roman Breviary* points at, when it says thus. "*Tho-*
"*mas*

"*mas* stretched out his powerful hand to un-
"usual and unheard-of wonders; for even
"they that were deprived of their Eyes, and
"of those parts by which Man-kind is propagated *, by his
"merits had the favour to receive new ones.
I dare trust this miracle with any Reader to
believe it if he can: But me-thinks it had
been better contrived, if the circumstances of the *last Story*
of *Thomas* his Friend, had been reserved for *this wonder*:
it had been enough to declare the *power* of the Saint, to have
received a full recovery of these parts; but it might, and
ought to have been referred to his *discretion*, whether it
would not be more for the health and profit of the Patients
Soul, to return presently into his *castrated estate*, wherein
this *fomes peccati* would be extinguished, and his after chastity better secured; and more perhaps for the good of the
World, it should be so; since it might be hazardous, what
kind of Race might spring up from a drunken Thief, thus miraculously inabled to propagate a-new.

Brev. Roman. antiqu. Lect. 9.

* Membris geni- talibus privati.

The Reader has seen a pleasant part the Monks of *Canterbury* have played, in setting up *Thomas* for a *Saint* and *Martyr*: and they did it so successfully, that we are told of a
Hundred Thousand People, that in some
Years have come to pay their Devotions to
his Shrine: nay more, that their zeal to-
wards him was so hot, as sometimes they seemed to have but
little consideration of the Bl. Virgin her self, and none at all
of *Christ*. For there being *three* Altars in the Church of
Canterbury, one dedicated to *Christ*, another to the *Virgin
Mary*, and a third to *Thomas*; we are
told out of an old Leger-book of that
Church, that one Year the Offerings at
the Shrine of *Thomas* amounted to 954 *l.*
6 *s.* 3 *d.* when those to the *Bl. Virgin* came only to 4 *l.* 1 *s.* 8 *d.*
and to *Christ* nothing at all.

W. Sumner. Antiq. of Canterb. p. 249.

Cited by Foulis, Hist. of Popish Trea- sons, &c. pag. 17.

I wonder not that these things were countenanced and
promoted by the *Pope*, whose *Slave* he was, as well as his
Saint;

Devotions of the Roman Church. 229

Saint; but it's strange methinks, that all Christian Kings should not be concerned to vindicate the abuse to them all, in the most vile usage of our *K. Henry*, such as no example in any Age can parallel; by obtaining at least, that such a Rebel to his Prince should be blotted out of the Kalendar of *Saints*, and no longer publickly venerated as a *Martyr*.

Concerning Patron Saints; or, Devotions to Particular Saints, in particular Distresses.

To S. Apollonia for the Tooth-Ach.

Horæ sac. uſ.
Sarum. f. 80.

Antiphona.

VIrgo Christi egregia
  Pro nobis, *Apollonia*,
Funde preces ad Dominum
Ut tollat omne noxium;
Ne pro reatu criminum
Morbo vexemur dentium
Vel capitis torquentium.

GReat Virgin Apollonia,
  To God our Intercessor
    prove,
That he, when thou requestest,
    may,
All noxious things from Us
    remove;
Lest our great crimes be punished
With vexing pains of Teeth
    or Head.

Oremus.

OMnipotens & sempiterne Deus, spes & corona omnibus tibi fideliter servientibus; qui B. *Apolloniam* gloriosam Virginem & Martyrem, excussionem dentium

Let us Pray.

ALmighty and everlasting God, the hope & crown of all that faithfully serve thee; who didst crown in Heavenly places blessed Apollonia that glorious Vir-

Q 3

pro

pro tui nominis fide passam, in cœlestibus collocasti; tribue, quæsumus, omnibus memoriam ejus piè colentibus, perpetuâ pace gaudere, & à periculis tam animæ quàm corporis liberari.

Per Christum, &c.

gin and Martyr, who suffered the beating out of her teeth for faith in thy name; Grant, we beseech thee, that all who piously venerate her Memory, may rejoyce in perpetual peace, and be delivered from all dangers both of Body and Soul.

Through Christ, &c. *Amen.*

But this matter is still more express, in the *Horæ B. Virginis sec. usum Romanum*, p. 140.

Antiphona.

Beata *Apollonia* grave tormentum pro Domino sustinuit; primò, tyranni extraxerunt dentes ejus cum malleis ferreis; & cum esset in illo tormento, oravit ad Dominum Jesum Christum, ut quicunque nomen suum devotè invocaret, malum in dentibus non sentiret.

Blessed Apollonia sustained great torment for the Lord; First of all, the Tyrants drew out her Teeth with Iron Hammers (a new way of drawing teeth) and when she was in that Torment, she prayed to the Lord Jesus Christ, that every one that should devoutly invocate her name, might feel no pain in their Teeth.

Vers. Ora pro nobis beata Apollonia.
Resp. Ut digni efficiamur promissionibus Christi.

Vers. Pray for us, O Blessed *Apollonia.*
Ans. That we may be made worthy of the promises of Christ.

Oratio.

Omnipotens sempiterne Deus, qui Beatam A-

The Prayer.

Almighty everlasting God, who didst deliver
pollomam

polloniam, Virginem & Martyrem tuam, de manibus inimicorum suorum liberasti, & ejus orationem exaudisti ; te quæso per intercessionem ejus, & Beati *Laurentii* Martyris tui, simulque omnium Sanctorum & Sanctarum, ut dolorem à dentibus meis expellas, sanum & incolumem efficias, ut tibi gratiarum actiones referre valeam in æternum.

Per Dominum, &c.

S. Apollonia thy Virgin & Martyr, from the hands of her Enemies, and didst hear her Prayer ; I intreat thee by her Intercession, and the Intercession of S. Laurence thy Martyr, together with that of all the He and She-Saints, to expell pain from my Teeth, and to make me safe and sound, that I may return Thee my Eternal thanksgivings.

By our Lord, &c.

Apud Bollandum de S. Apollonia ad Feb. 9. p. 282.

O Sancta *Apollonia*, per passionem tuam impetra nobis remissionem omnium peccatorum, quæ dentibus & ore commisimus per gulam & loquelam ; ut liberemur à dolore & stridore dentium hic & in futuro, & diligendo cordis munditiem per gratiam Labiorum, habeamus amicum Regem Angelorum.

Amen.

O Saint Apollonia, by thy Passion obtain for us the remission of all the sins, which with Teeth and Mouth we have committed through Gluttony & Speech ; that we may be delivered from pain & gnashing of Teeth here & hereafter, and loving cleannefs of heart, by the grace of our lips, we may have the King of Angels our Friend.

Amen.

NOTES.

THis last Prayer (out of an *Utrecht Manuscript*) Bollandus thinks, was not recited in the Divine Service, for this reason ; because it is not directed to God. But we found in others before, formal Petitions made to her immediately;

diately; and the falsness of his observation is apparent, in abundance of Instances which I have given all along; and we shall meet with many more, when we come to the Devotions directed to the Bl. Virgin: The Reader may do well, as to this particular, to consult the Learned *Dallæus*, (in his Book, *De Latinorum cultu*; especially *Lib.* 3. *c.* 12.) who has given us abundance of Examples out of their proper Masses. And why should any one believe, that they should be shy in directing their Prayers to the Saints, when we find that they have joyned *God* and *them* together in their praises, and in the same *Gloria's?* Of which take this instance at present, in a Hymn upon S. *Lewis* Bishop of *Tholouse*, immediately before the first Lesson; where at the end of the Hymn is this *Gloria*.

Brev. Rom. antiq. 19 August.

*Trino Deo & simplici, digna laudum præambula
Sint; & tanto Pontifici, per infinita secula.*

That is,

To God *that's* Three, *and yet but* One,
  Give all the praises that are fit;
To Lewis, *let the same be done,*
  Through Ages that are Infinite.

I observe here farther, upon what sleight occasions, the *Roman Church* has advanced their superstition in the *Invocation of Saints*. *Eusebius* in the sixth Book of his History, Chap. 41. (*edit. Valesii*) has told us a very short story concerning her; how a Year before *Decius* his persecuting the Christians, (which *Baronius* places *an.*252.) in a Tumult raised at *Alexandria* against the Christians, among others that suffered, they laid hold on the Admirable *Apollonia*, an Aged Virgin (παρθένον πρεσβῦτιν) and struck out her teeth, and kindling a Fire in the Suburbs, threatned to burn her alive, unless she would pronounce certain impious words with them; she made a little demur, as if she deliberated with
her

her self, and then suddenly leapt into the Fire and was burnt. Upon this *plain Song*, it's very pleasant to observe what *descant* the Makers of the *Roman Breviaries* have run.

They have told us of the Noble Race she came of; of her chastity and humility in her younger Years; her Fastings, Prayers and Almes; her Examination before the Heathen *Prefect* with his Questions, and her Answers, which you may see in *Bollandus*, who cites a great many old Breviaries: but the *Breviary* of *Utrecht* has done their work, and made it very reasonable, that all should apply themselves, when they are afflicted with the Tooth-ach, when it brings in the Virgin praying for those that were in that distress, and that a voice came from Heaven, saying, *O Spouse of Christ, thou hast obtained those things thou hast asked of God.* And now there is nothing further needful to excite the Peoples Devotions, save only Reliques and Miracles. For Reliques, none can be more proper than her Teeth, and the parts about her Mouth; and here they are well furnished in abundance of places. (though the Saint lived so long ago.) At *Rome*, besides her Head and Arm, one Church has part of her Jaw, and *four* or *five* Churches I know not how many of her Teeth. At *Volaterræ* in *Etruria*, there is preserved her Mouth, part of her Jaw, and one of her Teeth. At *Bononia*, in *several Churches* they have her Teeth, and in *one* her Lower Jaw, which is solemnly venerated on the 9th. of *February*, by the *Legate* or *Vice-Legate*. At *Antwerp* they show a part of her Jaw, by which frequent Miracles are wrought. At *Mechlin* they have part of a Tooth, and at several places in *Flanders* whole ones: At *two* places in *Artois* a remarkable portion of her Lower Jaw. At *Colen*, one Monastery has *four* of her Teeth, another has a Rib, and a Tooth, and Shoulder-blade; the *Carthusians* her Jaw, S. *Maurice*'s Church a Tooth, and S. *Albans* in the same City her Lower Jaw. At *Lisbon* in the Church of S. *Roch*, one of her Teeth, and other Reliques of her. At *Placentia* in *Spain* are two Reliques preserved of her, and there this Prayer is also recited.

Loc. citat.

Deus

Deus qui B. *Apollonia* in tenero * & puro corpore dira tormenta vincere tribuisti; da quæsumus, ut carnis illecebris superatis, nulla mundi adversa formidemus.

Per, &c.

O God, who didst inable S. Apollonia in a tender and pure body to overcome grievous torments; Grant us, we pray thee, that overcoming the allurements of the flesh, we may be afraid of none of the Worlds adversities.

Through our Lord, &c.

* *Here they forget what* Eusebius *says of her Age, and suppose her, as* Mantuan *does, to be,* Viridi vix nubilis ævo, *a young Virgin.*

Now though after this Catalogue of Reliques, one would have thought it strange that any Saint should have had more Jaws than two, or an old Virgin be furnished with such a number of Teeth, as they presume to shew for hers; yet we are farther told by *Chemnitius* *, that a grave and learned Man, one *Andreas* (*Abbas Amelunxbornensis*) used to relate, that King *Edward* was once troubled with the Toothach, and commanding that the Teeth of S. *Apollonia* should be sent to him, which were every where preserved in his Kingdome; "There were, says he, heaped together so ma-"ny Teeth of *Apollonia*, out of the Reliques of one King-"dome, that several *great Tunns* could not contain them.

* *Exam. Concil. Trid. part. 4. pag. 12.*

As for Miracles; that which *Bollandus* recites in the forenamed place, (though he dares not either affirm, or deny the truth of it) will serve in stead of a thousand, to fright the *Living* people into devotion towards this Saint, when such a mark of displeasure for neglecting her, was inflicted upon the Body of the *Dead* Bishop *Ernestus*; who suffering an edifice dedicated to her to run to ruine, when he was dead, all the Teeth of his Head were struck out, so that not one remained in his Mouth; that it might manifestly appear, that he was punished in that, in which she was wont to relieve all those, who did not blot her out of their memory.

To

To St. Anthony *the Hermit, for Inflammations, commonly called S. Anthony's Fire.*

Hor. B. Virg.
sic. us. Rom.
p. 138.

Antiph.

VOx de cœlo ad *Antonium* facta est; Quoniam viriliter dimicasti contra mundum, ecce ego tecum sum & faciam te in toto orbe nominari.

A *Voice came from Heaven to* Anthony, *saying, Because thou hast fought manfully against the World, behold I am with thee, and will make thee famous in all the Earth.*

Oratio.

The Prayer.

DEus qui concedis, obtentu B. *Antonii* confessoris tui, morbidum ignem extingui, & membris ægris refrigeria præstari, fac nos propitius ipsius meritis & precibus à Gehennæ incendiis liberatos, integros mente & corpore tibi fœliciter in gloria præsentari.

O GOD, who by the means of thy Confessor *S.* Anthony, dost vouchsafe the extinguishing of the Fiery disease and refreshments to sick Members; mercifully grant, that we being freed by his Merits & Prayers from the flames of Hell, may be happily presented sound in mind & body to Thee in glory.

Per Dominum.

Through our Lord, &c.

Missal.
Sarum.
Vers.

O *Antoni* Pastor inclyte,
Qui cruciatos reficis,

SAint Anthony, *thou Pastor great,*
To the tormented thou giv'st ease,

Morbos

Morbos sanas & destruis,
Ignis calorem extinguis;
Pie Pater ad Dominum
Ora pro nobis miseris.

Heal'st and destroyest their Disease,
Extinguishing all Fiery heat;
Pray for us wretches, holy Father, we intreat.

Secreta.

SAcrificium nostrum, quæsumus Domine, benignus intende; quo sicut B. *Antonii* precibus cruciatus temporales sanare non desinis, ita exui misericorditer impetremus ab æternis.

Per Dominum.

We pray Thee, O Lord, graciously to look upon our sacrifice; that as by the Prayers of S. Anthony thou ceasest not to cure torments that are temporal, so we may obtain to be mercifully freed from those that are Eternal.
Through our Lord, &c.

NOTES.

HE that had a mind to dispute about the truth of those Miracles, which *Athanasius* has told us were wrought by S. *Anthony*, in his Life; might think some of them justly liable to be questioned; as that which he tells us of his being beaten by the *Devil*, till the greatness of the pain took away both all his motion and speech, and that he was so cruelly handled, that he was at one time just a dying: and that other story, how when he was going into a Ship, he complained to his Companions of a grievous stink, and presently one possessed with a Devil, cryed out; whereby they gathered, that he perceived the Devil by his smell: (as *Bollandus* in his notes upon the place, says, S. *Pachomius* knew by the stench the presence of an Heretick.) But my business is not to detract from the Saint, or to lessen his due esteem: Only one thing I observe, that he seems in his life-time to have had a more than ordinary care, to prevent all that after-veneration of his Reliques, which is now practised

ctised in the *Roman Church*, which we know both gives life to their Devotions, and raises expectation of his help in those that apply themselves to him for relief in their distresses. For the forenamed Father tells us, that he gave a strict charge to those that attended him when he dyed, *that they should not carry his Body into Egypt, lest they should reserve it in their Houses* *, which he explains a little before, *that they did not commit the Body to the Earth, but wrapped it in Linnings, and putting it in a Bed, kept it in their Houses, thinking thus to honour the Dead*; (which is neither lawful nor pious) this, he says, *he had blamed, and dehorted from the usage of it*. (and no doubt he would have blamed the present *Roman* customes as well as the old *Egyptian*; for why is it worse to keep those Remains in *Beds* above ground, than to place them upon *Altars*, or keep them in *Boxes*?) *Bury therefore*, says he, *my Body, and cover it with Earth, and observe this charge that no man but you alone know the place of my burial*: which they did, says Athanasius, and no man hitherto, save those two Persons that ministred about him, knows where he was buried. But the *Roman Trade* cannot be driven with this *Secrecy of Interment*, many a good Market would thus have been spoiled: Digged therefore he must be out of his Grave, and if the *Monks* be so sullen, as not to discover where the place is, *Visions* and *Revelations* will not fail to do it; and though it was near 200 Years before a discovery was made of it, yet *Colen* that got the *three* Kings, hath got too S. *Anthonie*'s Beard; and we are told of a wonderful translation of his Body into *France*, which deserves relating: * One *Joceline* was ingaged by the Testament of his dying Father to go in Pilgrimage to *Jerusalem*: which he neglecting to perform, in a Battel he was sore wounded, and carried for dead into a Chappel of S. *Anthony*'s; where when he began to revive, a Multitude of Devils appeared to him, and for not performing his vow of the Pilgrimage, were preparing to drag him

* Athanas. in vit. Anton. p. 503.

* In Histor. Aymeri Falconis apud Bolland. ad Januar. 17.

to Hell, and one of them casting a Halter about his Neck, was ready to strangle him: In this strait S. *Anthony* the Guardian of the place, appeared, and chid, and drove away the Devils; commanded him to go his Journey to *Jerusalem*, and after that, in requital of his kindness, to carry his Reliques away, out of the *Eastern*, into the *Western* parts of the World; because there *Christ* would have him to be more highly venerated in time to come; all which he performed, and begging the Body of S. *Anthony* of the Emperour, brought him from *Constantinople* into *France* (though how his Body was brought to *Constantinople*, we are yet to learn.) But we are not to think that his whole Body was brought thence by *Joceline*; for in the Year 1231. *Lambertus* from the same place brought part of his Arm to *Bruges*: At *Colen* (as was said before) they show S. *Anthony*'s Beard, and a remarkable part of his Hand: they have some part of him at *Tourney*, and the *Jesuites* have two of his Reliques at *Antwerp*. At *Rome* one of his Churches is famous for his Sack-cloth, and some others for pieces of his Garment of Palmes, artificially weaved, which S. *Anthony* wore on high Days, and some say belonged before to *Paul* the *Hermit*: but the most part of that famous Garment, we are told, is preserved and shown at *Vienna* in *France*.

These Remains of his, we are informed, have wrought mighty Miracles for the Curing that Fiery Disease, which like a Pestilence swept away so many in *France*: nay (as *Aymerus* relates, *loc. citat.*) his Reliques being dipt into Wine, the Wine so sanctified, proved a present Remedy against that Disease; and therefore the *Pope* gave a Patent to the Monastery of S. *Anthony*, where his Reliques were kept, that *they* should make that sanctified Wine, and none else. Neither did this benefit, by the intercession of S. *Anthony*, accrue only to Men, but to Cattel also; and from hence, we are told, the custome arose of picturing this Saint with a Hog at his Feet, because, as the same Author says, on this animal, God wrought Miracles by his Servant; and in honour

honour of his memory, they used in several Places to tye a Bell about the Neck of a Pig, and maintain it at the common charge of the Parish, from whence came our *English* Proverb of *Tantony Pig.*

To St. Sigismund *for Feavers, or Agues.*

Breviar. & Missal. sec. us. Sarum.

OMnipotens sempiterne Deus, qui per sanctos Apostolos & Martyres tuos, diversa sanitatum dona largiri dignatus es; da quæsumus, ut præsentem famulum tuum N. qui à febrium vexatione fatigatur, per intercessionem famuli tui *Sigismundi* regis & Martyris, tua medicina erigat ad salutem, & ad sanitatem pristinam clementer revocare dignetur.

Per Dominum, *&c.*

ALmighty everlasting God, who by thy holy Apostles and Martyrs hast vouchsafed to bestow divers gifts of healing; Grant, we beseech thee to thy Servant N. here present, who is wearied with the vexation of Feavers, that by the intercession of thy servant Sigismund King and Martyr, thy Medicine may raise him to health, & mercifully vouchsafe to restore him to his former soundness.

Through our Lord, *&c.*

Secreta.

OFferimus tibi Domine munera sancta in nomine electi tui *Sigismundi* Regis & Martyris tui; ut à præsenti ægroto *N.* febrium ardores repelli jubeas, & exinde tuo semper in omnibus muniatur auxilio.

Per Dominum.

WE *offer unto thee, O Lord, holy gifts in the name of thy elect* Sigismund *the King and thy Martyr; that thou wouldst command Feaverish heats to be repelled from this sick Person* N. *here present, and that also he may always be defended in all things by thy help.*

Through our Lord, &c.

NOTES.

NOTES.

BY these Prayers any one would be apt to think, that this King had made some glorious confession of Christ, before the Opposers of his Religion, which he had sealed with his Blood, and thence had obtained the stile of King and Martyr: but when we examine the short story of his Life, which is given us by *Baronius* out of *Gregory Turonensis*, we shall see but little reason to venerate him for a Martyr, or to have any great expectations from his Patronage. He was converted, we are told, from *Arianism* to the *Catholick Faith*, by *Alcimus Avitus* Bishop of *Vienna*, in his Fathers Life-time. After his Death, he and *Godomarus* his Brother reigned over the *Burgundians*. He had one Son by the Daughter of K. *Theodoric*, called *Sigericus*, but she dying, he married a second Wife; who, upon a great falling out with this Son, perswaded *Sigismund*, that *Sigericus* sought to possess his Kingdome, and without making him away he could not be secure; whereupon one Day commanding him to lye down and sleep when he was drunk, he caused him to be strangled; for which fact he afterwards was extreamly penitent: But the Divine vengeance presently followed him. For K. *Clodomerus* making War against him and *Godomarus*, they were overcome by him, and *Sigismund*, with his Wife and Children being taken Prisoners, he together with them was slain, and his Body thrown into a Pit. This Death of his, which was a just retaliation of his former crime, can scarce, one would think, amount to Martyrdome. But now, so acceptable was his repentance, that his Body being taken up out of the Pit, and buried in the Monastery of *Agaunum*, it was presently famed for working Miracles. For now, says *Gregory*, if those

Baron. Annal. Ecclef. ad an. 509. p. 600.

Id. ad an. 526. p. 120, 121.

Greg. Turon. de glor. Martyr. c. 75.

"that are afflicted with Agues, do devoutly "celebrate Masses in honour of him, and "offer an oblation to God for the rest of
"his

" his Soul, presently their shakings cease, their Feavers are
" extinguished, and they are restored to their former health.
But this is not the first Fable that he (and you may put in his
Contemporary, Pope *Gregory*) has took upon trust, and reported from common fame; and I am the more suspicious
of it, because these *Masses* to be said in *honour of him*, and
Oblations for the *rest of his Soul*, look as if a Trade were
going forward to be menaged by the Monks inventions.
But methinks they were ill-advised in these doubtful circumstances, to pitch upon him for a Patron in the case of Feavers, when there was an elder Saint, and a more unquestionable Martyr, already in the office before him; I mean
S. *Pantaleon*: For thus I find it in the *Hours* of *Sarum*.

De sancto Pantaleone *Martyre.*	Of S. *Pantaleon* Martyr.
Anaphona.	
SAncte *Pantaleon* Martyr Christi	CHrist's *Martyr* blest Pantaleon
Militari ordine fuisti, quo præeminuisti,	*Was first in Armes, and honour won.*
Demum Heremeticam vitam acquisisti,	*Poor Hermits life at length he chose,*
Tu vero Hydropicum sanum reddidisti.	*By Dropsie's cure more famous grows.*
Missus in equuleo ungues perdidisti.	*By tortures racks, his Nailes he lost,*
Costas cum Lampadibus adustus fuisti.	*With burning Lamps his ribs they roast:*
Collum subdens gladio pronus pertulisti.	*He bow'd his Neck to th' fatal blow,*
Fundens lac pro sanguine vitam sic finisti.	*Milk from the wound for blood did flow.*
Cunctas febres dilue à plebe tam tristi,	*Cure all their Feavers, who to thee complain,*

R   Qui

Qui cœlestis gloriæ regna meruisti.   Thou that in Heavenly glory now dost reign.

Vers. O Sancte *Pantaleon* ora pro nobis.
Resp. Ut ab omnibus liberemur febribus.

Vers. O Saint Pantaleon pray for us.
Ans. That we may be freed from all Feavers.

Oremus.   Let us Pray.

Deus qui humilium vota respicis, ipsorumque cernis preces; adesto plebis tuæ precibus auctor: ipse pietatis; & præsta, ut qui beati *Pantaleonis* Martyris tui memoriam agimus, ab omnibus febrium generibus efficaciter liberemur, & ad gaudia æterna te ducente pervenire mereamur.

Per te Jesu, &c.

O God, who hast respect to the vows of the humble, and beholdest their Prayers; be present to the prayers of thy People, thou that art the Author of pity; and grant, that we who celebrate the memory of Bl. Pantaleon thy Martyr, may be effectually delivered from all sorts of Feavers, and by thy conduct may merit to come to the joys that are Eternal.

Through Jesus, &c.

To St. Sebastian *for removing the Plague.*

Hora B. Virg. sec. us. Rom.

Egregie Christi Martyr *Sebastiane*, princeps & propagator sanctissimorum

O Sebastian thou famous Martyr of Christ, the Prince and Propagator of præ-

Devotions of the Roman Church. 243

præceptorum ; ecce nomen tuum in libro vitæ cœlestis adscriptum est, & memoriale tuum non delebitur in secula.

most holy Precepts: behold thy Name is written in the Book of Heavenly Life, and thy memorial shall not be blotted out for ever.

Vers. Ora pro nobis B. Martyr *Sebastiane.*

Resp. Ut mereamur pestem Epidemiæ illæsi pertransire.

Vers. O Bl. Martyr *Sebastian* pray for us.

Ans. That we may merit to pass through the Plague unhurt.

Oratio.

OMnipotens sempiterne Deus, qui meritis B. *Sebastiani* Martyris tui gloriosissimi, olim pestem Epidemiæ generalem omnibus mortiferam revocasti; præsta supplicibus tuis, ut qui pro simili peste revocanda sive cessanda, sub tua confidentia ad ipsum refugiunt, ejusdem meritis & precibus, ab omnibus nocumentis venenosis, nec non ab omnibus corporis & animæ periculis; ac à subitanea & improvisa morte, & ab omnibus inimicis visibilibus & invisibilibus singulis diebus, horis, atque momentis, liberemur.

The Prayer.

ALmighty everlasting God, who by the merits of thy most glorious Martyr Sebastian, didst in time past remove a general Pestilence deadly to all; grant to thy suppliants, that we who for the recalling or ceasing the like Plague, flie to him, confiding in thæ ; by his merits and prayers we may be delivered from all poysonous harms, as also from all dangers of Soul and Body, and from sudden and unforeseen Death, & from all enemies visible and invisible, each Day, Hour and Moment.

Per Dominum.

Through our Lord, &c.

R 2 *Prosa.*

Missale Rom.
antiqu. & Missal.
sec. us. Sarum.

Prosa.

Omnes unà decantemus
Et Martyris personemus
   Laudem *Sebastiani*;

Hic à deo est electus,
Per quem morbus est ejectus
   Languoris pestiferi.

Nam se Christo totum vovit
Qui vult nos hunc venerari,
Christus eum nunc promovit
   In patria cœlesti:

Cunctis hic subvenit mæstis,
Statim est sedata Pestis
   Sui causâ meriti.

Ipsum si nunc deprecemur
Nomen quoque veneremur
   Martyris sanctissimi,

Morbus iste non nocebit,
Sed mortiferum delebit
   Populum qui tenuit:

Nos pro nostris tantis malis
Jam absorbet pestis talis
   Quod tota gens gemuit.

Sancte Martyr *Sebastiane*
Salva nos à morte Epidemiæ:
Nostra gravia ob peccata,
Terra ista desolata
   Non sit piè quæsumus;

Sebastian the Martyr's praise
Let's sing aloud, by God elected,
Through whom the languishing decays
Of deadly Plagues should be corrected.
He to Christ himself devoted,
Christ would have our worship grace him,
Whom he has so far promoted,
As in Heav'nly Seats to place him.

Our sorrows all by him are eas'd,
Sebastian's Merits were so great,
He once a raging Plague appeas'd;
And if we now his help intreat,
His name will prove sufficient charm
To keep us from this threatning harm.

The Pestilence now gives no Quarter
All the sad people in despair
Grone and cry, O holy Martyr,
Now save us from th' infected Ayre.
Let not our crimes our ruine prove

Sed

Sed nos considera	As for our guilt they justly may,
Et in nobis cessa	
Pestem jam te petimus.	But think on us, with speed remove
Ista per te gens sit tuta,	This heavy Plague, we humbly pray.
Et ne noceat acuta	
Febris hac in patria.	May we from this sharp Feaver's rage
Ex quo nostra spes est tota	Safe and unhurt hereafter be,
In te Martyr, nunc remota	Whose deadly influence asswage
Sit pestis mortifera.	Since all our hopes are plac'd in thee.
O Sancte *Sebastiane*	Be thou our early Guardian Saint,
Nostræ gentis sero manè	
Conservator & tutor sis;	Shield us from mischiefs when 'tis late,
Et Dominum deprecare,	Intreat Heav'n graciously to grant
Ut à nobis revocare	
Valeat vesana pestis.	A revocation of our Fate.
	Let this disease when thou dost plead
Ex tua sancta prece	
Ne sit morbus nobis nece,	Obtain no farther leave to slay men,
Sed recedat ab hac domo.	
Amen dicat omnis homo.	But conquer'd from each house recede;
	To which let every Man say, Amen.

NOTES.

THis last is a rare piece of Devotion; and if you observe it, most admirably accords with what we find, *Psal.* 50. 14, 15. *Offer unto God thanksgiving, and pay thy vows unto the most High, and call upon me in the day of trouble, I will deliver thee, and thou shalt glorifie me.* Here is calling upon a *Saint* in trouble, expecting deliverance from a *Saint*, praising and glorifying a *Saint*, without any taking notice of *God* at all, only that he would do it for them. I would fain know, whether if all this had been said to *Aaron* by a Jew, it would not then have been accounted deservedly Idolatry; and if so, What makes it a less sin, or none at all in a Christian? I am sure Idolatry is now condemned by the New Testament, as well as by the Old; and I would fain understand where our *Saviour*, or his *Apostles* have given us a new notion of it, different from what Men had of Idolatry before.

But here again, we are sent to *Visions* and *Revelations*, and *they* must bear out the worship of this Saint, though never so absurd, and set him up for a powerful Intercessor in the case of the Pestilence. For *Baronius* has made us understand the secret, out of *Paulus Diaconus, ad An.*680. *num.*58. " *Tuncque visibiliter multis apparuit, quia bonus & malus* " *Angelus, &c.* (speaking of the terrible Plague at *Rome* and *Ticinum.*) " Then it appeared visibly to many, for a " *good* and a *bad Angel* by Night went through the City, " and by the command of the *good Angel*, the *bad*, who " seemed to carry a Hunting-staff in his hand, as often as he " smote with his Staff the Door of any House, so many " People dyed out of that House, the Day following. Then " it was said by *Revelation* to a certain Person, that this " Plague would not cease, till the Altar of S. *Sebastian* was " placed in the Church of S. *Peter ad Vincula*; which being " done, and the Reliques of S. *Sebastian* brought to *Rome*, " presently upon the placing the Altar in the said Church, " the Plague ceased. *Baronius* adds, that the Altar it self " remains yet entire, as also the Image of the said holy " Martyr in Mosaick work. And from hence this piece of " Religion is propagated to Posterity, that in time of the " Plague, by way of vow, the Image of the said S. *Sebastian*, " is wont to be painted in divers places, and Altars to be e- " rected to his memory, yea and Churches to be built.

We are also further informed by *Bollandus* (ad *Januar.*20. *in vit. S. Sebast.*) what rare vows were made to him by those of *Milan*, in a great Plague, *An.* 1575. They chose him

for

for an especial Saint to implore, not only because he had conferred like benefits heretofore in other places; but chiefly because his Mother was of *Milan*, and there also he was educated; and they vowed, if he would succour them, to build a new Church in Honour of this Martyr, and settle a maintenance for daily offices to be performed in it; to celebrate his Annual feast, with a Fast the Day before; to bring solemn oblations to his Church yearly, on the Day of this vow, (*viz.* on the *Ides of October*) and also on the Day of his Feast: to offer a precious Vessel, to be a decent receptacle for the Martyrs bones; and several other things of like nature, which you may be sure were so obliging to him, that they could not fail of the desired success.

Neither does the Church want his Reliques, or *they* their miraculous effects; for though he lived so long ago (*viz. An.* 287.) that hinders not, but that in several Countreys and Cities, they have got remarkable portions of his Body; nay, more than one of those very Arrows with which he was transfixed at his Martyrdom, are shown at this day. We are told, that in a Church of *Capua*, this Saints Reliques sanctifie *Water* (as we heard before S. *Anthony's* did *Wine*) which is preserved for the infirm, & is so often called for, that they are fain thus to Consecrate it, more than once a Year: at *Ebersberg* in *Bavaria* they have the Top of his Scull, which is venerated with great Religion all over *Germany*, and is a certain amulet against the Pestilence; it being so included in Silver, that People may drink out of it, and in it Arrows are Consecrated, which are great preservatives against the Plague.

To S. Rocch *in time of the Plague.*

Horæ B. Virg.
sec. us. Sarum.

O Quàm magnificum est nomen tuum Beate *Rocche*, qui tuis intercessionibus multitudinem languentium nôsti salvare, & omnibus nomen tuum gloriosum commemorantibus, te propitium exhibere; veni & salva nos à morbo Epidemiæ. & aeris temperiem nobis concede.

Oremus.

OMnipotens sempiterne Deus, qui meritis & precibus Beatissimi *Rocchi* Confessoris tui, quandam pestem generalem revocâsti; præsta supplicibus tuis, ut qui pro simili peste revocanda, ad ipsum sub tua confugiunt fiducia, ipsius gloriosi confessoris tui precamine, ab ipsa peste Epidemiæ & ab omni perturbatione liberentur.

Per Dominum, &c.

Antiphona.

O Blessed Rocch, how magnificent is thy Name, who by thy intercessions knowest how to save a Multitude of languishing People, and to show thy self propitious to all that commemorate thy glorious Name; come and save us from the Plague, and grant to us a good temperature of Ayre.

Let us Pray.

ALmighty everlasting God, who by the Merits and Prayers of the most Blessed Rocch thy Confessor, didst remove a certain general Plague; grant to thy Suppliants, that they who for the removing the like Plague, fly to him, confiding in thee, by the prayer of this glorious Confessor, they may be freed from the Pestilence, & from all perturbation.

Through our Lord, &c.

But

But more fully in the *Horæ Sec. uſ. Rom* and in the end of the office of the Bl. Virgin, *Paris* 1615.

Anaphona.

AVe *Roche* sanctiſſime, nobili natus sanguine,
Crucis signaris schemate siniſtro tuo latere :
Roche peregre profectus, peſtiferos curas tactus,
Ægros sanas mirificè, tangendo salutiferè.
Vale *Roche* Angelicæ vocis citatus famine,
Qui potens es Deificè, à cunctis peſtem pellere.

ALL hail St. Rocch, to noble blood ally'd,
Markt with the sign o'th'cross on thy left side;
Plagues felt thy vertue in a forreign Land,
The sick were cur'd toucht by thy saving hand.
Farewell great Saint, whom Angels greet, we may,
Whose power, like Gods, does drive all plagues away.

Oremus.

DEus, qui Beato *Rocho* per Angelum tuum, tabulam eidem afferentem promisisti, ut qui ipsum piè invocaverit, à nullo pestis cruciatu læderetur ; præsta quæsumus, ut qui ejus memoriam agimus, ipsius meritis & precibus, à mortifera peste corporis & animæ liberemur.

Per Dominum, &c.

Let us Pray.

O God, who didſt promiſe to bleſſed Roch, by an Angel that brought a Table to him, that he who piouſly invoked him, ſhould be hurt by no tormenting Plague ; grant we beſeech thee, that we who keep his memory, by his merits and prayers may be freed from the deadly Plague both of Soul and Body.

By our Lord, &c.

NOTES.

NOTES.

THe *Legend* upon which these Prayers are founded, is set down in a large *Prosa* (as they call it) in the *Mass de S. Roccho*, which we find in the old *Roman*, and *Salisbury Missals* and *Breviary*, which begins thus. *In honore salvatoris sancti Rocchi confessoris agatur memoria.*

Where it mentions his being born with the sign of the Cross on his left side; and that, as a token of his future Sanctity, when he was a Child, on *Wednesdays* and *Fridays* he would never suck but once a day, (so keeping these as fasting days, by which we may guess at the likelihood of the rest of the story, as) that he cured Men of the Plague, by onely making the sign of the Cross upon them; and how a little *Dog* brought him Bread, & an *Angel* healed himself of the Plague: And then follows the story of his being in *Lombardy*, where he dyed, and how an Angel delivered him a *Table*, written in *Golden Letters* by Gods own hand, with the name of S. *Rocch* in it, and a promise that whosoever did commemorate this Saint, should be delivered from, or cured of the Plague, and it ends thus.

Tu qui Deo es tam charus, Et in luce valdè clarus, Sana tuos famulos;	O thou great Saint, who art to God so dear, And brightly shin'st in light above so clear;
Et à peste nos defende, Opem nobis ac impende Contra mortis stimulos:	Heal us thy servants, and from Plague defend us, Against its killing Darts thy succor lend us.
Vir tam potens, tam beatus Cum honore collocatus In cœlesti curia,	Well may we venerate a man so great, So blest, with honour plac'd in heavenly seat;
Voto, voce vereretur Ut per ipsum nobis detur Christi frui gloria. Amen.	Our vows and pray'rs we make to him, that we Hereafter may by him Christs glory see. Amen.

This

This Saint is venerated upon the same account with S. *Sebastian*, for delivering many Cities of *Italy* from the Plague by the sign of the Cross; and you may well think there was something more than ordinary in his *signing*, when *Surius* (in his life) tells us, that to preserve a Cardinal from the Plague, he made a cross upon his Fore-head, and the impression of it pierced his skin, as if the cross had been burnt in with a hot Iron. His veneration was decreed with great solemnity, by the Order of a *General Council*. For so *Baronius* informs us, (upon the *Roman Martyrologie*, Aug. 16.)

" In the Year 1414, (about an 100 Years after his death)
" the Fathers of the Council of *Constance*, for the driving a-
" way a Plague that was begun, decreed that the honours
" due to the Saints, should be bestowed on him; for with
" solemn pomp they brought his Image through the City,
" all the People accompanying it, which being done, the
" Plague presently stayed. And from thence was the ex-
" ample taken, that every where his venerable Images, Al-
" tars, Chappels, and lastly Temples were erected.

To St. Marguerite for Women with Child.

THere is a famous Legend of this Saint in the old *Roman* and *Sarisbury Breviaries*. (on the 26. of *July*.) In which these passages are remarkable. She desired of God, that she might have a conflict face to face with the Devil, that hitherto had been her secret and hidden enemy. Then the Devil appeared in the terrible shape of a *Dragon*, and swallowed her up: but she presently arming her self with the sign of the Cross, the *Dragon* burst asunder, and the *Virgin* came unhurt out of his Belly. Afterwards she saw another Devil, like a black man sitting, whom she catching by the Hair, threw him to the ground, and put her right Foot upon the Crown of his Head, and bid him tell
her

her what he was. The Devil said, lift up your Foot from my Crown, that I may speak: Then he told her, that he was one of those Spirits which *Solomon* shut up in a brazen Vessel, and the *Babylonians* coming, and thinking to have found Gold in it, broke it, and so we flew away. She also made him confess his arts of fraud and wickedness, and why he so miserably tempted the Christians; *Et pedem virgo sublevans, mox velut fumus evanuit*, and lifting up her Foot, presently the Devil vanished like smoak. [This was a notable trick of S. *Marguerite*, thus by putting the Devil to pain, to make him confess the Secrets of his own Trade and Rogueries; but S. *Bernard* made a worse fool of him, and cunningly over-reached the Devil, to the discovery of a secret which concerned Mens salvation, and such a Secret, as no good Angel ever told any Man, out of his own pure good will, the like. For thus I find it in a Rubrick of the *Salisbury* Hours. (*fol.* 123.) *Whan Saint Bernard was in his Prayers, the Dyuell said unto him; I know that there be certeyn Verses in the Sawter, who that say them dayly shall not perish, and he shall have knowledge of the day that he shall dye. But the Fende wolde not showe them to S. Bernard: Than said S. Bernard, I shall say dayly the hole Sawter. The Fende consideringe that S. Bernard shall do so moche profyte and goode labor; so he shewed him thys Verses.* The Verses are there set down, which begin thus, *O bone Jesu. Illumina oculos meos, &c.* Before every Verse, as if it was intended for a charm, is set commonly, a hard name of *Greek* or *Hebrew*; as, *O Adonai. Locutus sum, &c. O Heloy. Periit fuga à me &c.* And so before others, *O Emanuel, O Agyos, O Raby, O Tetragrammaton:* and there also, among the rest of the precious Devotions, (which were all taught him I suppose by the Devil, for I find no distinction mentioned) is that unintelligible and nonsensical Prayer, (which was mentioned at the beginning of the Book) *Peto Domine Jesu, &c.*] When she came to dye, she prayed of God, that whosoever writ, read or heard of her passion, might obtain pardon of his sins, and whosoever would build a Church to her honour, and
minister

Devotions of the Roman Church.   253

minister Candles out of his just labour for her service, might have whatsoever he asked that belonged to his salvation: and in a more especial manner (*signanter*) she prayed for *Women in Labour*, that when they invoked her *Patronage*, they might have a speedy *Delivery*, and escape the *Danger*, and that the Infant might be born without any defect of its Members. When she had done praying, there was a great Thunder, and a *Dove* came from Heaven, saying, Blessed art thou *Margaret*, the Spouse of Christ, behold, thy Petitions are granted thee by Christ, come into the rest of the Heavenly Countrey.

If these Requests and Answer can be supposed to be true, *Saint Marguerite*, for my Money; I see no need of any other Saint to pray to: and indeed I must commend the wisdome of the Later *Popes* in leaving all this out of the *present Breviaries*; for this one story would else have been enough to have spoiled the Market of the other Saints.

If any one have a mind to see this at large, and much more, let him consult her Life, written in *French* Verses, at the end of the *Office of the Bl. Virgin*, Printed at *Paris*, 1615. To which also the Women with Child are beholden, for furnishing them with a Prayer to her, though the Publick Offices of the Church are very sparing herein, being willing, I suppose, that the Bl. Virgin should have all the custome in this case, as you may hear more hereafter. The Prayer is this which follows, which I will not trouble my self to translate into *English Meeter*, because so many now a-days understand the *French*.

Oraison de S. Marguerite, *a dire pour les Femmes grosses.*

Madam Saincte Marguerite,
Digne vierge de Dieu eslite,
Qui le servis des ta jeunesse,
Plein de grace & de sagesse;

Qui pour l'amour de Dieu nostre sire,
Souffris tourmens & grief Martyre;

Qui

Qui le Dragon parmy Fendis,
Et du Tyran te deffendis;
Qui vainquis l'ennemy d'enfer
En prison fermee de fer;
Qui a Dieu fis mainte re-
queste
Quand on te voulut couper la
teste,
Et par speciale, que Femme
Grosse d'enfant,qui à toy Dame
De cœur devot retourneroit,
Et qui ton aide requerroit,
Que Dieu de peril la gardast,
Et de l'aider point ne tardast.
Si te supplie Vierge honoree,
Noble Martyre & bien heuree,
Par ta piteuse passion
Et ta Saincte petition,
Que Dieu vueilles pour moy
prier
Et doucement luy supplier,
Que par pitié,il me conforte,
Et douleurs qu'il faut que je
porte,
Et sans peril d'ame et de corps
Face mon enfant yssit hors,
Sain & Sauf, et que je le voye
Baptisé à bien & à joye;
Et si de viure il à espace
Il luy doint son amour et grace
Parquoy si sainctement il serue
Que la gloire des cieux des-
serue;
Et aux autres en cas sem-
blable,
Soit par toy amy favorable.
Ainsi soit il.

There is one thing I must farther remark, which we meet with not only in this story of S. *Marguerite*, but in *Twenty* other Lives of the Saints beside: *viz.* The *Admirable Petitions* they made to God before they dyed; together with the *promises* and *priviledges* they obtained in answer to their requests. God was very free, you will say, in a *grant* he made to *S. Oringa*; when he communicated to her one of his own properties, *viz. The knowing peoples thoughts*, as a reward of her modesty and chastness, and this too without her asking: (*that we read of*) For, we are told, that God promised to her, that because she had never cast her eyes upon the face of any man, she should (*for the future*) be able to see into the inmost secrets of the heart of any Man, whose face she would look upon. But commonly the *Priviledges* they boast of given to the Saints, were in answer to their Petitions; though most of them are such, as are no ways becoming

Bolland.ad 10 Januar. pag.651.

ing any Saint to *ask*, nor God to *grant*. To instance in a few here: (passing over many that have been named already, and others which we may have occasion to mention afterwards.) We are told of *four* Petitions that S. *Maidoc* made to God, which according to the plain sence of the words, express either little Piety or Charity, but all of them, a great regard that he had to himself: and yet these Petitions are said to be made, after that he had fasted *Forty* Days and Nights, without tasting any food.   *Colganus vit. S. Maidoc. 31 Jan.*

The 1. Petition was, *That whosoever of the Kingly race of the* Lagenienses, *especially of the Seed of Brandubius, should sit in the Seat of Maidoc, and dye in it, might not be with him in Heaven.* This sitting in the Seat of *Maidoc*, *Colganus* explains, by violent seising upon the possessions of his Church at *Fearna*, and holding them in possession without repentance to his death; he prays that such a one might not be saved: which is either a very foolish Prayer, or very uncharitable. To pray that a Sacrilegious Person, dying in impenitency, may not come to Heaven, is like praying that a stone may not fly upward into the Ayre: the weight of such a ones sins will depress him, without any other hinderance to keep him down: but if the Prayer refers to such a severe punishment of his crime, that he may never have the grace to repent, and be saved; this is not becoming any Christian to desire towards his greatest enemies; much less fit for this Saint to wish it, towards the race of this *King*, who (as his Life tells us) was his mighty *Benefactour*, and had bestowed upon him that Land, whereon he built his *Monastery*.

The 2*d*. Petition breaths the same fiery spirit; *That whosoever of his Monks should deny him, and prove a fugitive from him, such a one, in like manner, might not be with him in Heaven.* The 3*d*. Request was; *That Hell might not imprison those after the Day of Judgment, who should be buried in his Church-yard.* This, says *Colganus*, is to be understood of *Catholicks*, devoutly desiring to be buried there: but, by his

his favour, the words are so general, that I cannot see, but that an *Heretick* may have as much benefit by this grant as any other Person; especially since the rule of interpretation in this case is, that *Favores sunt ampliandi, Favours are to be understood in the largest sence*; and it's to be hoped, that S. *Maidoc*, if he had any foresight in him, took care before he dyed, to Consecrate a good large burying place; since, without doubt, if this was a known grant, there was like to be great crowding hither from all parts, and People would not be more careful, in their last Will and Testament, to commend their Souls into God's hands, than to commit their Bodies to be buried in this sacred ground: Only I observe one good help in this case; that the same priviledge, *totidem verbis*, was granted to S. *Kieran*, another *Irish* Saint; whose Church-yard, I suppose, had as much holiness and vertue in it, as this of S. *Maidoc*'s had, and so might have as much custome.

Colgan. vit. S. Kieran 5. Mart. Num. 38.

The 4. Petition was, *That he might every day deliver one Soul out of Purgatory, until the Day of Judgment.* This was a pretty request for a Saint to ask, that he himself might do it; and argues that he had no mean opinion of his own merits, but thought that he was furnisht with a full stock and treasury of them, that Souls might spend upon them thus daily, even till the last day: S. *Kieran* was a little more modest in another request that he made *, (because the favour depended upon a condition, and was not absolute, as this was) viz. *That whosoever honoured the Festival of his Birth day, might be rich in this World, and obtain rest in the World to come.* But who can believe, that God was as *free* in his *Grants*, as these Saints were *foolish* in their *asking* ? I may then believe, that all the *Irish Devoto's* to this last Saint were *saved*, when I can be perswaded that they were all *rich*; but till then, the Defender of these ridiculous stories, must not think that he has made them good, when he has told a great many others like them. It may not be amiss however to

* *Colganus, ibid.*

relate

relate some of those special Priviledges, that we may a little better understand to what heights of folly superstition may advance. We are told then, that *Gregory Turonensis* mentions *Christ*'s Grant to S. *Laurence*, that every *Friday* he should deliver one Soul out of Purgatory pains. The *Cistersians* boast, that it was granted by the Intercession of the *Bl. Virgin*, that the Devil should have no power over any one, who at his death was cloathed in their habit: and we are informed, that it had like to have cost a Monk of that Order very dear, who by the indiscretion of his Attendants, who did not consider sufficiently *Monastici habitus Sacramentum, the Sacrament of his Habit*, had pull'd off his *Cowl*, to give him some relief in the heats of his Feaver, and so he dyed unhabited: who though he was conducted very civilly by good Angels, to the Gates of Paradise, yet the Keepers that stood there, refused to give him any entrance; no not though his conducting Angels urged much his good Life and strict Devotion, yet all this would not do; for it was answered, that by an Eternal Law it was established, that no *Monk* should enter in at those Gates without his *Hood*; and so the Gates being shut upon him, he stood trembling without, expecting every moment to receive the sad sentence of damnation; Onely Christ the Judge was so merciful, that he restored him to life again, for so long a time, till he repenting of this neglect, might be habited in his *Cowl*, and so be fit without impediment to enter into Paradise. *

Colgan. in notis ad vit. Maidoc. ad num. 33, 34.

Bibliothec. Patrum Cisterciens. p. 171.

* *To insinuate the better, how safe a Man is, and secure of going to Heaven, when he is habited aright; they bring stories, to perswade people, that the Devil watches, as a Cat does for a Mouse, to find any one throwing off his habit, that he may have then a prey of him. For thus I find* Thom. Cantipratanus (Lib. 1. de Mirac. sui temp. cap. 7. s. 4.) *telling such another Fable as this.* " *How a Monk in the heats of a great Fea-*
" *ver, had put off his Cowl; and suddenly such a noise and crack was*
" *heard, as if the whole building was tumbling down; which a holy*
" *Man hard by at his prayers, being terrified with, the Devil appeared to*
" *him,*

S

"him, saying: I raised this great noise in indignation, because thou hin-
"deredst me by thy Prayers, from snatching that Monk bodily to be tor-
"mented, who had thrown off the Habit of his Order. So little wit
these Inventors of Lies have, to bring in the Devil too, discovering secrets
to his own prejudice, when he need not; for any one may see, that this appearance and discourse of his, would for the future prevent all his opportunities of seizing upon such careless People at unawares.

The *Carmelite Friers* also, are this way as well secured of their salvation, as they can wish: for in the Year 1250. one *Simon Stock* an *English-man*, and General of their Order, did daily supplicate the Bl. Virgin, that this Order which was honoured with the special Title of the Virgin, might be guarded by some singular priviledge of her donation; and he daily repeated with *great devotion* these words,

Gononus in Chron.
SS. Deipara. p. 256.

	Thou flower of *Carmel*, and thou flowring Vine,
Flos Carmeli, vitis florigera, Splendor cœli, virgo puerpera Singularis.	Whose glorious Face makes Heaven brighter shine, Virgin and Mother both, without compare.
Mater mitis, sed viri nescia, Carmelitis da privilegia Stella maris.	A Mother mild, who yet no Man didst know, On us poor Carmelites deign to bestow Some special boon, who art the Sea's bright Star.

This Devotion was so pleasing to the *Bl. Virgin*, that she appeared after this to him, accompanied with a multitude of Angels, holding the *Scapulare (a Garment)* of that Order in her hands, and said: This shall be a priviledge to thee, and to all *Carmelites, Whosoever dies in this habit shall escape Eternal Fire, whosoever dies in this shall be saved.* There is also another famous priviledge granted to the *Carmelites Scapular*, that *Whosoever should be buried therein, should not be held in Purgatory*

Colganus, ut supra citat.

gatory pains, beyond the Saturday next after the day of his death.

This priviledge was approved and confirmed by several Popes. *John* XXII. in his Bull from *Lyons, March* 3. and in the 6*th.* Year of his *Popedome*, has these words: *I by the power I have received do confirm this indulgence on Earth, as Christ for the Merits of the Bl.Virgin has granted it in Heaven.* This was also afterwards confirmed by Pope *Alexander* V. by *Clement* VII. *Sixtus* V. *Gregory* XIV. and *Clement* VIII. The Bull of Pope *Clement* the VII. dated *May* 13. 1528. (which begins thus, *Dilecti filii, &c.*) has these words in it. *Mary the glorious Virgin and Mother of God, on the Saturday* (which is the Virgins day) *after the death of such Persons* (so habited) *will visit them, and free their Souls from the pains of Purgatory.* Where by the way we may make one new discovery, that though, for ought I know, *Sunday* may be a good day of the Week to be *born* on; and may be a very comfortable day whilst one *lives*; yet it is, according to this, a very sad and ill day to *dye on:* For, let a Man have never so much favour shew'd him, you see he must lye almost one whole Week in Flames, if he chance to go out of the World on that Day.

But there is nothing of this nature, has made so great a noise, as the priviledges granted by our Saviour's own mouth to *Seraphical S. Francis.* As 1. *That whosoever shall love his Order in his heart, how great a sinner soever he be, he shall find mercy from the Lord.* *Colganus ut supra.* 2. *That none in the Habit of a Franciscan, can make an ill end, and that whosoever shall chuse to live ill in that Order, shall not be able to continue in it long.* The 3d. is more known than any of the other, *viz.* The Priviledges granted by Christ to his Church near *Assisium* in *Italy*, called *S. Maria de Angelis,* or *Portiuncula*; and in memory of the grant, a Festival was appointed on the 2d. of *August*, which even after the reformation of the Breviary by Pope *Pius* V. was allowed by him to be still observed by the *Franciscans*; and has a place at the end of his Breviary in the

the *Proprium Festorum ordinis Minorum,* under the Title of *Festum Consecrationis Ecclesiæ S. Mariæ de Angelis, quod appellatur Festum Portiunculæ.* The story is worth the setting down, out of the Lessons of that Feast, and out of *Gononus* his *Chronicon,* where the circumstances are given us more at large; which is as follows.

Gononus in Chron. p.217.

"In the Year 1221. as S. *Francis* one Night "was praying for sinners, an Angel of the Lord "appeared to him, commanding him to go to "the Church aforesaid; for there Christ with his Mother, "and a Multitude of Angels expected him. The Message "filled him with incredible joy, and he presently arose and "went to the Church, whither when he came, and saw *Christ* "and his Mother standing on the right hand, with fear and "reverence he fell flat upon his face, unto whom *Christ* spake "thus, as he lay prostrate. O *Francis,* thou and thine are "very sollicitous for the salvation of Souls; therefore I "give thee leave to ask something of me, for the common "consolation and salvation of Souls, and for the honour of "my Name; for thou art given for the salvation of Nati-"ons, and for the reparation of my Church : S. *Francis* "being a while in a rapture, at the contemplation of so great "Majesty, when he came to himself, he prayed thus. O our "most holy Father, I miserable sinner beseech thee, that thou "wouldst vouchsafe to bestow this grace upon Mankind, that "all and every Person that comes to this place, and enters "this Church, may obtain an Universal Pardon and Indul-"gence of all their sins, which they shall make confession "of to the Priest. I also intreat the Bl. Virgin thy Mother, "the Advocate of Mankind, that for the obtaining this re-"quest, she would vouchsafe to intercede with thy most glo-"rious Majesty. The Queen of Heaven being moved by "the Prayers of her Servant *Francis,* began immediately "to pray to her Son in this manner. O most High and "Almighty God, I intercede with thy Deity, and humbly "beseech thee, that thou wouldst vouchsafe to grant the re-"quests of this poor *Francis.* The Lord *Christ* presently "replyed;

Devotions of the Roman Church. 261

"replyed; *Brother Francis*, it's a great thing thou hast
"asked, but thou shalt obtain greater. Know therefore
"that I admit thy Petition; but I will have thee to go to
"my *Vicar*, who has the power of binding and loosing in
"Heaven and Earth, and require this Indulgence of him in
"my Name. On the morrow after S. *Francis* went to the
"*Pope*, laid open before him *Christ*'s mandate, intreating
"him, that *what* pleased Christ, whose   Lect.6.in Fest.consecr.
"place on Earth he held, and whose per-   S. *Maria de Angelis*.
"son he represented, that that might not
"displease him. The *Pope* at first did not think his request
"reasonable, because it was altogether free, that is, without
"any oblations; it was the greatest request, and also abso-
"lute and perpetual. He said, that it was requisite, that he
"who would obtain pardon of his sins, should some ways
"deserve it; and the *Pope* denyed that ever the *Roman Court*
"was wont to grant such an Indulgence: The Cardinals also
"that were present, opposed the grant; saying, That the con-
"sequence of it would be, that the Indulgences of the *Holy*
"*Land*, and of the Holy Apostles, S. *Peter* and *Paul*, would
"be neglected. But the *Pope* at length understanding, that
"it was the Divine pleasure it should be so, he granted to S.
"*Francis* a plenary and free and perpetual Indulgence; but
"it was to take place only on one natural day of every year,
"that is, from the *Vespers* of the *Calends* of *August*, to the
"*Vespers* of the next day, which was the *Anniversary day*
"of the said Churches *consecration*.

By this one Revelation to S. *Francis*, here are so many
doubtful Points determined, (concerning Indulgences, the
Authority of the *Pope*, as Vicar of Christ, the necessity of
private confessions to the Priests, the intercession of the Bl.
Virgin) that may well give us *Protestants* just cause of suspi-
tion, that the *Pope* had a greater hand in this grant, than
Christ had. As for those of this Church, who are bound
to believe the truth of that, which has been confirmed by 15.

Martyr. Francis.   Popes (and which one of the later of them,
pag. 324.   viz. *Urban* VIII. *an.* 1624. gave so much cre-
                         S 3   dit

dit to, that in a Year of *Jubilee*, when he suspended all *other Indulgences*, this was declared by his Letters, to be excepted and left untouched) I can only pitty the wretched temptation, which the common people especially are perpetually exposed to, by such grants, of laying as much stress upon the keeping of a day, visiting an Altar, or a Church, dying in such a Habit, and being buried in such a place, to procure the pardon of their sins, and to promote their Salvation, as upon inward moral goodness, and purity of heart and life. In the former cases, Miracles and Revelations are rung in their Ears, to give a mighty reputation to those little and easie observances; and the defects of the Later are pretended to be supplied by the use of the other, as the imperfection of Attrition by the Sacraments of the Church: but when were they told, that a balking of these usages, would not prove dangerous to a person otherwise studious of piety? No, no; the contrary is the business of this Church; amidst a great loosness of manners, which they connive at and tolerate, they furnish the People with frightful stories, to oblige them to all the exactness and care imaginable, about postures and habits, and trifling rules of Orders. Here now, a Convert did but happen in the hot Summer time, to sleep in a posture not modest enough (though no body saw it till afterwards) and the Devil, they are told, appeared in the shape of a *Nun*, and while he so slept, took him about the Neck and kissed him, whereupon he presently fell sick, and dyed within *three* days after. At another time, they are informed, that the Bl. Virgin went round all the Monks Beds, and blessed them all save only one, whom she neglected, and did not care to look upon (a grievous offence, one would imagine, this Monk had been guilty of; alas no) the business was, he lay in his Bed irregularly; either his Girdle was laid aside, or he had put off his Hose, or unloosed his Coat, the Relator could not tell which, but one of them it seems it was, and a fault so great, as to deserve to lose the Bl. Virgins blessing. Another, who in the judgment of

Cæsarius Dialog. distinct. 5. c. 33.

Id m ibid. dist. 7. c. 14.

all

all was thought a very fit Person to be preferred, and by common consent was just ready to be chosen an Abbot, the choice of him by a Divine revelation was forbidden, onely because one time he had presumed to sleep with his Stockings off.   But this punishment was but a small one, in respect of another which was inflicted (in another Stocking story) upon a Convert, who in one of the Granges of *Claravall Abbey*, presumed to wash his stockings without his Masters leave (the miserable Man, says the Relator, not considering how grievously they offend, who in the least things do violate the purity of the Sacred Order; *it seems the purity of his Order was nastiness, if it was a crime to wash his stockings*) but as the Man was doing this, he heard a Voice cry, *Smite him, Smite him*; and immediately he felt two grievous blows given him, one on his Head, the other on his Feet; whereupon he returned pale and trembling to his place, confessed humbly his fault, and described his invisible strokes, how that both of them crept inwardly along, one from his Head, and the other from his Feet, and that he should dye, when those strokes were joyned in his heart; and so it proved, for he dyed of them in a short time.   These and 20. other such ridiculous stories they tell; the effect of which is, the frighting Men into silly and superstitious fears and observances, whilst the undoubted commands of our Saviour are more neglected, and lye unregarded.

Biblioth. Patrum Cisterc. Tom. 1. distinc. 4. c. 25.

Ibid. cap. 24.

To S. Cosma *and S.* Damian, *for success in taking Physick.*

Horæ sec.
us. Roman.   *Anaphona.*

INclyte *Cosma* vale, salveq;
  sacer *Damiane,*
In quibus enituit gloria
  Martyrii.
Sumite nostrarum petimus
  jubilamina laudum.
Et nobis medicam ferte sa-
  lutis opem.

GReat Cosma and blest
  Damian, *all Hail*;
Whose Heads are grac't with
  Martyrs glorious Bayes;
Receive the Tribute of our
  joyful praise,
And bring your Med'cines,
  healing every aile.

Oremus.

INfirmitates nostras, tam
  mentis quàm corporis,
respice quæsumus Omnipo-
tens Deus; & dignare intercedentibus sanctis Martyri-
bus tuis *Cosmâ* & *Damiano,*
cunctis nostris mederi lan-
guoribus.
  Per Dominum, *&c.*

Let us Pray.

ALmighty God, look we beseech thee upon our infirmities both of mind & body, and vouchsafe upon the Intercession of thy holy Martyrs Cosma and Damian, to heal all our diseases.

  By our Lord, *&c.*

NOTES.

THe great credit of these Saints to help in this manner, was built partly, I suppose, upon their profession, being both Brothers and Physicians, (as the old *Roman Bre-viary* tells us) who might the more willingly be still employ-ed in the Art they were so well versed in before, and have a
  natural

natural inclination to look after sick Patients, that addressed themselves to them: but especially, upon the Miracles that are said to appear at their death. As, that when they were chained together, and thrown into the Sea, an Angel loosed their Bonds, and delivered them; *Brev. Rom. antiq.Lec.3.* after this, they were thrown into a great Fire, but upon their Prayers, the Fire lost all its power *Lec.4.* to hurt them: then they were hanged upon a cross, and command given to stone them, but the stones *Lec.5.* rebounded back upon those that threw them: and so in like manner, when Arrows were shot at them, they received no harm at all, but many of those that shot them, were thereby slain. Most of which stories are still retained in the present *Roman Breviary*, and seem to be taken out of *Usuardus*, or *Ado's* Martyrologies, who lived in the 9. Century, the proper Age (as I told you before) for rappers. The worst is, that *Baronius* himself, upon the *Roman* Martyrology (*Sept.* 27.) is forced to confess, that there are abundance of their Acts extant in *Simeon Metaphrastes* and *Surius*, which abound with falshoods, and ridiculous stuff: and if he would have been sincere, he could have told us, that it was not an easie matter, to determine which were true, and which false: but it's all one, Lies have set up many a Saint to good purpose in the Church of *Rome*.

To S. Nicholas *in dangers especially at Sea.*

Horæ Sec. us.Sa-um.   *Antiphona.*

Beatus *Nicolaus* adhuc puerulus, Multo jejunio macerabat corpus.

S. Nicholas *with much fasting did begin,
Though but a Child, to make his Body thin.*

Vers. Ora pro nobis, &c.   Vers. *Pray for us,* &c.

Oremus.

Oremus.

Brev. Rom.
Dec. 6.

DEus qui Beatum *Nicolaum* Pontificem tuum innumeris decorasti miraculis; tribue quæsumus, ut ejus meritis & precibus, à Gehennæ incendiis liberemur.

Per Dominum, &c.

Brev. Sarum.
Dec. 6.

DEus bonitatis Author & bonorum dispensator; concede propitius, ut qui Beati *Nicolai* Confessoris tui atque Pontificis Solennitatem veneramur, ejus Patrociniis atque suffragiis Majestatis tuæ propitiationem consequamur.

Per Christum, &c.

Ibid. O Per omnia laudabilem virum, cujus meritis ab omni clade liberantur, qui ex toto corde quærunt illum.

Let us pray.

O God, who didst grace thy Bishop S. Nicholas with innumerable Miracles; vouchsafe we pray thee, that by his merits and prayers we may be delivered from the flames of Hell.

By our Lord, &c.

O God, the Author of Goodness, and the Dispenser of good things; mercifully grant, that we who venerate the solemnity of thy Confessor & Bishop S. Nicholas, by his Patronage and suffrages may obtain the propitiation of thy Majesty.

Through Christ, &c.

O Man, in all things praise-worthy, by whose Merits they are delivered from all destruction, who seek him with their whole heart.

NOTES.

THere is no great difference in substance, concerning the Acts of this Saint, betwixt the *Old* and the Reformed *Breviaries*. Only the ancient ones, say *more* miraculous

Devotions of the Roman Church. 267

lous things concerning him, the new *fewer*. But we are likely to be excellently informed about him, when *Simeon Metaphrastes* has a hand in his story; concerning whom *Bellarmine* himself has passed this censure, *Illud observandum, à Metaphraste scriptas fuisse historias de vitis sanctorum, multis additis ex proprio ingenio, non ut res gestæ fuerunt, sed ut geri potuerunt.* *De Scriptor. Eccles. ad an. 850.* i. e. Observe, *that the Histories of the Saints Lives were written by Metaphrastes, many particulars being added out of his own head, not as the things were done, but as they might possibly be done.* And a little after, *He has added many and great Miracles, of which there is no mention among the ancient Historians.* I think we may well reckon in this number, that which is mentioned in the first *Antiphona*, and is still retained in the *Breviary* (Les. 4.) "When he was "an Infant, though on other days he suckt his Nurses milk "frequently, yet on *Wednesdays* and *Fridays* he would suck "her but once *, and that in the Evening, which custome "of Fasting he always observed the rest of his Life: which thing is also mentioned in the *Prosa* of the old *Roman* and *Sarisbury* Missals;

* These *sucking Miracles,* I perceive they are much pleased with, for thus they tell us that S. *Katherine* the *Swedish Virgin*, as a sign of her after chastity, refused with cries and tears to suck the milk of incontinent Women, as if it had been Wormwood. *In vit. ejus apud Bolland. ad Mart. 24.*

Qui in cunis adhuc jacens servando jejunia, A papilla cœpit summâ promereri gloriâ.	*Who yet in Cradle rockt, obtain'd the praise Of strict observing usual fasting dayes; An early Saint! not half so much in Love With Nurses milk, as with the joys above.*

We need not therefore think it strange, that a Saint who began so early to be famous, should grow in wonders with his

his Age, and at last come to be invoked as an Universal Deliverer from all dangers. I confess, when I read the first Prayer, which is the proper Collect both in the *Breviaries* and *Missals* for this Saint, it seemed to me a very cross-grain'd one, that when by the story that is told of him, his Talent, one would imagine, had lien peculiarly in helping and saving Men out of the distresses of *Water*, he should here be invoked to free them from the *Fire of Hell*: But I quickly corrected my fancy, when I considered, that nothing need seem impossible to the prayers of him, who fasted in his Cradle twice a Week, especially when it was (as you heard) upon *Wednesdays* and *Fridays*; for no *Astrologer* could have erected a Scheme of the Heavens more propitious for Miracles, than these two days are; (as we found before in S. *Roch*, of whom the same is affirmed.) Besides too, there is this affinity betwixt the *Sea* and *Hell*, that they are each of them a great *Abyss*; and it is so common and Proverbial to express all dangers by *Fire* and *Water*, that it was great pitty, that he who had such great command over the *one*, should have no stroke in matters that related to the *other*. Passing therefore over other things which the *Breviary* mentions, (as his miraculous Election to be Bishop of *Myrea*, not by the intervening of *Lots*, as in the choice of *Matthias*, but by a *voice from Heaven*, bidding them make him Bishop, who first entered the Church next Morning, telling them his Name should be *Nicholas*, which he first did, as if sent by God) Let's only see, whence his fame arose for a Deliverer in distresses at Sea. Thus then the *Legend* informs us.

Brev. Sar. lec. 7. & Brev. Rom. antiq. Lec. 9.

"Certain Mariners being in great danger by a suddain Tempest that arose at Sea, they began to cry out; O *Nicholas* the Servant of God, if those things be true which we have heard concerning thee, now succour us; that so being delivered from this danger, we may render thanks to God and thee. While they spake these words, one appeared, saying to them; *Behold I am here, for you called me*; and he began to help them in ordering

"dering their Cables and Sailes and other Tacklings; and a
"while after, all the noise of the Sea was quieted, and the
"Tempest ceased * : The Mariners when they came to shore,
"presently inquired where *Nicho-*
"*las* was; and when they learnt
"that he was in the Church, they
"went in thither, and, which is
"wonderful to be related, they im-
"mediately knew him, without any
"bodies showing, though they had
"never seen him before; and fal-
"ling prostrate at his Feet, they
"paid their thanks to him, relating
"how by his suffrages they had
"been delivered, when they were
"even at the brink of Death.

* The same is set down in a Prose of the Old *Roman* Missal. 1520.

O beate Nicola,
Nos ad portum maris trahe
de mortis angustiis;
Trahe nos ad portum maris
Tu qui tot auxiliaris
Pietatis gratia. (sum
Dum clamarent nec incas-
Ecce quidam dicens, Assum
ad vestra præsidia :
Statim aura datur grata
Et Tempestas fit sedata
Quieverunt maris.

And now I hope, after this story, none will wonder, when he hears of that Prayer to this Saint, (though otherwise it might seem a strange one) which we find cited by *Chemnitius*, out of the Hours of the Church of *Hildensheim*, in his *Examen Concil. Trid. Part.* 3.

Credo pie Sancte *Nicolae*, tuis me precibus esse salvandum, ideo ad te clamo, & te precibus meis licet indignis pulsare non desisto, ut te intercedente, ab imminentibus periculis, à peccatis & offensionibus meis, quibus quotidie affligor, merear liberari: Salva me supplicem famulum tuum, amice dei *Nicolae*, de præsentibus angustiis & tribulationibus, quia

O Pious S. Nicholas, I believe that I shall be saved by thy Prayers, therefore I cry to Thee, and cease not to importune thee by my prayers though unworthy ones, that I may merit by thy intercession, to be delivered from imminent perils, from my sins & offences, wherewith I am daily afflicted: Save me thy supplicating Servant, O Nicholas, thou Friend of
in

in te confidit anima mea, ut per te me salvet qui te sibi elegit.

God, from present straits & Tribulations, because my Soul trusteth in thee, that he may save me by thee, who hath chosen thee to himself.

Who need boggle now at the words of the *Hymn* mentioned by the same Author, and also by *Cassander*, p. 252. of his Works?

O Venerande Pontifex
Pius nec tardus Opifex
Cunctis, qui corde credulo
Te quærunt in periculo;
A*b*er mortis dispendia,
Confer vitæ stipendia,
Quò post carnis exilia
Tecum simus in gloria.

S. Nicholas *thou venerable Bishop,*
Inclin'd to pitty and to help not slack,
When dangers threaten thou ne'er failest his hope
Whose forward faith about to thee does tack,
From Deaths expensive losses us defend,
The pleasing gains of life unto us give;
That when the crosses of this flesh have end,
With thee we may in Glory ever live.

How edifying and Spiritual is the Application of all that is said of this *Sea-Patron*, which the *Prosa* in the forecited *Roman Missal* gives us?

Nos qui sumus in hoc mundo
Vitiorum in profundo
   Jam passi naufragia,
Gloriose *Nicolae,*
Ad salutis portum trahe
   Ubi Pax & Gloria.

We that in this World impure
In Seas of vice are almost drown'd,
Blest Nicolas bring to Port secure,
Where Peace and Glory's to be found.

To

To S. Barbara, *for to be Confest, and to receive the Eucharist, before Death.*

Horæ sec. us. Rom.   *Antiph.*

Virgo fide sana
  De stirpe creata profana
Gaudia mundana
Postponit & Idola vana.
  Ora pro nobis, &c.

This Virgin found in Christian Faith,
Though sprung from race that was profane,
All worldly joyes despised hath,
And undervalued Idols vain.
  Pray for us, &c.

Ibid. & Horæ sec. us. Sar.   *Oremus.*

INtercessio quæsumus Domine Beatæ *Barbaræ*, Virginis & Martyris tuæ, ab omni adversitate nos protegat, ut per ejus interventum, gloriosissimum Sacrosancti corporis & sanguinis Domini nostri Jesu Christi Sacramentum, ante diem exitûs nostri, per veram pœnitentiam & puram confessionem, percipere mereamur.

    Per Dominum, &c.

Let us Pray.

We pray Thee, O Lord, that the Intercession of S. Barbara, thy Virgin and Martyr, may protect us from all adversity; that by her means we may, by true repentance and pure confession, merit to receive before the day of our death the most glorious Sacrament of the most holy body and blood of our Lord Jesus Christ.

    Through our Lord, &c.

NOTES.

THere is scarce any Saint in the *Kalendar*, of whom more incredible things are told, than of S. *Barbara*, in the *old Roman Breviary*; nor indeed more ridiculous.

Lef. 1. She is said to be the only Daughter of One *Dioscurus* a Heathen, in the Reign of *Maximianus* (or, as *Baronius* will have it, of *Maximinus*) and is placed in the Year 230. and said to be instructed in the Faith by *Origen* (though it's strange so famous a Martyr should be pretermitted by *Eusebius*, who in his *Ecclesiastical History* (lib. 6.) mentions several Women, whom Origen converted to Christianity, but does not so much as name her among them.)

Lef. 2. Her beauty was so great, that to defend it, her Father built a Tower, only with *two* Windows, and a place to Bath in, curiously contrived and adorned, where she was put.

Lef. 3. There, while she was in Meditation, an Angel stood by her, and explained to her all things belonging to the Catholick Faith; and when the Angel opened the Mystery of the Incarnation, to her great joy, *Jesus* appeared in the shape of a Child. And now being more strong in faith, in the absence of her Father, she commands the Workmen to make a third Window in the Tower towards the East, she being a worshipper of the Trinity, saying, That only by 3 Windows (so it is in *Metaphrastes*) every one that comes into the World is enlightned: and this she said, signifying the Majesty of the H. Trinity (as *Metaphr.* has it) and when her Father was angry at this talk of hers, and at the addition of the third Window, she pointed with her Fingers, and said, *Behold the Father, Son and Holy Ghost.* [A fine discovery this is of the Trinity, by one that had been newly instructed in the Catholick Faith by an Angel: Like to which is that blasphemous Picture, in the *Salisbury Hours*, where the Trinity is represented by 3 Heads upon one Neck of a Mans Body. And with the like prophaneness and folly, the *Festivale**

---

* Festiv. in die Trinit. *which is taken out of* Durandus, *who giving a reason why the Bell tolls thrice, at the death of a* Man; *says, It is because the Trinity was first found in Man:* Primo enim formatus est *Adam* de terra, deinde Mulier ex *Adam*, postea homo creatus est ab utroque; & ita est ibi Trinitas. *Durand. Rational. lib. 1. c. 4. f. 13.*

discourses:

discourses: "*Adam* our Fore-father that came out of the
"Earth, one Person; and *Eve* of *Adam* the second Person;
"and of them both cometh the third Person, as their Child;
"thus the Trinity was found in *Man*. But methinks the
Nuns have found the Trinity better than thus in *Woman-
kind*. For in the Life of S. *Clara de monte
Falconis*, we are told, that in her heart, *Apud Ribadeneir.
Inter vit. Extra-
vag. p. 261.*
when it was opened, were found the impressions and marks of the passion of our Savi-
our, *viz.* a Crucifix with *three* Nayles, the Spear, Spunge,
and Reed on one side; and on the other, the Whips, Rods,
Pillar, (*at which he was scourged*) the Crown of Thornes;
and these signs of our Saviour's passion, did consist of strong
and hard Nerves. But (which I cite it for) they found that
which was still more wonderful, three Balls in her Gall, as
it were three Filberts, of equal weight, colour and bigness,
which (*says her life*) was a plain Testimony of the H. Trinity, to which this Virgin was wholly devoted: Which is
more fully exprest by *Bernardinus de Bustis* *, whose words
are these; "In her heart was found
"a Crucifix ingraved, with all the ** Cited in the Martyrolog.
Franciscan. 17 Aug. p. 352.*
"Mysteries of the Passion; and in
"her Breast were found *three* little Balls, one of which does
"weigh as much as two of them, nay as much as all three
"together; and all three together weigh no more than one
"alone; by which is signified, that she had a continual re-
"membrance of the passion of Christ, and a perfect belief
"of the Unity of the Divine Essence, and of the equality of
"the *three* Divine Persons. (*Which I take it is the most my-
sterious Relique that ever was found in Flesh, if any one can
believe it.*)

The *Festivale*, a little after, explains the Trinity by Water, Ice and Snow, which three, says he, be divers
in substance, yet all is but Water. "The Water *fol. 47.*
"is so full of might, that is to understand the Fa-
"ther: by the Son *Jesu Christ*, ye shall understand *Ice*, that
"is, Water congealed hard and brittle; that is *Jesu Christ*
"very

"very God and Man, that took the substance and frailty of "Mankind: by the *Snow*, ye shall understand the H. Ghost; "for right as Snow is but Water and Ice and Light in the "Ayr, but how, no Man can tell, so cometh the H. Ghost "from the Father and the Son. *Capgrave* also gives us a Narration, how when *France* was troubled with the *Arrian Heresie*, that Errour was reproved; and that God in *three* Persons, was of *One* and of equal substance, was shown by this plain Miracle of *three* drops clearer than Crystal, that fell upon the Altar, as it were from the Roof of the Church, which drops were of equal magnitude, and being joyned together, made one most fair Gemm.] *But to go on with the Story of S. Barbara.*

<small>Capgr. in vit. Egberti, f. 122.</small>

Less. 4. Upon the Marble of the Bath, she made the signs of the Cross, which remain to this day: (*Metaphrastes* says more expresly, *That she made the sign of the Cross with her Finger on the Marble, which made a remaining Impression, as if it had been graved with Iron*) and in the Bath, God so ordering it, upon her Prayer she was wonderfully baptized by *John* the *Baptist*.

Less. 5. Her Father perceiving, by the alterations she had made in the Tower, and by her discourses, that she was a Christian; drew out his Sword, in indignation, to slay his Daughter: but upon her Prayers to God, a great Stone opening it self, received her into its Cavity, and attended * her to a Mountain full of Caves, where she thought to have hid her self, but was discovered by a Shepheard, who was punisht for it miraculously, he himself being changed into a Marble Statue, and all his Sheep into Locusts, (or, as *Metaphrastes* says, into Beetles) which to the perpetual accusation of the crime, continually fly about her Grave.

<small>* Tecum virgo lapis volat. Prosa in Missal. Roman. Antiqu.</small>

Less. 8. She was, after this, brought before the Heathen President, who after Scourgings and beating with Clubs, commanded her Breasts to be cut off, and to b- led naked through

through all the City. But upon her Prayers, that her naked Body might not be exposed to the *Pagans*, an Angel came and covered her with a white Garment, and so healed the wounds of her Body, that not so much as a Scar appeared.

Les. 9. After this, her Father cut off her Head with his own Hands, and was severely punisht for it; for as he went down the Hill where the Murder was committed, Fire descended from Heaven, and so consumed him, that not so much as any Dust of his Body remained. (*Thus far the Lessons.*)

I cannot omit here the relating an extraordinary Miracle brought to confirm the efficacy of Prayers to S. *Barbara*, for obtaining the *Eucharist* and *Confession* before Death. It is recorded by *Surius* thus. In the Year 1448, at a Town called *Gorcum* in *Holland*, one *Henry Kock* by an accident of a Candle that fell into the Straw, had his House set on Fire in the Night, and he himself hardly escaped in his shirt, which began to burn in *two* places: but he remembred that he had left Money in the House, and would return into it again to save it; but before he could come to the place where it lay, the House fell upon his naked Body: when apprehending present Death, though the scorching Flames tormented him, yet he was more afflicted, because he had not been fore-armed against Death, by the Sacraments of the Church; and in this distress, he betook himself to S. *Barbara* for Soul-remedies, praying thus. *O S. Barbara, succour a miserable wretch, and one dying in his sins, which thing thou art now able to perform by thy Spouse: Let that be done by thy Prayers in me, which was of old promised by Heaven to thee, as thou wast a dying for Christ: Let thy Spouse be mindful of thy rosie and Virgin blood, let him remember thy chast and Virgin love, that my Soul may not go out of my Body, till it be purged by the Sacrament of Confession, and fore-armed with the saving Viaticum.*

Thus you must believe he prayed, (though it seems to be too long a Prayer for one whole Body was actually burning

Surius in vit. Barbaræ 4 Decemb. mentioned also by *Ribadeneira* in her life.

in Flames) but see the effect. S. *Barbara* being thus invoked, immediately presents her self, in such a form as she used to be pictured within Churches; and with her Garment, she quenched presently the Globes of Fire, and with her white Hand, brought him through the Straw-roof, and setting him in a safe place, spake thus to him. *Because thou hast often offered acceptable Devotions to me, and now implored the Divine mercy by my Patronage know that by my means thy life shall be prolonged till Morning, in which time thou mayst be confest, and receive the Sacraments of the Eucharist and extream Unction.* After which words, S. *Barbara* disappeared: all was performed as she said, though *Henry* was so burnt, that scarce any Flesh was left on his Bones unconsumed, and that which remained was as black as a *Negro*'s; only his Eyes, Tongue and Heart, remained untoucht. Testified by *Theodoric* the Priest that confest him; a credible Witness no doubt. *

* *Such another foolish story the* Golden Legend *gives us in her Life; that a Man that was thought to be starved to death, and by a Rope cast about his Neck, was drawn to the top of a Tower, and thrown off from thence, when he came to the ground, he rose up upon his feet; and gave this account to those that wondered how he was alive (having so long continued without any Meat) and how he could be preserved in his fall; he told them that S Barbara preserved him in all his straits; and in his fall from the Tower sustained him with her holy hands, and that he cou'd not dye till he was confest, and received the Eucharist and extream Unction.*

This story puts me in mind of another miraculous one, concerning the *Communicating* of S. *Brigid* before she dyed.

<small>Colganus vit.
S. Nennidii ad
18 Januar.</small>
It is thus. S. *Brigid* told Saint *Nennidius*, a Convert of hers, that on the day of her death, she would receive the Eucharist from his hand. He answered her, Would to God you might live till that come to pass: she replyed, that so it should be. Upon which when *Nennidius* was gone from her, he provided for his hand (with which he was to give the Eucharist) a strait Brass Glove (some say a Silver one) with a Lock and Key for it, lest it should touch his Body, or his Hand be
touched

touched by any unclean thing: And farther, believing what S. *Brigid* told him, and being willing to prolong her life for the common good many Years, he undertook a Pilgrimage to *Rome*; and entring a Ship, he threw the Key of his Glove into the Sea. *But there is no wisdom nor counsel against the Lord*: for some while after, returning into his Countrey, he was admonished by an Angel, that the day of S. *Brigid's* death was at hand, and that he must give to her, her last *Viaticum*: The Night following lodging at a *Fisherman's* House, his Landlord found a Key in the Belly of a Fish, that he had opened, which Saint *Nennidius* knew to be the very same he had thrown long before into the Sea; and so understanding that it was the will of God he should go over to S. *Brigid*, he did so; and found her almost expiring, to whom he gave the Eucharist before she dyed.

To St. Marus *Bishop of Triers, for Palseys and Convulsions*, &c.

Brev. Eccl. Trev. apud Bolland. ad 25 Janu r.

Deus, qui S. *Mari* Confessoris tui atque Pontificis intercessione, homines ipsum invocantes, à quavis morbida corporis membrorumque contractione, atque Paralysi liberare præservareque dignaris; concede nos ejusdem Sancti meritis, sic corporalis vitæ sanitate potiri, ut æternæ animarum salutis remedium in cœlestibus inveniamus. Per Christum, &c.

O God, who by the intercession of S. Marus thy Confessor and Bishop, dost vouchsafe to preserve & deliver Men that invoke him, from any diseased contraction of the body & members, and from the Palsey; Grant that we, by the merits of the same Saint, may so enjoy health of bodily life, that we may find the remedy of the eternal salvation of our Souls in Heaven. By our Lord, &c.

S. Blasius

S. Blaſius for removing Bones that ſtick in the Throat.

THe *Salisbury Breviary* informs us, that when this Saint came to be beheaded, he prayed to God in this manner: "O God, hear me thy Servant, that if any one remembring me, ſhall fall down and worſhip Thee; if any Fiſh-bone, or any other Bone ſhall ſtick in his Throat; or if he fall into any Infirmity, Tribulation, or Danger, receive, O Lord, I beſeech thee, his requeſt. The Lord ſaid, I will fulfill all thy Petition. The Invocation of this Saint, is a preſent remedy in ſuch caſes, preſcribed by a *Greek* Phyſician, ſays *Ribadeneira*, who alſo directs, that taking ſuch Perſons by the Throat, theſe words ſhould be pronounced aloud: viz. *Blaſius the Martyr, and the Servant of Chriſt ſays, either come up or elſe go down.*

Brev. Sar. Lec. 3. S. Blaſii ad Feb. 3.

Ribadeneira 3 F. br. p. 90.

S. Emetherius and S. Celedonius, for allaying Hail-ſtorms and ſudden Tempeſts.

THeſe two Saints are venerated in *Spain*, as having great power to allay Hail-ſtorms. "For, we are told, that in ſuch caſes, the Clergy of the Place, where their Chappel is, make a ſolemn Proceſſion thither; they put lighted Candles upon their Altar, and after they have ſung the Hymn with the *Antiphona*, they ſubjoyn the praiſes of "theſe

Bolland. Act. Sanc. 3 Mart. p. 234.

"these Saints, and the desired Calm follows. The truth is, by that time all these things are done, especially if the Priests do not cut short the praising work, but give these Saints their due commendation; a violent Tempest of Hail may cease naturally, without the help of them, or any other Saint besides.

S. Venisa, *for the Green-sickness, & pro Ordinandis menstruis, and Bloody Fluxes.*

THis Saint has a Chappel dedicated to her in a Village hard by *Roan* in *France*, and a Feast kept to her Memory, the day before *Ash-Wednesday*. And at *Valentiana* in *Hannovia*, there the Women implore her Patronage in the forenamed Cases; binding themselves about, for 9. days together, with Purple or white Swathes, according to the several proper kinds of this Disease; when they are cured, they hang them up near the Statue of S. *Venisa*; and by reason of the Multitude of those that frequent the place, the heap of such Oblations does so increase, that they are fain to remove them. The Women do the like at *Tourney*, and other places. Some conjecture with probability, that this S. *Venisa* (or *Venica*) is the same with S. *Veronica*, only her name contracted; and that all this Devotion comes from the common Opinion, that she was the Woman, whom Christ in the Gospel cured of the *Bloody-Flux*. There are many other Saints whose Patronage they implore, besides these I have named, as S. *Lucy*, for sore Eyes; S. *Leonard*, for Prisoners and Captives; S. *Hubert*, for biting with mad Dogs, or any venomous Beasts, *&c.* whose stories, I shall for Brevity omit, and only add one more.

Bolland. de S. Veronica. 4 *Febr. p.* 454.

S. Anthony of Padua, *for the recovery of lost Goods.*

THis is the last Example, I shall mention, of *Patron Saints*; but his veneration is so great in the Church of *Rome*, his Preaching and Miracles so famous, that it will require something a larger Discourse than I have bestowed upon the rest. He was a Contemporary and Disciple of S. *Francis*, to whom he was so dear, that he used to call him *his Bishop.* (as *Trithemius* tells us.) The present *Breviaries* have only *three* short proper Lessons for him, *Jun.* 13. and the following *Collect*:

ECclesiam tuam, Deus, beati *Antonii* Confessoris tui solennitas votiva lætificet; ut spiritualibus semper muniatur auxiliis, & gaudiis perfrui mereatur æternis. Per Dominum, *&c.*	O God, let the much desired solemnity of Bl. Anthony *thy Confessor* glad *thy Church*; that so it may be always defended with spiritual aids, and may merit the fruition of eternal joyes. Through our Lord, *&c.*

But the *Franciscans*, even after the Reformation of the Breviary, by Pope *Pius* V. obtained from him the priviledge of having *Proper Offices* for some *famed Saints* of their own Order, which were Printed a-part, at the end of his Breviary; among which, this S. *Anthony* has a large place, where I find *Twenty* Lessons of the old Breviary concerning him, still retained without alteration; and I hope the following *Popes* have not been so unkind, as to debar them from rehearsing those pleasant and beloved stories of S. *Francis*, and his great Followers, nor contracted their

Devotions

Devotions into a narrower room than that *Reforming Pope* did. I leave the Reader to confult the *Hymns* there, which they fing in Honour of him; and come to the bufinefs of his Patronage in the cafe of loft goods.

This is affirmed by many Authors. *Guillelmus Pepin**, a *Paris* Doctor, fays; "This Saint has "a priviledge from the Lord, in refe- "rence to loft goods; which by his me- "rits are often recovered, which I my "felf have frequently experienced. *Pelbartus*, a Francif- can, fays the fame; "That God, as he made him wonder- "ful in his life, by giving him the grace to be able to reco- "ver *loft Souls*; fo now he is in Heaven, he has granted "Men the favour wonderfully to recover by his merits *loft* "*goods*. But none I meet with, has given fo particular an account of it, as *Ribadeneira*, whofe words are thefe; "Chriftian piety does implore the Patro- "nage of S. *Anthony*, efpecially when afflict- "ed with the lofs of Goods, and his merits "work wonderous effects in this Cafe. The Original of "this Devotion feems to be this: A certain *Francifcan* "*Novice*, throwing off his Habit, ran away from the Mo- "naftery, (in which the Saint lived) and ftole away with "him a Pfalm Book, written with S. *Anthony*'s own hand, "and explained with Marginal notes, which S. *Anthony* "often ufed, when he privately expounded the Scriptures to "the Friers. As foon as *Anthony* perceived his Book to "be ftollen, he falling down on his Knees earneftly prayed "God, that he would reftore the Book to him again. In "the mean time the Apoftate Thief having his Book with "him, as he prepared to fwim over the River, met the "Devil; who with a drawn Sword in his hand, command- "ed him immediately to go back again, and reftore to S. "*Anthony* the Book he had ftollen from him; threatning "to kill him, unlefs he did fo: The Devil required this "with fo terrible an afpect, that the Thief being aftonifhed, "prefently returns to the Monaftery, reftores to the Saint
"his

* *Citat. inter Elogia prafix. vit. S. Anton. apud Joh. de la Hay.*

Ribaden. vit. S. Anton. 13 Jun.

"his Book, & continued in a religious course of life ever after.

I see the Church of *Rome* will never be at a loss for ways to promote this their Superstition. The most common Method we have heard of hitherto, has been *Revelations* and *Voices*, pretending gracious grants from God, to the merits of such and such Saints, that Persons in their particular distresses should find desired relief, when they did invoke them: this seems to be a pretty plausible incouragement, and to require only satisfaction in one doubt, how to be secured, that God spoke such words; for if he did, who will not readily determine his practice, by the plain significations of his heavenly will and pleasure? But as for the occasion here mentioned, there are, methinks, a great many discouraging circumstances in the story; so that the greater opinion a Man had of this Saint, the less expectation should he, in all reason, have of recovering his losses by the choice of this Patron, if this be all that can be produced to assure him, that his addresses to him in this case shall not be unsuccessful. For, 1. Few Mens losses are of that importance, that S. *Anthony's Psalter* was, especially with his admirable *Divinity* noted in the Margin: And again, few Mens merits, if all be true that is told of him, could equalize his; and why then should every one presume that their Prayers shall be extraordinarily heard, because his were? To which may be added this main doubt, that I believe that this is one of the first instances that can be given of the Devils threatning, and frighting any one into honesty, and into Devotion; and, considering his interest, it's very likely to be the last of the kind: and for any one now to tell us (as *Pepin* did) that he has found the success and benefit of such addresses, would be only to set all the cunning Men, and all the *Astrologers* a laughing (whose trade for discovering lost goods, seems to be threatned, by setting up this Saint for a *Patron*) for they would be ready, I dare vouch for them, to forswear their Art, if S. *Anthony* had ever helped so many to their lost goods, as they will tell you they have done.

But it may be, it is not so much this foolish story which

Riba-

Ribadeneira has pitched upon, (or at least not this alone) as the mighty fame of S. *Anthony*, and the reputation he has got in the *Roman* Church, partly as a powerful and prophetical Preacher, and partly as a worker of Miracles, that has invited them to a strange veneration of him; and then you may give them leave to chuse what way to express it in; and so many having been possessed before him of other Offices, this might fall to him of course.

That which I shall therefore do farther, shall be to give the *Reader* some account of the admirable things that are reported of him in his life; which *Ribadeneira* has given us more concisely, and *Surius* more at large; and more lately (*an.* 1641.) *Joh. de la Haye*, (who has given us S. *Anthony's* works) has put that Life in *Surius* before them, with some *additional Miracles* after his *Canonization*, and has divided it, for the Readers greater ease, into Chapters, whom therefore I shall cite all along in the following Discourse. To pass over other less material things concerning S. *Anthony*, I shall only consider what relates to his *preaching* and *miracles*.

The first occasion of his being noted for a Preacher (who was before accounted an illiterate person, and to have no farther skill than to say the Church-offices, and had submitted to the mean imployments in the Kitchin, of washing Dishes, and scowring Kettles, and used to sweep the *Friers* rooms) was, when he took sacred Orders with certain *Dominicans*, who being put upon it to Preach at that time to the People, excused themselves that they were altogether unprovided of a Sermon; whereupon S. *Anthony* was intreated to Preach (though it was *ex tempore*) whatsoever the spirit should suggest to him: His modesty was such that he also would fain have declined it, telling the *President* (who urged it) how little Learning he had, and that having been condemned to such humble Offices, he was better acquainted with *Potts* and *Besomes*, than *Scholastical Subtilties*; all this would not bring him off, but Preach he must:

Concerning S. *Anthony's* Preaching.

Ribaden. in vit. Anthon. 13 *Jun.* p. 247. *Et in vit. ejus apud Joh. de la Haye, c.* 6.

must: At the beginning of his Sermon he spoke to them simply and plainly; but in the progress of his discourse, he used such elegancy of words, such heights of mystical sentences, that rapt all his Auditors into admiration, especially because it was beyond all their expectation.

Orsus est simpliciter ad eos dicere.

And now the next thing we hear of him is, that he receives commission from the *Minister General* to Preach abroad; and he is so busie in this new work, that he runs up and down from one City and Town to another: The *Churches* were not sufficient wherein to spend his Zeal: but *Camps* and *Streets* and *Fields* are the Places where he chuses to Preach in; which course of his the Jesuite *Lorinus* would fain countenance, from something he fancies like it in the *Apostles*; but the resemblance is far greater betwixt him and our *Quakers*; who are a restless Generation, troublesome, and furious in their heats, of an ill-guided Zeal, and endeavouring to be popular by the pretences of extraordinary humility.

In vit. Antonii. cap. 7.

Lorinus in Act. 2. v. 6.

He preached at *Rome* one time before the *Pope* so much to his content and wonder, that he called him *Arcam Testamenti*, the *Ark* of the *Testament*: and well might he call him so, (says the Author of his Life) for he had the Scriptures so fastned in his Memory, that he could from thence have wholly restored them, if all the Books of Scripture had been lost. But whether the *Pope* had any great skill in Sermons or no, to be sure S. *Francis* had: and we are told that when S. *Anthony* was preaching one time upon the passion of our Saviour, S. *Francis*, though he was far distant in another Countrey, yet he appeared to his Children after a wonderful manner in the Ayre, for he seemed to stretch out his Arms a-cross, as it were approving *Anthony*'s Sermon, and showing what the *Friers* ought to imitate, and blessing them, he made the sign of the Cross over them.

Vit. Ant. c. 8.

Ibid. c. 10.

But we hear of a wonderful approbation of him for a
Preach-

Preacher, which was given him by the Inhabitants of the Sea, more astonishing than this Apparition in the *Ayre*. For as he was preaching at *Ariminum*, which was a Nest at that time of Heretiques, and few or none regarded his Doctrine, he went out of the *Ribadeneir. p.247. Francis. Mendozius inter Elogia præfix. vit. S.Antonii.* City, and sat him down by the Sea-side, and called to the Fishes in this Language. "Do you at least lift up your "heads, in regard to my words, since the Heretiques deny "to hearken to me. He had scarce left off speaking, when a Multitude of great and little Fishes thronged to the shore where he sate, lifting up their heads out of the Water, as it were to signifie their attention to his words. Then the Holy man, after he had saluted them by the name of *Brethren*, (a complement he learnt from S. *Francis*) he rehearsed to them the benefits for which they were indebted to their Creator, what gratitude they owed Him, and what serviceable offices they might perform towards him. (What pitty is it that this edifying Sermon should be lost, and since his skill was so great, that he did not leave a Treatise behind him upon this Subject, concerning *The whole Duty of Fishes* towards God?) When he had concluded his Sermon, the Fishes bended their heads, as if they asked his blessing, and went back into the Sea. And now it is no wonder to tell you, that the People were astonisht at the Miracle, that the Heretiques that were present, were struck as mute as Fishes, as to any farther opposition and contradiction; only they fell at his Feet, declaring their embracing the Orthodox Faith, and their Conversion. We are farther informed that a Prophetick Spirit accompanied his Preaching, of which they tell this story.

S. *Anthony* preaching at the Funeral of a certain *Usurer*, took that place for his Text, *Where your Treasure is, there will your Heart be also.* In his Sermon, among other things, he said. "This Rich man is "dead, and is buried in Hell: Go to his Treasure, and you "shall find his heart in the middle of it, though his Body "be

Vit. Anton. cap. 19.

"be buried: The Parents and Friends of the Man, went and searched, and they found his heart yet hot in the midst of his Money.

It will be now, after all this, no strange thing to be told, that all People were very desirous to hear such a Preacher, or to find him frequently engaged in this Work, when he is so much admired, that sometimes *Thirty Thousand People*, or more were present at one of his Sermons. When he preached a *Lent* course, the Church could not hold the Number of his Auditors, so that he was fain to hold forth in the open Fields. Thither from all Quarters People flock in crowds to hear him; They rise before Day, and strive which shall get first to the place, where the Sermon was to be: There you might see Souldiers and Noble Matrons, and such as used before to lye long in Bed, running in the dark, and watchfully expecting the Preacher. The Tradesmen would not open their Shops, or sell their Wares, before his Sermon was over. The good Women in devotion, cut off pieces of his Cloaths with their Sizzers, laying them up for Reliques, and he counted himself happy that could but touch the Hemm of his Garment. It was admirable to observe in this great Concourse of People, no ill behaviour, no laughter, no Children crying, no disturbing noises; all their Ears were attentive, their Eyes perpetually fixed upon the Man of God, all waited to hear him with untired patience, and much devotion, as if not any Man, but an Angel descended from Heaven spoke to them. The fervour of the Preacher was such, that his speech came from his Mouth, as from a hot Furnace; the effect was, that he wonderfully affected his Auditory, penetrated into the very marrow of their Souls, raising in them much devotion and compunction, hatred and detestation of their Vices: so that People were heard to say one to another, with much sighing; Ah miserable wretch that I am! who never till now thought such a thing to be a sin, and if I had known it to be such, would never have committed it: they

Ibid. cap. 12.

Ibid. cap. 13. & 21.

Devotions of the Roman Church.

they excited one another to make *confessions*, to undertake *Religious Pilgrimages*, to fast on certain days in honour of the *Mother of God, &c.* He sent so many of both Sexes to confess their sins, that neither the *Friers* nor *Priests*, though many did attend him, were enow to hear all their Confessions. Then first Men began to go in Procession by Troops, beating themselves, and singing pious Canticles * ; and this laudable custome proceeding from such an Author, increased more and more; so that almost in all the parts of *Italy*, it is strictly observed to this day.

* Ribadeneira *(p.248.) says, that the People at* Padua, *upon his Preaching at the time of the Spring-Fast, were so melted into sorrow and tears, that in great Companies unbaring their backs in the very streets, they severely whipped themselves, Crying out to God,* Mercy, Mercy.

And now I cannot but fancy, after this huge noise concerning such an *Angelical Preacher*, it will be a very seasonable Gratification of the *Reader*, to acquaint him with S. *Anthony*'s way of Preaching : That he may understand,

Quid dignum tanto feret hic promissor hiatu;

If his Strong sense by charming Tongue apply'd,
Makes good what Fame proclaims with mouth so wide.

And since it has fallen out so luckily that S. *Anthony*'s Sermons have out-lived him, and have been put forth as great Jewels and Rarities by their own Men; I shall only do the part of a *Rehearser*; not engaging my self to give you every word of the Sermons I mention, for (notwithstanding all that has been said in their commendation) I am sure the dulness of them would tire and cloy the *Reader*; nor shall I add any thing of my own, but faithfully translate his words, that no Man may object that I have plaid tricks with him. And since I find *Trithemius* has commended his *Sermones de Tempore*, upon those words, *Erunt signa in sole,&c.* And his

his *Sermone de Sanctis*, as most elegant and ardent discourses; I'le chuse to give the *Reader* a tast of each: And though they are all of a piece, yet since it may be presumed that the first Sermon in his Works, is not the worst, I'le begin with that.

S. Anthony's *Sermon on the* 1. *Sunday in Advent.*

Luc. 21. v. 25.

There shall be Signs in the Sun, and in the Moon and Stars; and on Earth distress of Nations.

"HEre are *Four* Things observable, according as there "are *Four* Advents, *viz.* Into Flesh, into the Mind, "to Death, and to the final Judgment. 1. The coming in-"to Flesh, and this is the Assumption of humane Flesh, in "those words, *There shall be Signs in the Sun*; for the *Sun* "is the *Son of God.* The 2d. (*Advent*) is into the Mind "spiritually; and this is the purgation of our Mind, or pro-"tection against Sin, or bestowing Vertues on us. In these "words; *There shall be Signs in the Moon.* The 3d. is, *In* "*Death,* which is the division of Soul and Body: in these "words, *And in the Stars.* The 4th. is, in the end of all "things, when there shall be a discussing of Merits, and pu-"nishing of Vices: in these words, *And on Earth distress* "*of Nations, &c.*

"*There shall be Signs in the Sun.*] The *Sun* (so called be-"cause it shines alone, *Sol quod solus luceat*) is *Christ,* who "dwells in Light inaccessible: in compare with whose san-"ctity and brightness, all that of the Saints suffers diminu-"tion: Therefore it's said, (Esa. 64.) *We are all become un-*"*clean, and all our Righteousnesses like menstruous Clothes.* "*This Sun* (as it is *Revel.* 6.) *is become black as Sackcloth*
"of

"*of Hair.* For with the Sackcloth of our Humanity, he covered the Light of his Divinity. *I have made Sackcloth my clothing*; (Pſal. 68.) And what has the Son of God to do with Sackcloth? With this Garment, not God, but the ſinner; not the Creator, but the offendor ought to be clothed. It is the Garment of the Penitent, not of him that forgives ſin. What haſt thou therefore to do with Sackcloth? It was very neceſſary for ſinful Man: becauſe it *repenteth me that I have made man*, that is, I am puniſhed for the ſake of man. Hence (Eſa. 43.) *Ye have made me to ſerve with your ſins, &c.*

Non Deus ſed reus, non Creator ſed peccator.

Pœnitet me feciſſe hominem, i.e. Pœna tenet me pro homine.

"The Sun therefore was black as Sackcloth of Hair. Under the Sackcloth of Fleſh, the brightneſs of Eternal Light hid it ſelf. Concerning whom it's ſaid, (Eſa. 45.15.) *Verily thou art a God that hideſt thy ſelf.* And, Eſa. 53. *His face was as it were hidden.* And well is it ſaid *Hidden.* For the *Hook* of the *Divinity*, was hidden in the *Bait* of *Humanity.* That (as Iſa. ſays, cap. 27. v. 1.) *He might ſlay the Whale*, (that is, the Devil) *which is in the Sea*, (that is, in the ſalt and bitter world.) Hence it is ſaid, Job 40. *In his eyes, as with an hook he ſhall take him*: that is, *Behemoth.* The humble takes the proud; our little Infant, the old Serpent. Therefore it's ſaid, Iſa. 11.

In oculis ejus quaſi hamo capiet eum. vulg. Latin.

"*The ſucking Child ſhall play on the hole of the Aſp, and the weaned Child ſhall put his hand on the Cockatrice Den.* Our *Infant* wrapt in ſwadling Bands, laid in a Cratch, by his powerful hand draws the *Aſp* and the *Cockatrice*, that is, the *Devil*, out of his *Hole* and *Den*, that is, the *conſcience* of a ſinner. The Sun therefore became black, as Sackcloth of Hair: O the firſt! O the laſt! O the high one, and yet humble and vile! *And we* (ſays Iſa. 53.) *counted him as a leprous Perſon, ſmitten of God and humbled.* Concerning whoſe humbled ſublimity ſpeaks Iſa. 6. *I ſaw the Lord ſitting upon his Throne, high and lifted up.* Obſerve,

V

'what

'what his fitting is, what the high Throne, what the sign of
'the Lord lifted up.   His fitting *, is the humble inclina-
'tion of the Divinity in the Humanity.   Thus *Ecclesiastic.*
'38. v. 19. *The Potter fitting at his work, and turning the*
'*Wheel about with his Feet, is always carefully set at his*
'*work.*   The *Potter* is the *Son of God*; concerning whom
'(Pfal. 32.) it's said, *Who fashioneth their hearts one after a-*
'*nother.*   He sits in flesh, to wit, he humbled himself to
'(*i.e* for the sake of) his work: i.e. our Salvation. Hence
'Isa. 28. *That he may do his work, his strange work, &c.*
'*Greg.* He shall come into the World, that he may do his
'work, that is, redeem Man-kind.   But it is his strange
'work: for it was not agreeable to the Divinity, to be spit
'upon, whipped, crucified.   He with the feet of his huma-
'nity turns about the Wheel of our Nature, which before
'ran to death; that to whom it was said before, *Earth thou*
'*art, and thou shalt go to Earth*; now it may be said to him,
'*Blessed art thou, and happy shalt thou be.*   The Gospel
'plainly enough declares, in what sollicitude he always was
'the space of 33. Years, for the perfecting of his Work.
'Whence *Pfal.* 61. it's said, *I ran in thirst.*   For he ran
               'to the Cross with such eagerness, as to a Fur-
Cucurri in   'nace, for to strengthen and consummate his
fiti.vulg.Lat.
               'work there, that he made no answer to *Pilate*,
'left the business of our salvation should be hindred.

* *Thus in another Sermon (pag. 454.) Christ's fitting upon a She-ass,
when he rode to Jerusalem, is interpreted, his assuming our Flesh. For
the She-ass (as it is in the Margin) is put for* humane nature. *Asina pro
humana natura.*

               'The *Throne*, (so called from its solidity) is the Humanity
               'of *Christ*, which leaning upon *Seven* Pil-
Solium, quasi 'lars, remains every ways constant and solid.
solidum dictum.
               'Hence it's said *Isa.* 4. *In that day seven*
'*Women shall take hold on one Man, saying: We will eat our*
'*own Bread, and wear our own Apparel: only let thy name be*
'*called upon us, take away our reproach.*   The seven Women
                                                        'are

'are the seven *gifts* of the H. Ghost; they are called *Women*,
'because no Man is begotten to God, but by the H. Spirit.
'The *Man* is Christ; *one man*, i. e. one alone, without sin;
'whom the seven Women shall take hold of, *i. e.* the seven
'gifts of the H. Spirit, that they may firmly hold him, and
'not let him go. These all pass unto *Christ*; they lay hold
'on none else, for there is no other Man that sinneth not;
'in all others the Spirit has the *lodging* of Tribulation, not
'the *mansion* of Rest: for the Spirit was in the Prophets,
'and other just Men, but because they were Men, and there-
'fore sinners, *it was in them*, but did not *abide in them*.
'Whence it is said only of Christ, *John* 1. *Upon whom thou*
'*shalt see the H. Ghost descending and abiding, he it is that*
'*baptizeth with the H. Ghost*. They shall take hold of one
'Man, saying, *We will eat our own Bread, &c.* There the
'Gloss, *He that hath bread and cloathing, needs nothing. We*
'*will eat our own bread, and wear our own apparel*; it signi-
'fies, that the H. Ghost possesses all things equally with the
'Father, and is not in want of any thing. *Let thy name be*
'*called upon us*, that is, let them be called *Christians* from
'thee, who desire to enjoy thine Incarnation. *Take away*
'*our reproach*; lest by the stench of Vices being expelled
'out of Mens hearts, we be farther often forced to change
'our Lodging.

'The Humanity therefore of *Christ*, (in which the Divi-
'nity sate, as in a Throne, *i.e.* humbled it self, was *high* and
'*lifted up*. High, in the incomparable sanctity of his life.
'Hence, Joh. 3. *He that cometh from above is above all*, viz.
'in excellency of Life: and *lifted up*, that is, on the Tree of
'the Cross. Whence, Joh. 12. *If I be lifted up, I will*
'*draw all Men unto my self*, viz. by the Hook of the Cross.
'In which our Sun being covered with Sack-cloth, was
'signed with *five* Signs. Therefore it's said, *There shall be*
'*signs in the Sun*: which signs were the *five* wounds in
'the Body of *Christ*. These are the *five* Cities which are
'spoke of, *Isa.* 19. *In that Day there shall be five Cities in*
'*the Land of Egypt, speaking the Language of Canaan,&c.*

'One

'*One shall be called the City of the Sun.* *Egypt* is, by inter-
' pretation, sorrow, or darkness. The Land of *Egypt,* that
' is, the flesh of Christ was in sorrow. Heb. 5. *Offering*
' *with tears and strong crying,* &c. In this Land were five
' Cities, that is, five wounds, which are Cities of refuge, to
' which whosoever flees, shall be delivered.—— It follows,
' *Speaking the Language of Canaan*; The wounds of *Christ*
' cry to the Father for mercy, not vengeance.——It follows,
' *One shall be called the City of the Sun.* The wound of his
' side is the City of the Sun: For, in the opening of the
' Lords side, the Gate of Paradise was opened, through
' which the splendor of Eternal Light shined to us. The
' Naturalists say, that blood drawn from the side of a *Dove,*
' clears the Eyes of blemishes. Even so, the blood of *Christ*
' drawn by the Souldiers Lance from the side of *Christ,* il-
' luminated the Eyes of such as were born blind, that is, of
' Man-kind.

Thus far the Explication of Signs in the Sun.

' It follows,

' *There shall be signs in the Moon.*] Concerning which it
' is said, Apocal. 6. *The Moon is become all as blood.* And,
' Joel 2. *The Moon shall be turned into blood.* God made
' two Luminaries, the greater Luminary and the lesser. The
' greater is the Angelical Spirit, the lesser is the Soul of
' Man. Whence it is called the Moon, as if you should say,
' one of those that shine. For the Soul of

Dicitur luna, quasi lucentium una.

' Man was created for this end, that relish-
' ing heavenly things, it might praise the
' Creator, as one of those blessed Spirits, and joyfully sing
' with the Sons of God. But by reason of its too great
' nearness to the Earth, it has contracted blackness, and has
' lost its clearness: therefore it is necessary, if it would re-
' cover its brightness, that it should first be wholly turned
' into *blood*: which *blood* is *contrition of heart*: Of which
' it's said, Heb. 9. 19. *Moses taking the blood of Calves and*
' *Goats, with Water and scarlet Wool and Hyssop, he sprinkled*
' *both the Book and all the People.*——*Moreover he sprink-*
'*led*

'led likewise with blood both the Tabernacle, and all the Ves-
'sels of the Ministery: and almost all things are purged with
'blood, and without blood-shedding there is no remission: Be-
'hold how all the Moon becomes as blood. But what does
'*Moyses* signifie? What the *blood*? What the *water*? What
'the *scarlet wool*? &c.

'When the merciful and pittying *Jesus Christ* comes in-
'to the mind of sinners, then *Moyses* takes the blood. *Moy-*
'*ses* is a sinner, now converted from the Waters of *Egypt*,
'who ought to take these *Five* things.

'Viz.
⎧ The *blood* of sorrowful contrition.
⎪ The *water* of weeping confession.
⎨ The *wool* of innocency and purity.
⎪ The *scarlet* of Brotherly kindness.
⎩ The *hyssop* of true humility.

'With these he ought to *sprinkle the Book*; that is, the se-
'cret of his heart, and all *the people* of his Cogitations; and
'the *Tabernacle*, that is, his Body; and all its *Vessels*, that
'is, the five Senses. By the *blood of Contrition*, all things
'are cleansed, but still with a purpose of *Confessing*: But
'without *Contrition* there is no remission of sin. Let it
'therefore be said, *There shall be signs in the Moon*. By
'the outward signs of the Penitent, are discovered the in-
'ward signs of Contrition. When *Chastity* shines in the
'Body, *Humility* in deed, *Abstinence* in food, *Vileness* in
'cloathing, they are the forerunners of *inward sanctifi-*
'*cation*.

'Hence it is, that the Lord promises these four to a Pe-
'nitent Soul: Isa. 60. 13. *The glory of Libanus shall come*
'*unto thee, and the Fir-tree, the Box-tree, and Pine-tree toge-*
'*ther, to beautifie the place of my holiness*. The *glory of Li-*
'*banus* is the chastity of the Body, of which the Soul glo-
'ries, *Ecclus*. 24. 13. *I am exalted as a Cedar in Libanus*,
'which signifies by interpretation, *whiteness*. The Cedar
'Tree drives away Serpents by its smell. In *Libanus* there-
'fore,

'fore, that is, in a chaft Body the Soul is exalted, as a Cedar
'Tree; becaufe by the Odour of an holy Converfation, it
'drives away the Serpents of Demoniacal fuggeftion and
'carnal concupifcence. —— The *Fir-tree* which grows high-
'er than other Trees, fignifies Humility, which lifts up it
'felf higher than other Vertues.—— The *Box-tree,* which
'is of a pale Colour, fignifies abftinence in Meat and Drink:
'Of which, *Ifa.* 30. 20. The Lord fhall give thee fcant Bread,
'and fhort Water: And *Verf.* 24. *The young Affes* (that
'is, the Penitents) *which till the ground* (that is, afflict their
'flefh) *fhall eat commixtum migma, mingled food.* Migma
'(*in the vulgar Latine*) is Barley with the Chaff, whereby
'is fignified hard fare. The *Pine-tree,* out of which pitch
'is drawn, fignifies meannefs of Apparel, *&c.*

I cannot methinks proceed farther with fuch filly myfti-
cal ftuff, upon the other Heads of his Sermon, concerning *figns in the Stars,* and *diftrefs of Nations*;
but fhall leave the Reader to confult it. Proceed we
now to the other commended Inftance of S. *Anthony's*
Sermons *upon the Saints:* Of which take that one,
Pag. 443.

SERMON II.

Concerning all the Saints.

Animæ juftorum in manu Dei funt. Sap. 3.
The Souls of juft Men are in the hand of God.
Wifd. 3. 1.

'NOte here, that *Noble Perfons* are wont to carry *Se-*
'*ven* Things in their Hands: viz. a *Ring,* *Gloves,*
'a *Hawke,* a *Looking-glafs,* a *Rod* to correct, a *Flower* or
'*Apple* to fmell to, and a *Scepter* to fhow their dignity.
'The

'The Souls of juſt Men are in the hand of God, like to all
'theſe.

'1. As a *Ring*, by faith : Oſe. 2. *I will betroth thee to*
'*me in faith.* The ring of juſt Men, is hope of Heavenly
'things founded in Faith : but becauſe faith without works
'is dead, and availes not to life Eternal, therefore it's ſaid,
'Jerem. 22. *If Jeconias were the Ring on my right hand, I*
'*would pluck him thence* ; becauſe he did not perform the
'worthy works of faith.

"2. The righteous ought to be in Gods hand as *Gloves*, by
'works of mercy : for he covers the Lords hand, who free-
'ly gives Almes to the Poor, and leaves it naked, who is
'unmerciful : for what thou putteſt in the hand of the poor,
'thou putteſt in Gods hand : Matth. 25. *What ye have done*
'*to one of theſe my little ones, ye have done to me.* The five
'fingers of this Glove, are five things that are required in
'Almes. 1. That it be ſpeedy. 2. Large. 3. Of the beſt
'and choiceſt things. 4. Of Goods lawfully gotten. 5.
'Diſcreet : to thoſe that are indigent. Concerning theſe
'five, *Zacchæus* ſaid, Luc. 9. *Behold half of my goods I give*
'*to the poor.* Behold, there's his *readineſs* ; half, there's
'the *largeneſs* ; goods, there's the *beſt things* ; my goods,
'there's his *property* in them : to the *poor*, there's *diſcretion.*
'But becauſe works of mercy profit little, unleſs they be
'done in Charity ; Therefore,

'3. They ought to be in the hand of God, as *Hawkes*.
'God's *Hawke* is a *heart* full of *Charity.* Thence it draws
'to it ſelf with the *foot of affection* all the good and evil of
'its neighbours, and makes advantage thereby, delighting in
'their good, ſympathizing with their evils, and bearing
'thoſe that are inflicted on it. Deut. 11. *Every place where*
'*your foot ſhall tread, ſhall be yours.* The *two feet of Cha-*
'*rity*, are *patience*, whereby it ſuffers evil things, and *benig-*
'*nity*, whereby it loves their good : 1 Cor. 13. *Charity is*
'*patient, is kind.* Note, that ſome are *Kites* and *Crows,*
'that fix only upon entrals and carcaſſes : Lament. 4. *They*
'*have embraced dung.* But the *Hawke* only ſeizes upon a
'noble

'noble prey. Also note, that a *Hawke* ought not to be
' carried without *Gloves*, because charity w.thout the expres-
' sion of good works, *viz.* works of mercy, outwardly, is
' worth nothing ; for the proof of affection, is action :
' 1 Joh. 3. *He that hath this Worlds goods*, &c. And be-
' cause charity ought to proceed from a pure heart, and a
' good conscience, 1 *Tim.* 1. Therefore,

' 4. Thou must be in the hand of God, as a *Looking-glass*,
' by purity of conscience ; that thy Soul may be the Daugh-
' ter of *Sion*, which is by interpretation a *Glass*, a glass of
' God's Majesty without spot, and the Image of his good-
' ness ; *Wisd*. 7. in which it may see God plainly by his
' image and likeness. But observe that there are several
' things that hinder the reflection of an Image in a Glass :
' *viz.* the dust of pride ; the inspection of a menstruous
' Woman, that is, of carnal concupiscence ; the dirt of a-
' varice ; the rust of rancor and anger ; the breath of de-
' traction, &c.

' Also because from a conscience purified from sin, a Man
' arises to the joy of contemplation, for *Blessed are the pure*
' *in heart, for they shall see God*, Matth. 5. Therefore,

' 5. We ought to be in the hand of God, as a *Flower* or
' *Apple* to smell to. For a sweet smell goes forth from the
' Soul, as from a *Flower* or *Apple*, and all its affection, cogi-
' tation and delight, rests in God ; so that it says with the
' Psalmist, *O Lord, all my desire is before thee*. And that
' Cant. 1. *When the King was at his Table, my Spikenard gave*
' *its smell : We will run in the favour of thy Ointments*.
' Concerning such a Soul the Spouse may say that Cant. 3.
' *Who is this that ascendeth like a Pillar of smoke of perfumes?*
' And, Cant. 4. *The favour of thine Ointments is better than*
' *all Spices*. And, Cant. 7. *The smell of thy mouth is as the*
' *smell of Apples*. And, Gen. 27. *Behold the smell of my Son*
' *is like the smell of a Field, which the Lord hath blessed*.

' But because some are so wholly intent upon contempla-
' tion, that they neglect the care of their neighbours ; there-
' fore the Soul is raised from contemplation, to be

'6. A

'6. A *Rod* in the Lord's hand, to correct others. As
'*Paul* says, 1 Cor. 4. *Will ye that I come to you with a rod,*
'*or in love and the Spirit of meekness?* But note, the *rod* is
'turned into a *Staff* and a *Serpent*, as *Moyses* his Rod was,
'while he that corrects, exceeds his measures: Isa. 10. *Woe*
'*to Ashur the rod of my fury, and a Staff is he, &c.* Because
'he that ought to have been a *rod*, was become a *staff*. Now
'the Saints are like a soft and tender *twig*, while they re-
'prove sinners with meekness; but in the Day of Judgment
'they shall be a Rod of Iron, judging the reprobate with-
'out mercy, when the Saints shall judg the Nations.

'Who if they be now in the Lord's hand as a *Rod*, they
'will be hereafter in the Lord's hand,

'7. As a *Scepter* to show their dignity: Esa. 62. *Thou*
'*shalt be a Crown of Glory in the hand of the Lord.* Psal. 2.
'*The Scepter of thy Kingdome is a right Scepter.* Matth. 19.
'*Ye shall sit upon twelve Seats, judging the twelve Tribes of*
'*Israel.* Thus the Souls of righteous Men are in the
'hand of God.

'And well is it said, that righteous Men are in Gods hand:
'for as that which is contained in ones hand is a *small* thing,
'so the blessed are *small* in number, compared with the re-
'probate: Matth. 20. *Many are called, but few are chosen.*
'Eccl. 1. *The number of fools is infinite.* Also a thing in
'hand is always in readiness, and is carried at the pleasure of
'him that holds it, so the Saints conform their will to the
'Divine will: thence in the *Lords Prayer, Thy will be done.*
'And Jer. 18. *As Clay is in the hand of the Potter, so are*
'*you, O House of Israel, in my hand.* Also as things in hand,
'are in perpetual remembrance, so the Eyes of the Lord are
'always upon the just: Esa. 49. *Can a Woman forget her*
'*sucking Infant, &c.*

This is the whole of S. *Anthony*'s admirable Discourse
upon this Subject, and sure it needs no comment to
show the ridiculousness and impertinency of it.

It

It were easie to make a Volume, to show how this fam'd Preacher has by his mystical Expositions, and straining of similitudes, spoiled the sence of Scr. in a hundred places, and talked more childishly concerning the gravest and most serious Arguments, than any School-boy would have done. For what Man of understanding can with any patience hear one trifle with such a noble Subject, as that, *Matth.* 11. *Take my Yoke upon you,* &c. He begins his Sermon with this Question. What are the *Apostles* then *Oxen*? And the most of his Discourse is to show that the *Apostles* are *Oxen*; for seven Reasons. Some of which are these. ' 1. Because the ' Apostles were sent by *pairs* like *Oxen*: Act. 13. *Separate* ' *to me Saul and Barnabas, &c.* 2. Because an *Oxe* is a ' *strong* and *laborious animal.* So S. *Paul* says, *He laboured* ' *more abundantly than they all.* 3. An Oxe *spends little,* ' though it *labours much*: and one of the Apostles sayes, ' 1 Tim. 6. *Having Food and Rayment, let us therewith be* ' *content*: but some Prelates in our time are *Palfreys*, that ' spend much, and labour little. 4. Because an Oxe has ' two Horns: and that which answers in the Apostles to ' these two Horns, is *Doctrine* and *Life*. Whence that ' Preacher is an *Unicorn*, who has but one of these: With ' this Horn Preachers ought to blow, that is, with good ' Doctrine in preaching; which yet often profits little, un- ' less it be accompanied with the other horn, that is, good ' life. Another reason is; because there is nothing in an ' Oxe unprofitable; so neither in the life of the Apostles: ' Of the Hide of the Oxe shooes are made, and from the ' conversation of the Apostles an example is taken, which ' fortifies the affections, as a Shoe does the Feet; *Cant.* 7. ' *How beautiful are thy goings in Shoes.* ' The Flesh of Oxen affords food. The ' Flesh of the Apostles are their carnal ' words and deeds: as *Peter* said carnally, Matth. 16. *Far be this from thee, O Lord.* Also because they loved him too carnally: By these we are nou-
'rished

*Serm.*8.*de Apost.*
pag. 428.

Quàm pulchri sunt gressus tui in calceamentis. vulg. Lat.

Devotions of the Roman Church.

'rished to caution. Besides, with the *dung* of Oxen the earth
'is fatned. The *dung* of the Apostles is their sins before
'conversion and after: as S. *Peter*'s denyal, &c. By which
'we are fatned to hope of pardon.

In another Sermon upon this Text, *Their sound went out into all the Earth.* The whole Discourse is spent in comparing the Apostles to *three* things that sound loud, and are heard afar off, viz. *Thunder, Trumpets* and *Bells*; and upon the last he is very large; and all that can be thought of about Bells, the Mettle they are made of, and whence it is digged, the Fire they are melted in, the Mold they are put into; The properties of their sound; The uses they are put to; to raise from sleep; to allay tempests; to quench fires; to cover fires, and give notice of Bed-time; to call People together; to give warning of death; to signifie the approach of Persons of honour, &c. All these are applyed with horrible straining, and absurdity to the Apostles preaching. *Serm.2.de Apost. pag. 420.*

But it were well if this were the worst in S. *Anthony*'s Sermons, that he talked foolishly concerning the *Apostles* and *Saints*; for I know not how he can be excused from this charge, in reference to *God* and our *Saviour*. Upon those words, Luc. 11. *If I by the finger of God cast out Devils,&c.* He descants in this manner, so as I think no body ever had the confidence to do before him. 'Christ by the Finger of God *Serm. Domin. 3. in Quadrag.p.179*
'cast out Devils. The Finger of God notes the difference
'of his work. For the hand signifies work, and the fingers
'placed in the hand are the difference of works. But now
'because the Lord either has wrought, or will work for the
'future with all his fingers; it is to be noted, that as there
'are five fingers, so there are five works of God. The first
'is called the *Thumb*, in which the strength of the hand con-
'sists: by vertue of this finger the Lord wrought in the
'Creation of the World, and the dispersing of Men, in the
'time of the Deluge, in the working of Miracles in *Egypt*,
'and therefore the *Magicians* said, *The finger of God is here*,
'Exod.

'Exod. 8. The 2d. finger is the *fore-finger*, called *Index*,
' *ab indicando*, from pointing, and to this wisdome is attri-
' buted: with this God wrought in the giving of the Law,
' when he wrote it with this finger in Tables of Stone,
' *Deut. 9*. The 3d. is called the *middle-finger*, and this is
' the finger of clemency and mercy, whereby God's revenge
' is deferred, and which joyns God with the Creature:
' with this Finger God wrought, when he drove out the
' Devil by it. Whence S. *Augustine* upon *Matthew* says,
' *With the finger of God*, that is, by the Holy Ghost. For
' the *Father* is the Arm in which is power, the *Son* is the
' hand in which is industry; and as the hand works by the
' fingers, and the Arm by the hand, so the power of the Fa-
' ther by the Son: Joh. 1. *All things were made by him*.
' Mark also the difference in the fingers, which signifies dif-
' ference of Graces, though it be the same spirit. The 4th.
' finger is the *Ring-finger*, that is, the promise of Glory:
' So, Luk. 15. *Put a Ring upon his hand*; i. e. on his Finger.
' With this finger he now works by his *promise*, and at the
' end of the World will work by *bestowing* of Glory. The
' 5th. is the *little* or *Ear-finger*. (*auricularis*.) This is that,
' which makes the Ears tingle: 1 King. 3. *Behold I do a*
' *work in Israel, which whosoever hears, both his Ears shall*
' *tingle*. This is the Finger of Judgment *hereafter*, and of
' threatning at the *present*. With this finger *Christ stooping*
' *down, wrote on the ground*, Joh. 8. But when he shall des-
' cend to Judgment, he will write in every ones heart a sen-
' tence against them: This is that *Little-finger thicker than*
' *his Father's Loines*, 3 King. 12. In the Loines of the back
' the vertue of generation does consist, and it signifies the
' kindness bestowed by God the Father upon ungrateful sin-
' ners, but the Judgment that is given to the Son shall ex-
' ceed all those.

What *Divinity* they of the *Roman* Church will call this, I know not, but one might expect sure as good as this from every *Kitchin*; and if these be the admirable strains of his Preaching, I think S. *Anthony* had better have kept to his

old

old imployment of washing Dishes, and scouring Kettles there, than ever have entred into a Pulpit. For I think never any Man before him took such *Starts* from the Scripture to let loose a number of foolish fancies, which he had not the discretion to restrain, even when they bordered upon Blasphemy.

Upon those words of S. *Mark*, cap. 7. 33. where our Saviour cured the deaf and dumb Man, by *putting his fingers into his Ears, and Spitting and touching his Tongue*; we have such another descant upon the five fingers, on the hand of *Christ* the Word incarnate. 'The *Thumb* in his Conception, 'which because it is shorter than the rest, does signifie the 'humility of the Son of God, who shortned himself in the 'Womb of the Virgin. The *fore-finger* in his Nativity, for 'then the Angel did, as with a finger, declare salvation, 'saying, *To day is born a Saviour, and this shall be a sign, &c.* 'The *middle-finger* in his preaching. The 4*th. finger* (cal-'led *annularis* & *medicus*) in the working of Miracles. The '*little-finger* (*auricularis*) in this Days Miracle, *viz.* of cu-'ring the deaf Man.

Serm. Domin. 12. post Trinit. p.365.

But upon that which follows, of Christ's *Spitting* and *touching his Tongue*, never any Man had the impudence before him, to talk of the *Saliva divinitatis*, & *Sputum Dei*: For these are his words, '*Sputum namque Dei est sapor* '*divinæ sapientiæ, quæ dicit*, Eccluf. 24. *Ego ex ore Altissimi prodii.*

I should tire my self and the Reader, if I should set down the thousandth part of his Allegorical and Mystical Divinity, which one may every where (let him dip where he will) meet withall; and such as I could scarce believe, upon report, any Man of sence would ever have fastened upon the Scripture, (so prodigious is their Absurdity) if I did not read them with these Eyes.

A few instances more of this kind shall conclude this Discourse about S. *Anthonie's* preaching.

Upon those words of the Gospel, Joh. 2. *There were there*

Serm. in Domin. 2. post Epiph. p. 116. there *six Water-pots* of Stone, (viz. in *Cana* of *Galilee*) *holding two or three measures a piece.* He discourses thus; 'In 'Cana of *Galilee*, that is, in a Soul, which by the zeal of 'love hath passed from Vice to Vertue, there are six Water-'pots: Contrition, Confession, Prayer, Fasting, Almes, 'and forgiveness of injuries; these are they which purifie 'the *Jews*, i.e. Penitents from all sins.——Then afterwards he concludes. 'Behold six Water-pots of Stone cut out of 'the Stone which the Builders refused, which is cut out of 'the Mountain without hands. How full they are unto 'the brim with saving Water, holding two or three mea-'sure a piece. In the *two measures* is signified the Love of 'God and our Neighbour. In *three measures* the Confes-'sion of Faith in the Holy Trinity, which in all the forena-'med things is necessary: Mark therefore these six Water-'Pots.

S. *Matthew*, c. 8. tells us, that *Jesus entered into a Ship, and his Disciples followed him.* S. *Anthony* begins his Sermon thus. * 'That Ship is 'the Cross of Christ, this is a Merchants 'Ship, in which he keeps his Marts, setting forth his glori-'ous Wares; viz. Patience, Indulgence, Meekness, suffer-'ing wrongs and reproaches, &c. Hence it is said, *Prov.* '31. 14. *She is like a Merchants Ship, bringing her Food 'from far.* By the help of this Ship we come to the shore 'of the Heavenly Countrey.——Note, that to the govern-'ment of a Ship, Four things are necessary; viz. the Mast, 'the Sail, the Oares and Anchor. In the Mast is signified 'contrition of heart. In the Sail, confession of the mouth; 'for as the Sail is fastned to the Mast, so confession ought 'to be tyed to contrition. The Oares denote works of 'satisfaction, to wit, Fasting, Prayer and Almes. The An-'chor, remembrance of Death.—— Whosoever therefore 'would pass over from the shoar of Mortality, to that of 'Immortality, that is, would come to *Jerusalem*, let him 'go into such a Ship of Repentance.

* *Serm. in Domin. 4. post Epiph. p. 120.*

Upon

Upon those words of the Gospel, Matth. 23. 2. *The Scribes and Pharisees sit in Moses Chair, all things therefore whatsoever they bid you observe, that observe and do, but after their works do not.* He has this excellent comment. 'The *Pharisees* are so called from a word 'that signifies *Division*, and may denote   *Serm. Fer. 3. Hebd. 2.* 'those sins that divide and separate us   *in Quadrag. p. 166.* 'from God. Isai. 59. *Your iniquities have divided betwixt* 'you and God.

'But here arise three doubts: 1. How sins are called 'Scribes. 2. How they are said to sit in *Moses* Chair. '3. How we ought to do according to what they bid us ob-'serve. It's worth hearing how this rare *Casuist* deter-'mines it. As for the first, *Isaiah* answers, cap. 10. 1. '*The writers have writ unrighteousness, that they might op-'press the poor in judgment.* Also there are Books, and 'Letters, and Writings against a Man in the last Judg-'ment.——— Sins therefore may be called Pharisees, not on-'ly as they divide, but as they condemn; and also because 'they inroll a Man into the Family of the Devil. Thence 'in *Revel.* 19. they are called, *The mark of the Beast.*

'As for the 2d. Doubt: How they are said to sit in the 'Chair, it is plain enough. The *mind of man* may signi-'fie the *Chair of Moses*, in which the divine Law ought to 'sit.——— *The Soul of the just man is the Seat of Wisdome:* 'Or else we may say, that they sit in *Moses* Seat, whilst by 'sin they kill the divine Law; Esa. 14. *I will sit in the 'Mountain of the Testament*, that is, in the height of the 'perfection of the Divine Law.

'As for the 3d. How we ought to do all that they bid us. 'That of the Gloss, is to be noted. *All things*, viz. which 'are profitable to Salvation: for we are to do all such 'things, but we must not do according to their works. For 'we must know that every vice commends its opposite ver-'tue: *ex. gr. Anger* commends Patience, Gluttony Tem-'perance. Therefore though the works of vices are evil, '(*and so ought not to be done*) yet they commend the contrary
vertues,

'vertues, as appears, because every vice would cover it self under the cloak of vertue, as appears in Pride. Thus therefore, *Whatsoever they say unto you do, but do not after their works, &c.* Sin condemns it self, and yet does not cease to infest the Soul, and therefore it follows well, *They bind heavy burdens, &c.*

Was there ever such a wild nonsensical fancy, as he has pinned upon those words of the Prophet to the Widdow of *Sarepta?* 1 Kings 17. 13. *Fear not, go and do as thou hast said, but make me a little cake first, &c. For the meal shall not wast, nor the cruise of oyl fail, till the Lord sendeth rain upon the Earth.*

Serm.in fer.2.Hebd.3. in Quadrag. p. 182.

This is his mystical sence. 'Go, return, *viz.* into thy conscience. Take Meal from the Barrel, that is, thoughts from the heart, which are ground between two Mil-stones hope and fear; and take the Oyl of Devotion, and make me the Bread of repentance baked under the ashes, *viz.* of humility; and then afterwards thou shalt make for thy self and thy Son, because feeding God with the food of repentance, thou shalt feed thy own Soul and Body in Life Eternal. Fear not, for if thou dost this to God, that is, to Divine Reverence, it shall never fail unto the Day of Rain, that is, of Glory.

I cannot omit another pleasant interpretation of those words, Matth. 4. *Jesus was led by the Spirit into the Desert.* Upon which, according to his usual way, he discourses thus.

Serm.2. in Domin.1. in Quadrag. p. 270.

'We are to consider morally what that Desart is, and by what Spirit we are to be led into it. The Scripture mentions a 7. fold *Desert*.

'1. *Desert* is Heaven; because it was deserted by Apostate Angels. This is that Wilderness, *Luc.*2. in which the Heavenly Shepherd left the 99. *viz.* the Company of Angels, that he might seek the lost Sheep, that is, humane nature, *&c.*

'2. *Desert*

2. *Desert*, is the heart of man, because it is deserted of
'Angels, and inhabited by Beasts, that is, bestial cogitati-
'ons: this is the wilderness of *Cades*, which is by inter-
'pretation, the fountain of judgment; *Psal.*28.*The voice of
'the Lord shaketh the wilderness of Cades*; which is, when
'the heart in the preaching of the word is made contrite by
'compunction.

3. *Desert*, is that of *penitence*: both because sins are
'here deserted, as also because there ought to be here as in
'a desert, rest from disturbing thoughts, hard cloathing,
'dry diet, &c. *John* the Baptist was in this desert, cloa-
'thed with Camels hair.

4. *Desert*, is Religion, in which the world is deserted
'by the vow of poverty, the flesh by the vow of chastity,
'and the active will by the vow of obedience. Concerning
'this, *Cant.* 8. *Who is this that cometh up from the wilder-
'ness, leaning upon his beloved?* For he that perfectly for-
'sakes the world, leans only upon God.

5. *Desert*, is the cross of Christ; in which all deserting
'him fled away. This is the desert of *Ziph*, which is by
'interpretation, *flourishing*, because the cross bore the flo-
'rid body of Christ the *Nazarene*, *i. e.* flourishing: Here
'the desert flourished by the *blood of Christ*, as it were *with
'roses*; by the *humanity of Christ* as *with Violets*, and by
'*his purity* as *with Lilies*.

6. *Desert*, is the world, forsaken by every good man,
'in which the Children of *Israel* wander and are afflicted.

7. *Desert* is Hell, deserted of all hope of freedom; for
'in Hell is no redemption. These ways *desert* may be ta-
'ken in Scripture.

'Now to the purpose; by what Spirit ought a man to be
'led, and into which of these deserts ought he to enter?
'The answer is, there is a sevenfold Spirit which is menti-
'oned *Isa.* 11. *The spirit of wisdom and understanding, the
'spirit of Counsel and fortitude, the spirit of knowledge and
'pity, and the spirit of the fear of the Lord*: By every one of
'these a man ought to be led into one of those deserts fore-
'named.

'named. Into the 1. Defart, that is Heaven, a man ought
'to be led by the *Spirit of wifdom*, by the contemplation of
'celeftial things. Into the Second, (viz. *the heart*) man
'muft be led by the *fpirit of underftanding*, by the confide-
'ration and difcuffion of his fins. Into the Third (viz. *of*
'*penitence*) he muft be led by the *fpirit of Counfel*, becaufe
'penitence is to be had by the counfel of the Prieft; *Matth.*
'*8. Go and fhow your felves to the Prieft.* Into the Fourth
'Defert, that is, of a *Religious profeffion*, men enter by a
'difficult way, therefore it is faid to fuch profeffors: *Be*
'*valiant in battel.* Into the Fifth, that is, the *Crofs*, men
'muft be led by the *fpirit of pity* and compaffion. *Lament.*
'*1. O all ye that pafs by, behold if there be any forrow*, &c.
'Into the Sixth Defert, that is, *the world*, a man muft be
'led by the *fpirit of knowledge*, that he may fee how he
'ought to walk cautioufly in the midft of an evil and per-
'verfe Nation. Into the Seventh, that is, into Hell, a
'man muft be led by the fpirit of fear, that fo he may con-
'fider, that there fhall be weeping and gnafhing of
'teeth.

I dare fay the *Seven wife men* of *Greece* would never have found out thefe Seven Deferts, if the Bible had been their ftudy all their life long. But S. *Anthony* had a peculiar Gift, (which I am fure none of the feven *Spirits* forenamed helped him to,) to bring any thing out of any thing. Such is his fearching invention, that he can find a figure of the day of *Pentecoft* in *Noah's ark*, becaufe we read, *Gen. 6.* that the *Ark was* 50. *Cubits in breadth*: He can find the *five fenfes* of man, in the *five chambers* of this Ark: The firft of which fhall fuffice, to fhow how refined this preachers *inward fenfe* was. "The firft chamber of the Ark was cal-
"led *Stercoraria*, where the dung lay; this is the
"*tongue* of the mouth, through which in confeffion
"we ought to fend forth all the *dung* of our fins. This is
"the *dung-gate* mentioned *Nehem.* 3. 14. The mind of
"man being infected with the Devils ordure (*ftercore Di-*
"*aboli*)

Serm. in die Pentecoft. p.312.

Ibid.

" *aboli*) is to be purged by the gate of confession, &c.

But, that I may not be endless, one instance more shall conclude this discourse about S. *Anthonie*'s Sermons. Upon those words, *Cant.* 6. 2. *My beloved is gone down into his garden, to the beds of spices, to feed in the gardens, and to gather Lilies.* He comments thus. "The garden of the *Serm. in Domin. 20. post Trinit. p. 399.*
" beloved, is the Soul of a righteous man, in which are
" two beds of spices, that is, *humility* the procurer of
" other vertues; and *Lilies*, that is, *double continence*, and
" therefore he descends into such a garden and feeds there.
" Note, that there is a fourfold Garden, *viz.* of *Nuts*, of
" *Apples*, of *Vines*, and of *Spices*. There are also seven
" gifts of the Spirit, (*which he reckons as we heard a little*
" *before.*) The Soul of a righteous man, by the *spirit of*
" *fear*, becomes a *Garden of Nuts*, which have three
" things in them, *viz.* *bitterness* in the *husk*, *hardness* in
" the *shell*, and *sweetness* in the *kernel* : The *Garden of Nuts*
" is *repentance* ; which has *bitterness* in the *flesh*, *hardness*
" of tribulation in the *long-suffering of the mind*, and the
" *sweetness* of spiritual joy, in *expectation of a reward*. Also by the *spirit of knowledge* and *pity*, the Soul becomes a
" *garden of Apples*, which has the *sweetness of mercy*. Also
" by the *spirit of counsel* and *fortitude*, it becomes a garden
" of *Vines*, having the *fervor of charity*. And by the *spirit*
" *of wisdom* and *understanding*, it becomes a *garden of Spi-*
" *ces*, sending forth its *sweet smell* in the Gates.

I hope the Reader by this time is pretty well assured that S. *Anthony* was no Conjurer, as to making of Sermons : That whomsoever he took to imitate in his mystical and moral expositions of Scripture, he was the dullest and the most nonsensical certainly that ever appeared in this way. That the way it self of his preaching was childish beyond measure, mere toying with the word of God ; had nothing in it to make any one a jot the *wiser*, nor fitted to move any thing scarce within a man, save only his *Spleen* : that it is an unpardonable impudence in the writers of his

Life,

Life, to cry him up, as if he was an Angel in the Pulpit, when there is not one page among all his Sermons worth any wise mans reading, and every line almost gives them the lie. That though there is no defence to be made for the foolish preaching of our own *Enthusiasts* at home, and the Papists may think they have a mighty advantage against us when they object it; yet this I will say, that there is not one of *our men* so ridiculous in Print, let them chuse where they please, but may be play'd for any wager against *their* S. *Anthony*, and will come off better.

But it is more than time to proceed to the other Head, of *his Miracles*: half of which, I think at least, seeing they concern his preaching; (being either tricks the Devil play'd to discourage and disturb his Sermons, or wonderous things God wrought, to give credit both to him and them:) We have gained thus much by producing his Sermons, that sure no wise man can believe a word of those stories, but will look upon them as Idle Tales and fictions; since he may see by the spirit and strain of them, that they have no tendency to do the Devil *much harm*, nor God any *considerable service*. If the evil Spirit receive any contentment from the impertinency and silly discourses of a preacher, I cannot but imagine that some of S. *Anthonie*'s have been like *Nuts* and *Apples* to him: but I have met with nothing likely to put him into any great chafe, unless it were the slovenly similitude, we lately noted, of the *Devils dung* *: So that when I am told, that once as he was preaching, the Devil tumbled down the *cover* of the *Pulpit*, with a great force and noise; I am ready to conjecture that the Pulpit

Concerning S. Anthonie's miracles.

Ribaden: vit. Anton. p.249.

---

* For thus they tell us, that the Devil was mightily vexed, because a Painter used to draw him in a most ugly shape under the feet of the Bl. Virgins; and as he was at this work one time upon his Scaffolds in a Church Porch, the Devil brought such a whirl-wind, that threw down all the Scaffolding, and the Painter had broke his neck, if the Image of the Bl. Virgin had not seasonably stretched out its hand, and kept him from falling till help came. Gononi Chronic. pag. 136.

was set up in some haunted place, (for we heard before that S. *Anthony* did not always preach in Churches) and that the Devil was disturbed in his usual walk: only one circumstance speaks it rather to be a fable, when it's said, in the story, that the fall of it neither hurt nor so much as frighted any body; for S. *Anthony* had forewarned his Auditors, that they should not be terrified, if they should chance to hear any noises; and it was an extraordinary speech indeed, that could prevent, when this happened, the womens frights and fears. But we are told of a worse accident, that through the Devils spight, happened to *himself* at the beginning of Lent; for after he was wearied with his labours, and had laid him down to sleep to refresh himself; the Devil set upon him cowardly, and griped him so fast by the throat, that he had almost choaked him; till invoking the Bl. Virgin, and making the sign of the Cross, and (which was the hardest work when the Devil had him fast by the throat) singing the Hymn, *O gloriosa Domina*, &c. he saw his cell filled with the brightness of Heavenly light, which the Devil not being able to indure, departed. One would wonder at the many spightful and *Dog-tricks* which, they tells us, the Devil served many of their great Saints. The other S. *Anthony* the *Hermit* (as we heard before) was almost beaten to death by him. S. *Benedict* had a *Bell* which was tied to a cord, by which bread was let down into his Cell, and gave warning to him when to receive it; this *Bell*, by throwing a stone at it, the Devil broke in pieces, thinking (I suppose) to starve the Saint. S. *Bartholomew* the *Monk*, as he was intent at his prayers, the Devil leapt upon his feet and legs, and at last throwing himself wholly upon him (as he dealt with our S. *Anthony*) got him fast by the throat and held him so long, till he was almost dead by the load that oppressed him; at another time

Rib.id. ibid. & in vit. Ant. cap. 12. Brev. Rom. Antiq. ad Jun. 13. Lect. 8. & 9. infra Octav.

Brev. Rom. Ant. ad Mat. 21. Lec. 4.

Capgrav. vit. Bartholom. f. 32, 33.

he drew him along by his Cowl, and threw him a great way into an entry; and when the Monk took up a stick to strike him, he stood and laught at his blows. S. *Ethelwold* was severely handled by him, when envying his zeal for the promoting the worship of God, as he was intent upon the building of a Church, the Devil by casting a Beam upon him, threw him down head-long, so that (though he was not killed out-right, yet) he broke one of his ribs. But S. *Godrick* was as much abused by his tricks, as any Saint I read of.

Ribadeneira vit. S. Ethelw. Aug. 1.

One time the Devil mocked him when he was singing Psalms, and calling him *Clown*, told him he could sing as well as he: When he was upon his knees at his Prayers, the Devil entring the Oratory, sought to disturb him, but S. *Godrick* would not so much as look towards him. Then the Devil threw the Pix at him, which had the *Hosts* in it; after that spilt a horn of Wine upon him, then threw a pitcher of water at him and a piece of wood with a Cross upon it; but when thus all night abusing him he moved him not at all, he departed from him; only he left such a stink behind him, as could scarce be endured by man: Another time, as he sate by his fire-side, the Devil gave him such a box on the ear, that almost fell'd him flat to the ground. Another bout they had, when S. *Godrick* (suspecting he was no man, though he appeared in that shape) catechized him, and asked him whether he believed in the Father, Son and Holy Ghost, and bid him worship the Bl. Virgin: The Devil surlily bid him not to trouble himself about his belief; and told him that he had nothing to do to inquire into it. Then *Godrick* took out his book which had the pictures of *Christ*, Bl. *Mary*, and of S. *John* in it, and clapping it hastily to his mouth, bad him if he believed in God, to kiss devoutly those pictures: The Devil not being able to indure any longer, did, as it were, spit upon the book, and disappeared mocking of him. He also another time abused him in the shape and habit of a Hermit, and

Capgr. vit. Godrice Hermit. f. 159, 160.

chouled

Devotions of the Roman Church.

choufed him of his bread and money; and prayed him to touch his ulcerous body, for he hoped he should have ease thereby: the Saint in great compassion touched his Body; which felt just like the body of a Goose with the Feathers off. But (though we are beholden much to him for that discovery, yet) this touch so inflamed him with obscene temptations, that it had like to have cost him the loss of his Chastity. But nothing grieved the Saint more, than that he had bestowed his gifts on the Devil, and he had carried them away with him; which cost him many tears, and great penances. He also much wondered that he stood the sprinkling of Holy Water, yea and kneeled down and prayed with him, and entred into the Church. But the Devils business was, not to be overlong godly; for the next appearance to him (as he was gathering Apples) was as *filthy*, as this was *devout*; for he went away in a stink, showing him his posteriours, and something else besides, which was so horrid, that it made the good Man's hair all stand up on end, like Hogs bristles. But the most terrible assault, was when the Saint lay in his Bed, and could not, through Age, raise himself up in it without help: then the Devil stood by him, and crying out, brandished a flaming Weapon against him; out of his Mouth proceeded Fire, as out of an Oven, & the breadth of his Eyes exceeded the measure of two Cubits: but such was the Saints courage, that he rose alone to fight with him; the noise of their skirmish might have been heard a great way off; and this single combat lasted, from *One* to *Nine* a Clock; the Devil, we are told, thrice assailed him, and thrice he was overcome by this Souldier of Christ.

Capgrav. ibid. p. 162.

Capgr. ibid. f. 163.

Ibid. f. 164.

But the Devil has been often paid home in his own Coin, and served trick for trick. The forenamed S. *Bartholomew* made him run into a corner, by the sprinkling of Holy-water, and at last casting a Bason of that Water full in the Devils face, made him turn into divers forms and vanish away. S. *Vodalus* made

Capgr. in vit. Barthol. f. 33.

quick

quick dispatch with him, when he cast him out of a possessed Person, only by giving him a box o' th' ear. S. *Cuthbert*, being molested by the Devil, took a great Club in his hand, and persecuted the enemy from place to place, till he drove him headlong (*to the endangering his neck*) from the top of a mountain; there to this day remain the impressions of both their foot-steps to be seen in the stones; where the Devil's *tread* is broad and crooked; great and distorted; which place no woman may enter without hazard. And it was a pretty trick of S. *Bertholdus*, when the Devil came down the chimny in the form of a *Hog*, to drive him away only with a *wisp of straw*. S. *Lupus* too, I think, was even with him, when the Devil came and disturbed his singing one night, and afflicted him with a sore thirst; he called for a pot of water, and perceiving the Devil busie about it, watching his opportunity, he clapt a cushion (signed with the sign of the Cross) upon the mouth of the vessel, and shut the Devil in; who all night continued there howling sadly, till the Sun was up; and then he that came to tempt him, was let go, and departed very much ashamed. But never was the Devil so handled, nor came off so shamefully, as when he came to tempt S. *Juliana*, in the form of an Angel of Light, and perswaded her to avoid farther torments, by sacrificing to the Gods: upon which, in indignation she laid hold on him, and threw him to the ground, held him howling a whole night; and after dragging him along with her through the Market-place, though he begg'd hard, and hung back very much, yet she threw him into a *Privy* hard by: He could never forgive this usage, you may be sure; and therefore when she came to the place of her suffering, the Devil incited them not to *spare her*: and yet he was

Bolland. in vit. S. Vodali. 5 Febr. p. 592.

Capgrav. vit. Cuthbert. f. 69.

Surius in vit. Berthold. 27. Julii.

Surius vit. S. Lupi Senonens. 1 Septemb.

Breviar. Rom. antiq Febr. 16. Lec. 2, 3 & 6.

Lef. 6.

so frighted with what had past, that when she heard him say so, and lookt upon him; he cried out that he was undone, for she would catch him again; and so ran away and vanished out of sight.

But to return to S. *Anthony*. As I cannot believe, that his Sermons were of such a strain, as to provoke the *Devil* to owe him a greater spight, than other preachers; so much less that God did ever give such wonderful attestations to the truth and excellency of his doctrine, as they would bear us in hand he did (though we should abate for the silliness of many of the stories.) Can any man of sense be perswaded, that the *Pentecost miracle* show'd upon the *Apostles* when they spake with diverse tongues, should be renewed, that people might understand the *Trifles* and *Toys* of his Sermon? Yet we are told, that when an innumerable company of people of diverse Nations came to *Rome* to obtain *Easter Indulgences*; the Pope put S. *Anthony* upon preaching a Sermon to those strangers: The Grace of the H. Ghost did so instruct the Tongue of the holy man, that every one heard and understood the language of his own country wherein he was born; which *Vit. S. Anton. cap. 15. & Ribadan. p. 248.* seems to say, that in one Sermon S. *Anthony* spoke all those languages at one time; and then indeed the miracle was greater than of the *Apostles at Pentecost*, for there were more than one to speak those several languages, and none of them spoke more than one language I suppose at the same time. *Ribadeneira* indeed would have it, that he spake but one language in his Sermon, but the Sermon was as well understood by all the hearers, as if he had preached in the language of their several Nations; and so considering the effect, this gift was equall to that of the Apostles: But in another respect he far out-did them: for though they spake with many tongues, yet I never read that their tongues were louder than other mens: (for the *two sons of Thunder* were called *Marc. 3. 17.* so for another reason, than because of their

loud

loud voices.) But, they tell us, that a *good woman* that would fain have followed S. *Anthony* out of the City to hear him preach, was hindred by her husband; which so grieved her, that she could not be satisfied, till she went to the top of her house, and viewed however out of a window the place appointed for the Sermon: and though the place was two miles distant, yet there she heard him preach distinctly; which occasioned a longer stay there than her husband could bear, who chid her for it; but when he understood the miracle, he also went up, and was a partaker of the same happiness, and from that day, neither of them were ever absent from his Sermons.

Vit. Anton. cap. 17.

Another *noble Matron*, as she was crouding among a multitude of people going out of Town to hear him preach in the fields, fell into thick dirt, being apparell'd in new and costly clothes; but in her fall, commending her self to God and to S. *Anthony*, she arose again, with her clothes unsoiled, to the great wonder of all. And as we are to believe such wonderous preventions of ill accidents that might have hindred peoples devotion *from hearing him*; so a great many more preventions of misfortunes *in hearing* him. For as he was preaching another time in the open fields, suddenly the Heavens gathered blackness, and great thunders and lightnings threatned a mighty storm of rain, so that the people were preparing to go away to save themselves from it. But S. *Anthony* bid them not to stir, for not a drop of rain should touch them; whereupon, believing him, they all stay'd; and the fierce shower of rain and hail, left them untouched, and did not so much as wet the place where they stood, though it seemed to compass them round like a wall *.

Ibid.

Vit. Anton. c. 18. Ribaden. p. 248.

* *Thus they tell us, that S. Anthony going a journey to Vicentia, a great shower of rain fell; and he having nothing to defend him from it, he put his Rosary upon his head, and prayed to the Bl. Virgin; and as if the Rosary had been turned into an house, it so covered him, that not one drop of rain fell upon him all the way.* Gonom: Chronic. p. 244.

And

And that no body might complain that they lost any thing *afterward*, by attending upon S. *Anthonie*'s Sermons; we hear of a woman, who disliking the wine that the good people had sent in to S. *Anthony* after his preaching, ran home to fetch better; she was in such haste that she left the vessel open, bringing the Spigot along with her in her hand, and the wine, when she returned, was all run out in the Cellar: but she trusting in the merits of the Saint, she put the Spigot into the vessel again, and it was presently filled with wine, that it ran over: which is more Romantick, than the story of the Sister, that was drawing wine, who being hastily called by S. *Adelheidis*, her obedience was so quick, that she ran with the Spigot in her hand, and yet when she returned, not one drop of wine was run out: It being easier to stop the wines running, than to fill the emptied vessel anew till it run over. *Vit.Anton.ibid.* *Bolland. 5.Feb. p.719.*

These apparent forgeries and Fables hitherto mentioned, concerning S. *Anthonie*'s preaching and miracles relating thereunto, must needs take away all credit from other stories told of him, if nothing else did: for he that will go about to deceive me with his lies, in a matter where I can easily detect him, deserves to be disbelieved in other things, where his cheats cannot so plainly be discovered, but yet is carrying on the same design.

Such are the stories of this Saint about *Confession*. As when they tell us, that he used in his lifetime to appear to persons as they lay in their beds, and say to them; *Arise Martin, arise Agnes*, go to such a one, and confess to him this or that sin, which thou didst commit in such a place, to which none is privy but God only. Also, that of a man of *Padua*, who among other things confessed to S. *Anthony*, that he kicked one time his mother to the ground: which when the Saint heard, he said to him in great zeal; *That foot which* *Vit.Anton. cap. 21.* *Ibid.*

smites

smites a father or mother, deserves presently to be cut off: The simple man construing his words amiss, presently went home, and cut off his foot, which being told to the *Saint,* he goes to the man, and after he had prayed and made the sign of the Cross, he joyned his foot to his leg, and immediately it was whole again. For the same man to perform several offices at the same time in distant places, is no easie matter to be credited; yet thus we are told, that S. *Anthony* preaching at *Mompellier,* after he had begun his Sermon, he remembred that it was incumbent upon him, to bear a part in the singing Service, in another Church, and he had forgot to speak to any one to supply his place; at which being troubled, he covered his head with his Cowl and leaned back in the Pulpit, making a stop in his Sermon for some while: at which time he appeared in that other Church, and performed his office there, and then coming to himself again (you must suppose he was in the Pulpit as in a trance) he went on where he left, with his discourse.

Vit. Anton. cap. 16.

S. *Antoninus* in his History relates this story also; and concludes, that because a man cannot be at the same time in more places corporally, we must understand, that he that sang the office in the other Church, was an *Angel,* not *Anthony.* But *Marturus* the *Jesuit* in his notes upon this passage of *Antoninus,* tells us, that it is a doubtful Question among the *Divines,* whether by the Divine power the same body may not be in several places *circumscriptivè.* S. *Thomas* indeed, he says, is of *Antoninus* his mind. *Sotus* seems to leave both parts of the question equally probable: But *Scotus, Biel* and others, are for the *affirmative,* proving that it implies no contradiction, because the body of *Christ* may be in diverse places, as they prove from its existence in the Eucharist. *Sanctesius,* he says, is of the same mind, for this reason (and it is worth the naming) because in controversies of Religion *that* ought to be lookt upon as the more *probable opinion,* which *depresses sense* and *nature,* and

Part. 3. Tit. 24. c 3. sec. 2.

or

Devotions of the Roman Church. 317

on the contrary *advances God* (as this does) if so be the Scripture in no other place opposes it, (as it does not.)

This I mention by the way, to show that there is no *foolish fable* told in that Church, though never so improbable, but they have *Divines* with as *foolish reasons* ready to dispute for it, and defend it. But whether S. *Anthony* could be in *two places* or not, at the *same time*; yet we are to believe that he was in *two very far distant places*, in *less time* than any would imagine. For when his Father, who dwelt at *Lisbon*, was clapt into Prison with his whole Family, upon suspicion of Murder, because a Youth that was slain, was found buried in his Garden; the Spirit gave him notice of it, and in one Night he was carried from *Padua* (the place where he was) to *Lisbon*, and appeared before the Judge the next Morning, desiring him to let go those innocent Persons; which he refusing, he then prayed to let the Body of the slain Youth be brought to him; which being granted, he commanded him to rise up, and tell whether *his Parents* murdered him, or no: the dead Body hereupon arose, and said, that they were all innocent of his slaughter; and so they were released, and the next Day he was brought back to *Padua* by the Ministry of an Angel. We are to suppose that this was a good Angel, whose Ministry he used; but methinks, considering how scurvily the Devil had before used S. *Anthony*, it had been better if they had told us, that he sadled the Devil for this Journey; as he was served once by S. *Antidius*, who having business with the *Pope*, got upon the Devils back, and made him carry him to *Rome*, and there attend at the *Pope*'s Gate, till he had dispatched his affair; and then made him carry him back again to the place from whence he came. But the hardest thing to be believed, in the foregoing story, is, that rather than the Parents of this Saint, should suffer unjustly, (though it has been the fate of many as good Men before them, both as to their good Names and Lives) a dead body must be raised to life, to clear their Innocency, and to disco-

Vit. Anton. cap. 20.

Vincentii Speculum lib. 19. cap. 3.

ver

ver the truth. The Writers of the Lives of the Saints, I observe, are very Liberal of Miracles in such cases; and he that can give credit to *them*, shall have my leave to do the same to *this* of S. *Anthony*. We are told, that a poor Man complaining to S. *Vedastus*, that one had stollen a Sheep from him, and he could not find out the Thief: the Saint first took this course, to admonish the People of it, when they met on Sunday at Church; but he that was the guilty Person being present, and yet, notwithstanding *Vedastus* his admonition, not confessing the fact, suddenly the Gloves in his bosome (which I suppose were made of that Sheeps skin) bleated in the Peoples hearing, and he was discovered thereby. S. *Mel* lying under a suspicion, that he had too great familiarity with his Kinswoman named *Lupita*, he cleared himself this admirable way before S. *Patrick*, by fishing and catching Salmons in the furrows of plowed ground: and she removed all jealousies on her part, when she took hot burning Coals into her Lap, and yet did not hereby singe her Cloathes. A Noble Matron of *Sardinia*, having brought forth a Child like a Blackmore, when she and her Husband were both fair, was suspected of Adultery with her Servant that was a *black*: *Guillelmus* a *Speluncato*, a famous Preacher there, discovered the true Father thus. He caused the married couple, the Child, and the Blackmore, all to stand forth before the People; Then from the Pulpit he commanded the Child in the Name of Christ, that without any help it should go to its true Father; immediately hereupon the Infant, though otherwise uncapable of walking * (it being scarce a Moneth old) leaving the Blackmore, went to the Womans Husband, whereby he was freed from his jealousies, and she from the suspicion of her crime; and not without great reason sure,

Bollandus ad 6 Febr. p. 813.

Colganus vit. S Melis. 4 Febr. p. 261.

Martyrol. Francisc. 17 Novemb. p. 542.

---

* *As uncapable as a Child is of understanding, and speaking at 40 days old, yet S. Amandus catechized one no older, and it pronounced clearly the word Amen, and was baptized by him.* Bolland. ad 6 Febr. p. 856.

the

the Child being so wise at that Age, as to know his own Father. But the worst is, so free the Monks were of their wonders in former days, that we read of as great a Miracle as any of these, of which I can see no other end, but to conveigh a false perswasion into Mens minds, for it served to clear no truth in Question. It is that which *Capgrave* relates concerning the Mother of S. *Kentigern*; who admiring the *Bl. Virgins* fruitfulness without the knowledge of any Man, rashly prayed to God daily, to be like her both in conceiving and bringing forth: a while after she was found with Child, and magnifying God, simply believed that her desires were fulfilled; for she often asserted, yea and swore, that she knew not *by whom*, nor *when*, nor *how* she became with Child: and the People of S. *Kentigern*'s Diocess to this day assert, that he was conceived and born of a Virgin. He calls them indeed *Fools* for saying so; but I think he was as great a *Fool*, for proclaiming the following wonder, which if true, might well confirm the People in their belief. He says then, that the *King* her Father coming to inquire of her, both by threats and fair words, who got her with child, she again protested with an oath, that she never had the company of any Man. At which the King being offended, would have the *Law* in this case to pass upon her; in which it was of old ordained in that Countrey, that a Maid committing fornication in her Fathers house, and proving with Child, she should be cast head-long from the top of a Mountain, and he that corrupted her should lose his head: This Law he commanded to be executed upon her, (with a design I suppose chiefly to find out him that had dared to corrupt the King's Daughter, which it might well be imagined she would confess before she dyed.) She was placed then on the brow of the Mountain called *Danpelder*, and thrown headlong down from thence; (without confessing any thing.) She descended to the ground with a pleasant easie sliding, and not any Member of her Body was broken, or so much as hurt. The *Pagans* (*Capgrave* says) ascribed this to Magick, and there-

Capgrave vit. S. Kentigern, f. 258.

therefore with the King's consent put her into a little Vessel made of Leather, and having brought her some Miles off from shore, they committed her alone to fortune and the Sea, for there were no Oars, or Men to help to guide it: but notwithstanding this danger, she did not miscarry; for her Vessel went faster than if it had had the benefit of Sailes and Oars, and she was brought safe into the Port. What could a Christian think of this double Miracle, but that she was innocent of what was laid to her charge, that she had neither fornicated, nor was forsworn? But then what becomes of the truth of what is so often said and sung in the *Roman* Church, (and owned by all Christians) that the Mother of our Saviour only had this priviledge, and that she was *Virgo puerpera singularis*? I am afraid it will prove a hard task to bring this off well. But to return to S. *Anthony.*

After all these miraculous things that are told concerning him, who can doubt, but that his sanctified breath might work such a wonder, as we hear he wrought upon a Religious Novice; who being frequently tempted by the Devil to forsake his Order, and discovering it to the Saint, he only opened his mouth and blew into it, saying, *Receive the Holy Ghost,* and immediately he was freed from all his temptations, and persevered in the Religious course he had undertaken. Another Monk that could not extinguish lustful heats, by fasting or prayers, or the use of the Sacraments, complaining of it to S. *Anthony*; he only made him put on *his Coat,* and thereupon all his evil desires were extinguished, and he never felt them more all his Life. Thus they still take care, that their new Saints, not only may equalize, but out-do the old ones, nay even Christ and his Apostles. I gave some instances of this kind before *, and here we have another such. It was a mighty Vertue that went out of our Saviour, which cured the Woman of her *Twelve* Years distemper, who only touched the Border of his Garment:

Ribaden. ibid. p. 149.

Idem ibid.

* *pag.* 89, 90, *&c.*

ment: but that garment was upon the body of our Saviour when it wrought the cure; this garment of S. *Anthonie*'s did so, when it was put upon another, and taken off from his body: *That touch* removed a *bodily* infirmity; this must be supposed to have influence upon the *Soul*, to correct a depraved fancy, and stop the course of imagination, and dry up the spring of evil desires; a harder thing by much than to stay a flux of blood. We read of S. *Paul, that from his body were brought unto the sick Handkerchiefs or Aprons, and the diseases departed from them, and the evil spirits went out of them.* But we are informed, that the very *Chord* of S. *Maria de Turribus* (which touched not her body but her clothes) dispossessed Devils: and even *one thread* unripped out of the Garment of S. *Leobinus* *, that was new mending, casts out an evil spirit. Nay farther, the very *water* in which S. *Francis*'s Chord was dipped, cured abundance of diseases: Insomuch that one of their famous preachers, *Ludovicus Granatensis*, comparing S. *Paul*'s Handkerchiefs and S. *Anthonie*'s Chord, gives the preference to the latter for wonder. *Verùm hìc aliquid video mirabilius*, &c. *Here I see something* (says he) *more wonderful, for the Lord not only bestowed such vertue* (of curing diseases) *upon the Saints Chord, but also upon the water, that had touched his Chord.* A man would imagine that Christ bore as tender a love as possible to his Disciples whom he conversed with upon earth, and gave them very good assurances and pledges of it, after he was ascended up to Heaven; but I do not read that they ever received such sensible tokens of it, as these *new Saints* have done: For though S. *Paul* indeed speaks of espousing the *Corinthians* to Christ as to their husband; yet which of

Luk. 8. 43, 44, &c.

Act. 19. 12.

Martyrolog. Franciscan. p. 414.

* Bolland. ad 14. Mart. p. 353.

See Martyrol. Francisc. p. 644.

2 Cor. 11. 2.

Y   them

them ever received by *his* hands, a gold Ring. as S. *Coleta* did by the hands of *John* the *Evangelist*, as a pledge of Christs love to her, and of his espousing her? S. *Peter* tells us of their loving him though they saw him not, and of their wonderful rejoycing, but it was by believing, when he was not present: but these *new Saints*, by their ardent love, bring him down from Heaven again, and he presents himself not to their minds only, but to their bodily eyes and other senses: insomuch that we read of two Sisters, S. *Ethnea* and S. *Sodelbia*, whose affections to him he rewarded, by appearing to them in the form of a most lovely Infant, putting himself into their bosoms to be embraced and kissed by them. Nay, our S. *Anthony* too had these caresses, (though I thought before I met with the story, that they had been the peculiar entertainments only of the *Melancholy Nuns*:) for his Landlord where he one night lodged, peeping into his chamber at a secret window, he saw Jesus in the form of a beautiful Child, first sitting upon his book, and from thence creeping into his Arms, whom the Saint embraced and kissed uncessantly, while Jesus smiled upon him, and with pleasing looks beheld him; but this was so Divine a favour (says *Ribaden.*) that when he understood by inspiration, that his Host was conscious of it, he begged of him, that he would not reveal it to any mortal man whilest he was alive; but, it's likely, when the inquiry was made into his miracles after his death, in order to his *Canonization*, this was then first produced. And that you may see that S. *Anthonie's* miracles from first to last, are all of a piece: we are told, that on that very day when the Pope Canonized him, this wonder happened at *Lisbon* (where he was born) that the men and women came out of their houses and sung and danced in the open streets, and all the Bells of the

the City rang out merrily of themselves, no hand moving them; neither could the people contain themselves from this mirth and dancing, though no body knew any reason for it, (and therefore admired the hidden cause) till certain *Friers* came thither from *Italy*, by whose relation and comparing circumstances they understood, that on that very day of their unusual joy, *Anthony* was put into the *Kalender of Saints*.

And now a great many fine stories are told us of miracles after his death, to convince some that doubted of the wonders that he was said to work in his life-time: One man would not believe, unless a glass which he had in his hand remained unbroken, after he had thrown it against a stone pavement; which he tried, and it received no more damage, than if it had been a hard Flint. *Vit. Anton. cap. 29.* Another chose this way for his satisfaction; finding a dried stalk of a Vine in the drinking-glass, he would believe, if he could fill his glass with Wine, *Ibid.* pressed from the Grapes that should grow upon that stalk; immediately it flourished with leaves, brought forth Grapes; and when he saw all done that he demanded, this miracle gave him a full and firm belief of all the rest. Nay, the senseless passions of a woman, which ended in a mad and foolish resolution, must be countenanced at the expence of a miracle, because S. *Anthony* must never fail any one that does invoke him. For as a woman in the company of her husband and several others was going to *Padua*, being transported too frolickly (as *Vit. Anton. ibid.* he thought) at a promise he had made her, of taking her along with him in a pilgrimage he was going; he, to curb her extravagant mirth, made as if he had now altered his resolution, and would not go the journey; upon which his wife was so exasperated, that she threatned, unless he would perform his promise, to drown her self in the name of *Christ* and S. *Anthony*, in the River that ran by. Which her husband looking upon as a coppy of her countenance,

nance, and calling her fool for talking so, and telling her he would persist in his new resolve; she presently invoking the name of S. *Anthony*, cast her self head-long into the River: The women that were in company, being amazed and seeing her float in the waters, forgetting the danger, ran after her into the River, laid hold of her, and brought her to land; where it was wonderful to see them all wringing upon the shore their wet garments, and not one thread of her clothes was in the least wetted, as if the waters had never touched them. " This action (says the relator) " though it ought to be ascribed rather to her folly than " vertue; yet the merits of this Holy Father prevailed so " far with God, that he who was always a friend to true " simplicity, preserved this simple woman, though a fool " (but I should count him a *greater* that believed it) un- " hurt in the midst of the waters. I cannot but here mention a concatenation of such wonders, which I meet with in the life of S. *Sedonius*, upon as trifling an occasion as this altogether, and in consequence of worse

Colganus in vit. S. Sedon. 10. Mart. p. 573.

passions than this woman exprest. " S. Se- " *donius* then, seeing one day a woman wash- " ing her Childs clouts in a Fountain be- " longing to the Monastery, cried out to " his fellow S. *Libernus*, of the shamefulness of this fact, " that she should thus defile that Fountain, from whence " they fetched the waters they used about the tremendous " mysteries of the sacrifice of the Mass. This moved such " a holy indignation in these Saints (though some may judge " it exceeded its bounds) that they imprecated the Divine " vengeance against the woman and her off-spring: The " Child of this woman, as it was playing upon an high " bank of the Sea, suddenly fell into it, where it was swal- " lowed up presently and appeared no more. Upon this " misfortune, the Mother comes crying and howling to " S. *Senanus* (whose disciples these two angry Saints were) " complaining how upon their curses her Child was drown- " ed. When *Senanus* heard this, he severely chides his

" sons,

"sons, as guilty of murder: and he commanded *Libernus*
"to go and stand upon a rock, placed in the neighbouring
"Sea, and there do his penance: As for *Sedonius*, he bad
"him go look for the drowned Child in the Sea, and not
"desist his search till he had found him and restored him to
"his Mother: They both of them obey this rigid sentence
"of the holy Father. *Sedonius* in his quest after the Child
"in the midst of the Sea, finds it (after it had lain there
"twenty four hours) safe and sound, playing in the waters
"and beating the waves with the palms of its hands, and so
"brought it to S. *Senanus*; who bad him go and fetch
"home *Libernus* from the rock, saying that he had found a
"very favourable judge; as indeed it proved, for the
"waters of the Sea that used to cover that rock at other
"times (*by the rising of the tide*) did not dare to touch
"him, but kept off the length of his staff round about
"him.

Thirty two years after S. *Anthonie*'s death, his body was translated into the Church where it now rests at *Padua*; there when they came reverently to examine and bring forth the holy Body out of the Coffin in which it had laid so long, they found the rest of his members turned to dust (says *Mendozius* *) only his Tongue was still fresh, and full of juice and blood, as if he had been alive: This S. *Bonaventure*, who was present, taking into his hand, broke out into these words. *O blessed tongue, which always did bless God, and taught others to bless him, now it appears of what merit thou wast*: After these words he reverently kissed his tongue, and then delivered it to the Magistrates of *Padua* to be laid up in a repository worthy of it. If they had told me that he was of so great merit, that he inabled the Fishes to use their tongues to bless God, as we heard before he taught them in a Sermon how much they were beholden to him; I should have as soon believed that the Fishes spoke, as that his Tongue alone remained uncorrupt

*Vit. Anton. c. 30
Ribadin. p. 251
S. Antoninus
ubi supr p. 738.*

* *Inter Elogia præfixa vit. S. Anton.*

Loco citat.

uncorrupt when the rest of his body was perished. The forenamed *Mendozius* indeed gives us some pleasant reasons, not only that it was so, but why it was fitting and ought to have been so, that his tongue should remain incorruptible. One is, to give his Country-men a sure pledge hereby that his intercession for them should never cease, but that his voice and prayers should be always imployed for their salvation: (by which reason all the tongues at least of the *Patron Saints* should have been preserved from corruption as well as his:) Another is, that the Tongue of S. *Anthony* was a preacher of truth, therefore it ought eternally to remain; for as S. *Ambrose* says rightly, *those things that are true are eternal*: which I shall then think to be a good argument, when I am certified that all those preachers tongues never rot in their Graves, which tell no lies in the Pulpit: But having heard before the little sence this tongue spake in Sermons, and how much he *corrupted* the true meaning almost of every Text of Scripture he medled with, I hope we may be pardoned, if, notwithstanding this reason, we believe this story to be a *lye*.

I have but one thing more that concerns S. *Anthony* to trouble the Reader withal, which I have reserved to be spoken to (though somewhat out of its due order) in the last place, because it's the most famed story that is told of him; mentioned by all the later Writers * of his Life: and particularly insisted on by *Bellarmine*, for the proof of the opinion of the *Roman Church*, concerning the Presence of the Body of Christ in the Eucharist; and it is called by him *miraculum insigne*, a notable miracle. I'le give it you in *Bellarmin*'s words, as he pretends to relate it out of S. *Antoninus* and *Surius*. "As S. *Anthony* was disputing concerning the truth of the Lord's Body in the Eucharist, with a certain Heretick in the parts of *Tholouse*, (for at that time the *Albigenses* vexed

Antoninus, Surius, Ribadeneira.

Bellarmin. de Sacram. Euchar. 9. lib. 3. cap. 8 prope finem.

"vexed the Church, and they with many more were in-
"fected with this error) the Heretick required of *Anthony*
"this sign, knowing him to be endued with the gift of mi-
"racles: (which last words are Bellarmines *addition, not
"to be found in his forenamed Authors; and a foolish one too,
"for if he knew him to have that gift, why was he not of his
"mind, without any farther trial?*) Says the Heretick, *I
"have a Mule* *, to which I will give no meat
"these three days: After the three days end,
"come thou with the Sacrament, and I will
"come with my Mule, and will pour out Pro-
"vender before it; if the Mule leave his
"Provender, and come and venerate the Sa-
"crament, I will believe.* These conditions
"were accepted, and after three days,
"S. *Anthony* being accompanied with a multitude of the
"faithful, and holding the venerable Sacrament in his hand,
"spake thus to the Mule. *In the vertue and name of thy
"Creator, whom I, though unworthy, truly hold in my
"hand, I require and command thee O Animal, that thou
"immediately approach humbly after thy manner, and show
"reverence to him; that so by this, Heretical pravity may un-
"derstand, that every creature is to be subject to his Creator,
"whom the Priestly dignity daily handles at the Altar.* Up-
"on the saying of which words, the Mule forgetting his
"Provender that lay before him, and his hunger, went to-
"wards the Saint; and bowing his head, and bending his
"knees, adored the Lord as well as he could, and confuted
"the Heretick.

* Jumentum, which I translate so, because both Antoninus and Surius call it afterward Mulus.

Though such ridiculous stuff as this deserves no Confutation, the very *relation* of it being sufficient to blast its credit: yet the *Relator* being of so great fame; for his sake, il'e a little enquire into its Age; for I believe we shall find, that this story (though by their later Writers more talked of * than any of the rest, yet) was either not so old, or not

* *Aldrovandus* has put it among the Histories concerning the *Mule*: Lib. de *Quadrupedibus Solidiped*. c. 4. tit. *Historica*.

so much credited heretofore, even in their own Church, as some other things they relate concerning him.

If this had been as current a Miracle in S. *Anthony*'s time, as it pretends to be publick, and to be a triumphant victory after a chalenge, and a set dispute with a Heretick; I am apt to fancy, that *Cæsarius* who pickt up all miraculous reports about the time he lived, would have met with it, & deliver'd it down to us in his Dialogues *, especially since his *Ninth Book* contains more such examples than one, concerning bruit creatures venerating the Eucharist. But if this could not come to his notice (as I am not peremptory in it) yet I am sure it might to another Writer of the same Age with *Anthony*, viz. *Thomas Cantipratanus* Suffragan to the Bishop of *Cambray*, who collected in the same manner the Miracles and memorable examples of his Time, and yet says not one word of this Miracle, though he also mention some of the same nature. But because this may seem too to have less force in it, since he says not a syllable of S. *Anthony* that I observe; I therefore add, that another *French*-man of this Age too, sc. *Vincentius* Bishop of *Beauvais*, whose *Speculum Historiale*, (libr. 30. cap. 131, 132, 133, 134, 135.) has a large account of S. *Anthony*; who also mentions his reasoning with Hereticks, and his converting an Arch-Heretick; yet he is wholly silent as to this of S. *Anthony*'s Mule, though said to be done in his own Countrey; which is a plain sign that this was not a story then in being, but coyned since; for if it had been done in his days, it could neither have escaped his knowledge, nor been omitted in his History, since it was the most remarkable thing that belonged to it. Which is still more confirmed, by another observation, that among six and thirty Lessons of the old *Roman Breviary* (where so many fine things are

* This I think not improbable, because he wrote his Dialogues so little a while before *Anthony*'s death, for he tells us that he was writing them, an. 1222. (and the Saint dyed 1231.) Cæsarius lib. 10. cap. 48.

Placed by Bellarm. an. 1265 de Script. Ecclesiast.

Placed an. 1250. Bellarm. ibid.

are told of him) this is not to be found; though in one of them I meet with these words. "*Anthony* con- "futed the perverse Opinions of Hereticks, by "the most congruous reasons; for at *Arimi-* "*num* (*a City in Italy*) he converted many Hereticks to the "soundness of Christian faith; among whom he reduced "to the light of truth, an Arch-Heretick called *Bonovillus*, "who for 30 Years space had been blinded with the dark- "ness of Pestilent errour. Where, by the way, you may correct either the wilful or ignorant mistake of *Ribadeneira*, who in the Life of *Anthony*, makes the dis- putation, wherein the Mule acted such a wonderous part, to have been betwixt the Heretick *Bono-villus*, and S. *Anthony*; whereas all that mention the vene- ration of the Mule, say expresly that this happened *in partibus Tholosanis*; and all that speak of *Bonovill's* story, deter- mine it to have been at *Ariminum*; that is, the one was in *Italy*, and the other in *France*; and his Life in *Surius*, men- tions both of them distinctly.

Les.3. infra Octav.

Ribaden. p. 247.

The summe of all I have now said put together, amounts to this. That if all those Writers of his Life, had agreed in the mention of this Miracle about the Eucharist, it would not have been a sufficient proof of its *Truth*; (since they are all known to abound with lies:) But so many of them o- mitting it, especially those of that Age, wherein it is pre- tended to be done, and whose design such a story would sin- gularly well have served, argues that then it had not so much as the credit of a common, or a current *Fable*. S. *Antoninus* who lived above 200 Years after *Anthony* (for ought I can find) was the first Writer that mentions it, and others seem to have taken it from him; so that nothing remains but Oral Tradition to help them out, which how fairly it has brought them off, we have seen in S. *Ursula*, and several other Instances named before.

Floruit an.1445. Bellarm.de Scrip. Ecclesiast.

I have but one thing more to Remark, which must not be omitted, and then I have done with this Saint. That is, the prodigious Licence they of this Church take to entertain the People with strange Miracles, in this of the Sacrament of the Eucharist, above all other Subjects. They have espoused the belief of a Doctrine contrary to the reason and sense of all Mankind, and it must be maintained in the same way that it was made. No mortal Man can invent any thing so extravagant and foolish, which they can pretend reason to boggle and stick at, who have once made *Transubstantiation* an Article of their Faith: I have no hopes therefore to make them ashamed in the least, by what I shall now say; yet however it may be useful to others who have not inslaved all their faculties, or committed themselves blindfold to the conduct of their pretended unerring Guide, to know what Diet their faith lives upon, and what hard morsels it must swallow down without any chewing at all. It were endless to enumerate the wonders they produce in the lives of Saints, and in Sermons, to procure veneration in Mens minds to the Eucharist; I shall content my self with giving a few Instances of Miracles that they tell us, have happened at the *presence* or *celebration* of it.

We know there is a certain time in the Mass, when they lift up the Host, and show it to the People, in order to their adoration of it. As S. *Ivo* was elevating it, a Globe of Light of wonderful splendor incompassed the Body of Christ, and also the Chalice, and after the elevation of both presently disappeared. *Catherina Gonzales*, though imployed at a distance in the Bakehouse, often saw the Host when it was elevated by the Priest, (*I suppose, that she might not lose the benefit of the adoration*) though there were many Walls between to intercept her sight. But, which is still more strange, S. *Sibyllina* though she was blind, yet knew when the Host was elevated by her inward sense; and one time as the Priest presumed to carry an unconsecrated Host to a sick Person, when through his negligence he wanted one consecrated, at the sound of the Bell

Brev. Rom. ant. Maii 19. Lec. 7.

Martyr. Francisc. p. 39.

Acta Sanctor. ad 19 Mart. p. 70.

as

fore she would adore it, she applyed it to her heart, and by a wonderful agitation she found there, she knew it to be a true piece of the Cross, and not counterfeit. It was a singular favour (you'l say) that was showed to S. *Bonaventure*; (who for several days through his great humility and fear had abstained from receiving the Communion) as he heard the Mass, and was meditating upon the passion *Brev. Rom. ant. Jul. 14. Lec. 4. infra octav.* of Christ, God having regard to his humility, mercifully put into his mouth a particle of the consecrated Host, which an Angel took out of the hand of the Priest. But it was a greater that was shown him, when he was near his death, and by reason of his weakness vomited up every thing he took. He was now in a great strait what to do, having a great desire to receive the sacred *Viaticum*, and yet durst not, out of reve- *Martyrol. Francisc. Julii 14. p. 288.* rence to it, and the danger of bringing it up again: However he resolved to have the Lord's Body brought to him; that he might dye more comfortably when it was in presence: he applied the Pix, in which it was carried, to his side, showing hereby his desire to receive it; and there his side opened in the form of a red Rose, at which place *Christ*'s Body starting out of the Pix, went in to his very heart, and his side closed again, without any remaining sign of its having been opened. *

* *This very thing is finely told under another name in these words of the old Homily.* "There was an Earl of Venice, called Syr Ain-
"bright, that loved the Sacrament of the Awter passing well,
"and did it all the worshyp and reverence that he might, so
"when he lay sick and should dye, he might not receive the Sa-
"crament for Castyng; then was he sory, and made do e;
"and then he let make clean his right syde and to cover it with
"a fayr clothe of sendall and layd Gods body therein, and sayd
"thus

"thus to the Host: Lord thou knowest that I love thee with
"all my heart, and would fayne receive thee with my mouth
"and I durst, and because I may not, I lay thee on the place
"that is next to my heart, and so I shew thee all the Love of
"my heart that I can or may; wherefore I beseech thee good
"Lord, have mercy on me: and even therewith in the sight of
"all the People that were about him, his syde opened and the
"host went there into his syde, and then it closed again, and so
"anon after he dyed. *Festival. in die corp. Christi, f.52.*

I had thought that the Eucharist had been designed only for the food of Souls, and that it never became a common repast of the Body: Yet S. *Nicholas de Rupe* it seems found it so, for we hear that he lived 20 Years without humane food, save only by the Eucharist received every Fifteen Days, and his Meditation on Christ's passion: (that is, upon the accidents of whiteness and roundness, &c. for the substance being, according to them, Christ's Body, can never nourish.)

Act. Sanctor. in vit. ejus. Mart. 22. p. 411. & 429.

But perhaps it may seem more proper to the instance before us of S. *Anthony*'s Mule, to hear a little more, concerning the strange effects its presence has produced upon *bruit Creatures*. "An ancient Priest as he was carrying the Sa-
"crament out of Town to a sick Person, met a Company of
"Asses laden with Corn in a very narrow,
"and deep miry way. He that went be-
"fore him with the Lantern, with much a-
"do, thrust by them. But the Priest seeing this, and consi-
"dering his age and weakness, began to look pale and trem-
"ble; and fearing that he might be tumbled into the Mire
"with the Sacrament by the Asses, he cryed out to them;
"*O Asses, what is it that ye do? what, do you not consider
"whom I carry in my hands? Stand still, fall down and give
"honour to your Creator, for I command it in his Name:*
"Behold, says the Relator, the wonderful obedience of these
"Animals. They all stood still, and fell down together;
"and, which added to the wonder, though the Asses could
"not fall down but with much difficulty, yet not one of the
"Sacks

Cæsarii Dialog. Dist. 4. cap. 98.

"Sacks of Corn did slide off from their backs. This fact is famous to this Day in the City of *Colen*. (a City as famous as the Story.) Saint *Coleta* had a Lamb that shew'd the same respect, and used, without teaching, to kneel at the Elevation of the Eucharist, and to rise when it was over. The Plow-man that early in the Morning was at work in the Field, and on a sudden with all his whipping could not make his Oxen stir a foot, and cryed out, that the Devil was in them; quickly found his mistake, when looking about him, he saw the *Pix* (with the Sacrament in it) lye before the feet of the Oxen (which some Thieves, that had broken open the Church, had stoln away and scattered there) and they in admiration stood still, and would go no farther; which veneration of theirs might well occasion, as we are told, the Priest of the Parish, and a great Multitude with Him to come into the Field, and with the Cross, censor of incense and wax lights, carry Christ's Body back again into the Church. The next story to it, of the Bees, must not be forgotten; A Woman who kept Bees that did not thrive, but dyed apace, was counselled to place the Lord's Body in the Hive, and that would stop the Plague that was among them; she went therefore to the Church, and receiving the Communion from the Priest; as soon as she went away from him, she took it out of her Mouth, and put it in one of the Bee-hives. But oh the wonderful power of God! the Bees acknowledging their Creator, built a Chappel to this their sweet Guest of an admirable structure, where they erected an Altar, and put the most holy Body of Christ upon it; and God blessed their works. All this mystery appeared when the Woman took up her Hive; for then in great fear she ran and confessed to the Priest what she had done, and what she saw; who coming thither with the Parishioners, drove away the Bees that flew about, and humm'd the praise of the Creator; and admiring the Chappel-walls, Windows, Roof, Steeple * (*Aldrovandus* adds Bells) door

Act. Sanct. ad Mart.6. p.554.

Cæsarius in Dial. dist. 9. c. 7.

Cæsar. ibid. cap. 8.

* *Aldrovand. de insectis l.1.cap.1. Historica de apibus.*

and Altar, they brought back the Lord's body with praise and glory. *Thomas Cantipratanus* relates a parallel fable concerning *Bees*, how they had lodged the Sacrament in their Hive, in a Pix made of purest Wax; and how the owner of them saw in the night the whole Air brightned above them: only these Bees were more contemplative than the former, for they left off working, and gave themselves to singing, which they ceased not to do even in the night-time, contrary to their custom.

Lib. 2. de miract. sui temp. c. 40. p. 398.

But I'le pursue these follies no farther, only that we may make a good conclusion, I'le set down out of one of the Homilies of the Festival (so often cited before) the story of the *Black Horse*, which far exceeds that of S. *Anthonie*'s *Mule*, and all the rest I have named: and I'le give it you in the old English style as I find it.

Festival. in die Corp. Christ. fol. 53.

"In Devonshyre besyde Exbridge was a woman that lay sick and was nye deed, and sent after a holy person about midnight, to have her ryghts. Than this man in all haste he might arose, and went to the Church, and took Goddes body in a box of Ivory, and put it into his bosome, and went forth toward this woman. And as he wente through the Forest in a fayre mede that was his next waye, it happed that his box fell out of his bosome to the ground, and he wente forth and wyst it not, and came to this woman, and herde her confession. And than he asked her yf she wolde be houseled, and she sayd, ye Syr. Than he put his hande into his bosem and sought the box, and whan he found it not, he was full sory and sad, and sayd, Dame, I will go after Goddes body, and come agayne anone to you, and so he wente forth sore weppynge for his symplenes. And so as he came to a wylowe tree, he made there of a rodde, and strypped himself naked, and bette himself so that the blode ranne downe by his sydes,

"sydes, and sayde thus to hymself: O thou symple
"man, why haste thou lost thy Lord God, thy maker,
"thy fourmer and Creatour: And whan he had thus
"bette hymselfe, he dyd on his clothes and wente forth,
"and than he was ware of a pyller of fire that lasted
"from erth to heven, and he was all astonyed thereof,
"yet he blessyd him and wente to it; and there lay the
"Sacrament fallen out of the boxe into the grasse, and
"the pyller shone as bryght as the sunne, and it lasted
"from Goddes body to heven; and all the beestes of the
"Forest were comen aboute Goddes body, and stode in
"compasse rounde aboute it, and all kneled on 4 knees
"save one blacke Horse that kneled but one knee. Than
"sayd he, yf thou be ony beest that may speke, I
"charge thee in Goddes name here present in fourme of
"bred, tell me why thou knelest but on one knee. Than
"sayd he, I am a fende of hell, and wyll not knele and
"I might; but I am made ayenst my will; for it is
"wryten, that every knelynge of heven and of erthe shall
"be to the worshyp of the Lord God. Why art thou
"lyke a hors? And he sayd, to make the people to stele
"me, and at suche a towne was one hanged for me, and
"at suche a towne another. Than sayd the holy per-
"sone I commaunde the by Goddes fleshe and his blode,
"that thou go into wyldernesse, and be there as thou
"shalt never dysease crysten man more. And than he
"went his way he might no lenger abyde, and than
"this man went forthe to the woman and dyd he
"ryghtes, by the whiche she was saved and went to
"everlastynge salvacyon. To the whiche he brynge us,
"our blyssed Savyour Jhesus.

A

A Summary of some Wondrous Legends of the Saints, taken out of the Lessons of the Breviaries.

HAving thus given the Reader an account of their many *Fabulous Saints*; and several *Fabulous reasons* of their Devotions to the *true ones*: having seen also, in so many foregoing instances, their admirable addresses to *Patron Saints*, whom they invoke in particular cases and distresses; It is now time to draw towards a conclusion of my task: and though I have met before with several occasions, to mention the absurd Histories of the Saints, from several Lessons of the Breviaries (which being publickly read to the people as the Scriptures were, they intended sure, that they should believe them to be true.) I'le summ up here a few more of these Legends, without questioning the Saintship of those of whom they are affirmed; and afterwards add a few more of their Devotions to the Saints.

S. *Lucy.* Decemb. 13.

Les. 6. The *Reformed Breviary* says of her, That when the judge *Paschasius* commanded her to be carried to the Stews, and her chastity there violated, they could not move her from the place where she stood by any force. But the old *Roman Breviary* gives a more particular account of it, telling us, "That the H. Ghost fixed her with
Les. 7. "such

"such a weight, that when many tried to thrust her for-
"ward, they could not stir her: then they tied ropes to
"her hands and feet, and endeavoured to draw her all to-
"gether, but she was unmoveable as a mountain. Then the
"Magicians and Southsayers tried their skill upon her, but
"all in vain: After this they brought many yoke of Oxen,
"whose drawing neither could prevail to move her. At
"which *Paschasius* wondering, said, What is the reason
"that a tender Virgin drawn by a Thousand men cannot be
"removed out of her place? *Lucy* answered, Though thou
"shouldest imploy ten thousand men, thou shalt hear the
"H. Ghost speaking for me, *A thousand shall fall at thy
"side, and ten thousand at thy right hand.*

"After this a great fire by his command
"was kindled about her, and they cast Pitch   *Les.* 8, 9.
"and Rosin and scalding Oil upon her, the
"sooner to dispatch her, and yet she remained unmoveable
"and unhurt. At last they thrust a Sword into her throat,
"yet she stirred not in the place, nor gave up the Ghost,
"till the Priests had given her the mysteries of the Sacra-
"ment, and all the people answered, *Amen.*

S. Martina. Januar. 1.

"When they brought her into *Apollo*'s
"Temple by the Emperors command to Sa-   *Brev. Rom. an-*
"crifice: upon her Crossing her self and   *tiq. Les.*1,2.
"praying, by a great Earthquake the whole
"City was shaken, and the image of *Apollo* broken in pie-
"ces. The Devil that inhabited that Idol, rolling himself
"in the dust of it, cried out with a great voice: O Virgin
"*Martina*, handmaid of the great God, thou leavest me
"naked, and showest me deformed, and drivest me out of
"my habitation, in which I have dwelt now ninety eight
"years, having under me 472 most wicked Spirits, that
"upon my command offered daily to me the souls of men;
"And so with a great noise he departed.   Z   "At

Lef. 4. "At another time S. *Martina* was brought to him as an Inchantress, and refusing to sacrifice, she was commanded to be stripped, and her flesh to be slashed with swords, but the snow-white body of the Virgin by the dazeling splendor of it, dimmed the eyes of the beholders: out of her wounds milk flowed instead of blood, and dispersed a fragrant odour, like that of Spices: And when after this, by the command of the Emperor she was beaten with clubs; those whom he imployed cried out, their strength failing them, and beseeched him, saying, Deliver us from this Virgin, for the Angels of God do strike us again with Iron bars, and our flesh and bones are all on fire: But when the Emperor would still have the strokes continued, all they that beat her died. Then was she put in

Lef. 5. "prison, and when one *Limineus* sent by the Emperor opened the door, he saw a great light shining round about her, which as he entred compassed him like lightning, so that for fear he fell to the ground; and scarce being able to arise and enter, he saw S. *Martina* sitting in a glorious seat, and a multitude of men in white about her, holding a golden Table, in which was written; *Thy works are wonderful, O Lord, in wisdom hast thou made them all*: All which he related to the Emperor.

The rest of the Lessons are all such Romantick stuff, of *Diana*'s *Temple* by fire from Heaven consumed to ashes, together with her Priests. How a fierce Lion kept three days fasting, and set upon her to devour her, fawned upon her, and falling at her feet kissed them. How being thrown into a great fire she received no harm, but the flame dispersed it self and burnt those that stood round it, &c.

S. Sebastian.

S. Sebastian.   Januar. 20.

As S. *Sebastian* was speaking, one saw an Angel descend from Heaven, and hold a book before him, and all his speech flowed from the reading that book.   *Brev. Rom. Antiq. Lec. 4.*

S. Agnes.   Januar. 21.

When she was by the Command of the Prefect stripped naked to be carried openly in that manner to the Stews, God gave such a thickness to her dishevel'd hair, that she seemed better covered therewith than with her clothes. And when she entred into the Stews, an Angel compassed her with such a wondrous light, that none could touch or see her by reason of the splendor; and there appeared a white Garment before her eyes, with which she cloathed her self, and it so exactly fitted her body, that none doubted that it was prepared by an Angel, (*who no question if he undertake it, will shape a garment more exactly than the best Tailor.*) The son of the Prefect thinking to violate her chastity, ventured to enter into that light, but before he touched her, he was choaked by the Devil, and fell down dead.   *Brev. Rom. Antiq. Lec. 6, 7.*

S. Dorothy.   Feb. 6.

When she went to be beheaded, one *Theophilus* jearingly said to her, Thou spouse of Christ, send me either *Roses* or *Apples* from his Paradise; which she promising to do, and praying, behold a most beautiful Child, that   *Brev. Rom. antiq. Les. 5 & 6.*

seemed

seemed not to be above four years old, brought to her three Roses and three Apples, which she bid him carry to *Theophilus*; as he was deriding her promise, the Child comes and offers the promised presents, who receiving them was converted to the Faith; for they were sent in *February*. [*Bollandus* tells us, That in memory of these Apples, at *Rome*, where the body of *Dorothy* is preserved, there is a solemn benediction of Apples (on the 6th. of *February*) which the people run to receive. Just such another story as this we meet with in the life of S. *Kentigern*, how he produced a fresh dish of Mulberries in Winter, only because a foolish fellow made this request to the King, and would receive no other present at his hands; and this Saint thought the King's credit lay at stake, and would not have the other go away from him unrewarded.]

Vit. Doroth. Februar. 6. p. 773.

Capgr. in vit. Kenteg. fol. 211

S. *Tiburtius* & *Valerian*. April 14.

Brev Rom. Antiq. Lec. 1, 2.

An Angel brought two Crowns from *Paradise* made up of Roses and Lilies, and gave one to *Valerian*, and the other to *Cecily* his new married wife; the Angel added, Because *Valerian* thou hast consented to the counsel of chastity (*having been perswaded by* Cecily *not to violate her Virginity* *) Christ has sent me to thee to give thee leave to

---

* *The account of this matter is given us in the said Breviary, in the Life of S.* Cecilia, *Nov.* 22. *Lesson* 2. "*On the marriage night when* "Cecily *and her Spouse* Valerian *were alone together in the Bedchamber,* "*she spake thus to him. O sweet and most loving youth, I have a secret* "*to confess to thee, if thou wilt swear not to reveal it. Which* Valerian "*swearing to, she said, I have an Angel a lover of mine, who with the* "*strictest jealousie keeps my body, he, if he in the least perceives that thou* "*touchest me with polluted love* (an excellent character of the marriage "bed) *he will presently stir up his fury against thee, and destroy the flow-* "*er of thy Youth: but if he know that thou lovest me with a sincere and* "*immaculate*

"*immaculate love, and preservest my Virginity whole and untouched,*
"*he will then love thee as well as my self, and will express his favour to*
"*thee.* Valerian replied; *If thou wouldst have me to believe thy words,*
"*show me the Angel, and if I find that he is indeed an Angel of God, I*
"*will do as thou sayst; but if thou lov'st any other man better than me,*
"*I will slay with my sword both him and thee.* So perswading him to
"become a Christian and be baptiz'd, she showed him the Angel.

ask any petition of him. *Valerian* hearing this adored, and begg'd that his brother *Tiburtius* might become a Christian. *Tiburtius* afterwards coming into the house, he smelt the odour of the Roses and Lilies, but saw nothing; who as he was wondering whence it came, *Valerian* told him of their Crowns which he could not see as yet, but if he would become a Christian, he should see both them and the Angel of God also: whereupon he consented to be baptized, and thereupon obtained the grant of all which he had asked of God, and saw the Angels every day.

S. John of Beverley. May 7.

"S. *John* after he was well instructed in
"Learning, was made Bishop of *York*: He
"was praying one day in the Porch of S. *Mi-*   *Brev. Sarum,*
"*chael,* and a certain Deacon peeping in,   *L.f. 2.*
"saw the H. Ghost sitting upon the Altar, excelling in
"whiteness a ray of the Sun, whose face was burnt by the
"heat of the H. Spirit. The Bishop adjured him, that
"whilest he lived he should discover this vision to no man.

[*Capgrave,* who mentions this story in
his Life, tells us that this Deacons name was   *Capgr. de S.*
Sigga, and that it was *his face* that was   *Joh. de Beverl.*
burnt, and the skin of his cheek shrivell'd up   *f. 190.*
by the heat of the H. Spirit; and that his face was healed
by the touch of the Saints hand. Mr. *Cressy*
has passed over this miracle, though he has   *Church Hist. l.*
given us a great many others concerning   *22. c. 10.*

him; particularly this out of *Malmsbury*, that the fierceſt Bulls, as ſoon as they are brought into his Church-yard (at *Beverley*) immediately loſe all their fury and fierceneſs, and become gentle as Lambs, though before they endangered with their horns all that came near them: He might have added another remarkable one out of *Capgrave*; that when the K. of *Scots* made war againſt K. *Ethelſtan*, *Ethelſtan* prayed to God that through the interceſſion of S. *John* of *Beverley*, he would ſhow ſome evident ſign whereby both the preſent and future Ages might know, that the *Scots* ought of right to be ſubject to the *Engliſh*: The King with his Sword ſmote upon a rock hard by *Dunbar*, and to this day it is hollowed an Ell deep by that ſtroke.]

Cap. r. ibid.

S. Aldelme. May 25.

Brev. Sarum, Leſ. 7.

"The Fame of S. *Adelme* coming to *Rome*, "Pope *Sergius* by his Letters called him thi- "ther, and there received him honourably, "whom God glorified with miracles; for "on a certain day as he celebrated Maſs in the *Lateran* "*Church*, he reached his *Caſula* (*one of the Prieſts Garments*) behind him, thinking to deliver it to one of the "Attendants; but none being preſent, a Sun-beam break- "ing through the window, held it up from falling a long "time in memory of the Saint. [Juſt ſuch another ridiculous ſtory as this, is told us in the Life of S. *Gudila*, who as ſhe was praying in the Church, the Prieſt chanced to eſpy the naked ſoles of her feet; and in compaſſion to her, took off his Gloves, and putting them under her feet, went his way; which ſhe after taking up, as if ſhe had been injured by this kindneſs, threw them away from her; but the Gloves inſtead of falling on the ground, miraculouſly hung in the Aire; and *Surius* ſays, that they

they hung so the space of an hour. *Bolland. Act. Sanctor. ad 8. Januar. p. 516.*]

"It happened also at *Rome*, that a   *Les. 8.*
"Child being born of an incestuous Mother
"and uncertain Father, the Pope's fame was
"injured: which *Aldelme* understanding, he commanded
"that the Child which was but twenty days old, should be
"brought forth; whom S. *Aldelme* charged to confess,
"whether *Pope Sergius* was to be accounted guilty of
"incest. The Child answered, That he was inno-
"cent.

S. Christina. July 24.

"She was bound to a Wheel, and rosted
"at a Fire; and as they poured on Oil the   *Brev. Rom:*
"flame broke forth, and slew a thousand of   *ant. Lec. 2, 3.*
"the Heathens. She was again put in
"prison, and by an Angel that visited her was healed and
"refreshed. Then she was cast into the Lake *Vulsinus*, a
"great stone-weight being fastned to her body, but the
"Angel freed her from drowning. Upon her prayers the
"Image of *Apollo*, which she was commanded to worship,
"was suddenly reduced to ashes; by which miracle three
"thousand were converted to the Faith of Christ. After
"this she was put into a burning Furnace, where she re-
"mained five days unhurt, &c.

** S. Helena's Legend of the Invention of the Cross. May 3.

"When the Emperor *Constantine* had ob-
"tained a victory over the barbarous   *Brev. Sarum,*
"people, by the sign of the Cross show'd   *Les. 1, 2, 3.*

" him from Heaven;" he after sent his Mother *Helena* to *Je-*
" *rusalem* to find out the wood of the H. Cross. Who
" when she admonished the Jews to chuse those that knew
" the Law; they said, For what cause does the Queen im-
' pose this task upon us? *Judas* one of them answered, I
" know the reason, she will make inquiry about the wood
" of the Cross, upon which our Fathers hanged *Jesus*:
" see therefore to it, that none confess the matter to her.

" *Zacheus* my Grandfather did foretel this to my Father,
" and my Father when he died told it me, saying; Ob-
" serve Son, when inquiry shall be made after the wood of
" the Cross, to which our Ancestors condemned the *Messi-*
" *as*, manifest it before thou beest tormented. Then I said
" to him; Father, if they knew him to be the Christ,
" wherefore did they lay hands on him? He answered me,
" Hearken my Son, I never was of counsel with them, but
" because he reproved them, they crucified him; and after
" he was buried, he rose again the third day: Upon which
" my brother *Stephen* believed, and was stoned. Others
" of them said, We never heard these things before.

" When they were called before the Queen, and she
" commanded them to be burnt, they out of fear delivered
" *Judas* to her; to whom the Queen said; Show me the
" wood of the Cross. *Judas* answered, I know not so
" much as the place where it is, for I was not then in being.
" Upon which she commanded to cast him into a *Pit* with-
" out water, and that there he should remain without food.
" When seven days were past, *Judas* cried out of the
" Pit, saying, Draw me out, I intreat you, and I will
" show you the Cross of Christ. When he was drawn out,
" as he was going to the place, he said, O Lord
" God, if it be thy will that the Son of *Mary* shall
" reign, cause that from the same place a fume of
" Aromatick odours may ascend: After he had prayed,
' the fume of Odours did ascend. Then *Judas* said; In
" truth, O Christ, thou art the Saviour of the world.

[The

[The present *Breviaries* have now left out all this stuff, and their Lessons are perfectly the same with those of the Breviary of *Pius* V. who first reformed it after the *Trent* Council; and gives us a story, that has more Authorities to back it, but I question whether much more truth in it than the former. His Lessons tell us of *Helena's* being admonished by a Dream to go on this errand to *Jerusalem*; that there she found in the place of the Cross a Marble Statue of *Venus*. That when the ground was digged, they found *three* Crosses, and also the Title that was once fastned to the Cross of our Lord, but now was fixed to none of them, but lay by it self apart from the crosses; so that they knew not to which of them it did belong. But that doubt was quite taken away by a Miracle, for a Woman almost at Deaths dore, through a grievous Disease; when two of them were applyed to her by *Macarius* Bishop of *Jerusalem*, and she received no benefit at all, when the third was applyed she was presently cured. * It is also further observable, how *Pius* in his Reformation of the Breviary, took care to prevent all suspicion, that by putting in those new Lessons, the old ones should be lookt upon as fabulous; for in his corrected Breviary, after the Lessons, I find the substance of the old Legend still retained in several Antiphona's. For *ad laudes*, and *per horas*, these short sayings are mentioned. *Helena the Mother of Constantine, went to Jerusalem.* Alleluiah. *When she commanded them all to be burnt with Fire, and they in a fright delivered Judas.* Alleluiah. *Death and Life are set before thee, if thou dost not show me the Cross of Christ.* Alleluiah. *When Judas ascended out of the Pit, he went to the place where the holy Cross lay.* Alleluiah. *Judas prayed, O God my God, show me the*

---

* Jacobus de Voragine *here says; that when the Cross was thus discovered, the Devil with a loud voice cryed in the Aire, O Judas, Why hast thou done this? so contrary to what my Judas did: for he by my perswasion betrayed him, and thou against my mind hast found his cross: by him I gained many Souls, by thee I seem to lose those I had gained: by him I reigned over the People, by thee I shall be expelled out of my Kingdome. But I'le be even with thee, &c.*

Wood

Wood of the holy Cross. Alleluiah. *Ad Benedictus.* Antiph. *S. Helena said to Judas; Fulfill my desire, and thou shalt live upon the Earth: that thou show me the place which is called Calvary, where the Lord's precious Wood is hid.* Alleluiah.

It would be too tedious to discover the follies and contradictions of their stories about the *Invention of the Cross*, as it is very easie to do; and as for the Authorities they bring in, of *Sulpitius Severus, Ruffinus, Paulinus, S. Ambrose, Socrates, Sozomen, Theodoret, &c.* which I know are urged in this matter; I shall only in short oppose against them, the silence of *Eusebius*, and the censure of Pope *Gelasius*. The first mentions *Helena's* Journey to the Holy Land, and building two Churches, the one at *Bethlehem*, the other at Mount *Olivet*, (as I noted heretofore) but says not one syllable about her finding of the Cross, or seeking after it; and yet none can well imagine that he should not be acquainted with it, or that he should have balked this, if there had been any such thing done, or talked of in his days. The other (*viz.* Pope *Gelasius*) he must needs know all that was said by the other Authors I named, who wrote of this matter after *Eusebius* his time; and yet thus he speaks in his Decree about *Apocryphal Books*.

Euseb de vit. Constant. lib. 3. cap. 42, 43.

Concil. Rom. 1. in Tom. 5. Concil. Labbe. ad an. 494. p. 1263.

"Also the Writings concerning the "*Invention of the Lord's Cross*, and "other Writings concerning the *In-* "*vention of the head of John the Bap-* "*tist*, these are certain novel relations, and some Catholicks "read them: but when these shall come into the hands of "Catholicks, let that sentence of the Bl. Apostle *Paul* go "before; *Prove all things, hold fast that which is good*: which plainly intimates his suspicion of the truth of them. For a conclusion of this; I cannot but give the Reader the pleasure of understanding, how the old Homilies represented this matter heretofore to the People, by giving him the beginning of a Sermon upon this Subject. Thus I find it.

"God

"Good frendes, such a daye ye shall
"have the invencyon of the holy crosse; *Festival. de invent.*
"ye shall not fast the even, but come *Sanctæ crucis. p. 100.*
"to God and to holy Chyrche as chrysten people sholde
"do, in worshypp of him that dyed on the crosse. Than
"ye shall understande, why it is called inventio sanctæ
"crucis, the fyndynge of the holy crosse; the whiche was
"founde in this wyse as I shall tell you. Whan Adam
"our fyrste fader was seke for age, and wolde fayne
"have ben out of this Worlde; Adam sente Seth his
"sone to the Aungell keper of Paradyse, prayenge the
"Aungell to sende him the oyle of mercy to anoynt his
"body therwith whan he were deed. Than went Seth to
"Paradyse, and sayd his message to the Aungell. Than
"answered the Aungell, and sayd that he might not have
"it tyll the yeres were fulfylled. But have this braunche
"of the tree that thy fader synned in, and set it on his
"grave, & whan it bereth fruyte than shall he have mercy
"and not erste. Than toke Seth this braunche and came
"home, & found his fader deed: than he set this braunche
"on his faders grave, as the Aungell badde him do; the
"whiche braunche growed there tyl Salomon was kynge,
"& he made to fell it downe, for it was fayre to the werke
"of his Temple, but it wold not accorde with the werke
"of his temple. Salomon made to caste it downe into
"the erth, and was hidde there to the tyme that the By-
"shop of the Temple let make a wayre in the same place
"thereas the tree laye, to wasshe in shepe that were of'red
"to the Temple. Than whan this wayre was made,
"they called it in their Language Probatica piscina.
"To the which water came an Aungell certayne tymes
"fro heven, and dyde worshyp to the tree that laye in the
"grounde of the wayre, & meved the water; and what
"Man or Woman that came to the water nexte after the
"Aungell was made hole, what sekenes that ever he had,
"by vertue of the tree; and so endured many wynters to
"the tyme that Cryste was taken and sholde be done up-
            "pon

"pon the crosse. Than this træ by the ordynaunce of
"God swamme upon the water, and whan the Jews had
"none other træ redy to make the crosse of, for grete haste
"that they had, they toke the same træ and made thereof
"a cros, and so dyed our Lord thereon, and than the træ
"bare that blessyd fruyte Crystes body, of the whiche
"welleth the oyle of mercy to Adam and Eve, and all other
"of theyr offspringe. But whan Cryste was dede, and
"was taken downe of the crosse, for envy that the Jewes
"had to him, they toke the crosse and two other crosses,
"that the thebes were hanged on either syde of Cryste, &
"buried them depe in the erth, for Crysten people sholde
"not wyte where they were done, for to do it worshyp;
"And there it lay a yere and more unto the tyme of E-
"leyna, &c. That which follows, is the story I set down
before out of the *Breviary* of *Sarum*, which I will not
repeat.

The Feast of S. Peter ad Vincula, or in Memory of S. Peters Chains. August. 1.

Brev. Sarum, Lef. 1.   "Dear Brethren, we are to mark, where-
"fore the Feast of S. *Peter* (as it is called)
"*ad vincula*, is celebrated upon the Kalends
"of *August*. This is said by some to be the cause of it.
"A certain *Roman* Captain called *Quirinus*, had a Daughter
"whose name was *Balbina*, who had a di-
Gutturonosam.   "sease in her Throat*, (*Surius* in the
"Life of S. *Alexander*, *May* 3. says she
"had a Wen in her Neck.) This Captain kept S. *Alexander*
"the Pope shut up in Prison. This Maiden (*his Daughter*)
"went often to the Prison, where Bl. Pope *Alex-*
Lef. 2.   "*ander* was kept bound in Chains; and she kissed
"the Chains wherewith the Saint was bound, which
"she did, hoping to recover health thereby. To whom
Bl. *Alex-*

Bl. *Alexander* said, "My Daughter, do not kiss
"these Chains; but go and seek the Chains where- *Les.* 3.
"with S. *Peter* was bound, and kiss them, and
"thereby thou shalt be cured. She immediately came to
"her Father, and told him what she had heard from the
"aforesaid Pope. Which when her Father heard,
"he sent Messengers, to enquire for the Prison, *Les.* 4.
"where the Apostle had been bound, and from
"thence to bring with them S. *Peter*'s Chain; which
"they did; and the said Maiden kissing them, was pre-
"sently perfectly recovered. After this Bl. *Alex-*
"*ander* coming out of Prison, appointed this so- *Les.* 5.
"lemnity to be kept on the Kalends of *August*, in
"honour of S. *Peter*, and in his Name built a Church, which
"is called *Petri ad Vincula.* In which solemnity also, they
"say that his Chains are devoutly kissed by the People,
"through the help of our Lord Jesus Christ, who with the
"Father, and the holy Spirit, liveth and reigneth God
"throughout all Ages. *Amen.*

[These are taken, we are told, out of the *Gests* of S. *A-lexander:* but excepting this last Period of the Peoples devoutly kissing that, which they call at *Rome* S. *Peter's Chain*, (which *Ribadeneira* assures us they do) I know not whether there be any jot of truth in all the rest. For *Surius*, in the place forenamed, and *Baronius* *   **Baron.ad ann.*132. tell us quite contrary, to what is in the 3*d.* Lesson, that it was not S. *Peter*'s, but *Pope Alexander*'s Chain, that cured the Daughter of *Quirinus*. *Baronius* will assure us, (contrary to the 4*th.* Lesson) that S. *Peter*'s Chains were not found in S. *Chrysostome*'s   *Baron.ad an.* 439. time (and therefore denies that Encomium which *Surius* gives (*Aug.*1.) of those Chains, to be *Chrysostome*'s) much less in Pope *Alexander* I. time: And also that not *this Pope*, but *Eudoxia* built the Church at *Rome* called *Petri ad Vincula.* Let us now see how the *Present Breviary* mends the matter, since it has altered all the foregoing story,

or

or rather quite discarded it. Thus then we are informed. "In the Reign of the Emperour *Theodosius jun.* when his Wife *Eudocia* came to *Jerusalem* to pay a vow, there she had many presents made her; but above all the rest she received the gift of an Iron Chain, adorned with Gold and Jewels, which they affirmed to be the very same, wherewith the Apostle *Peter* was bound by *Herod*. *Eudocia* piously venerating the Chain, sent it afterward to *Rome* to her Daughter *Eudoxia*, who brought it to the Pope: And he again show'd her another Chain, wherewith the same Apostle was bound, when *Nero* was Emperour. Whilst the Pope was comparing the *Roman Chain*, with that which was brought from *Jerusalem*; it happened that those 2 Chains were so joyned together, that they seemed not to be two, but one Chain made by the same Artificer. By which Miracle, so great an honour began to be paid to those sacred bonds, that thereupon *Eudoxia*'s Church (which she built) was dedicated in the *Exquiline* Mountain, by this name of S. *Peter ad Vincula*, and to its Memory a Festival was instituted on the first of *August*."

Brev. Rom. Lef. 4, 5.

I am apt to think that we were as well before with our *Salisbury Story*, as with this new one of *Eudocia*. For granting that she sent it for S. *Peter*'s Chain to her Daughter *Eudoxia*, and that she received it for such at *Jerusalem*. Yet when I remember what other fine knacks she sent from thence, it abates much the credit of these Chains with me.

Hist. Ecclef. Niceph. lib. 14. c. 2.

For *Nicephorus*, though he mentions nothing of this Chain of S. *Peter*, (which yet is strange, when the Lesson informs us it was the greatest present to her) yet he tells us of other great rarities she sent from *Jerusalem* to *Pulcheria*, to be kept for her; such as the Divine Image of the Bl. Virgin, which *Luke* the *Apostle* left drawn in a Table, and her *Divine Milk,* * and her *holy Distaff* (or Spindle) and the *Swathes* of our Sa-

* Τό τε θεῖον ἐκείνης γάλα, καὶ τὸ ἱερὸν ἄτρακτον, καὶ τὰ τῦ Σωτῆρος σπάργανα.

viour.

Devotions of the Roman Church.   351

viour. As for the miraculous joyning together of the two chains into one, if you examine *Baronius* about it, who gives us the whole story, instead of citing any Authorities, he refers us only to the *Ecclesiastical Tables*; which though they may be as Sacred to him as the *twelve Tables* were to the *Ancient Romans*: yet till I know more of their Authentickness, they will not have much more credit with me, than the Table (now mentioned) S. *Luke* left behind him with the Blessed Virgins picture upon it. *Annal. Eccl. ad an. 439. p. 682.*

I know indeed that S. *Gregory* in his Epistles talks wondrous things of these chains, and sent some filings of them to King *Childebert* for a mighty present; but his own wretched superstition about them, is as remarkable as any thing else: For thus he says in his Epistle to him. *Epist. Greg. l. lib. 5. Ep. 6.* "We have directed to your excellency the *Keys* of S. *Peter*, in which something is included taken off from his chains, which being hanged at your neck, may they defend you from all evils. So in another Epistle to *Dynamius*. We have sent the Benediction of the Bl. Apostle *Peter*, a little Cross, into which is put in some benefits from off his chains, which bound his neck for a time, but may they loose your neck for ever from sins. Thus in another. I have sent a most holy Key to you, from the body of S. *Peter* the Apostle, which is wont to shine with many miracles upon the sick; for it has within it something taken off from his chains. Those chains therefore which bound his neck, may they sanctifie your neck being hanged there. *Lib. 2. Ep. 33. Lib. 1. Ep. 29.* In all these instances you may observe something joyned (a Key or Cross) to the chains, so that the miraculous vertue seems to be divided between them. But in another Epistle to *Theotista*, I find him speak of a miraculous destruction of a person that would with his knife have cut in pieces the Golden Key of S. *Peter*, *Lib. 5. Ep. 23.*

S. *Peter*; for being possessed with an evil Spirit, he says he stabb'd that knife into his throat, and so fell down dead; and he thus concludes to him: "This Key I have taken care "to send to your excellency, by which Almighty God shew "that proud and perfidious man, that by it you, who fear "and love him, may obtain present and eternal salvation. But I think S. *Gregory* in another place, has told us a more wonderful story concerning S. *Paul*'s chain, than I find any where in him of S. *Peter*'s; for thus he writes to *Constantina*, (or *Constantia*) the Empress. "I will make haste to send to "you some part of the chains, which S. *Paul* the Apostle "carried on his neck and hands, and by which many mi- "racles are showed on the people, if so be I can prevail to "take any off by filing: For since so many frequently come "begging a benediction from the chains, that they may re- "ceive a little of the filings thereof, therefore a Priest is "ready with a File: and when *some persons* petition for it, "presently in a moment something is filed off for them "from the chains: but when *some others* petition, though "the File be drawn a great while through the chains, yet "cannot the least jot be got off from them.

Lib.3.Ep.30.

And now methinks one may have leave to ask, Why should not this miraculous chain of S. *Paul* have a Festival appointed in memory of it, as well as that of S. *Peter?* you may take *Baronius* his answer to it, till you can meet with a better. "Truly the bonds of S. *Peter* seem not with- "out reason to be worshipped, though the bonds of the "other Apostles are not; for it is but fit, that since he has "the chief power in the Church of Binding and Loosing "other mens bonds, that his bonds also should be had in ho- "nour of all the Faithful.

Baron. in Mar.
Rom. ad Aug. 1.

S. *Donatus.*

S. Donatus.   August 7.

"S. *Donatus* was brought up by S. *Pig-* *Brev. Sarum,*
"*menius* the Presbyter, and instructed in   *Lef. 1.*
"Divine and Humane Learning: With
"whom *Julian* being ordained a *Subdea-*
"*con* *, rejecting this degree, aspired to the Empire; who
"keeping *Pigmenius* in custody at *Rome*, slew with the
"sword the Father and Mother of S. *Donatus.*

* *This story of* Julian *is exploded by* Baronius. *Notis in Martyrol. Aug. 7.*

One *Eustasius* came in great perplexity of
mind to *Donatus*, because in his absence his   *Brev. Rom.*
wife *Euphrosina* had hid a great deal of pub-   *ant. Lec.3,4.*
lick money, and she was dead before he re-
turned, and the Officers came upon him for it. *Donatus*
standing upon the Grave of his wife, cried with a loud
voice: *Euphrosina, I conjure thee by Christ Jesus that was
crucified, that thou tell us what is become of this money.*
She answered immediately out of her Grave. *The money
thou seekest after, lies buried in the entrance of the house:*
and so the money being paid, *Eustasius* was freed from all
calumny.

[This is pretty fair, to make one speak au-
dibly in her Grave. But *Vincentius* (and   *Spec. Historial.*
after him, S. *Antonine* and *Ribadeneira*)   *l.14.cap.36.*
hath told us of a greater miracle still; of one
raised by him to life; and the occasion of it also a money
matter as the last was. For as a certain man was carrying
out to be buried, another came and stopt the Funeral, having a writing in his hand, saying, That the dead person
was indebted to him twenty shillings (as that paper
show'd) and till he had his money he should not be buried.

Whereupon there arose a great murmuring in the company: but some that saw *Donatus* at a distance, counselled the widow to run and speak to the man of God. She falling at his feet, told her case to him, and assured him that the money had been paid by her Husband, only the Creditor had not delivered him in his Note. S. *Donatus* coming to the Bier, and taking the dead man by the hand, said to him, Arise and plead thine own cause, for this thy Creditor forbids thee to be buried. Immediately he rose up, and convinced the Creditor of his knavery, in denying the payment of the money, and taking his Note out of his hand, tore it in pieces: then he begged of *Donatus* that he would suffer him to die again, who granted it, bidding him go to his rest.

S. *Clara.* *August* 12.

Brev. Rom.
ant. Lec. 8.

One day in the Monastery of S. *Clare*, when meal-time came, she was told, that there was but only one loaf of Bread (and that no great one, says *Ribaden.*) to serve them all. Notwithstanding this, she commanded half of that loaf to be given in Alms to the Friers, and the other half reserved for her Nuns, to be divided into fifty parts, according to their number: This command, though a strange one, yet was humbly obeyed by her servant; and by the Divine gift these small portions did so increase in the hands of every one that brake them, that every one in the Convent had enough. [Though this is not formally made a Lesson now in the Proper offices of the *Franciscans* for S. *Clare*, yet the substance of it comes in among one of the Responses just before the *Laudes*.

De pane pascit unico turbam   S. *Clare*'s poor Nuns fed
sororum pauperum: largely to their mind,
                                                       Claret

Claret figno mirifico virtus *When with one loaf she the*
figuorum veterum: *whole Convent din'd.*
Dum cibat ex tam modico *And former powers in this new*
magni conventus numerum.   *wonder shin'd.*]

"When the hour of her departure out of
"the world drew near, behold about mid-   *Offic. propr. Mi-*
"night a troop of Virgins enter in clothed *norum in fest.*
"in white garments, having golden Gar-   *S Claræ, Lec. 4.*
"lands upon their heads; among whom one was fairer
"than the rest, and her brightness such, that she turned
"night into day: for it was the Virgin of Virgins, the
"Mother of our Lord and Saviour. This Queen of Hea-
"ven drew near to the bed, where the spouse of her Son lay,
"and inclining her self lovingly over her, gave her a most
"sweet embrace; the other Virgins (*in her company*)
"brought forth a wonderous rich Mantle (*Pallium*)
"wherewith they covered the body of *Clare* the Virgin,
"and adorned the room as if it had been a Bride-chamber.

S. Elizabeth Widow, the King of Hungarie's Daughter. Novemb. 19.

"On a time a noble Matron giving her
"a visit, it happened that a comely Young *Brev. Rom.*
"man, too fashionably habited, came along *ant. Lec. 6.*
"with her; whom S. *Elizabeth* admonished
"to despise the pride of the world. The young man made
"answer: Madam, I beseech you pray for me. To whom
"she said, If thou wouldest have me pray the Lord for
"thee, go thou and do likewise. So as they prayed toge-
"ther at some distance, the young man not being able to
"endure the flame of her prayer, nor the fervour of so
"great devotion, he began to cry out aloud, That
"she should wholly desist from praying, otherwise he
                    A a 2   "should

"should be destroyed by the fire of such a prayer, and
"immediately breath out his last. S. *Elizabeth*'s mai-
"dens then running to the young man, found him so all on
"fire, that they could not hold their hands upon his
"clothes, but were fain hastily to withdraw their hands with
"which they laid hold on him, by reason of the too great
"heat with which he burnt. But when S. *Elizabeth* had
"done praying, the young man not suffering the heat
"within him to cool again, he went into the order of the
"*Franciscans*.

[We heard before (*pag*. 108.) how cold water was
made so scalding hot, only by the prayers of S. *Fechinus*,
that his Butler not being able to endure it, was fain to fly
the Bath. Here is another, whose clothes are too hot to
be touched, only by the fervour of devotion. The *lying
Spirit* comes in so powerfully at certain seasons into the
Monks inventions, that you may as well stop the current of
a tyde as the progress of their fictions: and though you
may guess in the other case how high the water will flow,
yet it's impossible here to know when a Fable is advanced to
its height. An Anchoret did once make a vow never to
see a woman in the Island where he lived;
A man (and his wife) comes over into this
Island to inhabit, and would not be perswaded either by him or S. *Brigid* to depart
thence. I see no offence in all this, since the Island was
big enough to hold them both, and it's to be hoped the
woman was so civil as not to come and disturb him in his
Cell against his mind: It was but either going farther from
them, or keeping more close at home, which would have
saved the Monks vow, if it was necessary to be kept. But
now their fancies work higher than thus, and bring in a
mighty wind that blew him and his over Sea unto the next
Port Town; and bring him upon his knees confessing his
fault, and devoting himself after this Miracle to God and
S. *Brigid*, promising never to enter the Isle more without
the *Anchoret*'s leave.

*Bolland. vit. S.
Brigid ad Feb.
1. p. 129.*

For

Devotions of the Roman **Church.**

For some soft and tender hearted Saint to have the gift of weeping is no such great wonder; but to be able to communicate it to another, by touching, as one would give the Itch, that's a pretty feat; and yet thus S. *Malachias* gave that gift to one, by laying his Cheek to his. It's very possible for the consideration of *Christ*'s passion to draw many tears from a devout Penitent: but to bring in an Angel gathering into a Vessel two Pound weight of tears, that fell upon that occasion from the Eyes of S. *Veronica*, is such a stretcher, that no Romance ever ventured upon the like.

Ribaden. in vit. ejus. 3 Nov. inter Extravag. p. 325.

Bolland. ad Januar. 13. pag. 892.

S. *Kentigern* had a singular way too of kindling Fire, which I could never have hit upon; who being in hast to light the Candles for *Vigils*, and some having in spight to him put out all the Fire in the Monastery; he snatcht the green bough of an Hasel, and in the name of the *Holy Trinity* he blessed it, and blow'd upon it, and immediately, by a Fire sent from Heaven, the Bough produced a great Flame; but when he had lighted the Candles, the Light appeared no longer in the Wood. (whence, by the way, we may probably conjecture that Tinder-boxes are of a later invention than S. *Kentigern*'s days.) But what will you say, if the *Monk*'s invention may be screwed up still one peg higher? I think I have met with a Saint that out-did all this, *viz.* S. *Berach*: who when he came to the King's Palace about a cause that was to be determined before him, his Adversary a Magician, being in better Cloaths, was admitted in; but S. *Berach* being despicable and poorly habited, the Gate was shut upon him, where seeing a great heap of Snow, as he stood without, he called upon the name of God, and blowing upon the Snow, immediately the Snowy Pile kindled with a vehement flame, as if it had been dry Wood, insomuch as the Houses near the Gate, began to be set on Fire. If you can believe that

Capgrav. vit. Kentig. f. 208.

Colganus 14 Febr. in vit. Berach, p. 342.

this angry Prayer of this Saint could make Snow burn, you shall then have my leave to believe, that the more charitable Prayer of S. *Elizabeth* might set the young Man's cloaths into such a heat, as not to be endured. But I must not forget to tell the Reader, that upon farther examination of the matter, we shall find, I doubt, that no Bodies cloaths were burnt, save only S. *Elizabeth*'s; and that too, not by the heat of her Devotion, but as any ones cloaths besides might be burnt, by a Coal of Fire falling upon them. For *Vincentius*, who lived in the same Age with her, (and S. *Antonine* after him) tells us indeed, that she was so intent one time at her Prayers and Contemplation of Heavenly things, that a Coal of Fire fell upon her own Garment, and burnt a great Hole in it, which she never perceived, till one of her Maids smelling Fire ran in, and extinguished it, and by her cry made the Saint come to her self, and see her misfortune; which says he, she as carelesly repaired, by setting an ill-favoured patch upon it with her own hands: but he says not one syllable of the young Man's burning, or of his cloaths being singed by her fervent Prayer; this was invented afterwards, and came by Oral Tradition, I suppose, to the later Writers, such as *Jac. de Voragine, Surius*, and *Ribadeneira*.

Vincent. Spec. Hist. lib. 30. cap. 136.

And now I should have here inserted the admirable Legends, which the *Breviaries* gives us, of S. *Mary Magdalen*, and S. *Martha*, of S. *Francis* and S. *Dominick*, and some others; but that, to the Readers great advantage, I have been happily prevented herein by the late *Second Discourse* of the *Learned Dr. Stillingfleet*, concerning the *Miracles of the Roman Church*; whose *known exactness*, as well as *vast Reading*, gives him an easie Triumph over the Calumny of those *Ignorant Zealots* of the Party, who have had the Confidence to charge him with false Citation of Authors; but will not give us the pleasure, I doubt, of seeing them so much as attempt such a *publick Discovery* of it, as he has made of their Cheats; but will have more wit in their rage, than to start this *New Controversie*, whether we have the same

same *Books* and *Eyes* with theirs, since it is to be hoped we may challenge at least *equal honesty*.

From all that has been said, methinks we need not beg much favour to conclude, that we in this Kingdome have been much beholden to God Almighty for the *Reformation*, concerning which some Men speak so contemptuously: for since that, no attempts have been made, with any shew of Authority, upon our Faith by lying Impostures; no doubtful Saints put into our Kalendar, and commanded to be venerated; no religious worship paid to any thing but to God alone; no *dreaming Revelations* in any credit with us, nor any pass for current ones, but such as are on all hands unquestionable; no Temptation laid before Men to *infidelity*, by seeing the *Publick Devotions* conducted by incredible stories, and invented Fables; these mischiefs we know the Reformation has delivered us from: and I dare say, it could not be possible to allure and intangle us in those former snares again, if Religion were Mens concern equally with other matters, which they charge themselves soberly to menage.

For what wise Man that has due care of his health, will forsake the safe practice of a skilful and honest *Physician*, to run after every *Mountebank* that sets up a Stage, will listen to the idle stories he tells all day of his miraculous cures; or if he needs none of his Physick, yet throw up his Glove (as I have seen foolish People do) to receive *Balls* that shall take out all spots and stains out of their Garments, or things in the fashion of *Hearts* to procure Love; or countenance the *pretended Doctor*, by gaping upon the tricks of his *Jack-pudding*. Our Devotion is sober and safe; has no tricks in it, but much Honesty. We are besotted, if we shall attend to the *Romish Legends*, or value their *Beads* and *Rosaries*, if we trade with them for their *Indulgences* and *counterfeit Reliques*, or be taken with the *Pageantry* that commonly in that Church takes place at the time of the *Nativity*, *Good Friday*, and the day of the *Resurrection*.

I'le add no more, save only that sharp, and no less true censure of their own *Cassander* (in his *Consultatio de meritis & intercess. sanctorum.* Oper. p. 971.) *Est & hic error haud infrequens, &c.* "This is also a common error, that "the vulgar sort of People, neglecting almost the *old* and "*known Saints*, more largely and ardently venerate those "that are *new* and *unknown*; concerning whose Sanctity "the evid nce is more obscure, and some of them are be- "come noted only by Revelations; so that one may deser- "vedly doubt concerning some of them, whether they were "ever yet in being; whose Veneration the Fictions of Hi- "stories, and the Impostures of Miracles have wonderfully "increased, which Fictions have defiled the Histories, even "of the acknowledged Saints, *&c.*

More Instances of their Devotions to Saints.

THat *Cassander* judged aright, in every tittle of the foregoing censure, he that doubts of it, may quickly be satisfied, by a Prayer I find among the Devotions of the famous Church of *Salisbury*; the Preface to it shows, that they laid more than ordinary stress upon it; and yet (which is strange) there is no mention made of any *Apostle* or *Evangelist*, no not so much as of the *Virgin Mary*; but *obscure* and *Romantick Saints* we have good store. The *Rubrick* to it says thus.

> *Whosoever shall devoutly and frequently say the following Prayer, whatsoever he shall duly and justly ask, he shall obtain.*

Antiph.

Devotions of the Roman Church.

Antiph. The Saints by Faith overcame Kingdomes, wrought Righteousness, obtained the Promises. *Horæ sec. us. Sar. fol. 99.*

Verf. Let the righteous rejoyce before God.

Anf. And delight themselves in gladness.

Oremus.   Let us Pray.

OMnipotens sempiterne Deus, qui sanctorum tuorum *Dionysii, Georgii, Christophori, Blasii, Egidii, Antonii, Eutropii, Pantaleonis, Livini, Eustachii, Leonardi, Nicasii,* atque *Cyrici,* sanctarum virginum & matronarum *Katharinæ, Margaretæ, Barbaræ, Marthæ, Honorinæ, Dorotheæ, Wenefredæ, Christinæ, Fredeswidæ* atque *Julitæ,* & decem millium martyrum, & undecim millium virginum patrocinia invocantibus, tuum in angustiis promisisti succursum; tribue nobis, quæsumus, eorum intercessione salutarem nostræ petitionis effectum, & auxilium in cunctis necessitatibus opportunum.

Per Christum, &c.

Pater noster. Ave Maria.

Almighty everlasting God, who hast promised thy succour in straits to those that invoke the Patronage of thy Saints Denis, George, Christopher, Blase, Egidius, Anthony, Eutropius, Pantaleon, Livinus, Eustachius, Leonard, Nicasius and Cyricus, and of the holy Virgins and Matrons, Catharine, Margaret, Barbara, Martha, Honorina, Dorothy, Wenefrid, Christina, Fredeswide and Julita, and of the ten thousand Martyrs, and the eleven thousand Virgins; Give us, we beseech thee, by their intercession, the saving effect of our Petition, and seasonable help in all our necessities.

Through Christ, &c.

Our Father. Hail Mary.

That which I shall now farther do, shall be to give instances of their Devotions, immediately addressed to Saints; which cannot admit that pretence, whereby they of the *Roman* Church endeavour to excuse themselves, that they pray only

only to *Saints departed* to pray for them, though that also is more than they have any encouragement to, from the Scriptures.

A Prayer to S. Erasine (or Erasmus.)

Horæ sec. us.
Sarum.

SAncte *Erasme* Martyr Christi pretiose, qui in Die Dominico Deo oblatus fuisti, & de eo magnam lætitiam suscepisti; Suscipe hanc orationem pro salute corporis mei & animæ meæ; ut Deus per tuam orationem dignetur mihi tribuere victum & vestitum; in hora mortis meæ veram confessionem, contritionem, & salutare sacramentum cum unctione olei sancti, in bonis operibus perseverantiam, cum recta fide & intentione bene moriendi, cum illis quæ Deo & tibi placita sunt ad laudem & honorem, mihi autem ad consolationem. Modo sancte *Erasme* tibi commendo corpus meum & animam meam, ut Deus per tuam orationem dignetur mihi tribuere gratiam: & commendo tibi omne consilium meum, omnes actus meos, & omnia mihi subjecta; ut eruas me ab omnibus inimicis meis visibi-

O Saint Erasmus the precious Martyr of Christ, who wast offered to God on the Lords day, which was an occasion of great joy to thee; Receive this prayer for the salvation of my body & my soul; that through thy prayer God may vouchsafe to give to me food and rayment; in the hour of my death true confession, contrition, and the saving Sacrament with the unction of holy oyle; perseverance in good works, with a right faith & intention to dye well, with those things that are pleasing to God and thee, to thy praise and honour, and to my consolation. Now, S. Erasme, I commend my body and soul to thee, that God by thy prayer may vouchsafe to give me grace: And I commend to thee all my counsel, all my actions, and all things subject unto me; that thou mayst deliver me from all mine enemies visibilibus

Devotions of the Roman Church.

libus & invisibilibus, qui mihi cupiunt adversari; ut non possint mihi nocere in aliquo, vel ullum damnum inferre animæ meæ vel corpori meo, turpiter vel dolosè, occultè seu manifestè: Quia tibi deus promisit, ut quicunque nomen tuum invocaverit, quicquid petierit firmiter impetrabit. Suscipe me Sancte *Erasme* in tuam sanctam fidem & gratiam, & conserva me ab omni malo per hos octo dies; & præsta mihi illos peragere cum recta fide & omni prosperitate & gratia, ad finem vitæ meæ; ut non proficiat in me ulla inimicorum voluntas, tibi ad laudem & honorem, mihi autem ad consolationem & gratiam. Tibi Sancte *Erasme* commendo corpus meum & animam meam, & omnes mihi confessione & oratione vel consanguinitate conjunctos, & omnes actus meos, ut vivam cum omni prosperitate, pace & gaudio nunc & in perpetuum.

Amen.

Pater noster.   Ave Maria.

sible & invisible, which seek to oppose me; that they may not be able to hurt me in any thing, nor bring any damage to my soul or body, basely or craftily, secretly or openly: For God has promised thee, that whosoever shal call upon thy name, whatsoever he shall ask, he shall certainly obtain. Receive me S. Erasme into thy holy faith and grace, & preserve me from all evil all these eight days; and grant that I may pass them with a right faith, and all prosperity and grace, unto the end of my life; that no desire of my enemies may be accomplisht against me, to thy praise and honour, and to my comfort and grace. To thee, S. Erasme, I commend my body & my soul, and all those I am bound to, by confession & prayer, or consanguinity, and all my actions, that I may live in all prosperity, peace and joy, now and for ever.

Amen.

Our Father.   Hail Mary.

Devotions to Saint Claudius.

Horæ sec. u s. Rom.
6 die Junii.

O Desolatorum consolator, captivorum liberator, resurrectio mortuorum, lumen cæcorum, auditus surdorum, mutorum eloquium, tutor naufragantium, impotentium & languidorum sanator, medicinæ refugium, via errantium, salus omnium in te sperantium; Sancte *Claudi*, benigne confessor Christi, ora Deum pro nobis, qui te tot & tantis illustravit miraculis; nam pro tua sanctissima vita, quam tam piè & devotè gessisti in hac valle miseriæ, vana hujus seculi spernendo & cœlestia sectando, pro tuis meritis ad superna polorum gaudia collocavit, & innumeris decoravit miraculis.

Vers. Ora pro nobis beate *Claudi*.

Resp. Implora apud Deum pro nobis auxilium.

O Thou comforter of the desolate, deliverer of captives, resurrection of the dead, light of the blind, hearing of the deaf, speech of the dumb, tutor of the shipwrackt, healer of the impotent and languishing, the refuge of medicine, the way of the erring, and the salvation of all that hope in thee; O St. Claude the bountiful Confessor of Christ, pray to God for us, who made thee famous by so many and great miracles: for by reason of thy most holy life, which thou didst lead so piously and devoutly in this vale of misery, despising the vanities of this world, and following after celestial things, for thy merits he hath placed thee in the joys of Heaven above, and graced thee with innumerable miracles.

Vers. Pray for us Blessed Claude.

Ans. Implore Gods help for us.

Oremus.

Devotions of the Roman Church. 365

Oremus.

DEus, qui per donum sancti spiritus, in beatum *Claudium*, gloriosum confessorem tuum atque Pontificem, tantam gratiam & beatitudinem effundere dignatus es, quòd per illam ferè totus orbis Christianorum, pro suis necessitatibus ad ipsum affluit; & quicunque eum piè & devotè quæsierit, desolatus non remanebit: da nobis, quæsumus Domine, justa desideria postulare; ut quæ justè postulaverimus, suis meritis & intercessionibus, apud te jugiter valeamus obtinere. Per Dominum, &c.

Let us Pray.

O God, who by the gift of the H. Ghost, didst vouchsafe to powre forth so great grace and blessing into Blessed Claude thy glorious Confessor and Bishop, that thereupon almost all the Christian world runs to him for the supply of their necessities; and whosoever seeks him piously and devoutly, shall not remain desolate: Grant to us, O Lord, we beseech thee, that we may request just desires; and those things which we justly ask, by his merits and intersessions, we may continually be able to obtain from thee. Through our Lord, &c.

A Prayer to the Holy Innocents.

Hor. sec. us.
Sarum.

OMnes Sancti *Innocentes*, orate pro nobis. O beati pueri, flores munditiei, gemmæ cœlestes, consortes agni immaculati qui tollit peccata mundi. Respicite famulum (vel famulam)

O All ye Holy Innocents, pray for us. O blessed boys, flowers of purity, celestial gems, the consorts of the immaculate Lamb, that taketh away the sins of the world; look upon the servant of your sanctity; and express the
sancti-

sanctitatis vestræ; & ostendite super me vestra tenerrima præcordia pietatis; ut vobis intercedentibus, cum pura conscientia Domino præsentatus (vel præsentata) merear vobiscum laudare Dominum Jesum Christum in secula seculorum. *Amen.*

wards me your most tender bowels of pity; that upon your intercession, being presented to the Lord with a pure conscience, I may merit to praise the Lord Jesus Christ with you for evermore. Amen.

A Prayer to the Apostles and Disciples.

Ibid.

OMnes sancti Apostoli & electi Discipuli Domini, orate pro nobis. O venerandi Patres Ecclesiæ, fidei Christianæ doctores & mundi luminaria, quorum prædicationibus miraculis & exemplis, Christi nomen gloriosum magnificatum est in gentibus. Per ipsum vos deprecor quem tanto fervore dilexistis & secuti estis, me gratiosè solventes à vinculis peccatorum, perducatis ad patriam civium supernorum. Præstante eo qui vivit & regnat.

Pater Noster. Ave M.

O All ye holy Apostles and elect Disciples of the Lord, pray for us. O ye venerable Fathers of the Church, the Teachers of Christian faith, and the Lights of the world, by whose preaching, miracles and example, the glorious name of Christ is magnified among the Gentiles. I pray you by him, whom with so much zeal ye loved and followed, that mercifully loosing the bands of my sins, you would bring me to the Country of the Citizens above. He performing it, who liveth and reigneth.

Our Father. Hail Mary.

A Prayer to the Martyrs.

Ibid.

Omnes Sancti Martyres, orate pro nobis. O fortissimi milites Christi, Principes & Duces exercitûs Domini; quorum vita mirabilis erat & mors speciosa; per illam charitatem insuperabilem qua Deo conjuncti estis, vos deprecor, ne me patiamini perire in peccatis meis; sed in omni necessitate atque periculo sitis mihi advocati & defensores, ut passionum vestrarum intervenientibus meritis, particeps esse valeam æternæ felicitatis. Quod ipse præstare dignetur, qui vester amor est, vita, salus & præmium, Jesus Christus Dominus noster. *Amen.*

O All ye Holy Martyrs, pray for us. O ye most valiant souldiers of Christ, the Princes and Captains of the Lords Hosts, whose life was wonderful and death honourable; by that insuperable love, whereby ye are united to God, I intreat you, that ye would not suffer me to perish in my sins; but in every necessity and danger, you would be my Advocates and Defenders; that by the intervening merits of your sufferings, I may partake of eternal felicity. Which he vouchsafe to effect, who is your love, life, salvation and reward, Jesus Christ our Lord. Amen.

To the Confessors.

Ibid.

Omnes sancti Confessores, orate pro nobis. O Patres, præcipui flores Ecclesiæ, specula virtutum, imitatores Christi, & tabernacula Spiritus Sancti; in

O All ye holy Confessors, pray for us. O Fathers, the chiefest flowers of the Church, the mirrors of vertues, imitators of Christ, and Tabernacles of the H. Ghost; in whose

quorum

quorum mentibus abundavit charitas, in verbis veritas, in actibus pietas cum omni morum honestate floruit: Ecce ad vos confugio miserrimus ego peccator & indignus, vestram clementiam humiliter interpellans; ut mihi vestris precibus impetrare dignemini gratiam verè pœnitendi, in bono perseverandi, & ad vestrum consortium gloriosum finaliter perveniendi. Præstante Domino nostro Jesu Christo: Qui vivit & regnat in secula seculorum. Amen.

minds charity did abound, in whose words truth, in whose actions piety with all honesty of deportment did flourish: Behold I miserable sinner and unworthy fly to you; humbly imploring your clemency, that by your prayers you would vouchsafe to obtain for me the grace of true repentance, of perseverance in goodness, and finally to come to your glorious fellowship. Our Lord Jesus Christ performing it: Who liveth and reigneth throughout all ages. Amen.

To the Holy Virgins.

Ibid.

OMnes sanctæ Virgines & Matronæ, orate pro nobis. O sacratissimæ mulieres Christi sponsæ matres & filiæ; propter amorem & vobis innatum gratissimam pietatem miseremini mei peccatoris; & lapsum carnis fragilis benigna compassione recolentes, impetrate mihi à Domino Jesu, dilecto vestro & Salvatore meo, delictorum veniam, vitæ munditiam, & gloriam in futuro. Amen.

O All ye holy Virgins and Matrons, pray for us. O all ye most holy women, mothers and daughters, the spouses of Christ; for your love sake, and your most acceptable innate pity, be merciful to me a sinner; and calling to mind with gracious compassion the rase lips of frail flesh, obtain for me of the Lord Jesus, your Beloved and my Saviour, the pardon of my sins, purity of life, and glory hereafter. Amen.

A Prayer to all Saints.

O All ye blessed Saints of God, and blessed Spirits Angelical, whom God with his mellifluous countenance and blessed presence maketh joyful and everlastingly glad, pray ye for me: I salute and honour you; I give lauds and thanks unto our Lord, which hath chosen you, and hath prevented you in his Benedictions: O obtain for me forgiveness, obtain for me grace, and to be made one with God. *Amen.*

Primer in English in Queen Marie's time, Lond. 1555.

A Prayer to all the He and She Saints.

Horæ sec.us. Sarum.

O Vos omnes Sancti & Electi Dei, quibus Deus præparavit regnum æternum à Principio; vos precor per charitatem qua dilexit vos Deus, succurrite mihi peccatori miserrimo, antequam me mors rapiat; conciliate me antequam infernus me devoret. O beata *Maria,* mater Dei, Virgo Christi, peccatorum interventrix, exaudi me, salva me, custodi me; Obtine mihi, pia Domina, fidem rectam, spem certam, perfectam charitatem, veram humilitatem, castitatem, sobri-

O All ye Saints and Elect of God, for whom God from the beginning hath prepared an Eternal Kingdom; I intreat you by that charity wherewith God has loved you, that you would succour me a miserable sinner, before death snatches me away; reconcile me (to God) before the Grave devours me. O blessed Mary, the mother of God, the Virgin of Christ, who intercedest for sinners, hear me, save me, keep me; Obtain for me, merciful Lady, a right faith, a certain hope, perfect charity, true humility, etatem,

etatem, & post cursum vitæ meæ societatem perpetuæ beatitudinis. Tu etiam sancte *Michael*, cum omnibus millibus Angelorum, ora pro me, ut eripiar de potestate adversariorum meorum; Adjuva me, obtine mihi amorem Dei, cordis decorem, fidei vigorem, & cœlestis gloriæ jocunditatem. Vos quoque Sancti Patriarchæ & Prophetæ, poscite mihi à Deo indulgentiam, pœnitentiam, continentiam, sanctamque perseverantiam, atque vitam æternam. O beati Apostoli Dei, solvite me à peccatis, defendite me à pœnis inferni & de potestate tenebrarum, confortate me & ad regnum æternum me perducite. Precor etiam vos Sancti Martyres Dei, ut detur mihi à Deo charitas sancta, pax sincera, mens pura, vita casta, & peccatorum remissio. O gloriosi Confessores Dei orate pro me, ut per vos mihi tribuatur à Deo cœlestis concupiscentia, & morum reverentia, & criminum ablutio. Similiter & vos rogo omnes sanctæ Virgines Dei, adjuvate me, ut habeam bonam voluntatem cordis, corporis sanitatem,

chastity, sobriety, and after my life is ended the society of endless blessedness. Thou also, S. Michael, with all thy thousands of Angels, pray for me, that I may be delivered from the power of my adversaries: Help me, obtain for me the love of God, comeliness of heart, a vigorous faith, and the jocundness of celestial glory. Also ye Holy Patriarchs and Prophets, beg for me of God pardon, repentance, continence, and holy perseverance, and eternal life. O ye blessed Apostles of God, loose me from my sins, defend me from the pains of Hell and from the power of darkness, comfort me and bring me to the everlasting Kingdom. I pray to you Holy Martyrs of God, that God would give me holy love, sincere peace, a pure mind, a chaste life, and remission of my sins. O ye glorious Confessors of God, pray for me, that by you God may grant me heavenly concupiscence, reverence of behaviour, and the washing away of my crimes. In like manner

I

humilitatem, castitatem, & post cursum vitæ meæ societatem perpetuæ beatitudinis. O vos omnes Sancti & Sanctæ Dei, vos deprecor quoque & supplico, subvenite mihi, miseremini mei misericorditer, & orate pro me instanter, ut per vestram intercessionem tribuatur mihi à Deo conscientia pura, compunctio vera, & vitæ consummatio laudabilis; quatenus per merita vestra pervenire valeam ad æternæ beatitudinis patriam. Præstante Domino nostro Jesu Christo. Qui cum Patre, &c.

I intreat all you Gods holy Virgins to assist me, that I may have a good will of heart, soundness of body, humility, chastity, and after my life is ended the society of endless blessedness. And all ye He and She Saints of God, I pray also and beseech you, to be aiding to me, that you would mercifully pity me, and pray earnestly for me, that by your intercession, God would give me a pure conscience, true compunction, and that I may commendably finish my life; so that by your merits I may be able to arrive at the Country of Eternal blessedness. Our Lord Jesus Christ performing it. Who with the Father, &c.

Now for a Conclusion of these Devotions, I'le only add (besides a Litany) one instance more; but it is such a one, as can hardly be parallell'd: It is the commemoration of *Etheldreda* (an *English* Saint) which is given us by the *Salisbury Breviary*; where we have Three Lessons, consisting wholly of prayers to her, in a Latin style so unusually-fine, and so full of Courtship, as would tempt one to think, that the Monk (or whosoever he was) who composed them, had some fair Mistress, that strongly possessed his fancy, all the while before his thoughts: *They are these.*

Brev. Sarum, fol. 100.

Lect. 1. IN præsentis vitæ & fluctuantis seculi naufragio constituti; ad tui portum præsidii confugimus virgo piissima atque celeberrima *Etheldreda*; ut tuæ circa nos pietatis sentiamus viscera, qui de tua jugiter gratulamur presæntia. Respice igitur pia Mater & Domina pio intuitu ad exiguum (sed devotum) nostri famulatus obsequium : & quos premit humanæ fragilitatis immensitas, tuæ virginitatis (quæ sponso virginum placuit) relevet ac sustentet veneranda sublimitas. Credimus enim atque confidimus, te ab eodem sponso tuo qui speciem tuam concupivit, quicquid petieris impetrare ; quam in thalamo regis æterni collocatam, cum virginum choris de palma virginitatis certum est exultare.

We who are placed among the dangers of this present life and uncertain world, that threaten to shipwrack us; do fly to thy safe port, most pious and famous Virgin Etheldrede, that we may feel the bowels of thy compassions towards us, who do congratulate always thy presence among us. Look therefore thou compassionate mother and Lady with a pitiful eye upon the poor (but devout) obsequiousness of our service : and those who are oppressed with the immensity of humane frailty, let the venerable sublimity of thy virginity (which has been acceptable to the spouse of Virgins) relieve and sustain them. For we believe and are confident, that from that spouse of thine who has desired thy beauty, thou canst obtain whatsoever thou shalt ask; since we are sure thou art placed in the bride-chamber of the eternal King, and dost triumph with the Quire of Virgins in the prize of virginity.

Lec. 2.

*Lec.*2. Succurre Domina, succurre Mater misericordissima Etheldreda nostræ miseriæ: suffragiis precum tuarum, scelerum nostrorum maculas absterge; tibique famulantes tales effice, ut tuæ integritati puræ valeant deservire. Gregi tuo tuæ sollicitudinis atque protectionis semper assit custodia; ut sicut tui sacratissimi corporis incorruptione jugiter gaudemus atque præsentia, sic & de tua subventione gaudeamus assidua. Protege igitur mater filios, domina servos; ut qui se tuæ memoriæ ac venerationi profitentur obnoxios, tuæ largitatis & pietatis beneficia se gratulentur adeptos.

Succour, O Lady, succour, O Etheldrede, our misery thou mother of mercy; by the intercession of thy prayers, wipe off the stains of our sins; and make those that wait upon thee such, that they may be able to serve thy pure incorruption. Let the safeguard of thy care and protection always defend thy flock; that as we continually rejoyce in the incorruption and presence of thy most sacred body, so we may also rejoyce in thy daily aid. Protect therefore, O mother, thy children, O Lady, thy servants; that they who profess themselves devoted to thy memory and veneration, may rejoyce in having obtained the benefits of thy bounty and compassion.

*Lec.*3. Respice benignissima virgo *Etheldreda* ad nostras angustias, quas nostris meritis sustinemus; & per tuæ sanctitatis merita & intercessiones, & iram judicis placa quem offendimus, & veniam impetra quam non meruimus. Tuis precibus ad misericordiam

Look O most gracious Virgin Etheldrede upon our troubles, which we deservedly sustain; and by the merits and intercession of thy holiness, both appease the anger of the Judge whom we have offended, and obtain that pardon which we have not deserved. By thy inclina

inclina justitiam districti (sed justi) examinis; quia agni qui sponsus est virginum vestigia quocunque ierit virgo sequeris. Repræsenta quæsumus supernæ clementiæ gemitus nostros atq; suspiria, ut divinæ miserationis per te suscipiamus incrementa, quo tecum in æternum gaudere mereamur; te petente, illo largiente, qui te integritatis coronavit gloria, per cuncta seculorum secula. *Amen.*

prayers incline to mercy, the justice of his severe (but just) examination; because thou that art a Virgin shalt follow the steps of the Lamb, who is the spouse of Virgins, whithersoever he goeth. Represent, we pray thee, to the Divine clemency our sighs and groans, that by thee we may receive more of the Divine pity, whereby we may merit evermore to rejoyce with thee; thou asking and he granting, who has crowned thee with the glory of incorruption, throughout all ages.

      Amen.

A

A LITANY.

EVery one that is acquainted with the *Common Litanies* of the *Roman* Church, knows that they are ſtuft with the names of Saints, whom they deſire to pray for them; and are larger or ſhorter, according as more or fewer Saints are inſerted: and there being little or no difference beſides between the Older Litanies and the Later, I ſhall give the Reader one that was in uſe here in *England*, as I find it in a *Pſalter* Printed at *London* 1503. Whereby he will underſtand what a pretty number of Saints (and ſome of them very odd and ſtrange ones) they invoked in thoſe days, and applied themſelves to in their Prayers. After the uſual invocation therefore of God and the Holy Trinity, it goes on thus.

Saint *Mary*,
Holy *Mother of God*,
Holy *Virgin of Virgins*,
S. *Michael*,
S. *Gabriel*,
S. *Raphael*,
All holy *Angels and Arch-angels*,
All holy *Orders of Bleſſed ſpirits*,
S. *John Baptiſt*,
All holy *Patriarchs and Prophets*, } Pray for us.

S. *Peter*,
S. *Paul*,
S. *Andrew*,
S. *John*,
S. *James*,
S. *Thomas*,
S. *Philip*,
S. *James*,
S. *Matthew*,
S. *Bartholomew*,
S. *Simon*,
S. *Thaddeus*,
S. *Matthias*, } Pray for us.

S. *Bar-*

S. *Barnabas*,	S. *Eusebius*,
S. *Mark*,	S. *Swithine*,
S. *Luke*,	S. *Birinus*,
All ye holy Apostles and Evangelists,	All ye holy Confessors,
All ye holy Disciples of the Lord and Innocents,	All ye holy Monks and Hermits,
	S. *Mary Magdalene*,
S. *Stephen*,	S. *Mary the Egyptian*
S. *Linus*,	S. *Margaret*,
S. *Cletus*,	S. *Scholastica*,
S. *Clemens*,	S. *Petronilla*,
S. *Fabian*,	S. *Genouefe*,
S. *Sebastian*,	S. *Praxedes*,
S. *Cosma*,	S. *Sotheris*,
S. *Damian*,	S. *Prisca*,
S. *Prime*,	S. *Tecla*,
S. *Felician*,	S. *Afra*,
S. *Dionysius*, with thy companions,	S. *Editha*,
	All ye holy Virgins,
S. *Victor*, with thy companions,	All ye Saints,
	S. *Sixtus*,
All ye holy Martyrs	S. *Cornelius*,
S. *Silvester*,	S. *Cyprian*,
S. *Leo*,	S. *Marcellus*,
S. *Jerome*,	S. *Vitus*,
S. *Augustine*,	S. *Modestus*,
S. *Isidore*,	S. *Adrian*,
S. *Julianus*,	S. *Nichasius*, with thy companions,
S. *Gildarde*,	
S. *Medarde*,	S. *Eustachius*, with thy companions,
S. *Albinus*,	

Pray for us.   *Pray for us.*

All

All ye holy Martyrs,
S. Gregory,
S. Ambrose,
S. Remigius,
S. Donatian,
S. Eligius,
S. Audomarus,
S. Sulpitius,
S. Paternus,
S. Patrick,
S. Dunstane,
S. Grimbaldus,
All ye holy Confessors.
All ye holy Monks and Hermits,
S. Felicitas,
S. Perpetua,
S. Columba,
S. Christina,
S. Eulalia,
S. Euphemia,
S. Eugenia,
S. Ghertrudis,
S. Ragenfledis,
S. Batildis,
S. Anastasia,
S. Etheldrede,
All the holy Virgins,
All the Saints,
S. Laurence,
S. Tiburcus,

} Pray for us.

S. Valerian,
S. Prothus,
S. Jacinthus,
S. Abdon,
S. Sennes,
S. Timothy,
S. Apollinaris,
S. Saturninus,
S. Maurice, with thy companions,
S. Gereon, with thy companions,
All ye holy Martyrs
S. Hilary,
S. Martine,
S. Brice,
S. Amandus,
S. Vedastus,
S. Germanus,
S. Ausbertus,
S. Arnulph,
S. Wulfrane,
S. Silvinus,
S. Taurinus,
S. Cuthbert,
All ye holy Confessors,
All ye holy Monks and Hermits,
S. Agatha,
S. Susanna,
S. Brigid.

} Pray for us.

S. Bar-

S. Barbara,
S. Marina,
S. Martina,
S. Felicula,
S. Julita,
S. Sapientia,
S. Fides,
S. Spes,
S. Charitas,
All ye holy Virgins,
All ye Saints,
S. Vincent,
S. Gervase,
S. Prothasus,
S. Timotheus,
S. Simphorianus,
S. Felicissimus,
S. Agapitus,
S. Alban,
S. Gorgonius,
S. Achilles,
S. Hippolitus, with his companions,
S. Lucianus, with his companions,
All ye holy Martyrs
S. Nicholas,
S. Audoen,
S. Romanus,
S. Laudus,
S. Machutus,
S. Samson,
} Pray for us.

S. Placidus,
S. Columbanus,
S. Anthony,
S. Macarius,
S. Richarius,
S. Adelwolde,
All ye holy Confessors,
All ye Saints, Monks and Hermits,
S. Cecily,
S. Fidis,
S. Austreberta,
S. Emerentiana,
S. Potentiana,
S. Oportuna,
S. Sophia,
S. Juliana,
S. Beatrix,
S. Crescentia,
S. Walburg,
S. Ermenildis,
All ye holy Virgins,
All ye Saints,
S. Quintin,
S. Christopher,
S. Lambert,
S. George,
S. Marcellinus,
S. Theodore,
S. Valentine,
} Pray for us.

S. Gri-

Devotions of the Roman Church. 379

S. Grisogonus,
S. Felix,
S. Audactus,
S. Boniface, with thy companions,
S. Kylianus,
All ye holy Martyrs
S. Benedict,
S. Maurus,
S. Maiolus,
S. Egidius,
S. Wandregesile,
S. Wolmarus,
S. Filibert,
S. Bertinus,
S. Winnoc,
S. Judocus,
S. Petrocus,
S. Botulph,
All ye holy Confessors,
All ye holy Monks and Hermits,
S. Lucy,
S. Catharine,
S. Sabina,
S. Justina,
S. Euphrasia,
S. Fausta,
S. Monegundis,
S. Aldegundis,
S. Benigna,
} Pray for us.

S. Wilgefortis, (so I put it instead of Walburg, because I find her placed before Radegundis, in another Litany)
S. Radegundis,
All ye holy Virgins,
All ye Saints,
S. Calixtus,
S. Urban,
S. Magnus,
S. Menna,
S. Rufus,
S. Valerius,
S. Processus,
S. Martinianus,
S. Marcus,
S. Gordianus, with his companions,
S. Pancratius, with his companions,
All ye holy Martyrs
S. Aldelme,
S. Anianus,
S. Euurcius,
S. Basil,
S. Maurilius,
S. Germanus,
S. Mamertus,
S. Authbert,
} Pray for us.

S. Willi-

S. *Willibrord*,		S. *Helena*,
S. *Leonard*,		S. *Euprepia*,
S. *Athanasius*,		S. *Candida*,
S. *Oswalde*,	Pray for us.	S. *Basilissa*,
All ye holy Confessors,		S. *Cordula*,
		S. *Ursula*,
All ye holy Monks and Hermits,		S. *Victoria*,
		S. *Corona*,
S. *Agnes*,		S. *Sexburgis*,
S. *Benedicta*,		All ye holy Virgins,
S. *Martha*,		All ye Saints,

(right brace: Pray for us.)

 The rest of the Litany that follows these names of Saints, I forbear to set down, because it consists of good and wholsome petitions, which it is not my business to reprove; but rather shall commend one among the rest in particular,

Ut obsequium servitutis nostra rationabile facias.

where they pray, *That God would make their service to him rational.* This request, considering how absurd their Devotions are, was a very needful one, and was for some while continued in their Litanies; (for I find it in one of them, among the Hours of *Sarum*, printed 1530. and also in a Litany in Queen *Marie*'s Primer, printed 1555.) but they perceiving that it was never likely to be heard, because they were never likely to amend their follies to any purpose, they have since very wisely omitted it, and it is left out of all the new Litanies.

 It would be also too tedious to examine the foregoing Catalogue of Saints names. *Fides*, *Spes*, and *Charitas*, which were mentioned together, you must believe the *Roman Martyrologie* that they were *Saints*, and not the *Graces of Faith*, *Hope*, and *Charity*. But I cannot so easily grant this of one, which just goes before them, viz. S. *Sapientia*; for I cannot meet with her in the *Roman Martyrologie*, nor in that of *Ado*, or of *Usuardus*: only Mr. *Cressy*, I find, has

Devotions of the Roman Church. 381

has put her among the *Ursulan Virgins*; but their names (as we heard before) are most of them known only by those Revelations which he discards. It's well therefore if in this case there has not been such a mistake committed, as the sorry Priest, according to the story, was guilty of, who had *Sol in Cancro*, which he found in Red Letters in his Almanack, for an *Holiday*: and there too you may find *O Sapientia* set down, nine days before *Christmas*. But that refers to no *Saint*, but to certain *Antiphona's*, which are required to be used on those days; the first of which begins with, *O Sapientia quæ ex ore Altissimi prodiisti*, &c.

But if you ask me farther, what is the meaning of so vast a number of Saints put into this Litany? I can give no better answer than this, That they seem to have had the same fancy, which their old Homily admirably expresses thus.

"On Alhalowen day, our prayers shall be sooner herde than any other day: for this day all the Saints in Heven come togyder to pray to God for us; and therefore we may well knowe, that all coming togyder, shall be sonner herde, than yf they came but by one or two by themselfe."

Festival. in fest. Omn. Sanct. f. 148.

280

Hymns

Hymnes to the Saints.

HEre I shall wholly wave those Hymns, which are the most exceptionable, that are composed to the Bl. Virgin, till we come to treat of their Devotions to her; and only set down some of the many rare strains of Devotion to the other Saints, which sufficiently show, what thoughts they have of their power now, to confer both temporal and spiritual blessings on them, and what expectations they have from them, upon their addresses to them.

To S. Venantius, May 18.

Officia nova Sanct. 1672.

Bellator ö fortissime,
Qui perfidis tortoribus
E caute præbes poculum,
Nos rore irriga gratiæ.

Brave Warriour, of courage true,
VVho to thy Torturers a-thirst
Mad'st VVater from a Rock to burst,
VVater our Souls with grace's dew.

Ibid. ad Laudes.

Nunc Angelorum particeps
Adesto votis supplicum:
Procul repelle crimina
Tuumque lumen ingere.

Now thou dost Angels bliss enjoy,
Readily answer, when we pray;
Expell the Crimes that Us annoy,
Thy light into our minds conveigh.

To S. Teresa, Oct. 15.

Brev. Rom.
O charitatis victima!
Tu corda nostra concrema,
Tibique gentes creditas
Averni ab igne libera.

O thou that art Love's vi-
    ctime rare!
Pure flames into our hearts
    inspire;
Deliver from infernal fire
The Nations trusted to thy
    care.

S. Petrus de Alacantara, Octob. 19.

Offic. nov.
Sanctor.
Nunc preces audi, gemi-
    tusque nostros,
Integros nobis sine labe mo-
    res,
Et tuos nostris animis salu-
    bres
  Ingere sensus.

Now hear us when we sigh
    and pray,
Preserve our Lives in inno-
    cence,
And thine own good and ver-
    tuous sence
Into our hearts conveigh.

Ibid.
Decus Minorum suscipe
Laudes precesque supplicum;
Tuos ab alto mitiùs
Pater beate, respice.

Franciscan's Ornament, re-
    ceive
The Pray'rs we make, and
    Lauds we give;
Blest Father, with a gracious
    eye
Behold thy Children from on
    high.

S. Herme.

S. Hermenegildus, Apr. 13.

Brev. Rom.
Nunc nos è superum protege sedibus
Clemens, atque preces dum canimus tuâ
Quæsitam nece palmam
Pronis auribus accipe.

Now from the Heav'nly seat thou hast obtain'd
Protect us graciously, and while we joyn
To sing thy victory by dying gain'd,
Thy ready Ear unto our Pray'rs incline.

S. John Baptist, Jun. 24.

Brev. Rom.
Nunc potens nostri meritis opimis
Pectoris duros lapides repelle;
Asperum planans iter, & reflexos
Dirige calles.

Now thy rich merits do thy power raise,
The stony hardness of our hearts subdue,
Make plane the rugged, and our crooked ways
Direct and make 'em true.

S. Peter and Paul, June 29.

Brev. Rom.
Beate Pastor Petre, clemens accipe
Voces precantum, criminumque vincula
Verbo resolve, cui potestas tradita
Aperire terris cœlum, apertum claudere.

Peter! blest Shepherd! graciously
Receive our Prayers, our bonds of sins untye
By thy sole word, to whom the power is given
To open wide, and shut the Gate of Heaven.

Egregie

Egregie Doctor *Paule*, mores instrue,	*Great Doctor* Paul! *our manners rude instruct,*
Et nostra tecum pectora cœlum cape.	*And snatcht from hence, our hearts to heav'n conduct.*

St. *Peter* is also called in another Hymn, *Janitor cœli*, the Porter of Heaven.

S. *Genouefa*, Januar. 3.

Horæ sec.
us. Rom.

Nunc *Genouefa* virgo clemens te precantes respice:	*Look favourably towards those Blest* Genouefe, *who thee intreat;*
Tolle pondus culpæ, prementes hostes & clades abjice;	*Take off sins heavy load, our foes, And their intended harms defeat.*
Sanum corpus & cor mundum semper nobis tribue;	*A healthful body, and a heart That's clean and pure to us impart;*
Et pugnantes in agone cœlesti junge curiæ.	*And when our combat here is past, Unite us to the Saints at last.*

To S. *Agnes*.

Missal. Rom.
antiq. f. 51.

Agnes agni fœmina Nos intus illumina Radices extermina Peccatorum.	Agnes *who art the Lambs chast Spouse, Inlighten thou our minds within, Not onely lop the spreading boughs But root out of us every sin.*

C c

Singularis Domina,	O Lady singularly great,
Post mundi gravamina,	After this state with grief opprest,
Transfer ad agmina Beatorum.	Translate us to that quiet seat Above, to triumph with the Blest.

S. Clare, Aug. 12.

Offic. nov. Sanctor.

Jamjam in regno Luminum Patri (*sc. Francisco*) conregnas filia;
Da te sequentem agminum Recta fore vestigia.

Now Daughter in the place of light
Thou dost with Father Francis reign;
We pray thee to direct aright
The steps of all thy following train.

Ibid. ad Magnific.

Salve sponsa Dei, virgo sacra planta Minorum;

Tu vas munditiæ, tu prævia forma sororum:

Clara tuis precibus duc nos ad regna polorum.

Hail thou fair Spouse of Christ thou sacred Nun
Under that Rule S. Francis first began;
Vessel of purity and pattern great
Whom cloyster'd Sisters ought to imitate;
At length by thy prevailing pray'rs, S. Clare,
Bring us to Heav'n, where all the Blessed are.

But I'le a little rest my self from Rhithming, as the Latin does in some that follow; giving you for variety a little Blank Verse, till the Latin begins to chime again.

To S. Martina. Jan. 30.

Brev. Rom.

Tu natale solum protege, tu bonæ
Da pacis requiem Christia-dûm plagis;
Armorum strepitus & fera prælia
   In fines age Thracios.

Et Regum socians agmina sub crucis
Vexillo, *Solymas* nexibus ex-ime,
Vindexque innocui sanguinis hosticum
   Robur funditus erue.

Tu nostrum columen, tu decus inclytum,
Nostrarum obsequium respi-ce mentium;
Romæ libens vota excipe, quæ pio
   Te ritu canit & colit.

Do thou protect thy Native soyle, and give
A peaceful rest to all the Chri-stian Lands;
The noise of Arms and cruel Battels drive
   Into the Turkish Coasts.

Under the Cross unite the Troops of Kings,
The Holy Land from slavery redeem,
Revenge the blood of slaugh-tered Innocents
   And Hostile pow'rs destroy.

O thou our Stay and chiefest Ornament,
Regard the ready service of our minds;
Rome's vows receive, which in devoutest sort
   Do's praise & worship thee.

In Festo omnium Sanctorum.
Breviar. Roman.   *Hymnus.*

Placare, Christe, servulis
Quibus patris clementiam
Tuæ ad Tribunal gratiæ
Patrona virgo postulat.

On the Feast of all Saints.
Hymne.

Be reconcil'd, O *Christ*, to us
For whom the Virgin Patroness
Do's beg before thy gracious Throne
T'obtain the Fathers clemency.

Et vos beata per novem
Distincta gyros agmina
Antiqua cum præsentibus
Futura damna pellite.

Apostoli cum vatibus
Apud severum Judicem
Veris reorum fletibus
Exposcite indulgentiam.

Vos purpurati Martyres
Vos candidati præmio
Confessionis, exules
Vocate nos in patriam.

Chorea casta virginum,
Et quos Eremus incolas
Transmisit astris, cœlitum
Locate nos in sedibus.

Auferte gentem perfidam
Credentium de finibus;
Ut unus omnes unicum
Ovile nos Pastor regat.

Deo Patri sit gloria,
Natoque Patris unico,
Sancto simul Paraclito
In sempiterna secula.

Amen.

And ye, O blessed Company
Into nine ranks distinguished,
From ills past, present, and to come
Most graciously deliver us.
Ye holy Prophets & Apostles,
Prevail with God the Judge severe,
That we indulgence may obtain
Who wash our selves in briny tears.
Ye Martyrs who have shed your blood,
Ye Confessors that walk in white
Call us from our long banishment
Unto our most desired home.
And ye, O Quire of Virgins chast
And Hermits that to Heav'n are come
From solitary Wilderness,
Place us in those blest Mansions.
Remove perfidious people far
From th' habitations of the just
That in one fold Christ's sheep may lye
By that great Shepherd governed.
To God the Father glory be,
And also to his only Son,
And to the holy Paraclet,
Now and for evermore.

Amen.

Another Hymn.

Ibid.
Salutis æternæ dator
Jesu, redemptis subveni:
Virgo parens clementiæ
Dona salutem servulis.
Vos Angelorum millia,
Patrumque cœtus, agmina
Canora Vatum; vos reis
Precamini indulgentiam.
Baptista Christi prævius
Summique cœli claviger,
Cum cæteris Apostolis,
Nexus resolvant criminum.
Cohors triumphans Martyrum,
Almus Sacerdotum Chorus,
Et Virginalis castitas,
Nostros reatus abluant.
Quicunque in alta siderum
Regnatis aula Principes,
Favete votis supplicum
Qui dona cœli flagitant.

*O Jesu, who eternal life
Dost give, help thy redeemed
 ones;
O Virgin full of clemency,
Thy poor distressed servants
 save.
Ye Myriads of Angels, and
Assembly of the Patriarchs,
Ye Prophets, pray for guilty
 souls
That we indulgence may obtain.
Let John the Baptist, Christ's
 forerunner,
And the great Keeper of
 Heav'ns Keys,
With all th' Apostles, break
 the bonds
Of sin, wherein we fettered lye.
And let triumphant Martyrs, with
The goodly Quire of Sacred
 Priests,
And Virgins holy chastity,
Wash our polluted Souls from
 guilt.
All ye that with th' eternal King
As Princes reign above the
 Stars,
Favour the prayers of suppliants,
That humbly beg the boons of
 Heav'n.*

Virtus, honor, laus, gloria	All power, honour, glory, laud
Deo Patri cum Filio,	To God the Father and the Son,
Sancto simul Paraclyto	
In seculorum secula	And to the Holy Paraclete,
Amen.	Both now and evermore.
	Amen.

A Hymn common to any Martyr.

Brev. Rom.

Invicte Martyr, unicum	Unconquered Martyr, follower
Patris secutus filium,	Of Christ, the Fathers only Son,
Victis triumphas hostibus,	Triumphing o're thy vanquisht foes
Victor fruens coelestibus.	As victor thou to Heav'n art come.
Tui precatus munere	By mediation of thy prayers,
Nostrum reatum dilue,	Wash off the guilt of all our sin;
Arcens mali contagium,	It's sad contagion too prevent
Vitæ repellens tædium.	And tedious griefs of life repel.
Soluta jam sunt vincula	Thy sacred body's bonds uneasie
Tui sacrati corporis,	
Nos solve vinclis seculi	Are loos'd, and thou at liberty,
Dono superni numinis.	Now by the grant of God above,
Deo Patri sit gloria, &c.	From this worlds fetters set us free.
	To God the Father, &c.

A Hymn for any Apostle.

Brev. Rom.

| Exultet orbis gaudiis, | Let all the Earth now leap for joy, |
| Coelum resultet laudibus; | And let the Heavens with praise resound; Apo-|

Apostolorum gloriam	*The glory of th' Apostles name,*
Tellus & astra concinunt.	
Vos seculorum judices,	*Both Earth and Stars together sing.*
Et vera mundi lumina,	
Votis precamur cordium	*You that are Judges of the world,*
Audite preces supplicum.	
Qui templa cœli clauditis,	*And its true Lights that brightly shine,*
Serasque verbo solvitis,	
Nos à reatu noxios	*With heartiest wishes we intreat,*
Solvi jubete, quæsumus.	
Præcepta quorum protinus	*Our humble supplications hear.*
Languor, salusque sentiunt,	*Ye that do shut Heav'ns Temple gates,*
Sanate mentes languidas,	
Augete nos virtutibus.	*And by your word unlock the same,*
Ut cùm redibit Arbiter	
In fine Christus seculi;	*Our guilty souls from punishment*
Nos sempiterni gaudii	
Concedat esse compotes.	*Release, we pray, by your command.*

*For in an instant your commands
Sickness and health do both perceive;
Heal therefore our diseased minds,
And every grace in us increase.
That when our Saviour shall return
When time is past to judge the world,
His sentence may award to us
Those joys that never shall have end.*

For the *Apostles*.

Missal. Rom. antiq. in fine.

Cœli cives digni dici,
Christi Fratres & amici,
   Confessuri judices.
Quando dies erit ire,
Date nobis non sentire
   Flammas culpæ vindices.

Ye that are citizens of Heav'n
   above,
Christs Brethren and the
   Friends whom he do's love.
And shall together Judges
   sit.
When death our Souls shall
   from our body sever,
Secure us from th' avenging
   flames, that ever
Torment men in th' infernal
   pit.

But the most fulsome Courtship of Saints I meet with, are those strains that are directed to the Relations of our Saviour according to the flesh; of whom the Scripture speaks very little, (I except here the Bl. Virgin, whom I at present pass over) it neither tells us any thing of the piety of some of them; nor advances any of them in excellency or interest with God, above the rest of the Apostles and Disciples of Christ; you cannot but observe, that their unseasonable interposing in matters that related to the office of our Saviour, was repressed by him, rather than at all encouraged; as appears by his answer to his Parents that found him in the Temple; his answer to the people, that told him that his Mother and his Brethren desired to see and speak with him; and his answer to the Bl. Virgin her self, at the Marriage-Feast at *Cana*, when they wanted Wine. Yet such is the boldness (I may say prophaneness) of these worshippers of Saints, that they represent to God and them, as mighty prevailing arguments, the relation and kindred they had to our Saviour,

Luk.2.49.
Luk 8.21.
Joh.2.4.

our, and upon that account ask the greateſt boons. I'le inſtance only in thoſe to S. *Joſeph*, and to *Joachim* and *Anna* the Parents of the Bl. Virgin.]

To S. Joſeph.

Offic. Nova Sanct.
19. Mart.
Cœlitum, *Joſeph*, decus, atque noſtræ
Certa ſpes vitæ, columenque mundi,
Quas tibi læti canimus, benignus
    Suſcipe laudes.

Joſeph, Heav'ns ornament,
  the hope
That ſtays our hearts, the world's ſure prop,
Receive thoſe praiſes graciouſlie
  We gladly ſing to thee.

Ibid. ad Laudes.
Ergo regnantem flagitemus omnes
Adſit ut nobis, veniamque noſtris
Obtinens culpis, tribuat ſupernæ
    Munera pacis.

We therefore pray, now thou doſt reign,
Be preſent with us, and obtain
Forgiveneſs of our ſins, ne're ceaſe
  To give Heav'ns gifts of peace.

Hor. B Virg.
ſec. uſ. Rom.
Salve *Joſeph*; ſalvatoris.
Sancte Pater nomine;
Locum tenens tunc Tutoris,
Cum Maria conjuge;
Virgo cuſtos es uxoris
Vicem gerens gerulæ;

All Hail to thee, Joſeph, *our Saviours Father,*
Father in name thou art, but not in truth;
Thou hadſt the charge, or thy wife Mary rather,
To be the careful Guardian of his Youth;
Thou Virgin Keeper of a Virgin wife,
Who didſt like an officious Nurſe ſtand by;

Sponſus

Sponsus testis es pudoris
Sponsæ tantæ gratiæ.
Ad te Patrem putativum
Dolens fundo gemitum,
Ut me factum abortivum
Ad tutum ducas exitum.
* Cum securi, faber sancte,
Excide in me vitium,
Ut sim lignum adoptivum
Ad cœli Palatium.

* *These last Verses I have not left out here, though I occasionally mentioned them at the beginning of the Book.*

Thou strict observer of this Fair-ones life,
And faithful witness of her chastity.
To thee that art Christ's Father styl'd,
My sad and doleful sighs I send,
That me forelorn abortive child
Thou may'st conduct to happy end.
With Axe, O Carpenter so good,
Cut down my vices forward spring,
That I may prove adopted wood
Fit for the Palace of Heav'ns King.

Sutable to this, I find in the old *Roman Missal*, upon the Feast of the most Holy *Joseph* our Lord Jesus Christ's Foster-father, (*Nutricii*) this following Prayer.

DEus qui dedisti nobis regale sacerdotium; præsta quæsumus, ut sicut Beatus *Joseph*, unigenitum tuum, natum de Virgine *Maria*, suis manibus reverenter tractare meruit & portare; ita nos facias, cum cordis munditia & operis innocentia, tuis sacris Altaribus deservire.

Per eundem, &c.

O God, who hast given to us a royal Priesthood; grant we beseech thee, that as Bl. Joseph merited reverently to handle and bear in his hands thy only begotten Son, born of the Virgin Mary; so thou wouldest make us with cleanness of heart, and innocency of deed, to serve at thy sacred Altars. By the same, &c.

It

Devotions of the Roman Church. 395

It is also observable, that as in the Breviary, there is a set Office on Saturdays for the Virgin *Mary*; so also at the end of Diverse Litanies printed at *Colen*, 1643. there is a *Weekly Exercise* (*Exercitium Hebdomadarium* the Title is) collected by an *English* Priest, and set forth with Licence and Approbation; there you have for *Sunday* an *Office* of the H. *Trinity*: for *Munday* an *Office* of the H. *Ghost*: for *Tuesday* an *Office* of the H. *Name of Jesus*: for *Wednesday* an *Office* of the *Guardian Angel*: for *Thursday* an *Office* of the H. *Sacrament*: for *Friday* an *Office* of the H. *Cross*: and for *Saturday* an *Office* of S. *Joseph*, which is furnished with Hymns and Prayers, and the Devotions divided among the seven *Canonical Hours*; and it concludes with this *Recommendation* to him.

Has Horas Canonicas cum attentione	*I do these Hours Canonical repeat*
Dixi, sancte *Joseph*, tui ratione:	*For thy sake,* Joseph, *with attention great:*
Ut sis memor mei in oratione,	*That in thy pray'rs I may remembred be,*
Ut vivamus simul in cœli regione.	*And in Heav'ns glory ever live with thee.*

To S. Joachim.

In the old *Roman Missal*, (*Festo S. Joachim*) they make this address to him.

Vers. O *Joachim* sanctæ conjux *Annæ*, Pater almæ Virginis, hinc famulis confer salutis opem.	**O** Joachim **husband of S. Anne, and Father of the Bl. Virgin, from hence bestow saving help on thy servants.**

Then follows a long *Prosa*, as they call it, which concludes thus.

Vale

Vale Pater inclyte,	Farewel great Father,
Placa regem gloriæ	Heav'ns bleſt King appeaſe,
In hanc valle miſeriæ:	In this ſad vale of tears and miſerie:
Clarâ Dei facie	
Da frui in requie	Grant Gods bright face hereafter we may ſee
Sanctorum Sanctæ curiæ.	
O Pater Reginæ cœli nos adjuva. *Amen.*	In Heav'n where happy Saints have reſt and eaſe.
	O Father of the *Queen* of Heaven help us. *Amen.*

Brev. Rom. ant. de S.
Joach. Mart. 20.

O Pater ſummæ Joachim puellæ,	Joachim, Father of that bleſſed Maid, Who brought forth God, yet Virgin did remain;
Quæ Deum clauſo genuit pudore,	See our chaſte vows we make to God, be paid,
Promove noſtras Domino querelas,	And all our pray'rs promote, when we complain.
Caſtaque vota.	
Scis quot hic ſævis agitemur undis,	Toſt in this Sea with many a cruel wave,
Triſte quos mundi mare defatigat;	Thou know'ſt we weak and weather-beaten are;
Scis quot adnectat Satanas caroque.	Thou know'ſt what combats we are like to have, Which fleſh and Satan our ſworn foes prepare.
Prælia nobis.	
Jam ſacris junctus ſuperum catervis,	And now thou'rt plac'd among the bleſt ſo high,
Immo præcedens, potes omne, ſi vis;	Thou canſt do every thing thou art inclin'd to;
Nihil nepos Jeſus merito negabit,	Thy Nephew *Jeſus* ſure will not deny,
Nil tibi nata.	Much leſs thy Daughter, what thou haſt a mind to.

To *S.* Anna.

As they have thus advanced the *Father*, so I find them in a like strain, courting *this Mother* of the Blessed Virgin; of which I'le only give a brief instance or two, and conclude these Hymns.

Brev. Sarum
ad Jul. 26.
O vas cœlestis gratiæ,
Mater Reginæ Virginum,
Per te precamur anxiè
Remissionem criminum.
Memento Mater inclyta
Quàm potens es per filiam;
Et nobis prece solita
Procura Dei gratiam.

O vessel of celestial grace,
Blest Mother to the Virgin's
Queen,
By thee we beg in the first
place
Remission of all former sin.
Great Mother, always keep in
mind
The power thou hast by thy
sweet Daughter;
And by thy wonted prayer let's
find
Gods grace procur'd to us
hereafter.

In another Hymn, after high commendations of S. *Anne,* they conclude thus.

Ibid.
Ergo te rogamus
Rogantes supplicamus,
Ut quod potes, velis,
Prece da nos cœlis;
Placans nobis natam
Mundo per te datam;
Illa Natum suum,
Tu Nepotem tuum.

Therefore still asking we re-
main,
And thy unwearied suiters are,
That what thou canst, thou
would'st obtain,
And give us Heaven by thy
Prayer.
Do thou appease the Daughter
thou didst bear,
She her own Son, and thou thy
Nephew dear.

Devotions to Angels.

That the Devotions may be continued, and not interrupted by any large Discourse, I shall here go on, with such as I meet with, in their Books, that relate to *Angels*; and reserve what I shall say concerning the worshiping of Angels, to the Conclusion.

A Prayer to all the Quire of Angels.

Hora sec. us.
Sar. f. 92.

O Inflammati Seraphim ardentes dilectione. O illustrati Cherubim lucentes cognitione. O summi throni judicantes Dei sessione. O supernæ dominationes dominantes divina largitione. O inclyti principatus aliis præfecti gubernatione. O mirandæ potestates dæmones arcentes dei jussione. O claræ virtutes miracula facientes pro fidelium illuminatione. O sancti Archangeli magnis majora nunciantes. O boni Angeli curam hominum continuam habentes. Intendite

O Inflamed Seraphims burning with love. O Illustrated Cherubims shining with knowledge. O high Thrones, judging in the session of God. O supreme Dominations, bearing rule by the Divine gift. O famous Principalities, set over others in governing. O wonderous Powers, driving away Devils by Gods command. O admirable Mights, doing Miracles for the illumination of the faithful. O holy Archangels telling greater things to great persons. O ye good Angels, having continual care of men. Mind

mini-

Devotions of the Roman Church.

ministerium vestrum ad custodiam nostram; dirigentes cogitatus verba & actus nostros in viam salutis & prosperitatis; ut mandatorum dei voluntarii cultores, numerum vestrorum ordinum (qui casu Luciferi diminutus est) valeamus divina largiente misericordia feliciter adimplere.

your ministry for our custody, directing our thoughts words and actions into the way of salvation and prosperity; that so we being willing worshippers of the commands of God, we may be able happily to fill up the number of your Orders (which is diminished by the fall of Lucifer) the divine mercy granting it.

Another Prayer to the Holy Angels.

Ibid. OMnes sancti Angelorum ordines, orate pro nobis. O felices incolæ patriæ cœlestis, spiritus immortales, astra matutina, rectores orbis, amatores hominum, & summi Ministri divinæ voluntatis: qui de pestifero Dracone potenter triumphantes, ipso corruente manetis in gloria perpetuæ felicitatis. Vos, inquam, deprecor, ut me vestræ gratiæ conservum ab hostium incursu piissimè protegentes, misero morienti consolatores adesse dignemini; ne spiritum in angustiis hærentem violenter opprimat turba malignorum; sed ex omni parte vestro sultus præsidio, finaliter requies-

O All ye holy Orders of Angels, pray for us. O ye happy Inhabitants of the celestial Country, ye immortal Spirits, morning Stars, Governors of the World, lovers of Men, and chief Ministers of the Divine pleasure; who powerfully triumphing over the pestilent Dragon, though he tumbled down, yet you abide in the glory of perpetual felicity. To you, I say, I pray, that mercifully protecting me, who am a fellow-servant of your grace, from the incursion of enemies, you would vouchsafe to be present to comfort me miserable man when I am dy-

cam

Amen. very ſide being ſupported by your ſafe-guard, I may finally reſt in God my ſalvation. To whom be honor, glory, & dominion, throughout all Ages. Amen.

Another Prayer, wherein Angels are invoked, promiſing mighty things to thoſe that uſe it, as appears by the following *Rubrick*, in the Hours of *Sarum*.

Thys Prayer was ſhewed to S. Auguſtine, by revelacyon of the H. Ghoſt, and who that devoutly ſay this prayer, or hyre rede, or bereth aboute them, ſhall not peryſhe in fyer or water, nother in batyll or jugement, and he ſhall not dye of ſodyne dethe, and no venym ſhall poyſinne hym that daye; and what he aſketh of God he ſhall obteyne, yf it be to the ſalvacyon of his ſoule, and whan thy ſoule ſhall departe from thy body it ſhall not entre to Hell.

Oratio.	The Prayer.
Deus propitius eſto mihi peccatori; & cuſtos meus ſis omnibus diebus ac noctibus vitæ meæ. Deus *Abraham*, Deus *Iſaac*, Deus *Jacob* miſerere mei; & mitte mihi in adjutorium Sanctum Michaelem Archangelum, qui me defendat & protegat ab omnibus inimicis meis. Sancte	O God be merciful to me a ſinner, & be thou my Keeper all the days and nights of my life. God of Abraham, God of Iſaac, God of Jacob, have mercy upon me; and ſend me Saint Michael the Archangel to my help, who may defend me, and protect me from all

Michael

Michael Archangele defende me in periculo, ut non pereéam in tremendo judicio. O Sancte *Michael* Archangele, per gratiam quam meruisti te deprecor, & per unigenitum filium dei Dominum nostrum Jesum Christum; ut eripias me hodie à periculo mortis. Sancte *Gabriel,* Sancte *Raphael,* Omnes Sancti Angeli & Archangeli Dei, succurite mihi. Precor vos omnes virtutes coelorum, ut detis mihi auxilium & potentiam, ut nullus inimicus me condemnare possit in via, nec in aqua, nec in igne, nec subitanea morte me, nec dormientem, nec vigilantem opprimat aut lædat. Ecce crucem ✠ Domini, fugite partes adversæ: vicit Leo de Tribu Juda, radix *David.* Alleluja. Salvator Mundi salva nos, qui per crucem & sanguinem tuum redemisti nos. Auxiliare nobis te deprecamur Deus noster. Agios O theos, agios ischyros, agyos athanatos, eleison ymas. Sancte Deus, sancte fortis, sancte & immortalis miserere

mine enemies. O Saint Michael the Archangel defend me in danger, that I may not perish in the dreadful judgment. O Saint Michael the Archangel, I pray thee, by the grace thou hast merited, and by the only begotten Son of God our Lord Jesus Christ; that thou wouldst deliver me this day from the danger of death. O S. Gabriel, S. Raphael, all ye holy Angels and Archangels of God, succour me. I pray you, all ye powers of Heaven, that you would give me help and power, that no enemy may be able to condemn me in the way, nor in water, nor in fire, nor may oppress or hurt me by sudden death, neither sleeping nor waking. Behold the Lord's cross ✠, fly away ye adverse powers. The Lyon of the Tribe of Judah the root of David hath overcome. Allelujah. O Saviour of the World save us, who hast redeemed us by thy cross and blood. Help us, we pray thee, O our God. Holy God, holy strong, holy immortal, have mercy upon us. Holy God, holy strong, holy and immortal,

Dd   nobis.

nobis. Crux ✠ Christi sal- have mercy on us. O cross
va nos. Crux ✠ Christi pro- ✠ of Christ save us. O
tege nos. Crux ✠ Christi de- cross ✠ of Christ protect us.
fende nos. In nomine Patris O cross ✠ of Christ defend
✠ & Filii ✠, & Spiritus ✠ us. In the name of the Fa-
Sancti. ther ✠, and of the Son ✠,
    Amen. and of the Holy Ghost ✠.
           Amen.

  At the end of another Prayer to Christ they conclude thus.

Horæ. sec.
uf. Sar. f. 83.

 ✠ Sancte *Michael* esto mi- ✠ Saint Michael, be thou
hi lorica. ✠ Sancte *Gabriel* my Coat of Mail. ✠ S.
esto mihi galea. ✠ Sancte Gabriel be thou my Helmet.
Raphael esto mihi scutum. ✠ ✠ S. Raphael be thou my
Sancte *Uriel* esto mihi defen- Shield. ✠ S. Uriel be thou
sor. ✠ Sancte *Cherubin* esto my defender. ✠ S. Cherubin
mihi sanitas. ✠ Sancte *Sera-* be thou my health. ✠ S.
phin esto mihi veritas. ✠ Et Seraphin be thou my truth.
omnes Sancti Angeli & Arch- ✠ And may all the Holy
angeli me custodiant, prote- Angels & Archangels keep,
gant & defendant; & ad vi- protect and defend me, and
tam æternam me perducant. bring me to eternal life.
    Amen.   Amen.

A Litany, concerning the Holy Angels. After their Addresses to God, the Bl. Trinity, and the Virgin Mary, it proceeds thus.

Litaniæ variæ. Colon. 1643. cum Approbat.

S. *Michael*, who hast always defended the People of God.
S. *Michael*, who didst thrust down Lucifer with his rebellious complices from Heaven.
S. *Michael*, who didst cast the Accuser of our Brethren into the depth of Hell.
S. *Gabriel*, who didst open the Divine Vision to *Daniel*.
S. *Gabriel*, who foretoldest the Birth and Ministery of *John* the Baptist.
S. *Gabriel*, who wast the Messenger of the Incarnation of the Divine Word.
S. *Raphael*, who didst conduct and bring back *Tobias* in safety.
S. *Raphael*, who didst expell a Devil out of *Sara*.
S. *Raphael*, who didst recover the sight of *Tobias senior*.
O ye holy Angels. Pray for us.
Ye that stand upon the high and elevated Throne of God.
Ye that continually sing to God, Holy, holy, holy.
Ye that illuminate our minds, dispelling their darkness.
Ye that declare Divine things to Men.
Ye that have received from God the custody of Men.
Ye that always see the face of the Father which is in Heaven.
Ye that rejoyce over one sinner that repenteth.
Ye that smote the *Sodomites* with blindness.

Pray for us.

Ye that brought out *Lot* from the midst of sinners.
Ye that ascended and descended on *Jacob*'s Ladder.
Ye that delivered the Divine Law to *Moyses* on Mount *Sinai*.
Ye that brought tidings of joy to Men, when *Christ* was born.
Ye that ministred to *Christ* in the Desert.
Ye that carried *Lazarus* into *Abraham*'s bosome.
Ye that sate by the Sepulchre of Christ in white Garments.
Ye that when Christ ascended into Heaven, appeared to his Disciples.
Ye that shall go before Christ with the sign of the cross, when he comes to Judgment.
Ye that shall gather together the Elect at the end of the World.
Ye that shall gather all things that offend out of Christs Kingdome.
Ye that shall separate the bad from among the just.
Ye that bring the requests of them that pray, unto God.
Ye that assist dying Persons.
Ye that conveigh to Heaven the Souls of the Just, that are purged from all stain.
Ye that work Wonders and Miracles by the Power of God.
Ye that are sent to minister to those that long for the inheritance of salvation.
Ye that cure *Babylon*, and depart and leave her when she will not be cured.
Ye that are constituted Rulers over Kingdomes and Provinces.
Ye that have often dispersed the Hosts of Enemies.
Ye that have often delivered the Servants of God from Prisons, and other dangers of Life.
Ye that have often comforted Holy Martyrs in their Torments.

} *Pray for us.*

Ye

Devotions of the Roman Church.

Ye that are wont to cherish with a peculiar care the
   Prelates of the Church, and Princes that are Foster-
   Fathers of the same.
O all ye holy Orders of blessed Spirits. Pray for us.
From all dangers, by thy Holy Angels, Deliver us
   O Lord.

Pray for us.

The rest that follows is common with other Litanies, and therefore I omit it: but this is enough to show, how they court the H. Angels, and think to gratifie them very much (I suppose) when they tell them of their famous acts, and the noble Embassies they have been imployed in.

You may also take notice, that they have singled three by Name, out of all the Angels, *Michael, Gabriel* and *Raphael* (whom they call, in other Offices, all Archangels) peculiarly to invoke; and I find in the *Salisbury* and old *Roman Missals*, particular *Offices* and *Masses* to these three. To give a few instances, how they address themselves to each of them.

To *S.* Raphael *the Archangel.*

In the old *Roman* Missal, and also in the Missal of *Sarum*, I find a proper Mass of *Raphael* the Archangel: with the following *Rubrick* by way of Preface to it.

"The following Office of Raphael the Archangel,
"may be celebrated for Pilgrims or Travellers; that
"as he conducted and brought back (in his Journey) To-
"bias sound and safe, so he would bring back those for
"whom the Mass is said. It may also be said for all
"sick People, and such as are possessed with the Devil,
"because he is a Medicinal Angel, who restored sight to
"Tobias, and dispossessed a Devil out of Sara his Sons
"Wife.

Oratio.

Oratio.

DEus qui Beatum *Raphaelem* Archangelum *Tobiæ* famulo tuo properanti prævium direxisti, & inter hujus vitæ ac viæ varietates atque discrimina, donasti custodem: da quæsumus, ut ejusdem protegamur auxilio, quatenus & vitæ præsentis vitemus pericula, & ad gaudia valeamus pervenire cœlestia. Per Dominum, &c.

Versf. Angele Medicinalis, mecum sis perpetualis; & sicut fuisti cum *Thobia*, ita sis mecum semper in via.

Secreta.

MItte Deus Archangelum tuum *Raphaelem* cum medicamine opificem; qui sanitatem mentis reportet & corporis, misericordiæque cœlestis donum infundat, & quæ in nobis sunt adversa deponat; ut qui nostra ini-

A Prayer.

O God, who didst direct Bl. Raphael the Archangel to go before thy servant Tobias hastening (in his journey) and gavest him to be his Keeper, amidst the varieties and dangers of this life and way: grant, we beseech thee, that we may be protected by his aid, so that both we may shun the dangers of this present life, and may be able to come to the joys of Heaven. Through our Lord, &c.

Blest *Angel*, who art styl'd Medicinal,
Give us thy company perpetual:
And as thou wast a Guide to good Tobias,
So in our way, let no ill chance come nigh us.

O God, send thy Archangel Raphael a skilful worker with his medicine; who may bring health of soul and body, and infuse the gift of celestial mercy, and may put away those things that are contraries

quitate

quitate tabescimus, de tua, in us; that so we who waste quam non meremur, pietate away in our iniquities, lætari concedas. Per Do- thou wouldest vouchsafe to minum. comfort us with thy pity, which we do not deserve. Through our Lord.

A Prayer to S. Raphael.

Hor. sec. us. Sarum, f. 92.

Auxiliare mihi & tu Princeps obsecro eximie *Raphael*, animarum corporisque optime Medicator, & qui corporeos *Thobiæ* oculos præsentialiter medicando illuminasti, meos quoque spirituales & carnales oculos illustra, & cunctas mei cordis & corporis tenebras amputare cœlitus orando ne deseras.
  Pater noster, &c.
  Ave *Maria*, &c.

I Intreat thee also, do thou assist me O excellent Prince Raphael, thou best Physician of soul and body, and thou that didst presently inlighten the bodily eyes of Tobias by curing them; do thou also inlighten my spiritual and carnal eyes, and do not cease by thy heavenly prayer, to cut off all the darkness of my heart and body.
  Our Father, &c.
  Hail Mary, &c.

A Prayer before we take in hand any journey.

O Good God, whom it pleased to direct *Abraham*, *Jacob* and young *Tobias* in their peregrinations, and brought them in health and safety into their Country; Grant, I beseech thee, to be my director in this journey, which I would in no wise undertake (much less follow and finish) if I knew it any way contrary to thy holy will. Therefore, O Lord, give me *Raphael* for my conductor,

Manual of godly Prayers, at the end, 1610.

to whose custody I may be delivered, and thereby be brought with happy success to the accomplishing that work, whereunto I prepare and dispose my self. Direct my understanding, O Lord, to the end that my feet no where stray from the observations of thy holy commandments. In the name of thy beloved son Jesus Christ our Redeemer, who with thee, &c. Amen.

To S. Gabriel *the Archangel.*

Though I find no proper Office in the present *Reformed Breviaries* for S. *Gabriel*, yet there is a large one for him in the *Old Roman Breviary*, with Hymns and Lessons (and a *proper Mass* to him in the *old Roman* and *Salisbury Missal*) there you have this Prayer at the beginning.

ILlumina, quæsumus Domine, mentes nostras fidei claritate; ut beati *Gabrielis* annunciatione jocunda, & omnis militiæ cœlestis interventione continua in tuo semper amore crescamus.
Per Dominum.

O Lord we beseech thee, inlighten our minds with clearness of faith; that by the pleasant Annunciation of Bl. Gabriel, and by the continual intercession of all the Heavenly militia, we may always increase in thy love.
Through our Lord.

At the very end of the Office we have this *Antiphona.*

Ad nos veni Præco pie
Gabriel Dei cœlorum;
Ave dulce dic *Mariæ*
Tecum ducens cœli chorum;

Come Gabriel *Gods holy Cryer,*
And thy sweet Hail to Mary *say;*
Bring in thy train the Heavenly Quire;

Nosque

Devotions of the Roman Church.

Nosque serves in hac die
Ab insultu peccatorum;
Ambulemus ut in die
Per profectum meritorum.

*Save us from sin's assaults
this day:
That daily we may progress
make
In vertues meritorious track.*

The old *Roman Missal* has a great many admirable strains in a *Prosa de S. Gabriele*; of which take a few Verses.

*Missal. Rom.
antiq. f. 52.*

Nunc lætetur plebs fidelis
Recolendo Gabrielis
   Laudes & præconia;
Omnis homo omni die
Gabrielis & Mariæ
   Poscat beneficia.
Ex his manet fons virtutis,
Dulcor vitæ, spes salutis
   Et diffusa gratia.

*Now let the Saints be joyful
whilst they tell
The praises and renown of
Gabriel.
Thou that would'st ask good
boons and not miscarry,
Make thine address to Gabriel and Mary.
These are the spring whence
vertue flows apace,
Heav'ns hope, life's sweetness
and diffused grace.*

Then it follows a little after,

—— Ab aversis nos evelle
Sana morbos & expelle
   Pestes & Dœmonia.
Gabriel qui descendisti
Cum salute, servos Christi
   Ducas ad cœlestia.

*Heal our diseases, all afflictive
evils
Remove, and rout both Pestilence and Devils.
To earth thou cam'st salvation
to proclaim,
To Heaven conduct us to injoy
the same.*

A Prayer to S. Gabriel.

Hor. sec. us. Sarum.

PRecor & te ô Princeps egregie, *Gabriel* fortissime, agonista certantium; exurge mihi in adjutorium adversus malignantes: esto mecum contra adversarios meos, & contra omnes operantes iniquitatem: detege versutos hostes & contere violentos; ut omnes adversantes mihi tuo opitulatu victi fugentur; favente Domino nostro Jesu Christo. Who with the Father, &c. Pater noster. Ave Maria.

I Pray also unto thee, O excellent Prince, most valiant Gabriel, the champion of those that contend; rise up for my help against the malignants: be thou with me against my adversaries, and against all that work iniquity: detect the crafty enemies and break in pieces the violent; that all mine adversaries may be driven away, being overcome by thy help. Our Lord Jesus Christ favouring. To whom, &c. Our Father. Hail Mary.

To S. Michael the Archangel.

Anaph.

Hor. sec. us. Rom. Sept. 29.

PRinceps gloriosissime *Michael*, dux exercituum, susceptor animarum, debellator malorum spirituum, Ecclesiæ Dei, post Christum, dux admirabilis grandis excellentiæ & virtutis: omnes clamantes ad te ab omni libera adversitate; & in

MOst glorious Prince Michael, the Captain of (Gods) hosts, the Receiver of Souls, the Vanquisher of evil spirits, the Admirable General, next to Christ, of God's Church, of great excellency and power: deliver all that cry unto thee from all adversity; and make them to ad-
cultu

Devotions of the Roman Church.

cultu Dei facias proficere tuo pretioso officio & dignissima prece.

vance in the worship of God by thy precious office and most worthy prayer.

Anaph.

Alia Hor. sec. us. Rom.

Michael Archangele, Paradisi præposite, veni in adjutorium populo Dei, & velis nos defendere à potestate inimici, & tecum ducere in societatem Domini.

O Michael the Archangel, chief officer of Paradise, come to the help of Gods people, and be pleased to defend us from the power of the enemy, and bring us with thee into the society of the Lord.

Let us pray.

Hor. sec. us. Rom. 1570.

OMnipotens sempiterne Deus, qui saluti humanæ naturæ ex summa clementia tua gloriosum principem Ecclesiæ tuæ beatum *Michaelem* Archangelum mirabiliter deputasti; concede propitius, ut ejus salutari subsidio, hic mereamur à malis actibus efficacissimè tueri; & in futuro nostro obitu, ab omni tentatione liberari, & tuæ excelsæ majestati beatificè præsentari. Per Dominum.

ALmighty everlasting God, who out of thy great clemency, hast wonderfully deputed the glorious Prince of thy Church, blessed Michael the Archangel for the salvation of humane Nature; mercifully grant, that by his saving aid, we may merit to be most effectually defended here from evil actions; and when we shall dye, to be freed from all temptation, and beatifically presented before thy high Majesty. Through our Lord, &c.

A Prayer to S. Michael for the defence of the Church.

Manual of Godly prayers, 1610. with License.

O Warlike Prince, S. *Michael* Archangel, who hast gloriously triumphed over the infernal Dragon, and hast hitherto valiantly defended the Church of God, come unto the aid and succour of the Catholick people, and procure to the Church Militant, victory against the furious beast of Infidelity and Heresie: prevent and quite overthrow all their machinations and subtile devices, and drive them out of all Christian Kingdoms: and likewise defend us both in our life and death, against the assaults of the Devil; and bring our souls after death, to the place of everlasting repose: Through Jesus Christ our Lord and Saviour. *Amen.*

In the reformed *Breviary* of *Pius* V. upon the 29. September, on the Feast of S. *Michael*, I find this Hymn following, (to which I'le annex their own Translation in Meeter, for a taste of their *English* Poetry, as we have it in the *Manual of Godly Prayers*, 1610. p. 388.

Tibi Christe splendor Patris,
Vita, virtus cordium,
In conspectu Angelorum
Votis, voce Psallimus,
Alternantes concrepando
Melos damus vocibus.
Collaudamus venerantes
Omnes cœli milites;

Thy Fathers brightness Christ to thee,
Life and vertue of our hearts:
In goodly view of Angels all,
In vow and voice we sing our parts,
Sounding in ensuing course,
Musick to our speech imparts.
In worshipping at once we praise,
All the host of Heaven high;

Sed

Devotions of the Roman **Church.**

Sed præcipuè Primatem	But Michael *as the chiefest*
Cœlestis exercitus,	*Of the Heavenly company,*
Michaelem in virtute	*Who* Zabulon *his strength de-*
Conterentem *Zabulum.*	*stroyed*
Quo custode procul pelle	*With great forces utterly.*
Rex Christe piissime,	*Under whose guard expel*
Omne nefas inimici;	*away*
Mundo corde & corpore.	*Of our foes each wicked thing,*
Paradiso redde tuo	*With our hearts and bodies*
Nos sola clementia.	*cleansed,*
Gloriam Patri melodis	*O our holy Christ and King.*
Personemus vocibus;	*Vouchsafe by thy good grace*
Gloriam Christo canamus,	*alone*
Gloriam Paraclito.	*Us to Paradise to bring.*
Qui trinus & unus Deus	*Let us the Fathers glory sound,*
Extat ante secula.	*With well seeming melody;*
Amen.	*And let us glory unto Christ*
	Also yield in harmony;
	And glory to the holy Ghost,
	Ever God in persons three.
	Amen.

But besides all this, they have dedicated Feasts to S. *Michael,* upon the most fabulous stories imaginable, of his wondrous Apparitions, and revelations to particular persons, requiring them to build Churches to his Honour. The ridiculous original of one of his Feasts upon the Eighth of *May,* when he appeared to the Bishop of *Siponto* and the Drovers upon Mount *Garganus,* has been set down already, out of the Breviary, by Dr. *Stillingfleet* in his Book of the *Idolatry practised in the Roman Church.* And that you may see how one Fable propagates and spawns more of the kind, the *Breviary of Sarum* has given us another perfectly like it, of an Appearance of *Michael* upon Mount *Tumba,* and a Festival appointed for the memory of it, up-

Idolatry of the Rom. Church, c. 4.

on the Sixteenth of *October*. The story is told in short, by *Vincentius*; but is finely enlarged by *Jacobus de Voragine* (*de S. Michaele*) and out of him the *Salisbury Breviary* seems to have taken it: which because it is very extraordinary, I shall transcribe the Lessons.

Vincent. Spec. Hist. l. 23. c. 137

Lesson 1.

"After that the *French* Nation being converted to Christianity, had brought under the necks of the proud, through Provinces far & wide: *Michael* the Archangel, the chief officer of *Paradise*, who aforetime had showed that he would be worshipped in Mount *Garganus*; he showed also by many signs how he was to be honoured in this place, which by the inhabitants is called *Tumba*.

Brev. Sarum Octob. 16.

Les. 2. "This place was heretofore shut up by a dark Wood, but afterward was reduced to the form of a Sandy shore by the waters of the Sea that surrounded it. Yet the Sea with-drawing it self, does twice a-day afford a passage to devout people to go to the Church of *Michael* the Archangel.

Les. 3. "Now let us see how this place was dedicated by the Revelation of the Angel. After that *Authbertus* Bishop of the said place and beloved of God, had been twice admonished in his Dream to build a Church to the honour of S. *Michael* on the height of that place; it happened that the *Bull* of a certain man was hid there for a time by a Thief: The Bishop was warned a third time more sharply, to build a Church in that place, where the *Bull* was secretly tied.

Les. 4. "And when he desired to be satisfied concerning the largeness and quantity of ground (for his building) he received an answer in his dream, that the measure of his building should be that path which the *Bull* had worn in circuit with his feet, and he was commanded to see the Bull restored to his owner.

Les.

Lef. 5. "Then the Bishop being assured of the Vision, "went to the foresaid place, and caused it to be cleansed and "levelled. But in the middle of it, two Rocks stood out; "which when they could not remove by the labour of many "Workmen; a certain Man named *Bayno*, by a divine war- "ning, came to the said place with his *Twelve* Sons, and by "the help of S. *Michael*, he removed the Rock, of so great "magnitude, so that there seemed to be no weight there.

Lef. 6. "When the Bishop doubted still about the big- "ness of the Fabrick, at Midnight there fell a Dew upon "the top of the Mountain, but where the Foundations were "to be placed, there it was altogether dry. And it was "said to the Bishop, Go, and as thou seest it signed, lay "the Foundations.

Lef. 7. "Then the Bishop giving thanks to God, built "the Fabrick on the top of the Mountain, round like a "Vault, capable of holding, as is judged, a Hundred Men, "after the fashion of that in Mount *Garganus*.

Lef. 8. "After this, by the advice of Bl. *Michael*, Mes- "sengers were sent to Mount *Garganus*, to fetch thence To- "kens (*pignora*) of Bl. *Michael*; who being honourably "received by the Bishop and Abbot of the place, they "humbly declared the cause of their coming.

Lef. 9. "The things they came for were delivered to "them: *viz.* part of a red Mantle, (or short Cloak, *palli-* "*oli*) which Bl. *Michael* himself laid upon the Altar, which "he built with his own hand; and also part of a Marble- "stone, upon which he stood, whose foot-steps to this day "remain in the said place. Then the Bishop *Authbertus*, "honourably receiving the said Gifts, finished his work; "and appointed the Offices of *Twelve* Clergy-men there; "giving them *two* Villages out of his Bishoprick, for to su- "stain them.

You see from this Legend, that when People are mad with superstition, any story of a *Cock* and a *Bull*, will serve their turns to found a Festival upon, and to give occasion for

for the further Veneration of a Saint, or an Angel, though the circumstances are never so improbable. This of removing the Rock is a pretty stretcher, and is more plainly told in the *Festival*, the Names only varied.

Festival de S. Michaele, f. 144.

"Also Michael appered to another Byshop, and badde hym go to an hyll toppe unto the Mount of Gardell, and there as he founde a Bull teyed, he sholde make a Chyrche in the worshyp of God and Saynt Mychaell. Than were there two roches of stone on eyther syde, that the werke myght not up. Than Saynt Mychaell appered to a Man that hyght Haymo, and badde hym go and put awaye the roche and drede no thynge. So this Man went thyder and sette to his shoulders, and badde the roche goo utter in the name of God and Saynt Mychaell, and so the hylles wente utter as moche as neded to the werke."

And now that this work is thus wonderfully finished, you may be sure that S. *Michael* will not be wanting to give countenance and incouragement to his worship here, by his miraculous works. *Jacobus de Voragine* has recorded one fitly matched with those that have gone before.

Voragine de S. Michaele.

"When a great Multitude were going to this Church (for twice a Day, as we were told, the Sea that encompasses the Mount gives the People a passage) it happened that a big-bellied Woman, and near her time, went along with them: And behold the Sea returned with a mighty force, and all the Company in a great fright fled to the shore again; onely the Woman with Child, not being able to fly, was overtaken by the Waves of the Sea: But *Michael* the Archangel preserved the Woman unhurt; so that she brought forth her Child in the midst of the Sea, (*which was a fine lying in*) and taking her Child in her Arms there gave it suck; and the Sea making her a way, she came forth rejoycing with her Child.

I

I hope also that the precious piece of S. *Michael*'s red Cloak is forth-coming, if any have the curiosity to inquire for it, (as who knows but many a one may, especially those of *Jersey* Island, to whom this Church is so near) which they might be the more encouraged to, if those other remains of the Archangel (for his Reliques are since increased) his *Dagger* and his *Shield*, are to be seen; for so they were at the beginning of this Age; though one of their Historians, * *Lescarbotus*, who describes his Journey to *Michael's Mount* (which is the same with our Mount *Tumba*) says that *five* Years before he came thither (which was in the Year 1607) the Bishop of *Auranches* had forbidden his Shield to be any more showed: but who knows but some of the succeeding Bishops may have been better natured, and not have denyed this gratification to the desires of their gaping Devoto's.

* See *Dallee de object. cult. Relig.* l. 4. c. 18. *pag.* 683.

To the Guardian-Angel.

THe Guardian Angels had a place in the old *Roman Breviary*, upon the first of *March*, but the Office was not so formal, with Prayers and Hymnes, as it was since made by Pope *Paulus* V. who set out *Officium Angeli custodis*, an Office of the Guardian Angel, which was Printed at *Colen*, 1613. and there was joyned to it a Treatise, *de Angelo custode*, concerning the *Guardian Angel*, composed by *Francis. Albertinus*, a Jesuite, fitted for the younger Wits, which are infinitely desirous to know the conditions of those spirits above, but (as the Preface tells us) were not to be trusted, or counselled to lanch into the *deep Sea*, or to try to ascend the *inaccessible Mountain of Scripture* to find out their Nature, but must be condescended to by the method of humane interpretation, (to use his words.) And indeed the *Scripture* could never have furnished him with such bold and presuming speculations about this matter, as their

School-men could do; for howsoever some places may seem fairly to countenance this in the Scripture, and make it a probable opinion; that at some particular Seasons at least, there have been particular Angels deputed to preside over a Countrey or Province; and so also that they have had the charge of particular Persons; yet the evidence of it there, is not so cogent, as that it should be put as an Article of Faith into *Summs of Divinity*, or that *Prayers* and *Offices* should be made to them, and they religiously courted and worshipped under that notion. To determine, as this Author does, that every Church and Temple has a peculiar Angel to guard it, to tell us the like of Monasteries

cap. 2. and Colledges, and of every Family; nay, that every *Altar*, as soon as it is consecrated, is commit-
cap. 20. ted to the custody of a particular Angel; To know that *Adam* had such a Guardian Angel in innocency,
cap. 4. and that his Posterity would all have needed such, if he had never fallen; that Antichrist shall have one,
cap. 8. to keep him from doing greater mischief, and that Christ only neither needed, nor had one; to be able
cap. 5. to understand to what Hierarchy those Angels belong, that are Guardians; whether any, or how many of the Orders are exempted, that the Angel that comforted our Saviour in his Agony in the Garden, as well as that which admonished *Joseph* not to forsake the Bl. Virgin, and to fly with the Child *Jesus* into *Egypt*, was a *Seraphin*, and of no other Order of Angels. To know that the number of Archangels is greater than that of Angels; and to know how many times the number of Angels exceeds the number of all Mankind; These are things which the
cap. 3. useful plainness of Holy Writ meddles not with, but the impertinent curiosity, and trifling subtilty of the Schools is busie and forward to determine; and some of them are vouched by Revelations, of those whom they call Prophetick Women; as the last I named by S. *Brigid*, whom our Author cites in these words. "If all the Men that have "been born since *Adam*, to the last Man that shall be born
"in

Devotions of the Roman Church. 419

"in the very end of the World, should be computed; there would be found more than Ten Angels for every single man. (By which manner of speaking, this Prophetess, who is so exact a Computer, would have us, I suppose, to conclude, that it would be a great mistake to think that the number of Angels was either 9, or 11. for one of Men.) These are fine *Institutes* to season Youth withall, to whom the Bible would be a dangerous Book. After a great deal more such stuff as this, he pretends towards the conclusion to instruct us, by what means a Man may enter into a *holy familiarity* with his *Guardian Angel* (which I leave the Reader to consult him about) and at last gives us an example of addressing to this Angel, which he calls *Colloquium ad Angelum custodem*, which take in his words thus translated.   Cap. 20, 21, 22.

p. 221.

"O most holy Angel, my Companion and Guardian, I give thee thanks from the bottom of my heart, (who after God and his blessed Mother art to be loved by me, with the highest affection of mind) I give thee thanks, I say, for all the benefits bestowed on me, from that moment, in which thou undertookest the care of my Body and Soul: I also beg pardon for my forepast life, because I cannot hide the innumerable and shameful crimes, which I hitherto have committed before thine, and our God's most pure eyes; Humbly beseeching thee, that out of the Treasury of the Divine Goodness, thou wouldst vouchsafe to obtain for me readiness and fervour in things spiritual: for being so illuminated, I will begin a new life, and persevere in a conversation acceptable to God, and not unworthy of thy Presence. *Amen.*

This is a pretty improvement, you'l say, in devotion, and acceptable talk to an Angel; and this familiarity does increase daily, so that now the learned Men dedicate Books, as I remember *Schottus* the Jesuite does a Book of Mathematicks, to the Tutelar Angel. You cannot well imagine how this profaneness should arise higher, unless it be in one case,

Ee 2   which

which this Author a little after advances to, which relates to the Bl. Virgin, in a *Form of Oblation of ones self to her*, which I'le only add.

p. 224.

"O Most holy Virgin *Mary*, the Mother of God, I N. though most unworthy every ways, to be received into the number of thy servants, yet trusting in thy admirable pity, and being strongly moved with a desire of serving thee, I chuse thee this day, in the presence of my Guardian-Angel, and all the Celestial Court, for my peculiar Mistress, Patroness and Parent; and do firmly purpose to follow thee, to serve thee, and to endeavour, that others also may serve thee. I therefore humbly beg of thee, O mother of all clemency, by that most sacred blood, which Jesus Christ thy Son shed for me, that thou wouldest vouchsafe to admit me into the number of those, who have devoted themselves to thee, to be thy perpetual servant: and do thou obtain for me Grace from God, that in all my thoughts, words and actions, I may so behave my self, that nothing from me may at any time displease either Gods eyes or thine; and be thou mindful of me at the hour of my death. *Amen.*"

But it is high time to return into the road of their more publick Devotions to the Guardian-Angel.

A Hymn.

Brev. Rom. reform.
Offic. Angel. Custod.

Custodes hominum psallimus
   Angelos,
Naturæ fragili quos Pater
   addidit
Cœlestis comites, insidianti-
   bus

The praise of Angels Guardian we sing,
Whom God, our Natures frailty pitying,
Has given for our Companions, to oppose

Ne succumberet hostibus.	The power and skill of our insnaring foes.
Nam quod corruerit Proditor Angelus,	For since the Rebel Angel fell; from Heaven,
Concessis merito pulsus honoribus;	And granted honours there, so justly driven;
Ardens invidia, pellere nititur	He seeks from Heav'n to drive, inflam'd with spight,
Quos cœlo Deus advocat.	Those whom Gods goodness thither do's invite.
Huc custos igitur pervigil advola,	Thou watchful Guardian hither therefore fly,
Avertens Patria de tibi credita	And from that Countrey, where thy charge do's lye,
Tam morbos animi, quàm requiescere	Divert what ere may prove their minds disease,
Quicquid non sinit incolas.	And what disturbs the peoples quiet peace.
Sanctæ sit Triadi, &c.	To the blest Trinity, &c.

And in the *Antiphona* at the end of all the Office, they speak thus to the Angels.

Sancti Angeli custodes nostri, defendite nos in prælio, ut non pereamus in tremendo judicio.

O Ye holy Guardian-Angels defend us in battle, that we may not perish in the dreadful judgment.

I observe also that in the Proper Offices for the Church of *Lisbon*, granted by Pope *Sixtus* V. there is an Office for the *Guardian-Angel* of the *Kingdom of Portugal*, with a Mass to the same, after it, printed at *Lisbon* 1625. Also in the Proper Offices for the *Order of the H. Trinity, for redemption of Captives*, there is another Office and Mass for the Guardian-Angel of that Order, printed at *Lisbon* 1621.

In the *Roman Ritual*, a dying person is taught to pray thus.

Ritual. Rom. in visitat. infirm.

Sancte Angele Dei mihi custos assiste. Omnes sancti Angeli & omnes sancti intercedite pro me, & mihi succurrite.

O Holy Angel of God, assist me as my keeper. All ye holy Angels and all ye Saints intercede for me, and succour me.

A Prayer to the proper Angel.

English Primer used in Queen Maries days, 1555.

O Aungel which art my keeper by Goddes merciful providence, preserve, defend and govern me committed to thy cure: O thou swete Aungel which remainest with me, thoughe bodelye thou speakest not to me, save me bothe bodye and soule, I beseche thee; for that is the onely office committed to thy charge.

The Versicle.

O blessed Aungel the Messenger of our God.

The Aunswer.

Direct (or rule) my doings, according to the will of the highest God.

Let us pray.

O God whose pleasure is, to have certayne of the holy Aungels beningly appointed to thine assistance, and certen here in earth mercifully to minister unto men, graunt, I beseche thee, that the Aungel committed to kepe me, may direct me in goodnes, may stirre me up stil unto vertue, and most mightelie deliver me from the fitte of synnes, so that at the straighte judgement when there shall be but one folde or shepecote of men and Aungels

Aungels under that mighty shepherde, I may be founde worthy to be counted amongst the shepe of his flocke. Throughe oure Lorde Jesus Christ thy sonne, which lyveth and reigneth with thee verye God, world without ende. Amen.

>Let us pray.

O Holy Aungel of God, the minister of the heavenlye empyre, unto whome Almightie God hath committed and deputed the keping of me: humbly I beseche thee for his majestie and pities sake, preserve my bodye and soule and all my senses, from all wickednes and unlawful desiers, from all hurtful vayn and unclean thoughts, from all illusions of evil spirites, from defyling of body and soule, and from the deceites of all my enemies, as well visible as invisible, which seke destruction of my soule. And be thou my sure protectour and governoure, wheresoever I go daye or night, tyde or time. Conserve and kepe me in clennes and puritie, strengthen me in feare and love of Jesus Christ with all holy desires: and after this miserable and britel life, carye my soule unto eternal felicitie; where with God and all Sainctes I may joy worlde withoute end. Our Lord Jesus Christ graunting this: to whom be honour and glorye for ever and ever. Amen.

A Brief Conclusion concerning the Worshipping of Angels.

AS the design of this Book is to acquaint the Reader with the plain matter of fact, what kind of Worship and addresses they of the *Roman* Church make to Saints and Angels, rather than to enter into the large field of Controversie, and formally to state and dispute these things; there being scarce any thing more requisite to confute the usages of that Church, than plainly to expose them to a full view: So in this particular especially, concerning Worshipping Angels, less one would imagine should be needful to be said about it, when the Scripture has so plainly and punctually determined this case, both by express precept and example: So that I count it a vain and foolish thing to talk or argue with that man, who will maintain an opinion so directly cross to as full an evidence as can well be desired in the case: for it is certain he must act the part of a perverse Sophister, whose wit only serves him to shift off and evade the force of that truth that stares him in the face, and is never likely to examine any thing fairly and candidly. What can be a more plain caution against this Worship, than that of the Apostle? *Col.* 2. 18. *Let no man beguile you of your reward in a voluntary humility, and worshipping of Angels, intruding into those things which he hath not seen, vainly puft up by his fleshly mind. Not holding the head*, &c.

I do not wonder to hear *Baronius*, who defends the Worshipping of them, to cry out, that *this place is a very difficult one, not easie to be understood, and the difficulties cannot*

Baron. ad an. 60. Sec. 15.

not be overcome without an exact skill in the affairs of those times: and after a long inquiry into the opinions of the *Jews,* and *Simon Magus, Cerinthus* and the *Philosophers;* the great comfort is, that they have found out men that had such opinions about Angels, which the *Romish* Church has not, and such Worshipping of them as is far more *infamous* and *superstitious* than any thing can be charged against them. Whereas the text is plain against all Worshipping of Angels, and that others are *more guilty,* is no argument that they are *innocent.* . No more than because that the *Egyptians* or other Heathens thought that the very things they worshipped were Gods, therefore the *Israelites* were not guilty of Idolatry in the matter of the *Golden Calf,* in offering Incense to the *Brazen Serpent,* or in sacrificing to the *Calves* at *Dan* and *Bethel,* in which it was impossible that they should have such low and vile thoughts of God, or such high thoughts of those Images themselves, as the other had of theirs; but just such as the *Roman Church* has, who think they acceptably worship God *by them.* The truth is, the Church of *Rome* seems to be many ways concerned in that place to the *Colossians* about *Worshipping Angels,* and to be condemned by several things there spoken, (though we should grant, that the Apostle might have some *Hereticks* or *Philosophers* in his eye, when he spoke them, who practised what he there condemns.) The learned *Grotius* (whom no body accounts too severe against their opinions) seems to give as plain an account of them as any, in his Comments upon the place. *Intruding into those things that he hath not seen*] i. e. says he, " Penetrating into those " things which he hath not known; taking liberty to talk " about unknown things : They set Angels over what af- " fairs they pleased, they put names upon them, and distri- " buted them into Classes (and every one may know that the School-divinity about Angels, is very peremptory and presuming in this kind ; telling us in what place they were created, resolving whether the number that stood was equal to that of those that fell ; the way whereby they understand,

derstand, and the way how they communicate their thoughts one to another; how many orders of them there are, and the names that belong to each order. &c.)

Not holding the head] *i. e.* "Not holding himself to
" Christ, whom God has therefore given to be head to the
" Church, that by it we might bring our desires to him.
" Those many commenders easily give occasion to Schism,
" the Church retains unity. *There is one God and one Me-*
" *diator,* 1 Tim. 2. 5. *But to come to the main thing.*

Humility and Worshipping of Angels.] *i. e.* Humility in
" Worshipping of Angels. It has a show of modesty, not
" to dare to approach to God, but to bring ones prayers
" to Angels in order to their being brought to God: by
" which colour the Philosophers defended *Polytheisme,*
" which also *Celsus* did, as we learn from *Origen.* (From whom also *Grotius* cites several places, to show that the *Jews* did not worship Angels.) Which is also the very sense of *Theodoret.* "They, says

Λέγοντες ὡς ἀόρατος ὁ   "he, perswaded them to do this
τῶν ὅλων Θεὸς, ἀνέφικτος τε "(*i. e.* pray to Angels) using
καὶ ἀκατάληπτος, καὶ προσή- "the pretence of humility, say-
κει διὰ τῶν ἀγγέλων τὴν   "ing, That the God of the Uni-
θείαν εὐμένειαν πραγμα-   "verse was invisible and inaccef-
τεύεσθ. *Theod. in Coloss.* 2. 18. "sible and incomprehensible;
" and that it was fit we would procure Gods favour by An-
" gels. So also the same *Father,* upon those words, *Coloss.*
3. 17. — *do all in the name of the Lord Jesus, giving thanks to God and the Father by him*: He Comments thus:
" Because they commanded men to Worship Angels, he en-
" joyneth the contrary; that they should adorn their words
" and deeds with the remembrance of Christ the Lord; and
" send up thanksgivings to God and the Father *by him,* says
" he, not *by Angels.* The Synod of *Laodicea* also follow-
" ing this Law, and intending to cure that old Disease, de-
" creed that they should not pray to Angels, nor forsake
" our Lord Jesus Christ. This Law of the Council of *Lao-*
dicea Theodoret also takes notice of in the place forcited (in
Col.

Col. 2. 18.) in these words. Ἔμεινε καὶ τοῦτο τὸ πάθος, &c. "This vice (of worshipping Angels) hath continued a long "while in *Phrygia* and *Pisidia*; for which cause also the "Synod assembled in *Laodicea*, a City of *Phrygia*, forbad "them by a Law to pray unto Angels. And even to this "present are to be seen Oratories of S. *Michael* (the Arch- "angel) among them and their borderers.
Which last words, (notwithstanding all that *Baronius* has said in favour of those Orato- ries, from the wonderful prodigies which *Metaphrastes* mentions, were shewed at *Colosse* by S. *Michael*;) are the more remarkable, because that which *Theodoret* calls here a vice *in them*, is now a common practice in the *Roman Church* to dedicate Churches to the honour of S. *Michael*, and to worship him as a great Protector, as the Devotions we have set down have told you. The Law which *Theodoret* speaks of, is the Five and Thirtieth Canon of the Council of *Laodicea*, whose words are these. "Christians "ought not to forsake the "Church of God, and depart "aside, and name (or invocate) "Angels, and make meetings, "which are things prohibited. "If any man therefore be found "to give himself to this hidden "Idolatry, let him be *Anathe-* "*ma*, because he hath forsaken "our Lord Jesus Christ, and has "approached to Idolatry.

Baron. loc. ant. citat.

Ὅτι ὐ δεῖ Χρισιανὸς ἐγκαταλείπειν τ̀ ἐκκλησίαν τῦ Θεῦ, κ̀ ἀπιέναι, κ̀ ἀγγέλως ὀνομάζειν (which Theodoret called before εὐχὰς ἀγγέλοις) ἢ συνάξεις ποιεῖν, ἅπερ ἀπηγόρευται· εἴτις ἐν εὑρεθῇ ταύτῃ τῇ κεκρυμμένῃ εἰδωλολατρείᾳ σχολάζων, ἔςω ἀνάθεμα, ὅτι ἐγκατέλιπε τ̀ κύριον ἡμῶν Ἰησῦν Χριςὸν, τ̀ υἱὸν τῦ Θεῦ, κ̀ εἰδωλολατρείᾳ προσῆλθεν. *Pandectæ Canon. Concil. Laod. Can.* 35.

Aristenus his words upon this *Canon* are remarkable, who after he had mentioned the Heresie of the *Angelici*, who said that the world was created by Angels; he after this takes notice of some that taught, as S. *Paul* in his Epistle to the *Colossians* had shown, that Christ by reason of his Greatness was not so fit to bring us to God as Angels, which, says he, is a renouncing the
Divine

Divine Oeconomy under the shew of humility (and if the *Romanists* do not balk him wholly as *too great*, yet the joyning of this worship of Angels to that of our Saviour, argues as bad an opinion of him as they had, that is, that he is *less good*, not merciful and compassionate enough to be trusted alone in his mediation to God for us.) "He "therefore, says he, who joyns himself to them, and says "that the world was created by Angels, or that says that "by Angels we are brought to God and the Father*, let "him be *Anathema*, as one that relinquishes our Lord Je- "sus Christ the Son of God, and approaches to the opini- "on of Idolaters. He that would see more of the sence of the Fathers in this matter of worshipping Angels, may consult the learned Annotations of Mr. *Beverege* upon this *Canon*.

* Zonarus *upon this* Canon, *in like manner interprets the words of* S. Paul. *The crime he describes thus*; θέλων μετάγειν ὑμᾶς ἀπὸ τ̅ ὀρ-θῆς πίστεως εἰς θρησκείαν τ̅ν̅ ἀγγέλων, ἤγεν εἰς τὸ λατρεύειν τοῖς ἀγ-γέλοις ἐν ταπεινοφροσύνῃ· *which humility he explains*, ὡς ὑπὲρ ὑμᾶς ὄντ(ος) τῷ ἐπικαλεῖσθαι τ̅ κύριον, κỳ αὐτῷ χρῆσθαι προσαγωγεῖ πρὸς τ̅ αὐ-τ̅ πατέρα.

And now though we seem, one would think, to be pretty well secured both of the meaning of S. *Paul* and of this Council; yet our Adversaries have attempted to weaken the force of both, by pretty sleights both of *wit* and *knavery*. By the latter (for I can give it no softer name) they thought to prevent all mischief this *Canon* could do their Church, who in the late *Latin Collections* of the *Canons*, instead of *Angelos* put in *angulos*, there being but one letter difference between *Angels* and *corners* in the *Latin tongue*: wherein they show'd their good will to cheat the world; and if there had been no *Greek Canons* to discover it (where this trick can have no place, there being no affinity between *Angels* and *corners* in the words of that Language) it might have gone off with more credit, and have passed at least for a fine conjecture. But this has been exposed sufficiently by the

the *Reverend Primate of Ireland*, in his *Answer to the Jesuits Challenge*, pag. 470, &c. Their *Great Cardinal Perron*, thought to have done as much for S. *Paul* by *his wit*: for he had invented an interpretation wherein none went before him in the conjecture, which yet if he could have made it good, had quite enervated the force of all Arguments from that place to the *Colossians*, against *Worshipping Angels*. His conceit is this. " That S. *Paul* " in this phrase *Religion of Angels* (θρησκεία " ἀγγέλων) takes the *Genitive Angels* not " *objectivè*, but *originaliter* ; so that by that " word he understands not the Religion that is paid *to Angels*, but that which is received and delivered *by Angels*, " *viz*. the *Jewish Religion*, which the Apostle says, *was or-* " *dained by Angels in the hand of a Mediator* (Gal. 3. 19.) " and *the word spoken by Angels*, (Heb. 2. 2) So that according to this interpretation, the Apostle gives a Caution against no Religion or way of Worship, save only that of the *Jews*. But this fancy of the Cardinal has been as shamefully baffled as the former, by the great diligence of *Monsieur Dallee* ; who as he hath show'd the Novelty of it (having no countenance from the ancient Fathers to back it) and that it hath been exploded by the Learned of his own Church : So also shows, that the *Genitive* of θρησκεία, is never taken in his sence, but always in the other. Thus *Wisd*. 14. 27. *The worshipping of Idols* (εἰδώλων θρησκεία) *not to be named, is the beginning, the cause, and the end of all evil* : Where the worship of Idols, cannot signifie (in his way) the worship delivered by Idols, but the worship given to them. So *Jam*. 1. 26. *If any man bridle not his tongue*, τούτου μάταιος ἡ θρησκεία, *his Religion is vain*, not the Religion he institutes, but which he exercises : and *Acts* 26. 5. *after the most strict Sect* τῆς ἡμετέρας θρησκείας *of our Religion*, that is the *Jewish*, and that not the Religion that they were the

Du Perron Repliq. l. 5. c. 6. p. 909.

Dallee de object. cult. relig. adv. Latinor. tradit. lib. 3. c. 31.

Infandorum Idolorum cultura. Vulg. Lat.

Authors

Authors or deliverers of, but that which they practised. But I leave the Reader to consult him in the forecited place, who has said a great deal more, to show the absurdity of *Cardinal Perron*'s interpretation.

But if there shonld seem any difficulty in the Apostles words considered alone (though they are plain enough one would think till men begin to play tricks with them, and by that way any Law, though never so clear, may have some mists cast before the face of it, which may render it seemingly obscure till they be dispersed.) Yet now that the Scripture has given us precedents in the case, I mean examples of this adoration refused, even by those Blessed Spirits to whom it is pretended to be due: what can any one desire more for his satisfaction? The places are known to this purpose. *Revel.* 19. 10. *And I fell at his feet to worship him; and he said unto me, see thou do it not. I am thy fellow-servant and of thy Brethren that have the Testimony of Jesus,* worship God. And *Rev.* 22. 8, 9. *I fell down to worship before the feet of the Angel that shewed me these things; then said he unto me; see thou do it not; for I am thy fellow-servant, and of thy Brethren the Prophets, and of them which keep the sayings of this book: worship God.* Where you see the thing prohibited twice; and not only barely prohibited; but by the abrupt manner of the Angels speaking, "Ορα μὴ, in the Greek, he shows his hasty concern to prevent it; and that too with a reason annexed; *I am thy fellow-servant,* &c. which plainly concludes, that it was not the courtesie of the Angel, but the necessity of the thing, that made him so shye of accepting the profered honour; and if this reason holds good as to Angels themselves, then much more forceably doth it conclude against the religious worship of any Saint, who are all in a much stricter sence our fellow-servants than Angels are: Nay farther, if not only for this reason it be undue to them, but also unjust and sacrilegious as to God, the invading one of Gods properties, as the Angels last words imply, *Worship thou God*: (for if religious adoration were not such a *peculiar*

culiar of his, and not to be communicated to any other being, these words of the Angel might have received this easie answer; worship God? Yes, so I intend always to do, yet give me leave too to worship thee.) I say, if all this do not give satisfaction in this Question to an honest mind and plain-meaning person, it's hard to guess what will; and methinks it should do so in reason to our adversaries also, who professing to venerate Angels, ought to revere their determinations and judgment of things; and not to be so uncivil as to argue *Pro*, when an Angel is on the other side, and determines *Con*. But neither man nor Angel can stop the mouth of a cavilling Sophister, but something he will have to say, though little to the purpose.

It is so here in our case, we have *another Cardinal* (viz. *Bellarmine*) that is as busie with his fine Quirks and Sophistry, as the *former* was, to stop the mouth of these Texts from speaking one syllable against worshipping Angels; nay farther, (which is a bolder enterprize than that of *Perron's*) he would make us believe that they speak for it. For these are his words. *Bellarm. de Sanct.Beat.l.1. c.14. ad Quartum dico.*
" To the fourth example (which is this of
" S. *John* and the *Angel*) I say, it makes
" for us. For either *John* thought him,
" that appeared to him, to be God, or an Angel. If he
" thought him to be God, he was deservedly reproved: (Sayst thou so, great wit? If he in thy opinion deserves to be reproved, who worships that which is not God, even when he *thinks* him *to be God*; pray what dost thou deserve, who art for worshipping that which is not God (*viz.* a Saint or Angel) even when thou *confessest* that he is *not God?*) " If he thought him to be an Angel, and yet ado-
" red him; why are we reproved, who do what *John*
" did? Do the *Calvinists* know better than *John*, whether
" Angels are to be worshipped? There is none I dare say, whether *Calvinist* or not, that is advanced any thing considerably above a *Natural*, who can be in danger of being
hurt

hurt by this Horn of his *Dilemma.* For inſtead of asking, *why are we reproved for doing what John did?* One would think it's a more material queſtion to ask, Why was *John himſelf* reproved by the Angel for doing this, if it was, as you ſay, no fault, taking him to be an Angel, to worſhip him? Why do you worſhip Angels, knowing them to be ſuch, when *John* by an Angel was prohibited? What? do Cardinals know better than Angels, whether Angels are to be worſhipped?

One of theſe Queſtions, the Cardinal thinks fit to take notice of. Why *John* was reprehended? His firſt anſwer was conſidered before, which is, that per-
Bellarm. ibid. haps he eſteemed him to be Chriſt. The ſecond is more peremptory. "I ſay that " *John* did well to give due worſhip to the Angel, as he " remembred his Anceſtors *Abraham* and *Lot* had done, (which is a great miſtake, as *Origen* ſufficiently proves againſt *Celſus,* if he means it of any higher adoration, than was what cuſtomarily paid in thoſe Eaſtern Nations by proſtration to great perſons,) " but the Angel prohibited it, in " reverence to Chriſts humanity: for Angels before " Chriſts coming ſuffered themſelves to be adored by men ; " but after that God was made man, and that all the Angels " began to adore man in Chriſt, the Angels would not now " be adored by men, and eſpecially by the Apoſtles and " other great men. [Well, however one would think we had gained thus much, by this diſcourſe of the *Cardinal,* that now ſince the coming of Chriſt, all the old worſhip of Angels (if there was any) is at an end, and ought no more to be uſed; no ſuch matter, for he adds,] " Notwith- " ſtanding it does not follow that we do ill if we adore An- " gels; for we both rightly adore them, and they rightly " refuſe to be adored. A ſtrange Concluſion! If S. *John* at firſt did well in offering to adore them (before he knew that reaſon from our Saviours Incarnation, and the alteration of the Angels minds as to their willingneſs to be adored

red thereupon.) Yet he could not be said to do it (as he did) a second time rightly (when it's to be hoped, he knew that reason as well as *Bellarmine*, and the *Fathers* he cites) nor we, after that, to do it rightly, when the same reason still holds, and we may presume, that the Angels have not taken any toy, and changed their minds once more.

But the secret of it (which is all I shall add) is plainly this: That the reprehension which the Angel gave to Saint *John*, according to the *Cardinal*, was but a copy of his countenance, and only a *great complement*: And all that the Angel said to him in the forenamed Texts, comes but to thus much, if I may have leave to put it into other words, not injuring the *Cardinals* sence.

"*John*, I see you understand the excellency of our Na-
"tures, and know how to address your self to persons of
"our Birth and Quality; but at this time (under favour
"and with submission to your judgment) it is a little un-
"seasonable to make these *reverences*: for we have all
"made an agreement, out of our particular respect to *Je-*
"*sus* (whom we worship, and your nature in him) to
"wave all ceremonies of this kind from those of the same
"nature with him, and especially from you, that have had
"the honour to be of his Family and Attendance. Besides,
"it is no time for us to insist upon these Formalities, being
"now busie with you to advance *his name*, while you carry
"the Testimony of *Jesus* to the Gentiles: when his Reli-
"gion is established among them, then our *Prince Michael*
"will make some glorious appearances on Mount *Garganus*,
"*Tumba*, and some other places, and leave some *precious*
"*remains* to indear his and our memory to the world;
"then it will be a better season to renew these complements;
"and of the punctual time, *you*, if you live so long, how-
"ever *the Church* shall infallibly have due notice, from a
"*General Council*, or, which comes all to one, from the
"*Pope*: when they will be also directed, to prevent mi-

"stakes and scandals, to reserve the worship of *Latry* for
"the Holy Trinity, and of *Hyperduly* for the Blessed Vir-
"gin, and for the Humanity of Christ, and to pay to us
"Angels the worship of *Duly* and no more: In the interim,
"for once be ruled by me and forbear; and desire others
"to do so, and to pay their worship, where, in the
"present circumstances, it is more seasonable. Let it suf-
"fice, good *John*, that we accept the will for the deed,
"till that time come, when it will be your Duty to worship
"your *Fellow-servants*.

THE END.

An Index of Saints, &c.

Whether forg'd or abused by the Authors of those Fabulous stories and Superstitious Devotions, that are considered in this Book.

Those of more special Note are Printed in a Different Character.

A.

Adelheidis.	315
Adon.	36
Ædus.	221
Ængussius.	105.108
Agnes.	46.339.385
Aidan.	74.89
Aldelme.	341
Alexander. I.P.	348
Alexius.	170
Ambrose of Siena.	107
Anastasia companion of Ursula.	138
Anne, Mother of the Bl. Virgin.	46.64.397
Antony the Hermit.	235
Antony of Padua.	280
Antoninus, the sleeper.	99
Apollonia.	229
Audoen.	35
Audrey.	166
Austin the Monk.	88

B

Babcaris, compan. of Ursula.	35
Babyla.	165
Bado.	36
Baldred.	37
Balthasar.	17.66
Barbara.	271
Bartlemew, Monk.	309.311
Benedicta, companion of Ursula.	132
Benigna, compan. of Ursula.	132
Bennet.	151.309
Berach.	357

Ff 2   Ber-

An Index of Sain's.

Berthold. 312
Birinus. 78
Blasius. 278
Bonaventure. 325.331
Brendan. 182
Brigid. 36.83.105.276. 356

C

Carpophora, companion of Ursula. 132
Catharine. vid. Katharine.
Cecilia. 340
Celedonius. 278
Chelyndris, companion of Ursula. 132
Christina. 343
Christopher. 5
Ciriacus. P. 135
S. Clara de monte Falconis. 273
Clara, the Franciscan. 354.386
Clarus, the Ermit. 77
Claudius. 364
Clementia, companion of Ursula. 132
Coleta. 322.333
Colman. 44.150
Columba, companion of Ursula. 132
Columbanus, companion of Ursula. 134

Constantin, the sleeper. 99
Cordula, companion of Ursula. 34.132.146
Cosmus. 264
Cuanna. 108
Cuthbert. 80.104.312

D

Dadon. 36
Damianus. 264
Daria, compan. of Ursula. 35
David. 77.78.101
Decumanus. 77
Denis, Areopag. 68
Denis, the sleeper. 99
Donatus. 353
Dorothy. 339
Dunstan. 39.74

E

Eanswitha. 99
K. Edmund, a Martyr. 38
Eleutheria, companion of Ursula. 132
Eleutherius, companion of Denis. 69
Eleutherius, companion of Ursula. 134
Elias. 170
Elizabeth of Schonaw. 126

Eli-

An Index of Saints.

Elizabeth, *Widow.*	355
Emetherius.	278
Endeus, Monk.	59.90
Erasmus.	362
Etheldred.	166.371
Ethelfleda.	164
Ethelwold.	310
Etherius, Ursula's spouse.	140
Ethnea.	322
Exacustadius, the sleeper.	99

F

Fanchea.	59
Fechinus.	44.108
Fingar.	44
Finnian.	87
Fintanus.	86
Florentia, companion of Ursula.	132
Florentin.	44
Florina, companion of Ursula.	34
Francis of Assize.	121. 259.260
Fursey.	44

G

The Angel Gabriel.	401. 408
Genouefe.	385
Genulph.	83

George.	93
Gerasina, Q. of Sicily.	132
Gilbert.	176
Gildas Albanius.	102
Godrick.	310
Gonsaluus.	89
Gudila.	242

H

Haseca.	37
Helen, *mother of Constantin.*	343
Henry, *the Hermit.*	169
Hermenegild.	384
Hildutus.	80

I

Iamblicus, the sleeper.	99
James, *Bishop of Antioch.*	127.134
Jaspar, *one of the three Kings.*	17.66
Indract.	44
Innocents.	365
Joachim, *father of the Bl. Virgin.*	395
John the Baptist.	384
John of Beverley.	341
John, the sleeper.	99
Joseph, *husband to the Bl. Virgin.*	46.56.393
Joseph of Arimathea.	29

Jota,

An Index of Saints.

Jota, companion of Ur-
sula. 132
Juliana. 312
Ivo. 85. 330
Justinian. 77
Justus the Hermit. 42
Juthwara. 77

K

Katharin, *daughter of K.*
Costus. 153
Katharin of Siena. 46
Kentigern. 319. 340. 357
Kienan. 90
Kieran. 83. 256
3 Kings *of* Colen. 17. 66

L

Laurence. 256
Leobinus. 321
Lewis, Bishop. 232
Libernus. 324
Longinus. 11
Lotharius, companion of
Ursula. 134
Lucia. 336
Lucia, companion of Ur-
sula. 133. 138
Ludger. 150
Luke. 60. 64
Lupus. 312
Lutwin. 79

M

Macarius. 73
3 Magi. 17. 66
Maidoc. 74. 255
Malachias. 357
Malchus, the sleeper. 99
Margaret. 251
Mary the Bl. Virgin. 148. 149
Maria de Turribus. 321
Martian, the sleeper. 99
Martina. 337. 387
Marus. 277
Matrona. 165
Maximianus, a sleeper. 99
Maximilian, a sleeper. 99
Mel. 318
Melchior. 17. 66
Michael *the Archangel.*
401. 410
Mochoemoc. 44
Mochua. 86. 90
Moedoc. 222
Molua. 222

N

Nennidius. 276
Nicholas, Bishop. 265. 148
Nicholas de Rupe. 332

O

An Index of Saints.

O

Odilia, companion of Ursula. 132
Odo, Archbishop of Canterbury. 35. 72
Ositha. 77
Othmar. 124

P

Pachomius. 236
Panefredis, companion of Ursula. 34
Pantaleon. 241
Pantalus, Bishop of Basil. 132
Patrick. 42. 101. 318
Paul de Leon. 85
Peter and Paul. 384
Peter ad vincula. 348
Peter the Abbot. 84
Peter of Alcantara. 383
Pigmenius. 353
Pinnosa, companion of Ursula. 132
Prisca. 64

R

Radon. 36
The Angel Raphael. 401. 404
Regulus. 150

Roch. 248
Ruadanus. 87
Rusticus, companion of Denis. 68

S

Sapientia, companion of Ursula. 132
Sapientia. 380
Scutinus. 107
Sebastian. 242. 339
Secundus, companion of Ursula. 34
Sedonius. 324
Semibaria, companion of Ursula. 35
Senanus. 105. 325
Serapion, the sleeper. 99
Severus, Bishop. 91. 169
Sibilia, companion of Ursula. 133
Sibyllina. 330
Sigismund. 239
Simon Stock. 258
The Seven Sleepers. 98
Sodelbia. 322
Suibert. 76

T

Teresa. 383
Theliau. 36
S. Thomas Apostle. 17

Ff 4   Tho-

An Index of Saints.

Thomas Aquinas.	169
Thomas Becket.	184
Tiburtius.	340
Tresan.	45

U

Valeria, companion of *Ursula.*	34
Valerian.	340
Vedastus.	318
Venantius.	382
Venisa.	279
Verena, companion of *Ursula.*	127
Veronica.	35
The Eleven Thousand Virgins.	110.33
Ursula.	110.33

W

Walburg.	147
Wereburga.	81
William of *Speluncato.*	318
William, companion of *Ursula, Bishop.*	134
Wilgefortis.	2
Willibrord.	124
Winwaloe.	82
W.thburg.	168

Y

Ywanus, companion of *Ursula.*	134

A TABLE Of the Principal CONTENTS.

The absurdness of much of the Roman Devotions, the best reason why it should continue in Latin. Pag 1, 2.
Their Fabulous Devotions; such as to S. Wilgefortis, from her miraculous Beard. 3.
Instances of foolish allusions in their Prayers. 4
Devotions to S. Christopher. 5, &c.
Mr. Cressy's reviving the old Legend of S. Winefrid, who lived after her beheading. 9
Devotions to S. Longinus: with his Legend. 11, 12
His Reliques, with several others at Prague. 14
Of their corrupting the Gospel Text. 14, 15.
Their lewd Comments upon diverse places of it. 16, 17

Devotions to the three Kings of Colen. 17, 18, &c.
A reproof of the positiveness of their prayers, as to their number, names, and being Kings. 21
A digression concerning Reliques; their Legend how the three Kings bodies came to Colen. 23
This Legend confuted. 24, 25
The Follies of Mr. Cr.'s History about Reliques. 25, 26
Of the Spear and Nails of the Cross. 27, 28
Of Christ's blood sent, and brought hither by Joseph. 29
Of the Præputium of our Saviour. 30
The School-mens Opinion about the blood of Christ hypostatically united to the word. 32

Of

A Table of the Principal Contents.

Of the Reliques of S. Ursula, *and the* 11000 *Virgins.* 33

Mr. Cressy's instances, concerning Saints bodies. 37

Of the speaking Crucifix and moving Images. 39

The Gentile Religion boasted such Miracles. 40

Story of the Staff of Jesus *given to* S. Patrick, *and the good use of Mr.Cr. doubting about it.* 41

Five Stories of the staves of Irish Saints; and how the wood of S. Colman's Tree is a strange preservative. 44

The famous controversie about the Bl. Virgins Ring. 45

Other places pretend to it, and Miracles by it. 56

The ancient Hebrews used no Ring in Espousals. 57

Abuses of Scripture to countenance their Fables. 59

A cheat discovered about the Body of S. Luke. 60

The measure of the Bl. Virgins foot. 61

Cheating with counterfeit Reliques. 61, 62

A Catalogue of such Reliques out of Lassels. 63

Their Patron Saints an imitation of Heathenisme. 65

The three Kings of Colen *invoked by Travellers.* 67

Devotions to S. Denys, and his Legend. 68, 69, &c.

Of the appearances of Christ *in the Eucharist.* 72

Stories of S. Dunstan. 74

A Digression, about the Miracles in Mr. Cr.'s History. 75

That he knowingly cheated, in his History. 76

His Story of S. Birinus, walking on the Sea. 78

Of an Eagle over-shaddowing two Saints in a journey. 79

His Story of S. Eanswitha. ibid.

Of S. Cuthbert's body. 80

Of S. Wereburga and her Wild-geese. 81

Of Saints commanding and punishing Birds and Beasts. 83

Diomedes *his Birds, a parallel story.* 84

Of S. Ivo, and S. Paul de Leon. 85

Foolish toying and playing with Miracles. 86

The Miracle of Austin *the Monk considered.* 88

Scripture Miracles exceeded upon trifling occasions. 89

Devotions to S. George, and the Fables of his Acts. 93

Pleasant account of his, and other Saints names. 97

A prayer to the 7 Sleepers, & their Legend. 98

Confuted by Baronius. 100

A Table of the Principal Contents.

A Prayer to S. David, *and the Lessons of his life.* 101

Gildas *at a stand in his Sermon, at the entrance of* S. David's *Mother into the Church.* 102

How a Dove taught S. David, *and sang Hymns with him.* 107

Of Saints reciting their Devotions in cold water, and S. Fechinus *his heating it by his Prayers.* 107

Of a Hill rising in Wales under S. David, *as he preached.* 108

Devotions to Ursula, *and the* 11000 *Virgins.* 110

The Historical account of them out of Authors confuted. 114

Gildas *and* Bede *no witnesses in their case.* 118

The pretences of Oral Tradition *about them confuted.* 125

Reflexions upon the Lessons of the old Breviary about them. 128

Saints departed not concerned for their own veneration. 147

Tales of Visions and voices gave rise to some Festivals. 148

Feigned Miracles to countenance the worship of Saints. 150

Devotions to S. Catharine *of* Alexandria. 153

The Legend of her out of the old Breviary, &c. 157

Cassander's *censure of it as Fabulous.* 162

How her story is reformed in the late Breviaries. 163

Occasion taken from thence to reprove Mr. Cr. 164

S. Etheldred's *preserving Virginity after marriage.* 166

Their base reflexions upon a married estate. 166, 170

Marriage of Priests of worse account than keeping whores. 171

Of S. Hippolytus; *his Legend seems to be taken out of the fictions of the Poets.* 174

Reflections upon the foregoing Romances, and upon their easie ways of pardon and overcoming temptations to sin, and being saved by one good work. 176

Their admirable Legends seconded with dull Prayers. 183

Devotions to Tho. Becket *A. Bishop of* Canterb. 184

The occasion of the Quarrel betwixt the King and him. 186

To what height the contest was carried. 188

Mediations

A Table of the Principal Contents.

Mediations for agreement, and why unsuccessful. 197

A short account of the Progress of the Pope's power. 203

The humble Style of antient Popes, an argument that they claimed no Temporal Power over Emperours. 205

Examples of the Insolency of later Popes. 207

Their State above that of Emperours and Kings. 209

Ridiculous pretences of the honour of Christ, and humility. 210

Homage from Kings demanded by them, and denyed. 212

Concerning the death of Thomas. 215

The Kings strange penance at his Tomb. 216

Thomas no Martyr. 218

A full account of his Miracles after his death. 220

His worship obscured that of Christ and the Virgin. 228

Devotions to Patron Saints, as to S. Apollonia for the Toothache. 229

Her numerous Reliques, especially those of her Teeth. 233

To S. Anthony the Hermit, for Inflammations, &c. 235

His opinion was against Reliques, as appears by his charge to bury him where none should know. 237

His Reliques used to sanctifie Wine as a preservative. 238

To S. Sigismund for Feavers or Agues. 239

The sorry account they give of his being a Martyr. 240

S. Pantaleon a Patron for Agues before him. 241

To S. Sebastian for removing the Plague. 242

Their Devotions to him Idolatrous. 246

To S. Roch, in time of the Plague. 248

Some particulars of his Legend noted. 250

To S. Marguerite, for Women with Child. 251

Her vanquishing, and S. Bernard's over-reaching the Devil. 252

Strange Petitions of Saints and priviledges thereupon. 254

Priviledges to the Scapular of the Carmelites. 258

To S. Francis and his Church called Portiuncula. 259

More stress laid upon Habits, keeping Days, and visiting Altars and Churches, than upon moral goodness. 262

Devoti-

A Table of the Principal Contents.

Devotions to S. Cosma *&* Damian *in taking Physick.* 264

Devotions to S. Nicholas, *in dangers at Sea.* 265

To S. Barbara, *to receive the Eucharist before Death.* 271

Concerning her wonderous Legend. ibid.

Profane representations of the Bl. Trinity, *with absurd discourses and Miracles concerning it.* 272

Of miraculous preservations by invocating S. Barbara. 275

Ridiculous Story of communicating S. Brigid. 276

To S. Marus, *for Palseys and Convulsions,* &c. 277

To S. Blasius, *for bones in the Throat.* 278

To S. Emetherius *and* Celedonius, *for allaying Tempests.* Ib.

To S. Venisa, *for the Greensickness,* &c. 279

To S. Anthony *of* Padua, *for recovering lost goods.* 280

Concerning Saint Anthony's *preaching.* 283

The Popes calling him the Ark of the Testament. 284

His preaching to the Fishes. 285

Above 30000 *People present at his Sermons.* 286

What effects his Sermons had upon his Auditors. Ib. & 287

Instances of his foolish way of preaching ; his first Sermon upon Luc. 21. v. 25. 288

Another Sermon concerning the Saints, upon Wisd. 3. 294

Upon Matth. 11. *Take my yoke upon you,* &c. *where he compares the Apostles to Oxen.* 298

Another comparing them to Thunder, Trumpets & Bells. 299

His prophane discourse, about God's five fingers. 300

His descant also upon the five fingers of Christ. 301

His blasphemy of the Saliva Divinitatis, &c. 301

His Allegories upon the six Water-pots. 302

And upon Christ's entring a Ship, Matth. 8. 302

Upon Matth. 23. 2. *The Scribes and Pharisees sitting in* Moses *Chair.* 303

His mystical sense of the Prophets words, 1 Kings 17. 13. 304

Upon Jesus *being led by the Spirit into the Desert.* ibid.

Upon Cant. 6. 2. *My beloved is gone into his Garden.* 307

Con-

A Table of the Principal Contents.

Concerning S. Anthony's miracles. 308
The Spiteful tricks the Devil has served the Saints. 309
How the Devil has been served in his kind by them. 311
Instances of more miracles to attest his preaching. 313
His appearing in more places at the same time. 316
And in far distant places in very little time. 317
Admirable Miracles to clear doubts. 318
S. Anthony's miracles prefer'd before S. Paul's. 321
Christ in form of a Child putting himself in his Arms. 322
Strange Story of S. Sedonius and S. Libernus. 324
The miracle of the incorruption of Anthony's tongue. 325
The boasted Miracle of the Mule venerating the Eucharist in St. Anthony's hand, examined and confuted. 326
Their prodigious Licence to coyne Miracles concerning the Eucharist. 330
Story of the Host entring into S. Bonaventure's side, told by the Festival of an Earl of Venice. 331

More instances of Miracles upon bruit Creatures at the presence of the Eucharist. 332
The Story of the Black-horse out of the Festival. 334
A summary of wondrous Legends in the Breviaries. 336
Of S. Lucy. ibid.
Of S. Martina. 337
Of S. Sebastian, S. Agnes, & S. Dorothy. 339
Of S. Tiburtius and Valerian. 340
Of S. John of Beverley. 341
Of S. Aldelme. 342
Of S. Christina. 343
Of S. Helena's Invention of the Cross. ibid.
Account of the Invention of the Cross out of the Festival. 347
Of the Feast of S. Peter ad Vincula. 348
St. Paul's Chain. 64.352
Of S. Donatus. 353
Of S. Clara. 354
Of S. Elizabeth, the King of Hungarie's Daughter, and her setting a young man on fire by her prayers. 355
A wind blowing a man and his wife over Sea. 356
S. Kentigern's admirable way of lighting Candles. 357

S. Berach's

To S. Claudius. 364	Angel, 405
To the holy Innocents. 365	A Prayer to S. Raphael. 407
To the Apostles and Disciples. 366	To S. Gabriel the Archangel. 408
To the Martyrs and Confessors. 367	A prayer to S. Gabriel. 410
To the holy Virgins. 368	To S. Michael the Archangel. Ib.
A Prayer to all the He and She Saints. 369	Another Prayer to him for defence of the Church. 412
Three Lessons of admirable courtship to S. Etheldreda. 372	The Legend of his apparition in Mount Tumba. 414
A Litany, wherein a number of Saints are invoked. 375	The ridiculous Reliques of him they have shown. 417
Their leaving a good petition (that God would make their service rational) out of the new Litanies, that was in before. 380	To the Guardian Angel. ibid.
	The subtil speculations of the Schools in this matter. 418
	An instance of a Colloquy to this Angel. 419
A collection of several Hymns to the Saints. 382	Also of a prophane oblation of ones self to the Bl. Virgin. 420
Fulsome courtships of the Relations of Christ, viz. S. Joseph, Joachim and Anna. 392, &c.	A Hymn and Prayers to this Angel. 420, 421, &c.
	A conclusion, concerning worshipping Angels. 424
Devotions to Angels. 398	The plain caution of the Apostle (Col. 2. 18) against it. Ib.
A Prayer to all the Quire of Angels. ibid.	
Another Prayer to the holy Angels. 399	The exposition of Grotius and Theodoret. 425
Another, wherein Angels are invoked, with a Rubrick be-	The 35 Canon of the Laodicean Council. 427

The

A Table of the Principal Contents.

The cheat of some Latin Collectors of the Canons, putting angulos for angelos. 428
Card. Perron's Novel Interpretation of Col. 2. 18. 429
The instance of S. John forbidden by an Angel to worship him, urged. 430
Card. Bellarmine's Sophistry to evade the force of those places in the Revelations. 431
His strange conclusion set down, and exposed. 432, 433.

THE END.

A Brief Catalogue of Books newly Printed and Reprinted for R. Royston *Booksellerto his Most Sacred Majestie.*

THe Works of the Reverend and Learned *Henry Hammond*, D. D. containing a Collection of Discourses chiefly Practical, with many Additions and Corrections from the *Author's* own hand; together with the Life of the *Author*, enlarg'd by the Reverend Dr. *Fell* Dean of *Christ-Church* in *Oxford*. in large Folio.

Nova & Vetera:
Or, a Collection of Polemical Discourses addressed against the Enemies of the Church of *England*, both Papists and Fanaticks, in large Folio, by *Jeremiah Taylor*, Chaplain in Ordinary to King *Charles* the First of Blessed Memory, and late Lord Bishop of *Down* and *Conner*.

The *Christian Sacrifice*, and the *Devout Christian*, and *Advice to a Friend*, these last three Books written by the Reverend *S. P.* D. D. in 12.

www.ingramcontent.com/pod-product-compliance
Lightning Source LLC
Chambersburg PA
CBHW031957300426
44117CB00008B/803